Robert Needham Cust

Essay on the Prevailing Methods of the Evangelization

Of the Non-Christian World

Robert Needham Cust

Essay on the Prevailing Methods of the Evangelization
Of the Non-Christian World

ISBN/EAN: 9783744722513

Printed in Europe, USA, Canada, Australia, Japan

Cover: Foto ©Lupo / pixelio.de

More available books at **www.hansebooks.com**

EVANGELIZATION

OF THE

NON-CHRISTIAN WORLD.

PUBLICATIONS BY THE SAME AUTHOR.

ETON ADDRESSES TO KING WILLIAM IV. 1840.
HAILEYBURY-OBSERVER CONTRIBUTIONS. 1840–1842.
CALCUTTA-REVIEW CONTRIBUTIONS. 1845–1885.
MANUALS FOR GUIDANCE OF NATIVE OFFICIALS IN THE URDU-LANGUAGE. 1855 to 1859.
PANJAB REVENUE-MANUAL. 1865.
REVENUE-LAW OF NORTH-WEST PROVINCES OF INDIA. 1867.
LAND-REVENUE-PROCEDURE FOR NORTHERN INDIA. 1870.
MODERN LANGUAGES OF THE EAST INDIES. 1878.
MODERN LANGUAGES OF AFRICA. 1883.
MODERN LANGUAGES OF OCEANIA. 1887.
MODERN LANGUAGES OF THE CAUCASIAN-GROUP. 1887.
LANGUAGES OF THE TURKI BRANCH OF THE URAL-ALTAIC FAMILY. 1889.
LINGUISTIC AND ORIENTAL ESSAYS. Series I. 1880.
LINGUISTIC AND ORIENTAL ESSAYS. Series II. 1887.
LINGUISTIC AND ORIENTAL ESSAYS. Series III. 1891.
PICTURES OF INDIAN LIFE. 1881.
THE ROMAN CATHOLIC SHRINES OF LOURDES, SARAGOSSA, LORETTO, Etc. 1885 and 1892.
POEMS OF MANY YEARS AND PLACES. 1887.
THE SORROWS OF AN ANGLO-INDIAN LIFE. 1889.
NOTES ON MISSIONARY SUBJECTS. 1889.
BIBLE-LANGUAGES. 1890.
CLOUDS ON THE HORIZON, OR THE VARIOUS FORMS OF RELIGIOUS ERROR. 1890.
BIBLE-TRANSLATIONS. 1890.
AFRICA REDIVIVA, OR MISSIONARY OCCUPATION OF AFRICA. 1891.
ADDRESSES ON BIBLE DIFFUSION. 1892.

In the Press.

THE GOSPEL-MESSAGE.
FEATURES, WHICH APPEAR IN ALL THE RELIGIONS OF THE WORLD BEFORE ANNO DOMINI.

ESSAY ON THE PREVAILING METHODS

OF THE

EVANGELIZATION

OF THE

NON-CHRISTIAN WORLD.

BY

ROBERT NEEDHAM CUST, LL.D.,

AN OBSERVER IN THE FIELD, A MEMBER OF COMMITTEES, AN ALL-ROUND
READER OF MISSIONARY-LITERATURE IN FIVE EUROPEAN LANGUAGES,
AND ONE, WHOSE HEART, AND INTELLECT, HAVE BEEN DEVOTED
TO THE SUBJECT FOR FIFTY YEARS, INDEPENDENT OF
CHURCH, DENOMINATION, OR NATIONALITY.

"*Sunt bona, sunt quædam mediocria, sunt mala plura.*"

" Ἐν τῷ σπείρειν (1) ὃ μὲν ἔπεσε παρὰ τὴν ὁδόν, καὶ κατεπατήθη,
" (2) ἕτερον κατέπεσεν ἐπὶ τὴν πέτραν,
" (3) ἕτερον ἔπεσεν ἐν μέσῳ τῶν ἀκανθῶν,
" (4) ἕτερον ἔπεσεν εἰς τὴν γῆν τὴν ἀγαθήν."

LUKE, viii, 5-8.

" Arcis divinæ super muros humilis speculator cœli prœsagia prospicit, et
fideliter denuntiat."

LONDON:
LUZAC & Co., 46, GREAT RUSSELL STREET,
Publishers to the India Office.
1894.

HERTFORD
PRINTED BY STEPHEN AUSTIN AND SONS.

PRESENTED BY THE AUTHOR

TO

University of California

WITH THE EARNEST DESIRE, THAT THE COUNSEL AND CRITICISM OFFERED MAY BE ACCEPTED IN THE SPIRIT, IN WHICH IT HAS BEEN WRITTEN, OF LONG, EARNEST, AND SINGLE-MINDED DEVOTION TO THE

GREAT SUBJECT.

TO THE

MEMBERS OF THE MISSIONARY-CONFERENCE

OF THE

CHURCH OF ENGLAND,

ASSEMBLED IN LONDON, MAY, 1894,

THIS ESSAY

IS

DEDICATED.

CONTENTS.

	PAGE
Prefatory Remarks	1

Part I.

GOOD METHODS	10

Part II.

METHODS NOT RECOMMENDED	15
I. Secular	16
II. Spiritual	27

Part III.

BAD METHODS	42
I. Arm of the Flesh	43
1. Interference of Civil, Military, or Diplomatic, Power	43
2. Receiving Endowments from Taxes levied from non-Christians	60
3. Intolerance of other Religions, or other forms of the same Religion	62
4. Destruction (or Appropriation) of Buildings belonging to another Religion	68
5. Making a Mission a handle for Political Schemes	70
II. Modes of Conversion	72
1. Tribal, not Individual, Conversion	72
2. Purchase, and Baptism, of Slaves bought from the Slave-dealer	73
3. Securing Conversion by offer of Material Advantages	74
4. Omitting Bible-Teaching in the Vernacular	74

CONTENTS.

		PAGE
III. Difficulties attending Conversion		76
1. Degradation, or Imperfect Teaching, of the Gospel		76
2. Pagan Notions of Nominal Converts		79
3. Imposing New Conditions precedent to Baptism		80
4. Relapse of Converts into their Old, or adoption of a New, Religion		84
5. Low Culture, and Extreme Intellectual Denseness, of Converts		87
6. Questions connected with the Matrimony of Converts		89
7. Credulousness of any new Story		92
8. Injurious Influence of Western Education on certain Classes: Is Education a Necessary Part of Evangelization, or Civilization?		93
9. Evils arising from raising the Material Status of Converts		96
10. Objections to little Barracks for Converts		99
11. Dwelling too strongly on the Sins of non-Christian World		100
12. Asserting, that Missionaries have *Material* Help from God		105
13. Treating with Contempt the Parental Rights of non-Christians		109
14. Necessity of Union of Denominations into one National Church		111
15. Certainty of Opposition from Old, and New, Forms of Religion		117
IV. The Missionary-Home-Agency		124
1. The Board of Missions		124
2. The Association		125
(*a*). Its Relation to the Church and Public		125
(*b*). Its Relation to the Mission-Field		135
3. The Deputation		141
4. The Financial Department		147
5. The Publications		159
6. Sensationalism		167
V. The Mission in the Field		170
1. The very small Mission without resources		171
2. The Solitary Mission-Station		172
3. The Self-supporting Mission		174
4. (*a*). The Native Agents		181
(*b*). Independent Native Church		186
5. The Unpaid Agent		191

		PAGE
VI. The Missionary-Agent		193
1. The Untrained Agent..		195
2. Not gifted with the Grace of Winning Souls		201
3. Failing to Master the Vernacular Language		202
4. Losing Heart, and Desponding		203
5. Quarrelsome		204
6. Puffed up with undue Praise..		206
7. Meddler and Busybody; "Allotrio-Episcopos" ..		208
8. Marrying Early		210
9. Arrogant to the Natives		222
10. Devoid of all Sympathy, and Love, and Justice, to the Natives		227
11. Disloyal to the Home-Committee		234
12. Defying Laws and Customs of the Country		235
13. Tilting against Legal Native Customs		241
14. Throwing up his Vocation for his own Private Convenience.		243
15. Holding Secular Offices, or Honours		248
16. Living in Society of Secular White Men, and Keeping away from Touch of the People		251
17. Offending against intra-Mission Comity, whether Protestant, or Romish		252
18. Ridiculing and Speaking Ill of non-Christian Religions		260
19. Immoral		271
20. Importing Western Ideas		272
21. Undertaking Work not Belonging to his Duty		275
22. Introducing New Fads, such as Total Abstinence, etc.		276
23. Insulting, or Making Use of, non-Christian Places of Worship		276
24. Preaching to Prisoners in Public Gaols		278
25. Taking up New Work to Neglect of Old		278
Concluding Remarks ..		280
Appendices		287
I. Plea for the Poor non-Christian World		287
II. Five Signs of a True Missionary		291
III. Suggestions for Emendation of Missionary-Methods		292
Alphabetical Index of Parts, Chapters, and Sections		295

ERRATA.

PAGE.	LINE FROM TOP.	READ.
10	1	course *for* cause.
149	2	prayers *for* pages.
173	2	has *for* have.
216	40	occupations *for* occupation.
271	14	failure *for* failures.
276	17	liquors *for* liqueurs.
283	22	neo-Zoroastrianism *for* neo-Zoroastrian.
283	31	clings *for* cling.

PREFATORY REMARKS.

I commence with quotations from esteemed authors:
" He is the truest friend of any institution, who calmly but
" fearlessly points out its defects and its aberrations from the
" way of truth. The ostrich-policy of shutting one's eyes to
" patent facts may answer for a time, but in the end it is
" disastrous. 'Open rebuke is better than secret love,' when
" rebuke is needed. The only essential qualification is, that
" the rebuke or protest be uttered in a brotherly and Christian
" spirit."

" When the current of popular opinion seems to be running
" very strongly in one direction, many are tempted to follow
" the easy course of swimming with the stream. This may be
" pleasant and profitable, but it cannot be right. There are
" times, when even those, who most dislike controversy, may feel
" it a duty to speak if, as in the present instance, they are not
" invited to do so. If a cause seems to them to be a true one,
" it is mere pusillanimity to let the love of personal ease prevail,
" and to suffer it to be lost by acquiescence and default."

Some are content to swim with the tide, and never oppose abuses: In my youth I knew Clergymen, who held three or four livings, and Deaneries as well: they used to say that it would last their time: some have the misfortune to see further ahead, and to be about ten years in advance of their colleagues. Erasmus was one of these: "Bona verba quæso" is the motto of the compiler of a Missionary-Report: it is, in fact, of the same genus as an election-placard: Euphemism supplies the place of historical completeness, or intelligent criticism, for such might give offence to some supporter, or wound the feelings of the relatives of the individual Missionary, whose conduct is disapproved of.

It is complacently observed in some Reports, that in such matters the men and women actually engaged are the most competent judges of their own policy and proceedings. I took the trouble to make an analysis of the Reports of the six great Societies in 1889–90 and subsequent years. No one, who had read these Reports, would agree in the above opinion, for the men and women in the Field of the same Mission do not agree with each other. Those, who overlook a game of chess with a knowledge of the rules of the game, are better judges of the policy and skill of the players than those who actually play. No class, and no individuals, have such a narrow view of human affairs as the Missionary. The difference of language, which he has acquired in his youth, binds him for ever to one Field, one set of opinions, one environment of experiences and ideas. How wonderfully improved would be the Chinese Missionary, if he could take a term of three years in Africa! How small would seem the Opium-burden, which presses so heavily upon him, when replaced by Cannibalism, Witchcraft, Slave-trade, Murder, and entire Nudity of both sexes.

In my old age, as I sit musing in my Library, reflecting on God's gracious dealings with me during the last half-century, I recall this one of His greatest blessings, that there passes across the mirror of my memory a long procession of spiritual heroes, a stately band, of many of whom I have grasped the hand, while their thoughts and their utterances ring still in my ears: they have been of all denominations of Christ's Church from Rome to Moscow, from Canterbury to Geneva: and each one of them seems to look at me, as he passes by, recalling some opinion given not without profit, some nail driven well down by the Grace of God into the tablets of my Spiritual Life.

My main, my single, desire in these pages is to point out whatever appears to me entirely wrong, or defective, in the Methods in vogue, and suggest some improvement. It is extremely difficult to write on such matters without giving offence. I have endeavoured to guard against this by mostly making general statements. Baxter in his Preface to the "Reformed Pastor" writes: "I have excepted those, who are not guilty, and therefore hope that I have injured none." Like all things human every department of Mission-work is susceptible from year to year of improvement. No Mission has obtained any degree of perfection, however well satisfied the middle-aged Missionary may feel: the moral machinery of the world is always advancing.

I have read and annotated the Annual Reports of a certain number of Societies for a great many years: I think that I know one from the other without reference to the title-page: I am obliged to admit, that the art of writing such Reports has not been acquired yet: the style and execution of all leaves much to be desired. I read them, as it were, medicinally, and a great deal goes against my intellectual stomach. I am obliged to ask: Is the writer dealing with actual facts? If so, why does he write in such a non-natural way, and interlard the remarks with so many quotations from Holy Writ, and such sensational emotional padding? Is the Report merely a pious dream like the "Pilgrim's Progress?" However, I shall come to this subject in Chap. IV. of Bad Methods. I have for many years helped to rule vast Provinces in British India with Millions of inhabitants, and made Annual Reports on Judicial and Revenue matters to the Government: what profit could there have been, if Reports had been made of a non-real type with such sensational paragraphs? I conclude, that these Reports are fashioned to catch the taste of a peculiar emotional class: in some quarters a hit against the Church of Rome, the Ritualist, or the Opium-Trade are essential ingredients calculated to draw subscriptions, or perhaps the absence of such remarks would injure the Society financially.

Since the idea suggested itself to me of compiling this volume, I have carefully gone over a vast number of Pamphlets, Newspaper-cuttings, and Missionary Memoranda, which I had accumulated during the last fifteen years. Sermons of a chance Irish Bishop, called to preach an Annual Sermon entirely devoid of first-hand knowledge, the usual arguments being trotted out: Essays by the single-Mission-Enthusiast, who tries to bring all the multiform phenomena of the Kingdom of Christ into his own narrow lens: Books by one-sided devotees, who take a partial and partizan view, who denounce all the feeling after God, if haply they could find Him, evidenced by the poor heathen, of which Paul speaks so tenderly at Athens; who describe British India, or China, as the Kingdom of Satan, oblivious of the morals of the Cities of London and Paris. Such books do infinite mischief. We know too well by the example of British India, that the population of that Empire actually increases at the rate of three Millions annually, the vast majority of whom are non-Christians, while the whole Christian fold, Syrian, Romish, and Protestant, do not reach much beyond two Millions and three-quarters.

The usual arguments brought in the public Press against the present system, or absence of system, is that (1) the Missionary associations are divided among themselves, and abuse each other to the natives of the Region; (2) they require comforts, and luxuries, and furloughs, and pensions, and wish to live like secular men; (3) they wildly attack the whole Mahometan and Hindu system instead of those parts, which are vulnerable: in their ignorance they knock their heads against that substratum of Divine and Eternal Truth, which lies at the foundation of all systems of adoration of the Divinity by poor weak, ignorant, sinful man; (4) they dwell too much upon the miracles of the

Gospel-Epoch, while they have not that power themselves; (5) instead of adopting the example of Paul and dwelling on the essentials they at once go into details, and thus perplex their hearers. These are not my arguments, but I take notice of them as uttered.

Dean Stanley in one of his sermons in the Abbey on Christian Missions in 1873 remarks on "the necessity of a "vigilant endeavour to repress the exaggeration, to denounce "the fallacies and inaccuracies, which infect even the best "attempts of narrow and fallible, though good and faithful, "servants of the Lord."

Bishop Westcott remarks, "that it is a part, and a painful part, "of the work of the wise to control and correct the folly of the "good." In no departments of good work is this more evident than in the work of Evangelization.

Sometimes in a Report there comes a sentence or two, which go straight to the heart: I quote from a Church Missionary Society Report:

"It is in such circumstances as the foregoing, that we need "the prayers of the people of Christ at home. I often think, "that Missionaries get a great deal of false sympathy. I could "write pages of so-called Missionary hardships—mouldy bread, "lack of provisions when on tour, difficulties in travelling, etc.: "these things are nothing for Christ's sake, and only add a "charm to Missionary life. We need the prayers of the people "at home for the Native Christians themselves, in order that "they may lead pure and holy lives. They need greatly the "Holy Spirit's power to sanctify them; and also the moral "character and fibre of real soldiers of Christ, in order that they "may not hinder those, who would come into the Kingdom of "God."

"There are diversities of gifts, but the same Spirit, and there "are differences of administrations, but the same Lord, and there "are diversities of operations, but it is the same God, which "worketh all in all."—I Cor. xii, 4–6.

I am led to reflect upon the phenomena, presented by a survey of the Missions of the World. It is so strange to find men convinced, that their own system is not only the right one, and the best (the best for them no doubt), *but the only one*, and yet there is an extraordinary, a startling, diversity of practice. In some Associations the Missionary is petted, spoilt, encouraged to early matrimony, involving wanton expenditure of sacred funds; in others I find celibate Brotherhoods and Sisterhoods with the germs of great evils of a contrary tendency. In other quarters I find the Missionary, wife, and little children, turned off in a strange country, in a tropical climate, to support themselves by labour, such as teaching languages, keeping a store, digging yams and potatoes, or, as an American paper bluntly puts it: "Root, Hog, or die," and they do die, and, when an additional baby is born, it is counted as an additional Missionary. Another strange variety is the Knight-errant, without even a knowledge of the language, starting alone on a camel, or horse, to deliver God's message through an interpreter, himself a heathen, and then passing on. The great Associations have large resources, collected at a heavy percentage by an elaborate organization: they spend money freely, and send out men freely, often unsanctified, and untested men, and sometimes gross failures. Sometimes Missionaries are tied to a shibboleth of dogma, and a confession of Church-Government; at other times there is an amalgam of dogma, and a free-hand of Church-Government. Some allow their agents fixed subsistence-allowances, and subsidiary provision for Rent, Locomotion, Disablement, and Children. Others make a boast, that they do not, that the Missionary must make his own private resources go as far as possible, and that he will get a fractional portion of the income of the Society, varying each year, and nothing of any kind to fall back upon.

Dr. G. Smith in his "Conversion of India" quotes from an open letter from the Missionary Society in S. India the following words:

"Since the Spirit of God still abides in the Church, it is not "shut up by a mere imitation of Methods used in bygone days "by good men. God is with us now, as He inspired our fathers: "He places us in new and untried conditions, that we may "learn new lessons, and apply new Methods. There is no "finality, or rigidity, in the Methods now adopted." I entirely agree with this noble sentiment, but, when an untried Missionary band descend from Colorado, U.S., on the West Coast of Africa, or China, I ask them to make use of sanctified common-sense, sweet reasonableness, and collected experience.

What is my qualification for putting pen to paper? Just fifty years ago, in the Spring of 1844, Daniel Wilson, Bishop of Calcutta, taught me my lesson in Missions: I had received £80 as a prize for proficiency in some language, and I wanted to invest it, and the Bishop showed me how to do it to advantage by distributing it among Missions: it was the best investment that I ever made, for from the subject of Evangelization I have had joy, interest, and occupation, for half a century: in the Indian Field for a quarter of a century, inspection of Missions in Turkey, Palestine, Egypt, N. Africa, in the Committees of many Societies in London, on the platform, in the Press, making the acquaintance of scores of good men, not necessarily wise men, as things of this world go. I have had access to the periodicals and literature of all Missions, English or Foreign, Protestant or Romish, in the four modern languages of Europe, to which must be added for the Church of Rome, Latin. Besides all this I had the advantage of having been a Ruler of Millions for many years, and living alone among, and loving, my people, speaking their language as my own: I knew all about their customs and languages, and religious beliefs, and sympathized with the latter, as their expression of their belief in their Creator: all the stories of Missionaries about the multiplicity of gods among the Hindus is mere nonsense picked up: their number of real divinities is limited: as for the Mahometan it goes without saying, that he is a stern monotheist. I became aware of the tranquil happy life in the scattered Indian villages. My first district was a conquest made in the campaign, in which I had taken part in 1845–46, and my first duty was to tell my people, who had never seen a white man before, that I should not allow any burning of widows, killing of daughters, and burying alive of lepers: as to Caste, and Child-Marriage, and the re-marriage of the widows, whom we had saved from the funeral-pile, that was left to the people themselves: they were an ancient and civilized people at a time, when the Britons and the Anglo-Saxons were barbarians: the population has increased by so many Millions during the last half century, that child-marriage, and the non-marriage of widows, does not seem to have had a prejudicial effect on the number of births.

Up to this day I am totally opposed to the proselytizing of members of the Romish, Greek, Asiatic, or African, Christian Churches: and till ten years ago I took no interest in the conversion of the Jews: "they have Moses and the Prophets, let them hear them." I have twice traversed, at the interval of a quarter of a century, the length and breadth of Palestine from Dan to Beersheba, and during my last tour in 1885 it was brought home to me, that the conversion of the whole non-Christian world would be as nothing, if God's chosen people still remained outside the fold: so on my return I joined the London-Jews Society, spoke for it at the Annual Meeting in Exeter Hall, and have since visited every one of the Mission-Fields except that in Persia: I thus have tried to complete my knowledge of this solemn subject: and the question is brought home to me, why after the lapse of eighteen centuries only a fraction of the world has been brought to Christ, and I repeat in defiance of all the folly uttered by enthusiasts, that the great mass of non-Christians is numerically larger at the close of this century than it was at the commencement, and that in addition to the old dead Book-Religions, which date before the Christian era, and the great Religion of Islam, which has come into existence in modern times long after the Christian era, there is now a new birth of Religious conceptions, inculcating the highest morality, free from gross idolatry, not enslaved to Priesthoods, with a certain amount of spirituality in their essence, which are a hundredfold more dangerous enemies than the old moribund forms of worship. There is room for great humiliation in the Christian Churches. Where is boasting? it is excluded: there is not one single self-supporting Christian Native Church in any one of the four non-Christian Divisions of the World, free and independent of the spiritual domination of the alien European and American. The fallen Churches of Asia and Africa were not very spiritual, but still in spite of persecution and oppression they have kept their candlestick lighted, and depend for aid on no foreign Power, while in the event of the strong political Power of Europe and America being withdrawn the great majority of the new embryo Churches would be swept away, as has happened to the Church of Rome in S. America and W. Africa.

My Essay is ostensibly on "Methods," but I have been constrained to include certain features, which would be more accurately classed as "Environments" than "Methods;" but it is necessary, that attention should be drawn to these, for owing to the euphemistic, emotional, and semi-poetical, style, adopted in the Reports and periodical literature, the harsh phenomena, which surround the work of the Missionary, are obscured from sight: it is my desire, that the work should be understood as it is: my quotations are numerous and from Missionary-Reports. At present, if anyone really desired to know what the prospects of the warfare were, he would never gain it from the one-sided Reports, and Publications, of different Societies, and the authors of some of the volumes on the general subject are so sanguine, so full of worship of their particular Missionary-hero, they burn so much incense to their own Society, they are so unwilling, or fearful, to state the failures, the difficulties, the gross errors, that they are like the prophets, who deceived the Kings of Israel and Judah. I have tried to do my duty as a free-lance, a careful student, and one absolutely devoted for a lifetime to the one great subject of Evangelization.

Far be it from me to say, that because the number of non-Christians is now greater than it was before Missions commenced, that Missions are failures: nothing of the kind: for my own belief is, that the Truth of the great cause is evidenced by the large degree of success vouchsafed in spite of the very imperfect, and often very injudicious, Methods, adopted by a succession of men, all of whom have been good, but few only have been wise. I have seen the tree grow in British India, and the Turkish Empire, under my own eyes: If the Lord had not been on our side, the event would have been different. Besides, I am entirely opposed to the counting up of converts made, and the numbering of baptisms: we have done our duty, if we sow the seed in well-prepared ground: it is from the Lord that comes the increase. I think that I heard last year at an Annual Meeting of a Society, that they had not baptized one soul, and being a brotherhood and sisterhood, had not the false comfort of reporting, that they had baptized their own children: in fact their font was dry.

It is such a pity, that in all treatises a certain number of stock-names of Statesmen, or Military, and Civil, Officials, are paraded, without stating that some have been dead thirty or fifty years, that their experience was limited to one Field only, and possibly to one Mission, and that their remarks were made in the course of an Exeter-Hall-Speech, or some occasion, when all criticism, however friendly, was out of question: if quotations are to be made, let them be from the utterances of qualified persons in the Missionary Conferences, or carefully composed Essays prepared for print and criticism by others.

Even the Church Missionary Society, which is very emotional, very conservative, and rarely looks outside the door of its own Committee-room, seems in the appended quotation to feel a shaking of its dead bones, and to hear a sound of a going in the trees, and it expresses itself in the sweet Doric dialect of the Society with a copious use of the Divine Name, and semi-poetical gushing phraseology:

" God has owned old Methods of work. Destroy them not,
" for there is a blessing in them. In the light of accumulated
" experience, and under the influence of new environments, the
" old Methods have been, and will be, improved. God forbid
" that they should be abandoned.

" The call has come for new Methods and fresh experiments.
" That call can neither be lightly disregarded, nor lightly
" obeyed. The Committee is not frightened by the outcry
" against new departures. Rather they thank God, that the
" increased interest at home, and the growth of opportunities
" abroad, necessitate new departures. But all such new
" departures must be jealously safeguarded by rigid adherence
" to the old principles, which from its foundation have been the
" glory and strength of the Society.

" In view of the rapidly rising tide of intelligent, self-conse-
" crating, interest at home, and in view of the marvellous
" opening out of the Field abroad, the Committee is deter-
" mined, God helping them, to be found ready, first for the
" consolidation and strengthening of existing work, then for
" further expansion, as God shall provide duly qualified workers.

" With the Master's commission, 'Go ye into all the world,
" and preach the Gospel to every creature,' ringing in their
" ears, the Committee would say, 'God forbid that we should
" surrender the high privilege of holding ourselves in readiness
" to utilize to the utmost all the evangelical and evangelistic

" fervour and zeal, which God the Holy Spirit is awakening in the Church of England!'

"The constitution of the Society anticipated boundless development in the demands made upon her. There is no necessity to limit that development. Methods must be adopted to cope with the growing, worldwide demands, which in God's mercy are being made, and the laws of the Society permit of this being done. The Committee have had under consideration various schemes for easing the admitted strain; and are satisfied that the advance made is as rapid as is consistent with that due deliberation, which alone can secure continuity of principle in administration; and, above all, continuity of those great evangelical and spiritual principles, which permeate the whole work of the Society. For themselves, their prayerful aim will be, in dependence on the Spirit of God, to have the control so regulated and the procedure so ordered that, whatever the demand be, they may be enabled to respond efficiently and promptly."

No all-round student of Missions could doubt from what quarter these words emanated: a copious use of pretty phrases, and expressed readiness to let in a breeze of the outside air into their Council Chamber: a Vox clamantis, et promittentis, et

PRÆTEREA NIHIL.

Part I.

GOOD METHODS.

There are of cause various modifications of these great Methods, which must rest with the discretion of the agents: the population of the world is not on a dead level of culture: some recommend preaching for a few days, after the manner of Jonah at Niniveh, the first Missionary to the Gentiles, and then passing on to Regions beyond. I doubt.

I quote an extract from another point of view: "To what ex-
" tent should we use means? This is a point that has exercised
" many. It seems to us, that God intends us to use every means
" we can, provided the means are right and worthy of God. It
" is on this point that we are sometimes misunderstood. We
" gladly use every means we know of to make known the Gospel
" at home and abroad, and to obtain money and men to carry
" on the work, provided the means are not only right but worthy
" of God, but we decline to use means, that do not seem to us
" well pleasing to the Lord. Probably all Christians would
" agree that no means should be used that are immoral, but so
" great is the pressure in every good work, that there is a strong
" temptation to condescend to agencies that are unworthy."

Here again is a diversity of opinion: I have known a Missionary refuse contributions, or aid, from a man not living up to his idea of a godly life. Did even the Pharisees prevent the Publican from casting his mite into the Treasury?

Slow was the process, like that of a moving glacier, but there never was a period, when the movement entirely stopped: God's wheels grind slowly: even in the Evangelization of the World it is not the Method of God to give immediate results: let modern Missionaries take that fact to their comfort, and their guidance.

To men in the nineteenth century, dwelling in the midst of material civilization, the voice crying from the wilderness may have no effect: in his health and strength man scarcely thinks enough of the blessings of life: but to the sufferer on the sick bed, the dweller in the lone garret, the man bereaved of all his loved ones, the one, who cries aloud for his daily bread, to such a one in that terrible period, the story of the banks of Jordan, the happy land, the prospect of a future state, which cannot be worse than the present, the reunion with friends, the escape from the power of the tyrant, the enemy, the oppressor, had a reality, especially when preached by earnest men, who believed their message, and who talked about the undying worm, and the tortures of hell, as if they had had personal experience: all this touched the heart both of the first class, who had lost all confidence in their discredited divinities, and the second class, which was fresh and receptive of new doctrines, which *perhaps* they thought *might be true;* at least they were comforting.

In describing Xavier's work a Romish writer writes, and truly writes, that the first good Method of Evangelization was, that the Missionary should be a sample of a life of self-denial, mortification of the flesh, humility, combined with love of God, and zeal for the salvation of souls: whenever Missionary work has succeeded, is successful, or will ever succeed, it is only by such a Method as that of Xavier, which was also that of Columbanus, Boniface, Aidan, and all who were animated by their spirit and desired their reward. A kind of comfortable dilettante life to be given up, when the wife is sick, is worth nothing.

Let me first notice the Apostolic Methods: they require no comment.

    I. Preaching in the Vernacular, whether in the streets of the City, by the Hillside, on the banks of Rivers and Lakes, whether by parties of men, or of women, itinerating from village to village.

    II. Teaching the way of Salvation in private visits, in journeys, in walks, in small assemblies collected together, or in larger gatherings.

    III. Healing the sick, if not by the miracles described in the New Testament, at least by the miracles of Science, and loving care, and tender nursing. Such Missionaries receive no remuneration, and go great distances: what more perfect Charity can there be than the Hospital?

I now pass to post-Apostolic Methods:

    I. Reading and distributing portions of the Scriptures in the Vernacular to those, who are able to read.

    II. Visiting Hospitals, and talking to, or praying with, the Patients: visiting the women's apartments in great houses, and talking with them, reading the Scriptures, and praying with them.

    III. Visiting Leper-Asylums, where such exist, or similar Institutions for unhappy outcasts.

    IV. Founding and maintaining Orphanages for the reception of children abandoned in season of Famine, released from Slavery, or made over by the State to the Missionaries.

V. Founding and maintaining purely elementary schools for religious teaching.
VI. Reading and distributing Christian literature of a light and attractive character in the Vernacular.
VII. Training-Colleges to provide Native Pastors, Evangelists, and Teachers, and for such purposes providing Boarding houses, or Hostels, for their entertainment.

In the process of converting Europe the Monastery played an important and holy part: the institution had not then been abused: as time went on a bad name attached to it. It was at once an asylum, a hospital, and a religious school. Agricultural, and Industrial, occupations were superintended: the lives of the Missionaries were simple, devout, and devoted. Celibacy was of course the rule. The Church-services, however ritualistic, did something to elevate the character of the ignorant heathen: bad customs, loose morality, were shamed out of existence: lessons of self-denial, self-restraint, and gentleness, were thus given: intercession for mercy was made to rude Chieftains, and often with success: conciliation was effected between litigants: bloodshed protested against: an asylum offered to the victims of persecution. The new doctrines appeared in the outward form of a group of self-denying, patient, benevolent, altruistic brethren: it would appear ridiculous now, but it was a great instrument of good then. The corporate life of Brotherhoods and Sisterhoods represent this factor now. We should not allow a prejudice, arising from our knowledge of the abuse of the system, when maintained after the necessity had passed, to blind our eyes to the wonderful service rendered by it. Social life in Europe has changed, but the condition of affairs in Africa now is much the same, as it was then in Europe in the sixth or seventh century. It is all very well to talk of a Missionary's home with his wife, and six children, as a beautiful object-lesson of Christianity to the Natives; they cannot see it in that romantic light, nor could I, though I have visited scores of Missionaries in their homes. Altruism is the object of Missions: egoism is the very essence of family-life. I unhesitatingly pronounce Brotherhoods and Sisterhoods to be a good Method.

It requires Faith, Patience, deep-rooted Kindliness to argue with an inquirer. There was a book published forty years ago called "Dwij," in which a late Missionary at Banáras describes the death-struggle, which he had with a young Brahmin, finally converting him. I knew both the combatants, and remember the combat: it caused serious reflection in my mind at the time, and up to the present hour: he bought his Faith at a great price: I had the blessing of being born in the Faith.

The new conception of the Female-Evangelist promises to be one of the most blessed, and fruitful of blessings. I described

their appearance among the villagers ten years ago, and I can add nothing: "To the village-women the appearance of a
" Female Evangelist must be as it were the vision of an Angel
" from Heaven: to their untutored eyes she appears taller in
" stature, fairer in face, sweeter in speech than anything mortal
" they had ever dreamed of before: bold and fearless without
" immodesty: pure in word and action yet with features un-
" veiled: wise yet condescending to the ignorant and little
" children: prudent and self-restrained, yet still a woman loving
" and tender: such as they never appeared before to poor
" village-women, even in their dreams, until suddenly their eyes,
" their ears, and their hearts, seem to realize faintly and con-
" fusedly the Beauty of Holiness, when they begin to hold
" converse, only too brief, with their sweet and loving visitor,
" who, smitten with the wondrous desire to save souls, has come
" across the sea from some unknown country to comfort and
" help them. Short as is her stay, she has, as it were with a
" magic wand, let loose a new fountain of hopes, of fears and
" desires: she has told them perhaps in faltering accents of
" Righteousness, and Judgment, of Sin, Repentance, and Pardon
" through the blessed merits of a Saviour. This day has Salva-
" tion come to this Indian village." This is a good Method.

Among good Methods must be included a proper rule with regard to the return to Europe of Missionaries located in unhealthy regions, such as Equatorial Africa, and tropical countries generally. A living Missionary can do much, but a dead Missionary, or one with his health hopelessly shattered, can do nothing. The Civil Government as regards its own servants has laid down rules sufficient for health. In Africa three years is the very outside for a residence without a break. As it is, the deaths in the field are appalling: Furlough after ten years in India, China, and Japan, is amply sufficient, unless a Doctor's certificate orders an earlier return. It is false economy to throw away, or lose the services of, a trained and capable man.

The very presence of a Missionary, man or woman, is the symptom of a good Method. The Merchant from the West cannot be quoted as a sample of character. It is a surprise to an African to have a white man in their midst, who, if he chose, could ill-use them, carry off their wife and children and sell them as slaves, and yet does not do so: the wages, whether in cash or kind, paid regularly, cause a new sensation among people used to do forced labour: the kind word uttered, and assistance rendered in case of sickness, surprises them still more: Character does not go for much in old civilized countries, like India, China, and Japan, yet the people are led to reflect upon the wonderful phenomenon, that there are men and women living among them for a score or more years, not to rule the land like the officials, not to make money like the merchant, but to do acts of kindness, speak words of gentleness, encourage morality, and talk about God, and a Future State: I quote a letter from the Minister of the United States at Pekin, dated 1886:

"I am not particularly pro-Missionary: these men and women are simply citizens to me, as Minister: but as a man I cannot but admire and respect them. I can tell the real from the false. These men and women are honest, pious, sincere, industrious, and trained for their work by much arduous study: outside any religious question these people are doing a great work of civilizing, educating, and taking care of helpless thousands. They are the forerunner of higher Methods, and higher morality. I do not address myself to Churches; but, as a man of the world, talking to someone like himself, I think, that it is difficult to say too much good of Missionary-work in China from even the standpoint of the Sceptic." This also is a good Method.

Part II.

METHODS NOT RECOMMENDED.

Between the good Methods, and the bad, there are a certain number, which have come under my consideration, and which I cannot recommend, though unquestionably they are practised by good men: the question is one of expediency. I have divided them into two categories, I. Secular, II. Spiritual, and append a detached list of them, and now proceed to describe each, with my reasons for not recommending.

CAP.		
I.		SECULAR.
	1	Industrial Farms, Trades, Manufactures, Fisheries.
	2	Giving Western names to Natives of Africa, Asia, Oceania, and America.
	3	Giving Western Agents higher rates of emolument than Natives, except so far as life and health require.
	4	Interference with Slaveholders, and giving asylum to runaway Slaves.
	5	Adopting dress of Natives.
	6	Sensational and emotional proceedings.
	7	Intrusive Begging, Beehives, Bazaars, Old-World Fairs, Lotteries, etc.
	8	Preaching in Streets under circumstances calculated to entail a breach of the peace.
	9	Forbidding Converts to marry non-Christians.
	10	High-class Secular Education.
II.		SPIRITUAL.
	1	Baptism of Polygamists.
	2	Challenging, or accepting, public discussion on Doctrine.
	3	Substituting other elements in the Communion for Bread and Wine.
	4	Interfering with the ancient organization of the Asiatic and African Churches.

I. SECULAR.

1. Industrial Farms: Trades: Manufactures: Fisheries.

No one can doubt the benevolence of those, who undertake such enterprises; but I think most probably the spirituality of the manager must be driven out of him, and in these days of the fight of Capital against Labour, and the competition of Trade, it must needs be, that occasionally the Courts of Law, Civil or Criminal, must be appealed to, and my long experience of Courts of Law in British India makes me feel, that the white Missionary would cut a very sorry figure in such contentions: he at least cannot lie, or suborn witnesses, or practise the tricks of the Court, and it is difficult to say, whether he would be more alienated from his converts, if he came out of the Court triumphant, or defeated. The whole thing is so thoroughly contrary to Apostolic practice, and post-Apostolic experience.

The duty of the Missionary is to preach the Gospel, and nothing else, except what helps the preaching of the Gospel. His converts, and his Church, may be poor and uncivilized; that is not his affair: the poor have the Gospel preached to them: that is his sole duty. A great deal can be done incidentally by advice, and example, but all my experience of the last half century goes against any attempt in the least degree to ask a spiritual man to do secular duties, or to yoke secular and religious men in the same fellowship. I am entirely in favour of the Lay Evangelist, the Female Evangelist, the Medical Evangelist, wherever Gospel-preaching is the substantive work, but, when it is proposed to have a pious Industrial Superintendent, or an Evangelical tile-manufacturer, or a Low-Church breeder of cattle, or raiser of turnips, I draw my line, and fall back on the great Commission, Matt. xxviii, 19, 20, and sternly reject all external adjuncts. Let not our agents exchange their blessed names of Preacher, Teacher, Friend for those of Farmer, Trader, Employer: the latter may make more money; the former will save more souls, and that is the sole object of Christian Missions. The Missionary may not see the reward of his Soul in his lifetime, but his name will be mentioned with gratitude by generations still to be born, as the man, who opened the way of Salvation to them, who roused them from the long dark sleep of centuries, and perhaps had the blessed honour of dying in their midst. Augustine did not teach our Anglo-Saxon forefathers the art of building ships, or starting manufactories, or breeding oxen, but he did something better: he brought to a Nation, that was heathen, the knowledge of a Saviour.

Captain Lugard, in his book on "The Rise of our East African Empire," writes so strongly in favour of Industrial Missions, that it may be well to reproduce here the views held upon the subject by Missionaries of undoubted experience.

Bishop Steere says: "The main defect of travellers' talk about "Missions is, that they can only tell what they saw. Now there "are two very distinct systems of Mission-working. One is to "take the natives into tutelage, and make them live and move "by order, and work when and as they are bidden. This "system, well worked, produces fine plantations, good culti- "vation, well-kept houses, and a most respectful demeanour.

"The other system aims at giving the Native independence "and force of character. It leaves him free to cultivate and "build and live as he pleases, subject only to instruction, and a "moderate amount of Church discipline. The strong point of "this system lies in its development of a really native home- "grown Christianity, with a principle of self-improvement, which "works slowly and from within.

"It is morally certain, that nine travellers out of ten will "report better of Missions on the former plan, and therefore "say that they are more successful than any others. I doubt "the fact."

And Archdeacon Alan Gibson, who is Bishop Coadjutor-elect of Capetown, in a most interesting article on "The Gospel of Labour," in the *Kaffrarian Diocesan Quarterly* for January 1894, sums up as follows:

"It seems to me, that in the matter of manual labour the "Missionary must not take European countries for his guidance, "but must shape his course by the Bible, and by Christian "common-sense. A certain amount of manual labour is, of "course, necessary, and is practised. The Christians build "their churches and schools, cultivate crops sufficient for their "own support, and the payment of Church-dues, school-fees, "and Government hut-tax; and, with the constant enlargement "and improvement of kraals, have plenty to occupy them.

"Where they do so little as to neglect any of these Scriptural "injunctions, there the Missionary plainly has a duty; lest the "younger generation should grow up despising manual labour, "it would most likely be well to have some alteration in the "day-schools, which, however, probably only Government could "carry out; and more attention should be paid to the decent "housing of the family.

"In all these points the Church has a distinct mission; but "when the Missionary is told absolutely, that his primary duty is "to teach the native to work, he may well call to mind the old saying, 'Est modus in rebus, sunt certi denique fines.'"

I quote the opinion of my valued friend, the Rev. W. Gray, himself many years a Missionary, and many years one of the Secretaries of the Church Missionary Society:

"I dislike the system to which you refer: Our work as Missionaries, is to lead men to Christ: it is no business of ours to draw them away from the innocent secular callings, in which Christianity found them, and to find new employment for them: there is no need to organize Industrial or Mercantile Systems. The Church Missionary Society is often appealed to by Missionaries in India to help them in setting on foot some system for providing employment for converts. They are not encouraged. Lately a Corresponding-Committee encouraged the idea of going to Government to get a special Christian Regiment established: it was at once discouraged by the Committee: why should Native Christians be thus segregated? I oppose to the utmost of my power any attempt to introduce anything like the Basle-system into the Church Missionary Society's Indian or African Missions. We have hard enough work already to dispossess the minds of the converts of the idea, that they are conferring on Missionaries a great compliment, and benefit, by becoming Christians. The Basle-system must help to foster this idea, and it does not tend to foster the spirit of independence and self-help. I Corinthians, vii, 24, gives no uncertain advice: 'Let every man abide in the calling, in which he was called.'"

In 1890 certain friends of the Church Missionary Society at Keswick moved that Society to take steps in the direction of Industrial Missions. A Sub-Committee was appointed to consider the subject, and after a full inquiry submitted a most interesting and instructive Report to the General Committee, with the following recommendations:

    I. That no trading or industrial Mission should be carried on by the side of, and in close connection with, Missionary work.
    II. That Missionaries in uncivilized Regions should have some industrial training.
    III. That industrial training should not form a factor of educational work in *all* the Missions, still that there were certain places where it might be.
    IV. That simple industrial training should form part of the teaching in Africa.
    V. That the circumstances of Frere-Town in E. Africa are so exceptional, that there an Industrial Training Establishment should be maintained in full efficiency.

Bishop Smythies recorded his opinion, that "he regarded with "suspicion all industrial work undertaken by Missionaries unless "kept in strict subordination to Missionary ends, as tending to "lower the standard of spiritual life, and to turn Missionaries "into traders and planters."

The Rev. B. La Trobe of the Moravian Mission informed the Sub-Committee of the Church Missionary Society, that the industrial trading in Labrador and Greenland was carried on by a Society in connection with the Missionary-Society, but separate from it, the losses when they occurred being borne by the Mission, and the profits used exclusively for Mission purposes. On the whole, although industrial work would attract and benefit converts, and was absolutely necessary for the civilization of savage races, he thought his Committee would be glad to do without it. It appeared, however, that the objection arose specially from the trading operations necessarily involved. They feel, that trading and business principles ought to be taught, and that, although the expressions *Church heart* and *Store heart* were sometimes used, the contact with the Natives in business matters helped decidedly to get at their hearts, and gave opportunities for Gospel-teaching.

The Reports of Mission-work for Labrador have quite a flavour of Train-Oil and Deep-sea-Fishery. It is excusable, because the work lies amidst the lowest grade of the human race, and the Mission depends for its existence on its Industry.

The Rev. W. S. Price, who has had much experience in industrial training work at Nasik and at Frere-Town, was of opinion, that there should be no industrial training except in orphanages and other special institutions. In a unique country like U-Ganda he would found no training institutions, but merely give the lads sufficient instruction to start them in work.

I now quote the opinion of my esteemed friend Dr. Thompson of the American Board of Foreign Missions in a letter to me asking my opinion in 1890 :

"A distinction exists between manual labour (1) as an inci-
"dental thing, and (2) as the leading feature of a school. In
"most Missions to the young instruction is given in useful in-
"dustries, yet only as an adjunct, the leading notion being to
"raise up competent native helpers in pure Mission-work. On
"the other hand Industrial Schools contemplate remunerative
"secular occupation, and the training of labourers, who will be
"able to support themselves by handicraft, and enrich the com-
"munity. In such schools mental training, and religious edu-
"cation, are subordinated. Secular Industry is the distinctive
"feature : and manual skill, which is remunerative, is the object
"in view."

Such Industrial Schools are valuable, when conducted by the Civil Government, or by private philanthropy, but I doubt, whether they have a legitimate claim upon Missionary-Resources, and whether they can possibly be included in the sphere of Gospel-promulgation. I had no hesitation in my reply, that Industrial Schools were neither apostolic, nor expedient, when conducted by Missionaries.

The spiritual agent of Missions must stand entirely apart from the baser employments of human life: his vocation is to lead men to the Kingdom of God, not to make neo-Christians fat and comfortable in this world. Paul did indeed work with his own hands, so as not to be a charge to his converts: he had not a wealthy constituency behind him to supply his needed wants. Experience tells us, that it is better for the work to free the Missionary from vulgar cares, so that he may have more leisure and strength for his sacred duties: but this does not mean that he should start tile-works, or weaving establishments, or carpenter's shops, although our Lord Himself deigned to live, as the son of a Carpenter. Nor should his time be occupied in superintending Fisheries, although Peter and John were fishermen. To this extent there has been a social revolution in the world. The man of God would find his spirituality fairly squeezed out of him by contact with hard worldly business: which, quite commendable for secular laymen, is not suitable for those, whom the Holy Spirit has selected out of their contemporaries to carry the Gospel. It is not canny to hear of a Missionary shooting elephants on the Kongo, and making a pile of money by sale of tusks, or breeding ostriches, rearing cattle or sheep, raising turnips, oats, or cereals. Capital has to be advanced and risked; books have to be kept, profits to be accounted for, losses written off: accumulated wealth by a small Christian community might be a temptation to plunder: The only safe course for a Missionary to take is to live from hand to mouth, and to have nothing to offer the barbarian tribes, which might tempt them to plunder.

In the camp, which maintains the opposing views, I find the honoured and respected names of the Bishop of Sierra Leone, the Free Church of Scotland, the German Mission of Basle, the Missionaries of the Church of Rome; I proceed to quote from their reports.

I am not maintaining, that a Missionary should not be a handy man, able to build his own house, thatch his own roof: I quote Chrysostom, Dec. Soc. Lib. iv, § 4. "καὶ δεῖ τὸν μέλλοντα τὴν "πρὸς πάντας ἀναδέχεσθαι μάχην, τὰς ἁπάντων εἰδέναι τέχνας· καὶ "τὸν αὐτὸν τοξότην εἶναι, καὶ σφενδονιστὴν, καὶ στρατιώτην, καὶ "στρατηγόν, καὶ, πεζὸν, καὶ ἱππέα, καὶ ναυμάχην, καὶ τειχομάχην."
These are subordinate qualifications of the Christian warrior,

but there is no necessity to be the Manager of a Manufactory, or the leader of an agricultural colony.

The good Bishop of Sierra Leone cannot be called a Missionary, nor his Episcopal charge a Mission: if he find it in him to promote a benevolent industrial Mission, and funds are forthcoming distinctly for that purpose, by all means let him so employ them. The Church Missionary Society Lay Workers' Union was addressed by the Bishop, and a separate fund was started. It seemed to several of the members, that to
" assist the Bishop in giving his proposed Industrial Institution
" a fair start would be not only a pleasant way of commemorating
" his Lordship's visit, but also a work most appropriate to be
" undertaken by a Union of Lay Workers. It is indeed not
" impossible that, when the funds have been secured, one of our
" own members may go out as the Industrial agent. Under
" these circumstances we hope that the members will all unite
" to support this scheme. The sum required to start it will be
" £100 a year for three years. If each member will subscribe
" 3s. 4d. yearly for those three years, or 10s. in all, the amount
" will be secured, and we hope that all will make an effort to
" contribute this small sum, amounting to less than a penny a
" week. We shall, however, be glad to hear from the richer
" members of our Union, that they are willing to supply the
" place of some of those, whose income does not enable them
" to contribute this sum. A considerable sum was promised in
" the room at Salisbury Square, and we shall be very glad if an
" effective answer can be given before the Bishop leaves for
" his Diocese." It is unnecessary to state the Bishop's argument as to the need of Africa: it is self-evident: my point is, that it is not the work of a Society for the Propagation of the Gospel.

Mr. Stewart, of the Free Church of Scotland, the celebrated founder of the Industrial Mission at Lovedale in South Africa, writes that " Industrial work does not interfere with spiritual
"life in any greater extent than the same occupations do at
" home: it depends entirely on the man." Herr Oehler, Missionary-Inspector from Basle, gives the same testimony with regard to their Mission in India and Africa.

I quote from the Annual Report of the Free Church, 1890:

" *Re-organization of Trades' Department, Lovedale.* The
" change involves a much larger amount of time being taken in
" teaching of a purely technical or trade kind, and to placing
" the apprentices in groups so as to benefit by that Instruction.
" It also involves letting go some of the profits of the work, and
" affects the question of self-support."

Again:

" *The Artisan Evangelists and Teachers.* From the founda-
" tion of the Mission in Lovedale the Free Church has sent out

"godly young artisans, carpenters and masons, blacksmiths
"and engineers, gardeners and printers, to erect the Mission
"Stations, work the steamers, print the Word of God,
"evangelize the natives through the vernacular tongue, and
"teach their children. There were eleven such men in 1890."
And again:
"We are put to a heavy expense in and endeavour to carry out
"the requirements of the Educational Code of Cape-Colony,
"which requires Industrial Training in all Schools. Turning
"out carpenters and blacksmiths will stir up bitter opposition
"from the European settlers, who will consider the bread
"taken out of their mouths."

The Bishop of Sierra Leone is not alone as regards W. Africa: I regret that he and the Archdeacon wrote the words, recorded in the Report of the Church Missionary Society.

"The Bishop of Sierra Leone strongly urged on the Sub-
"Committee the necessity of industrial training forming an
"essential part of Mission-work in Africa. Archdeacon
"Hamilton considered that industrial training was most desir-
"able. He would have masonry and coopering at Sierra Leone,
"brickmaking and coopering at Lagos, carpentering and black-
"smiths' work at Abeokuta, taught in the Church Missionary
"Society Schools; this work not being supported by the
"Society, but by selling the goods made."

I now quote from the Reports of the Basle-Mission in Western India, 1890:

Industrial and Mercantile Establishments.

"Our Weaving Establishments in Mangalore, Cannanore,
"and Calicut, as well as our Tile-Works in Kudroli, Jeppu
"(Mangalore), Malpe (Udapi), and Calicut, are too well known
"to require any detailed description, as also our Carpentry
"Establishment at Calicut, our Mechanical Workshop at Man-
"galore, and three Mercantile Mission-Branches at Mangalore,
"Mercara, and Calicut respectively. But, although we have
"repeatedly explained the object and nature of these Estab-
"lishments, still we frequently meet with people who misunder-
"stand our motives. We would therefore briefly remark in the
"first place, that these Establishments have not been called
"into existence by our Missionary-Society, but by a separate
"Mercantile Committee, which has, however, among its members
"a number of gentlemen, who take a deep interest in Mission-
"work, with the object of giving a means of livelihood to our
"converts; and secondly, that if profit be made in the business,
"the Mission-fund gets a part of it; this, however, is not by
"far so large as some people seem to think, for some of them,
"like other Mercantile firms, have their losses. It is true that

"some of the Establishments were from the outset opened on a larger scale than was absolutely necessary for the purpose in view, and in consequence of this, a large number of heathen and Mahometans find employment side by side with our Christians and candidates for baptism, but these, however, are brought within the influence of the Gospel by means of the Scripture-reading and prayer held every morning in our Establishments before work is begun. We know of instances, in which these daily services have given the first impulse towards Christianity. Our lay brethren can also directly and indirectly do much for the furtherance of Mission-work. We are thankful to the Lord for all, that has been done in this direction, and trust that we may also in the future get faithful workers for this branch of the Mission. Faithfulness in little things the Lord will not leave unrewarded.

"These Weaving-Establishments have also in the past year continued to do their good work for the maintenance of our Christians, while at the same time they supply work to some of the new-comers and young men."

The same Missionary-Society has similar secular establishments in W. Africa. Amidst the African races the system may find an excuse, or a pretence. In India the people were acquainted with the arts of weaving, pottery, and carpentry, at a remote period when the Teutons, the common ancestors of Germans and English, were naked savages.

Do such establishments produce gratitude? I quote the Report:

"When we review the other portions of our Mission-Field we are painfully struck at the daily diminishing number of that band of noble men and women, who amidst much enmity and persecution, forsook their idols, their castemen, and their families, became the first fruits of our different Stations, and as such, the salt and light of the congregations. A new generation is gradually taking their place: most of these have not tasted the thraldom of idolatry and the enmity of the world, but have enjoyed all the privileges conferred upon them through the medium of Church and School. They feel their present elevated position; their energies, however, have not as yet found their proper channels. Many, especially of those, who till now have not experienced what a new birth is, in their desire to improve their circumstances, are impatient, that things develop so slowly and not in the very way they wish, and are often apt to suspect the *very* Missionaries, to whose instrumentality most of them owe their prosperity, and who leave untried no means and ways to push them on, as if it were they, who were keeping them down and hindering their progress.

"With deep regret we have this year to confirm these remarks. Reports have reached us from several stations of growing-up sons grieving their parents and teachers, and in one case, of having even ill-treated them. These unruly members were duly admonished, but finding all our remonstrances had remained fruitless, we had finally to excommunicate them. Very careful nursing and faithful looking after of souls is indispensable, if our congregations are to shine as lights amidst the heathen darkness around them."

The excellent arrangements of the Industrial Mission of the Missionaries of the Church of Rome on the mainland on the coast opposite the Island of Zanzibar, connected with the name of the much respected Père Horner, have been the object of praise by both German and English writers of judgment and distinction. When a Church can go so far as to purchase slaves of the slave-dealer in order to make up a Mission School, we can hardly weigh them in the same balance as regards Industrial Schools; they do not approach the subject of Evangelization with the same spirit. The Jesuit Missions on the Zambési go in for Industrial Missions in their worst form. They give out that real and lasting good can only be done among savages by the establishment of Christian villages, where the faith and habit of Christian life are gradually learnt; it is their desire to renew on African soil establishments, such as once existed in S. America, famous for their temporal prosperity. The British African Company has lately made a grant of a large tract of country in Mashona-land, and the Romish Missionaries appeal for funds to carry out their designs.

Contact with matters pertaining to money-making takes off the fine feeling of a Missionary. I have seen Romish Missionaries distilling liqueur; I have heard of them superintending the breeding of cattle, and selling the beasts, and it made me shudder. Of course, hand-work and loom-work for the use of the family is lawful, and working in the garden. Lay-brothers with a Missionary spirit would be useful here, in the school and in the pharmacy.

Finally, I have on my table a circular issued by a new Protestant Zambési Industrial Mission, intended to be self-supporting and self-propagating. This is the right kind of thing, and deserves every support. There is, however, a fatality, which seems to urge good people to do their work in the least wise manner, for the directors of this enterprise announce, that the chief and special work of the Industrial Mission is to set free A-Ngoni Slaves: it appears according to them that there are at least 300,000 slaves, and that the power of the Chiefs, who hold this mass of men in bondage, is to be destroyed; this means war, and a very speedy break-up of the so-called Industrial Mission.

2. GIVING WESTERN NAMES TO NATIVES OF AFRICA, ASIA, OCEANIA, AND AMERICA.

The Missionary should abstain from introducing among his flock the personal and local names of his distant country. Why not allow the people to use the same names as their non-Christian ancestors? Paul has set us this example. Tryphena and Tryphosa are not very spiritual names, and yet they were retained. Then the introduction of Bethel, and Bethesda, and such like Bible-names, is open to great objection. In a Missionary Report I read that one Ram Chandra, a Hindu, was at his baptism unwisely given the name of Paulus: after eight years nominal Christianity he had become a Mahometan Fakir, thus degrading his holy name.

It has been a mistake in Africa, but too late to remedy, to assume European surnames: why could not the late Bishop Crowther have been known by his own native name? It is distressing to read in the local papers of Sierra Leone, or Lagos, that a man named Henry Venn, or William Wilberforce, has been sent to prison for felony. The plurality of the name of Johnson, in honour of the first Missionary, is inconvenient. It is one of the signs of that peculiar British arrogance which, had it been possible, would have substituted the name of Johnson, or Smith, for Socrates and Cicero: why should a well-known Native Pastor in N. India have been called David Mohun, while others were allowed to retain the honoured names of Ram Chandra, Krishna Mohun Banerji, and Gopenath Nandi, all these names of the Indian Divinities, and yet sanctified by these good men bearing them. In the Acts we read of Apollos, who bore the name of a Greek Divinity, and was not required to change it when he was baptized. It is the same Chauvanism, which makes a French Missionary drag in "La France" into all his operations, and names his purchased slaves with French names, that induces Missionaries of the British middle classes to give to Hindu and Mahometan converts some name familiar to them in their home circle, or some name from the Old and New Testament, which is still more objectionable. Thus one of the most distinguished high caste converts of this generation is named Nehemiah Nil Kant, the last name meaning "blue-necked," a title of the Indian Divinity Siva. Our object should be not to make our converts ridiculous in the eyes of their countrymen, or to prevent their mixing upon equal terms with their non-Christian acquaintances. We have only to imagine an invasion of Arab Missionaries into these islands, and preaching the doctrines of Islam, and after circumcision giving them Mahometan names,

3. GIVING WESTERN AGENTS HIGHER EMOLUMENTS THAN NATIVES, EXCEPT SO FAR AS LIFE AND HEALTH REQUIRE.

This will be one of the difficulties of the next generation: when a Church is self-supporting, the question will at once arise why a white man should receive more than a dark-skinned, beyond what health, and protection of life, render necessary: for instance food, clothes, and house-rent. No doubt the simpler and more economical the unmarried life of the Missionary, the better for himself: a great advance has been made by the system of associated brethren, and a common table: in former centuries this was universally the practice: the luxury of the nineteenth century has caused the difference: if the style of living of the white man be raised up, it will follow that the dark-skinned man will desire the same thing. In the first Mission Congress at Lahore in 1861, some wonderful disclosures were made of this latent feeling: in the prayers of the Church men are declared all to be equal, and they wish to be so: we must practise what we preach. So long as pure Missionary work is going on to the non-Christian world, the white Missionary must be paid from Europe or America, but, when the next stage has arrived of the management of Native Christian congregations, the white man had better withdraw.

4. INTERFERENCE WITH SLAVE-HOLDERS AND GIVING ASYLUM TO RUNAWAY SLAVES.

Happily in Asiatic Mission-Fields such a status as that of a slave no longer exists, but in Africa the difficulty does arise: the status of slavery has not been abolished directly or indirectly in the British spheres, and for a Missionary to interfere in such cases is simply to oppose himself to the existing law, or custom having the force of law. The present period is one of transition, and within one or two decades probably the status will be abolished. A Missionary should not allow his house to be converted into a refuge for runaway slaves: Paul has left us an example how we should act: a conciliatory word to the slave-holder, who arrives to claim his property (technically legal) may induce him to remit the punishment of the runaway: at any rate the civil authorities cannot support the Missionary, as he is not above Law. I write this as a Member of the Committee of the British and Foreign Anti-Slavery Society, and one who is ardently striving to destroy the Slave-Trade, and mitigate the evils of Domestic Slavery. We are in the nineteenth century of the Christian era, and we must recollect, that in the nineteenth century before Christ, Abraham had domestic slaves: it is only during the last half century that the status of Slavery has been abolished in India.

5. Adopting Dress of Natives.

I read that in China some Protestant Missionaries, following the example of the Romish Priests, adopt the native garb, and maintain that the influence of so doing was beneficial. I cannot believe it. No Protestant Missionary in India has ever done so: it is not suggested, that a Missionary in Africa, and his wife, should dispense with garments altogether, according to the custom of that country, or in cold Northern climates adopt the costume of the Eskimo. Surely it is better, that each Nation should adhere to its own habits, its own dress, its own nomenclature, its own manner of food, its own peculiar culture.

This subject was mooted at one of the meetings of the Board of Missions in the Church House, Westminster, last year. The Primate read a letter, forwarded to him by the Foreign Office, from a British Consul in China, stating that the respectable classes of China were scandalized by seeing young British men and women going out in Missionary tours together in Native costume, who to the best of their belief were not husband and wife. I do not think that the opinions, and moral sensations, of a Chinaman are worth much, still I was glad to assure the Meeting, that such was to my belief not the practice of Church of England Missionaries, and the matter dropped. On the other hand I regret to say, that a few years ago two sensational young Missionaries of the Church Missionary Society adopted the practice on the Upper Niger, which is thus reported in the Church Missionary Society's Annual Report of 1891:

"The adoption of Native dress by the Missionaries is considered to have been a great help in obtaining a ready access to all classes of Natives, and the loose, flowing, Hausa garments are found much more comfortable and suitable to the climate than European clothes. Dr. Battersby wrote: 'The turban, I believe, is far the best protection from the sun; the tobe or gown, which is very loose, admits of free ventilation, and at the same time can be modified to suit almost any change of weather, except rain. Below we have the loose trousers and sandals for the feet, very comfortable.'"

Both the Missionaries died in a very short time, possibly from attempting with European constitutions to adopt native customs, the idea being more peculiarly ridiculous, because the Negro Bishop, Archdeacons, and Pastors, as well as the better classes of the laity, have long adopted European dress.

6. Sensational and Emotional Proceedings.

I would not willingly say a word against any attempt to spread the Gospel and save souls, yet some degree of sobriety in the Methods is necessary, and the practices and proclamations of the so-called Salvation Army seem to exceed all limitations of common-sense.

7. Intrusive Begging, Beehives, Bazaars, Old-World Fairs, Lotteries, etc.

This is part of the foolish, sensationalist, busybody furor of the age. Extravagant expenditure leads to the necessity of local unions, constant applications for funds, and every form of mendicancy. I quote a few:

"We drew attention a week or two ago to the unsatisfactory "means employed in some quarters to obtain money for Church "purposes. The latest instance of this kind is in connection "with a Church Missionary Society sale of work. The enter-"tainment provided was of a very singular nature. It seems to "have included 'a Witch's Cavern,' in which two young people "'practised palmistry,' and certain comic songs from the music-"halls, sung by a local celebrity. It is, perhaps, needless to "add that the arrangements of such entertainments are purely "local, and quite beyond the control of Salisbury-square."

"One of our secretaries, Miss E. M. Horton, Park House, "Shifnal, Shropshire, is skilled in the art of deciphering "character from handwriting, and is kindly willing to employ "this talent for the benefit of our Society. Her charge is 7*d*., "and we hope many of our friends will send specimens of their "writing and allow her to exercise her skill upon them."

"*Church Bazaars.* It would seem, that there are many and "various opinions on this subject; that while, on the one hand, "there are those who object *in toto* to bazaars and sales of work "for Church purposes, some clergymen, on the other hand, go "so far as to say, that such modes of raising money are actually "indispensable. It may help to clear the ground for a right "judgment, if one or two leading principles which govern the "whole subject be clearly stated and established:

"First, it is highly necessary to bear in mind, that *the gift of* "*God cannot be purchased with money.* Men talk hastily and "loosely about money being absolutely necessary for what are "called Church-purposes, but when we come to consider that "'Church-purposes' really mean, ultimately, *spiritual* objects, "the enlargement and the deepening of Christ's Kingdom in

"the hearts of His people, we cannot for one moment pretend
"to maintain that these things, the operations of the Holy
"Spirit, are purchasable with money.

"Of course it is true, that the outward machinery usually
"employed in Church-work, such as the fabrics and furniture of
"churches or mission-rooms, can be bought with money, and
"that money or money's worth is absolutely requisite for
"procuring such things. But here, again, it must never be
"forgotten, that these things cannot by themselves, by their own
"intrinsic worldly value, procure spiritual blessings any more
"than money can. Thousands of golden sovereigns may be
"converted into the fabric of a beautiful house intended to be a
"House of God, but neither the sovereigns nor the house have
"any power whatever of themselves to bring the grace of God
"to bear on a single human soul.

"A gentleman who takes scarcely the faintest interest in the
"object of a bazaar is induced to go to it, and when there is
"further induced to buy for five shillings a doll, we will suppose,
"which would cost four at a shop, and which he forthwith gives
"to his little daughter: has he then given five shillings to the
"Church-Restoration-Fund, or whatever the object may be for
"which the bazaar has been got up? No; he has *sold* five
"shillings, and has received his *quid pro quo*, viz., a doll worth
"four shillings, the pleasure of giving his child a present, and
"also the pleasure of gratifying the promoters of the bazaar,
"who are his friends, and especially the charming lady, who
"presides at the doll-stall. This may be called a severe
"opinion, and it may be that some such frequenters of Church
"bazaars do take a little interest in the good object, and are,
"therefore, willing to *give* some money, besides what they sell,
"for an equivalent.

"But though the purchaser may give little or nothing, yet there
"are others who give, and whose gifts may be blessed. The doll
"which was sold for five shillings may have cost one shilling,
"the material for its clothes may have cost another shilling,
"and the workmanship of them may represent time and labour
"equivalent to two shillings more. The lady who thus *spent*
"two shillings and *worked* two shillings has *given* four shillings;
"and if Church bazaars meant no more than genuine *sales of*
"*work* done by those, who convert time and labour into money
"for a good cause at the shop prices, there would surely be
"nothing to say against them."

The admonition of Paul should be felt by everyone, that it is
the duty of all to contribute something, and to provide for that
contribution; but the Lord loves a cheerful giver, and the
miserable shilling, wrung out of the unwilling contributor by the
man with the plate at the Church door, exhibits the very lowest

possible type of alms-giving. The Beehives, and Collecting Cards, and Missionary-boxes, have really become a bye-word as adopted in present practice. I remark in one Missionary periodical of this month, that the holder of a Missionary-box should seek contribution from the dwellers within the residence of the box-holder, as well as those without: this is sometimes forgotten.

8. PREACHING IN STREETS UNDER CIRCUMSTANCES CALCULATED TO ENTAIL A BREACH OF THE PEACE.

My attention was drawn to a notice in the Annual Report of the London Missionary Society, 1890, that Police-orders had been issued in Madras to prevent preachers of different religious beliefs, or different denominations of the same, taking up a position within two hundred yards of each other, so great had been the excitement. This points to the lamentable indiscretion of some Missionaries, who would run the risk of unseemly collisions of so-called Christians with each other in the streets of a non-Christian city. In all my experience of Northern India, as Magistrate of Banáras, or Amritsar, or Lahore, I never heard of such a disgraceful state of things, more worthy of Ireland than of India. The late disturbances in Indian cities between the Hindus and Mahometans, though neither of them can possibly have suffered persecution, or wrong, is a proof, that an epoch of unrest is at hand, and those, who know the character of the people of India, will feel that, if there be a trouble, the Missionaries will probably be to blame for not having considered the place, which they may have selected, or some other particular circumstance, which has ruffled the usual quiet of an Indian urban population.

9. FORBIDDING CONVERTS TO MARRY NON-CHRISTIANS.

In a light, easy way the Church Missionary Society Report of 1893 touches on this, one of the most difficult subjects in nascent communities:

"Intermarriage with heathens has been in the past, and is, a
"sadly common evil. Mr. Carr refers to one village of nearly
"3,000 people, most of whom were formerly Christians, but
"who have gone back to heathenism on account of the difficulty
"of getting wives or husbands, as the case might be, among the
"Christians. Discipline was enforced. Mr. Walker wrote:
"'For many years discipline has been sadly lax, and marriage
"irregularities, like evil weeds, have grown apace. After con-
"sultation with the Madras-Corresponding-Committee, and
"submission of the question to the Bishop of Madras, it was
"decided to face the evil at all risks, and endeavour to uproot

" it. Accordingly every case of marriage irregularity has been
" reported to the Bishop, and dealt with by him in the exercise
" of discipline. I grieve to say, that several hundreds of
" Christians have been thus excommunicated during the course
" of the year.'"

The writer goes on to say that a stern Nehemiah is required as well as a loving John. It is not asserted, that these men had put away their lawful wives, and taken new ones: there appears to have been a difficulty in getting wives, and the civil law of British India would recognize such *bonâ fide* unions. Was anything gained to Christ's Church by turning several hundred Converts out of the Church for an offence, which can only be purged by one still more heinous, viz. deserting the wife and offspring, and marrying a young Christian girl. In the Jewish Mission of the Church of England in London I found a few years ago the custom prevailing of each Jewish convert divorcing his Jewish wife, and starting fresh with a Christian girl. I remonstrated, and got together a Special Committee, and the practice was forbidden: it is earnestly hoped, that Missionaries will not interfere in such subjects, except in case of adultery, and unlawful relationship.

It is not practical also: the real remedy is that, if a Christian marry a non-Christian woman, and bring her to his home, a female Evangelist should visit her, and do her best, to persuade her to adopt her husband's religion: of course it is out of the question attempting this in the case of a Christian woman marrying a non-Christian man: this necessarily implies a withdrawal from the Christian Church. The distinguished convert, Ram Chandra of Dehli, lived to the day of his death with his non-Christian wife, when nothing would persuade her to be converted; but history tells us that it is possible, that a Christian wife may bring over a non-Christian husband. At any rate it is of no use for a Missionary to forbid a union, which the law of the land allows, and which involves no question of immorality. This must remain a thorn in the flesh of the neo-Christian Church in every land, as it was to the Jews, when Boaz married Ruth, and Salmon married Rahab, and Esther married the King of Persia.

The Metropolitan condemned in no measured terms a
" practice which had not been unknown amongst them: namely,
" that of a father giving his daughter in marriage to a heathen
" man because he could not find a Christian husband for her of
" his own degree. Such a man should be at once excommuni-
" cated." I cannot agree. I cannot find anything in the New Testament to justify: did not the Christian wife of the heathen King of Kent bring Augustine and Christianity to England?

Let Protestant Churches be warned the folly of the Church

of Rome, which forbids the marriage of a Romanist with a Protestant, and in Spain declares the marriage of Protestants to be concubinage.

The Bishop of Blumfontein in his charge, 1893, would allow catechumens unbaptized to intermarry with those who had been baptized. He also remarked as follows: "There is a growing " tendency on the part of Christian men to induce their " sweethearts to be married before the Missionary, even when " they are heathen. I hope to make four of these heathen " wives catechumens in a week or so, as they have been regular " in their attendance ever since their marriage. It is a good " sign, though, of course, too much might be easily said or " thought of it. It is a step forward." And a very important one. The Missionary must think less of Church-order and more of Purity, and Morality. Conversion will come in God's time. Uncleanliness leaves a permanent stain on the children not yet born, as well as on the Parents.

10. HIGH-CLASS SECULAR EDUCATION.

A great deal has been written on this subject: half-a-century ago Dr. Duff, of Calcutta, started his famous schools, and the Free Church of Scotland has distinctly adopted this as one of their Methods. Not very long ago they issued a Circular calling for opinions on the subject, and I gave my opinion, that High-Class Secular Education was not the Gospel-Message: the Method is not supported by any utterance of our Lord, nor is it of Apostolic practice. The Census-Returns of the population of British India, which amounts to two hundred and seventy-five Millions, tell us of the few, that are educated, and the Millions, who are in the grossest state of ignorance, and yet the Gospel has to be preached to, and is good for, all. When Dr. Duff started the idea, there was no State-Education-Departments: that is not the case now, and the existence of Missionary-Establishments has led to the opening of non-Christian Colleges. It is usual to say, that the educated youth of India are like the man, from whom the unclean spirit of Ignorance has been driven out, and who takes to himself spirits more numerous, and worse, than the old one: this probably is true; but will a small portion of Gospel-Truth, placed like the meat in a sandwich between Mathematics and Classics, help him? When the State first started their Colleges, the cry of the Student used to be, "You have taught me English: now give me bread to eat." Both Secular, and Missionary, Educationists, are touching the fringe of an enormous subject: in the half-European cities of Calcutta, Madras, and Bombay, success may be vaunted of, but those cities are small islands in the vast sea of the people of India.

Among good plans I unhesitatingly count the acceptance, by sincere and Christian men and women, of educational posts under the Government. Let them, however, count the cost beforehand: probable loneliness, in Japan the uncertainty of tenure, the limitation, (which must be loyally adhered to) which obliges them not to teach doctrinal Christianity during school-hours. Still, if, notwithstanding all these disadvantages, they are prepared to throw themselves enthusiastically, on the one hand, into the work of secular education, and, on the other, into the opportunities, indirect though they be, of making known the Truth, which these posts afford, then, I believe, such educationalists are to be counted among real and effective allies of the regular Missionary Staff. I could support this view by instances, which have come under my own notice. In one case, during six years, a considerable number of young Japanese, over thirty, were instructed and baptized by an educationalist, who was alike scrupulously observant of the conditions, under which his services were engaged, and careful to make use of the opportunities of work for God, which his position, and it alone, afforded him. Some English Churchmen, I gather, are suspicious of this mode of work, as if in it the claims of the Truth were subordinated to those of secular science. This fear is groundless, provided the teacher is possessed by a sincere and earnest desire for the Salvation of those under his charge. There is a small Mission of graduates at Tokyo, close to a great Native School, and its influence is being felt by Japanese youths.

In India another policy is in practice. In the neighbourhood of the great Secular Colleges of the State let there be special Missions, consisting of highly-educated English, who will seek the acquaintance of the Student, and let care be taken that the Education-Department does not allow improper books to be admitted to the classes of the State Colleges, or avowed Atheists, Agnostics, Theosophists be permitted as Professors to teach their views in the classes: let there be fair play all round.

The Church-Missionary-Society in its official organ in 1886 thus expressed itself, and it seems to be right:

" The question of Education in any country is not directly
" within the scope of a Missionary Society. The province of
" such a Society is the dissemination of the Gospel of our Lord
" and Saviour Jesus Christ, mainly by the oral teaching of
" living agents, who, as ambassadors for the Lord Jesus Christ,
" go forth in obedience to their Master's command, and make
" known His purposes of mercy and love to the souls of adults
" unconscious of them. The contents of the Bible may be
" viewed as their credentials. They are the living records, to
" which the servants of Christ appeal when questioned by what

"authority they assert their claim to be heard. There are
"well-recorded instances where, when these credentials have
"fallen into the hands of individuals, they have by their own
"intrinsic power become effectual to Conversion; but under
"ordinary circumstances the mode of bringing home the
"message of Salvation, described by St. Paul in his Epistle
"to the Romans, is still that, which has been found most
"universal and most efficacious, as it is most conformable
"to Apostolic practice. In all ages of the Church, men
"unlearned, and without education of any sort or kind, have
"thus had their hearts opened to receive the Truth, and have
"embraced it, to the saving of their souls."

In British India, under the Charter of 1854, subventions are made to Missionary-Schools by the State on the condition of a Report of the Secular Inspector: we may anticipate an early end of this. The Treasury of British India is nearly insolvent, and wholesale economies must be made. Moreover, the Missionary-Societies, in their remittances from Great Britain to India, make enormous annual profits by the fall of the Rupee, though they carefully refrain from noting this fact in their Reports. On the other hand some Societies have declined to accept the subvention on the condition of the Inspector. It cannot be expected, that in India the State should support two sets of schools, Secular and Religious, considering that the taxes devoted to the Missionary places of education are levied from the non-Christian world: if Protestants had to support an Educational Institution of the Church of Rome, they would soon cry out. If they are wise, the Societies will not ask for, or accept, subventions from a State, which distinctly is non-Christian: their object should be solely to teach Christ: everything else is supplementary.

A large Field is thus laid open and ready for a Christian Education-Society, analogous to the Christian-Literature-Society. In touch, and friendly intercourse, with Missionary-Societies of all Schools of Thought, the object would be distinctly not to catch souls, but to train the intellect in the same character of Christian Education as prevails in Europe.

Hear what, in the *Church-Missionary-Society-Intelligencer*, October 1886, Bishop Hodges, of Travancore, himself a Principal of a Missionary-College, says: "But besides and above all this,
"no Field of labour gives so abundant exercise for the personal
"influence of a Christian life, as the daily unambitious round
"of school-work. The educational Missionary is from day to
"day brought into close personal intercourse with his pupils,
"who cannot fail to be deeply influenced and to catch the tone,
"insensibly it may be, but all the more impressively, of his life
"and conduct. And this wholesome influence tells the more, as

"he joins them in their games and recreation, and gives them
"at all times a ready access and welcome to his house. Nor
"must the personal part, that he takes in their secular studies,
"and the general interest he shows in their temporal welfare,
"be held as a hindrance to his higher aims; nay rather, in
"many unseen ways it may only emphasize and recommend his
"more direct religious teaching."

I cannot conceive what advantage the cause of Missions, *i.e.*, the Conversion of souls, has gained by the Education-Commission of 1883. No doubt Education has derived advantage. The non-Christian public now see clearly, that the one only object of a true Missionary is Conversion. He wishes the State-Colleges to be closed, that he may start a Propagandist Institute. If a Priest of the Church of Rome had pressed the matter on Lord Ripon, when the Viceroy, and reminded him that the number of the Romish native converts far exceeded that of the Protestants, jealousy would have been aroused. The proportion of the number of Christians of all sorts in India to the non-Christian population is ridiculously small, $2\frac{3}{4}$ Millions to 282 Millions. What chance in Great Britain would a small column of Mahometans or Jews have in the School-Boards? If elective School-Boards were started in India, the Missionary would find, that King Stork had succeeded King Log. Young India would not long submit to any insidious form of propagandism under the guise of Secular Education. The Lord's battle must be waged openly, not in the form of a somewhat cheaper Secular Education. The Gospel-Message cannot submit to be enclosed in the wallet of a school-boy, tied up in the same strap with Philosophy and Mathematics.

It is not only in British India, but in Turkey and Persia, that the shoe pinches about the Missionary-Schools. Clearly a Sovereign-State has the control of its own Educational Department. Austria, Russia, France, Germany, and Italy, claim for the State the Monopoly of Public Instruction. If Missionaries act with conciliation to the local authorities, they can keep open their Schools, but it is of no use blustering, and claiming under a Treaty a right to open Schools avowedly to convert the Mahometans. I am not quite sure, that even in Free England large Mahometan Schools would survive the popular indignation, if opened avowedly to convert Christians.

Neander remarks, that "experience teaches us, that Christianity
"has only made a firm and living progress, where from the first
"it has brought with it the seeds of all human culture, although
"they have only developed by degrees." Had Neander experience of the Missions of the nineteenth Century amidst all the races of the world in every stage of civilization? He died in 1850, and his great work was written much earlier. I

humbly trust, that Christianity has a firm hold among races, of whom it cannot be said, that they have any culture at all, nor seem likely to develop it.

I have not stated the grounds of Dr. Duff's opinion, nor described his celebrated practice: it is so well known, that it would be a waste of time, and the Free Church of Scotland has recently laid down the principles with great precision.

My opinion is, that there is great objection to the prosecution of Education, which has not a strictly Missionary-object. It is not the duty of Missionary-Societies to give a cheap Secular Education to the natives of any country. School-teaching is a lawful expenditure of Missionary - Funds only when its sole object is Conversion of Souls. It may be that in some countries Education is the only Method available; still, if it cannot be conducted on strictly Christian principles, it should not be undertaken. The School must be opened and closed with prayer, and the Bible be taught without any reserve, or limitation. No conscience-clauses should be tolerated in a Mission-School. If State-Grants are saddled with such conditions, they should be refused: non-Christian teachers should not be employed, and, if the Missionary thinks, that he can only secure such success in secular studies, as will warrant a State-Grant, by sacrifice of Religious Instruction, he should give up the Grant. Unless the scholars attend the Prayers, and Religious teaching, they should not be admitted.

Education is the "hiding of power," that has done so much in primitive Missions for the Spiritual Kingdom. It may be a question, whether High Schools, and Colleges, excellent in themselves, are proper Apostolic Methods, and proper objects for money collected to preach the Gospel. If the Schools are intended to train evangelizing Agents, or to educate the children of Christian converts up to the level of *reading the Bible, and no further,* call them so. Knowledge is Power, and it cannot be right with Mission-collections to elevate the converts to a status in life above that of their friends. The fear is, lest in the midst of all the Educational tendencies, the direct preaching of the Gospel should fall out of fashion. All other matters are ancillary. In British India the Missionary might leave Education to the State, and care for the Education of his converts, and training colleges and schools. What has the ordinary Missionary to do with Higher Education? Is he qualified any more than an ordinary Minister in Great Britain, to superintend an Educational establishment higher than a Sunday School?

II. SPIRITUAL.

1. BAPTISM OF POLYGAMISTS.

The Missionary must be very cautious in meddling with the marriage-customs of the people, among whom he lives. The status of Polygamy is legal to the Mahometan everywhere, and his children are legitimate by the law of all lands: the same may be said generally of professors of other religions. Under no circumstances should a Missionary suggest the idea of a man putting away some of his wives: what is to become of her and her children? for her to cohabit with another man would be adultery. The Mahometan and Hindu Marriage is guarded by proper ceremonial of a religious character: among Pagan, and barbarous tribes, such is not the case: a man's family may be made up of slave-girls, who do not pretend to be married at all, by the widows of relatives, who have been passed to him by inheritance, who are not in any sense his wives: so after inquiry it may be found, that he has only two or three *bonâ fide* legal wives, married according to the custom of the tribe from their father's home, or after the death of their first husband, and he must not be encouraged to divorce them, except for the only reason, which would justify divorce, if he were a Christian.

The subject has been much discussed, and I have myself gone carefully into it, and come to the conclusion, that the baptism of a Polygamist is impossible, until there survives only one wife: he must remain a catechumen even unto the day of his death, but all his wives and children may be baptized. To admit a Polygamist to all the privileges of the Church would only encourage other baptized Christians to desire to have a plurality of wives also, and it is better, that one man should suffer than the purity of the Church should be defiled.

In British India the Civil Law allows a convert, whose wife has been taken away from him by her relatives, to summon her, and if she fail to attend, and show cause, why she should not live with her husband, the marriage is declared to be void. This law was passed, while I was in the Legislative Council of the Viceroy, and I opposed it, but it passed into law, and it will not be well for a Missionary to resist the law of the land.

The subject was brought before the last Lambeth-Episcopal Conference. I had forwarded a copy of my pamphlet to every one of the Bishops. On the day following the decision of the Conference on this point I met his Grace the Archbishop of Canterbury at a reception, and he told me, that the decision was on the lines of the view taken by me. It sounds so easy to do, as Bishop Selwyn the first said to a Chief, who wished to be baptized: he held up two fingers of his hand, and then slowly put down one, to indicate, that he must part with one of his wives: this will not work: is he to put away the oldest, the fattest, the one who is childless, or the mother of his children? A Polygamist had placed himself in a dilemma, and he must not make others suffer for his misfortune. Why did not Nathan call upon David to put away all but one of his wives? he particularly mentions, that Polygamy was not the sin complained of, but Adultery and Murder. In the case of the Hindus there is no lust in the matter of Polygamy; all the marriages take place, while the bride and bridegroom are in their childhood. We read in II Chronicles, xxiv, 3, that Jehoiada, the High Priest, took for the little king Joash, aged seven years, two wives; and in one case in conversation with a Hindu about the folly of his having two wives, his reply was, that he had not done it, for he was married to both as a child: he had children by both, and both were good women: he could not part with them. After the return from Captivity, Polygamy ceased among the Jews, and never existed among the Greeks and Romans, and even in British India, where it is legal, it is quite exceptional, but it would not be wise for the Government to interfere: the Christian Church is bound to say clearly, "No Polygamist shall be baptized."

Another very serious reason for maintaining this rule is the deliberate attempt now made by the Members of the Churches of West Africa at Lagos and Sierra Leone to introduce the custom into their Christian Churches: they maintain that Monogamy may be good, as it has always been good, for Europe, but it is not good, and never has been good, for Africa. Specious reasons have been brought forward to support these views, and I have now papers on my table of this very year from both Colonies discussing a subject, which was deemed absolutely settled: it would be an extreme danger, therefore, to allow Polygamists to be baptized: the sight of them seated in Church with their numerous wives and children would naturally suggest the inquiry, why a Negro born a Christian should not have the same privilege as a converted heathen: what is right in one, cannot be so far wrong in another.

We shall see further on, that some Missionaries made the putting away of all wives but one a condition precedent to baptism: to this I solemnly object, as cruel, and unjust, to the women. Another argument is, that the women are from their earliest youth impure, and deserve no consideration: such an argument is most unworthy on the part of men: if the women have sinned in their youth, it may be hoped that they have by marriage left off sinning. Other Missionaries have attempted to persuade the wives of Polygamists to refuse to cohabit with their husbands: this policy might lead to very serious consequences, and possibly to violent crime. The wisest cause is not to admit Polygamists into the Church.

2. CHALLENGING, OR ACCEPTING, PUBLIC DISCUSSION ON DOCTRINE.

This is not a desirable Method: it does not follow, that the Missionary may prove an able disputant, and while a defeat would be injurious, no possible advantage could come from a victory. I quote the following from the Annual Report of the Church-Missionary-Society:

"One Mr. Wilson, an Englishman, who has become a Mahometan Missionary, came from India. Meetings were held in various parts of the island. He boasted of having converted 7,000 Englishmen at Liverpool, and said he had come to Mauritius to do the same. At first a few Church of Rome Creoles pretended to be inquirers, and then some Hindus attended his meetings. Emboldened with this *soi-disant* success, he attacked Christianity with great vehemence. As the Mahometans were everywhere roused against us, I had to summon Mr. Wilson to a public discussion. He proudly agreed to it, appointed a day, and had notices in the papers to say, that he would point out the errors of Christianity, and prove the truth of Islam. When the day came, a large number assembled on the spot, but the controverter would not come. A few days afterwards he quietly left the island. However, this self-defeat has not disconcerted the Mahometans; they have, with fresh zeal, circulated a new supply of anti-Christian tracts, and challenged us to refute them."

3. SUBSTITUTING OTHER ELEMENTS IN THE COMMUNION FOR BREAD AND WINE.

The serious question must arise, how a Native Church is to provide itself with the elements for the Lord's Supper in countries, where neither the vine, nor corn, which were the staples of life in Palestine, are forthcoming. The inward and spiritual Grace should be the object of consideration, and it is distressing to read of the Native Pastor buying a bottle of wine at a low

European store, especially when it is desirable to keep the people free from the use of liquors, especially European liquors. One Missionary-Society has decided as follows: "The question " of foreign bread and wine being used at the Lord's Supper was " discussed, and, feeling the tendency of the Natives to regard " the Sacrament with superstitious feelings, and the desirability " of keeping it as simple and primitive as possible, and also of " using elements, that might be easily procured by the Natives, " we determined to use the *bread and wine of the country*, viz. the " beautiful yams, and the cocoa-nut milk, which is more Scriptural " than water, coloured with a little wine, and bread made from " the dregs of the Missionary's cask: the object is, that the " Natives should find the elements in their own land for the sus- " tentation of Christianity."

I can quite understand a great difference of opinion existing on this subject: we have to imagine regions, where corn and wine never existed, or have ceased to exist: in some islands intoxicating liquors are absolutely excluded: flour is unknown, except in the Missionary's cask imported from a foreign land. I recollect a poor dying soldier begging the Chaplain to administer the Sacrament to him: there was no wine in the camp: there was brandy and beer: the Chaplain used the former in water, but it was understood, that he was reproved by the Bishop. In looking forward to the increase of the members of the Church, these things rise up for consideration.

4. Interfering with the Ancient Organization of the Asiatic and African Churches.

I confess, that I am very sorry to witness such interference. These Churches have survived the persecution of Centuries, have kept their candlestick lighted, and copies of the Holy Scriptures in their vernacular: they are not very spiritual, and are certainly very unlearned, and quite justify their name of the Fallen Churches; and yet it goes against the heart to see them swept away, or converted into a parody of a European or American non-Episcopal Church: it goes without saying, that no Episcopal Church would approach them in a hostile attitude: it is a better policy to try to strengthen them, and reform them; to assist them to train their priests, to become more spiritual, to give them the Scriptures and other religious literature in the modern Vernacular: it is uphill work, no doubt, and the efforts of the Church of Rome are to sow dissension, and bring a portion into their obedience, making concessions to gain their object, such as sanctioning a married Priesthood, and the Sacrament to laymen in both elements: it is sad to think, that these monuments of God's Providence should perish after the strain of persecution has passed away. When first I became acquainted with them in Africa and Asia, in 1852, I had some conversation with American Missionaries, who told me that, when first they arrived in the country, they did try to reform and support these Churches, but experience had taught them, that it was hopeless, that there was nothing for it but to destroy them. It is quite clear, that no Episcopal Mission should adopt such a policy: it would be better to leave them alone, and receive into the Mission as proselytes those, who came voluntarily, and were determined of their own accord to leave their ancient Church: these again, when instructed, should be urged to go back again among their people, and try to reform the old and decaying fabric.

Part III.

BAD METHODS.

I now come to the Bad Methods: I have divided this Part into Six Chapters:

    I. Leaning on the Arm of the Flesh.
    II. Modes of Conversion.
    III. Difficulties attending Conversion.
    IV. The Missionary Home-Agency.
    V. The Mission in the Field.
    VI. The Missionary-Agent.

There is a further sub-division of each Chapter into a great many Sections, and to preserve regular and lucid order I attach at the head of each Chapter a list of the Subjects treated in each Section. There will be an alphabetical Index of Subjects, which will give facility of ready reference to every detail of this many-sided operation.

CAP. I.		Leaning on the Arm of the Flesh.
	1	Interference of Civil, Military, or Diplomatic, Power.
	2	Receiving endowments from taxes levied from non-Christians.
	3	Intolerance of other Religions, or other forms of the same Religion.
	4	Destruction, or appropriation, of Buildings belonging to another Religion.
	5	Making a Mission a handle for political schemes.

I. ARM OF THE FLESH.

1. Interference of Civil, Military, or Diplomatic, Power.

A relying on the Arm of the Flesh has been one of the sins of Missionaries from the earliest centuries to the present hour. I do not know which is more odious, the Arm of the Flesh against the promulgation of Christian Truth, or in favour of it: I really think, that the latter is the most odious: it affects the character of the Missionary: instead of relying on the Arm of God he learns to truckle to the Chartered Company, the Local Government, the Jack in office, the Consul; and this destroys his holy energy. " To me to live is Christ, and to die is gain : " that is no longer possible, when he joins armed forces, as at U-Ganda, or takes compensation, as in China, for the spoiling of his goods. I am obliged to speak strongly on this matter, because it is the prevailing disease of timid Missionaries, and short-sighted Committees. Why was the Church of Rome so intolerant, and bloody, at the time of the Reformation? Simply because it had worked its way to the Conversion of Europe by the sword, and slaughter of the heathen, and destruction of their places of worship. If Christianity be introduced by force, the dominant Church is sure to attempt the reduction of all other sects to subordination in the same way.

I should carry all with me in alluding to the use of the Arm of the Flesh against Christianity; my thesis is on the opposite side. It is one of the topics, which fascinate young Missionaries, and writers of articles in the Missionary-periodicals, to describe, or rather to assert, that Mahometanism was propagated by the sword. The Hindu, or Buddhist, might raise this objection: can the Christian? When the Mahometans conquered a country, they offered two alternatives: Conversion or additional Taxation: the great fact is patent, that India was eight centuries under Mahometan rule, and its Temples, Priesthood, and Religion, remained unaltered; and in Western Asia the Armenian, Greek, Syrian, and Nestorian, Churches, and in N. Africa the Coptic and Ethiopic Churches, have survived to our time. The Mahometans loathed the forms of Christian and Brahmanical Idolatry, which were presented to them, but they spared them; but in Europe not a vestige of Paganism survived the fearful persecution, which accompanied the introduction of Christianity: the Mahometans and Jews were nearly driven out of Europe, and their property was confiscated: all attempts to reform errors, or give rein to free thought, were crushed out by the scaffold, or the stake. Let us hear no more of Mahometanism being unique in its persecuting Methods. Each conquering Chief, whether it were Olaf of Norway, or Charles Martel of France, or the Khalif Omar of Arabia, or the Missionaries of the Church of Rome up to the beginning of this century, have taken as their rule the verse of Deut. viii: "Ye shall destroy their altars, and break down their images, and burn their graven images with fire." At the same time, if a hand were lifted up against the Christians, it was called wicked persecution. The Asmonean Dynasty of Judæa before the Christian era conquered Edom, Moab, and Ammon, and enforced circumcision on the population: so in Europe Baptism was the only symbol and condition of peace: to refuse Baptism was to be a rebel, and meant war. It was in vain, that men like Alcuin begged Sovereigns and Priests to pause. Death was the penalty of the absence of nominal conversion. This shows how completely the Arm of the Flesh was the understood weapon of aggressive Christianity. I quote the words of our own Boniface of Exeter to Daniel Bishop of Winchester (see Neander, III, p. 100), in reply to a letter suggesting a more lenient policy:

"Sine patrocinio Principis Francorum nec populum regere, "nec presbyteros, nec diaconos, nec ancillas, regere possum, "nec Paganorúm ritus, et sacrilegia, in Germaniâ sine illius "mandato et timore prohibere valeo." He stamped out all independent attempts at Evangelization, put a stop to the divergencies of the earlier British Missions, and substituted Italian Ecclesiasticism: if he never baptized by force, he destroyed the places of worship of the Pagans by force. All the religion taught by him was: (1) building churches, (2) hunting after relics, (3) securing protection of the Arm of the Flesh by gifts and ritual, (4) worshipping statues, (5) making pilgrimages. Later on, the Teutonic Knights completed the Conversion of Europe by killing down the heathen, very much as English free lances do to the Ma-Tabéle in 1894, and giving the land to German colonists. Centuries later a French Biographer of Xavier remarks, that the most efficacious means of Conversion, used by Xavier, was to gain to God those persons, who were most considerable in their truth and dignity. In 1843 a Bampton lecturer remarked, that such means were too much neglected by ourselves. Absit omen! Surely the great Charter is, that the poor have the Gospel preached to them: Paul did not commence with Cæsar's household. It is sad to think, that Augustine of Hippo quoted from our Lord's parable the words "Compel them to come in," as a justification of his cruelties, not against the Pagans, who knew not Christ, but against Sectarians of his own religion. A swift punishment came upon him, and the African Church; and I thought of these words of his, as I stood a few years ago on the spot, where he was buried, as he perished during the siege of Hippo.

"A Duke of Poland, who had himself become only in out-
"ward form a Christian at the request of his wife, determined
"that his subjects should be so also, and that anyone, who
"did not fast at Easter, should lose his teeth. A Bishop
"remarked on hearing of this order, that the roughest treat-
"ment was required for a people, who were no better than
"cattle; and that, as they were stubborn, religion must be
"beaten into them."—*Maclear*: *Slavs*, p. 111, S.P.C.K.

One writer remarks cynically, that "Conversions made by force
"were quite as permanent as those, which are made in the
"legitimate way. The Conversions made by Mahometans, and
"the Church of Rome, have been as stable as those made by the
"Conversion of individual souls. In one or two generations the
"new faith becomes hereditary, and in a blind, senseless way is
"clung to as tenaciously, as was the old exploded religious con-
"ceptions." I fear that in an epoch of intense ignorance this may be the case. What became of the Christian Churches of Syria, Egypt, and N. Africa? the great mass of the ignorant herd were swept into the Mahometan net, and there they remained. But in an age of higher intelligence, and faithful record, this seems to be impossible.

The opposition manifested against Christianity by the Slavs and Teutons far exceeded that offered by any Asiatic race in modern times: it is of no use attributing the crimes, which both the Pagans and Christians committed, to the epoch and the environment: if an attempt were made in modern times to spread Christianity by the same Methods, say in Zululand, or the Niger-Basin, or Tunisia, the result would be the same: to me the fault seems to be entirely on the side of the Christian Missionary: merciless intolerance, force, fraud, spoliation, destruction of temples, were the Methods used: there were no schools, nor hospitals, nor kindly visits to the village-homes, no exhibition of Christian example, no preaching in the Vernacular, or Bible-reading; the native languages were proscribed: foreign Priests drove an ignorant herd to be baptized by thousands in a river: a mere nominal Conversion was the result: and this was urged on by Christian Potentates in the name of Christ, while the same Potentates led evil, lustful, lives. We know now the pedigree of the Inquisition at the time of the Reformation: the lesson had been learnt from the original Conversion of the heathen: a Pope wrote to his agent in Servia to deal gently with the Pagan, but to allow no one of these nominal Christians to relapse without the extreme punishment: we complain of the Mahometan Law in Turkey and Persia: was not, is not, this still the Law of Rome?

No excuse can be reasonably offered. Life and liberty were as valuable then to the poor herd in Europe, as it is in Asia and Africa now: there was an individual existence of a body, soul, and spirit, in each of God's creatures then as now, but the spiritual Priest and temporal Ruler chose to overbear individual rights and feelings. When the Missionaries, and the compiler of the Mission-Report, use their favourite epithets "fanatic and bigoted," let them recollect to whom these terms more particularly apply. When the Mahometans in their hour of conquest played the same game in Christian countries, loud was the outcry against their Intolerance, and Cruelty, but the Christians had acted, and were still acting, in the same way: they were convinced of the truth of their own views, and had no scruple in enforcing them upon Mahometans, Pagans, and heretics: the Mahometans were equally convinced and equally unscrupulous. When learned Bishops undertake to show, that the progress of the Conversion of the world in the nineteenth century is proceeding as rapidly as, or even more rapidly than, the Conversion of Europe in the first thousand years of the Christian era, they should not omit to draw attention to the difference of Methods: there is now, with slight exceptions, entire Toleration on the part of all civilized Governments: the Intolerance of modern times is protection of old Faiths, rather than the Intolerance of a new Faith on the War-Path, as I have above described.

The saddest feature remains. In the presence of religious Intolerance all feelings of equity, pity, and patience, disappear. Even modern writers of esteemed works, and the whole host of compilers of periodical religious literature, appear to forget that deep-rooted principle of Justice, which springs from a firm conviction on their part of their own religious Belief, and the noble rule to do to, and say of, others what they would wish that men should do to, and say of, them. Historians speak with praise of a King, who in past centuries forbade his subjects to perform the rites of Paganism. Think of that: Missionaries in Turkey, Persia, and China, or Bishops like Augustine of Hippo, expelled so-called heretics from their churches, and deprived them of their means of living. They would loudly complain, as the Missionaries of Rome do now, of the least persecution of themselves. It makes me smile, when I read my weekly *Missions Catholiques* from Lyons in France of persecution perhaps in India, or the British or German sphere, in Africa.

Quis tulerit Gracchos de seditione querentes?

Cannot all Missionaries, Protestant or Romish, realize the fact, that God is a Spirit, and must be worshipped in spirit, and not at the point of the sword, or with the help of the Rifle and Maxim-gun, that He in His wisdom, and longsuffering, permits these non-Christian races to increase and multiply, and prosper, and that it is not good to be less merciful to them, than God.

I have dealt at length on this subject, for the tendency is so insidious: the story of U-Ganda sadly illustrates the danger: those, who have not read Church-History, as recorded in books published by the Society for the Promotion of Christian Knowledge, would say, that it was impossible, that Christians should in past centuries have acted in this way; but my experience of fifty years tells me, that it is in the heart of many men even at this day, that they have a right and duty to make use of every power, opportunity, influence, Method, just or iniquitous, to bring Salvation, after their conception of the word, to the non-Christian World.

I now practically apply the principles to the present Epoch.

The Empires of Austria and Russia allow of no Missionaries within their European dominions; and I heard, on the occasion of a deputation to the Foreign Office, Lord Salisbury remark, that all the Powers assert the unquestionable right of expelling Missionaries from their Colonies at their own good pleasure. France makes the conditions of Evangelizing in her Colonies so difficult, that the task is all but hopeless. No language but the French is allowed. A writer in 1889 blames the French Government for not having added to the conquest of Algeria the conversion of the inhabitants by force or influence: it was on the cards, but the deposition of Charles X and the elevation of Louis Philippe arrested the precious scheme. A Priest of Rome thus writes:

"Les indigènes s'y attendaient eux-mêmes, car chez eux "l'absurde idée de separer la religion de la conduite des choses "humaines n'est pas encore entrée dans les esprits, et le jour "même de la prise d'Afrique la population terrifié demandait a "grande cris, si on lui laisserait la vie sauve a condition qu'elle "embrasserait la religion des français."—*Missions Catholiques d'Afrique*, p. 11.

It is not often, that an opinion so abominable, based on facts so false, has been expressed. Directly the Franco-German war broke out in 1870, both sections of the Mahometan population of Algeria burst out into rebellion, and were with difficulty reconquered after the Peace.

British India presents the most extreme contrast. The Government treats Missionaries of all nationalities with the same impartial benevolence, interferes with none, asks no questions, enforces no orders, except the necessity of obeying the common law of the country, and makes grants for educational purposes to all indifferently on the same conditions, whether Protestant or Roman Catholic, British or alien. They may conduct their operations in the language, which suits them best; they may own lands, erect buildings, move to and fro just as they like; no passports are asked for; there is no jealousy of the Frenchman or the German on the part of the Briton; no ejection of Missionaries, as has been the case of Mr. Jones of the London Missionary Society, at Lifu in the Loyalty Islands, by the French; no expulsion of the whole Mission, as has happened to the British Baptists at the hands of the Germans at the Kamerúns in W. Africa; no exclusion of French Roman Catholics, as is the case in this same German Colony; no practical extinction of religious schools by State laws of education, as has happened to the American Missionaries in the French colony of W. Africa on the Gaboon, and to English Missionaries on the West Coast of Africa and the Gambia, and in the French colony of Algeria and Tunisia. I quote two speeches of Earl Northbrook, Viceroy of India:

"I believe that the natives of India are thoroughly satisfied,
"that the British Government has no desire to force upon them
"the Christian religion by any improper means, and that all that
"the British Government gives is a fair field to the Missionaries,
"who are in the country. That, again, to my mind, is a right
"and just principle, that Government should not interfere with
"religion. It received the cordial adherence of William Carey
"years and years ago. I find he used upon that occasion these
"words: 'Whatever Government may do, let it not touch my
"work. It can only succeed in making men hypocrites; I wish
"to make them Christians.' I say, then, that the natives of
"India understand the position of the Government. I can say
"more. I have come in contact with many Missionaries in
"India, and I have talked with them upon the condition of the
"people; and I am satisfied that many Missionaries, by not
"being connected with the Government, have more of the
"confidence of the people in India than is given to the officers
"of the Government; and I have, on several occasions, found
"advantage from obtaining from sensible Missionaries their
"opinion of the feelings of the people with respect to the
"measures of the Government."
And again:

"Nothing in my opinion could be more entirely alien to the
"feelings of Henry Venn, who of all men I ever knew was the
"most interested in Missionary-work, and the wisest conductor
"of Missionary-operations, than that Missionaries of any kind
"should be betrayed into using physical force to control the
"Natives of the country to which they are sent. Missionaries
"must be prepared, if they go to foreign countries, to carry
"*their lives in their hands*. They have lost their lives on former

"occasions, and it is needless to say, that a man in that posi-
"tion, taking the Message of God to the Natives of Africa, is
"bound to lose his life rather than use physical force."

I notice excellent remarks in the Periodical of the London Missionary Society, July 1881, deprecating the despatch of ships of war to avenge the slaughter of their Missionaries in Papua. In strong contrast with this appears the conduct of the American Board of Foreign Missions in the Caroline Islands, which belong to the Kingdom of Spain. The Missionary-Society complained to the Government of the United States, that their Missionaries had been turned out of the Island, very much as Mr. Jones was turned out of the Loyalty Islands by the French. The United States-Government sent a man-of-war, and restored the Missionary to his Islands. The Captain in his letter advised all Americans, whether Christians or not, to go down on their knees and return thanks to God for having been born a "free American." These alien Missionaries were encouraged by an alien Power to defy the constituted Authority of three hundred years: it may be wondered how the Gospel of Peace can be preached under such circumstances, and we cease to wonder, that the great Continental Powers assert the principle of exclusion. Germany, in starting her Colonial Empire, laid down the principle of only German Missions in German Colonies: the Missionary is to be chaplain to German subjects, to work for German interests, use the German language only, and make his converts good German subjects. The long-suffering Government of India puts up with the impertinent intrusions of ill-judging Missionaries in the conduct of secular affairs: it must be remarked, that in British India the Missionaries of Rome, whether French, Spanish, Portuguese, or English, have never given the least trouble, or meddled with subjects, which did not concern them. The Protestants are the busybody meddlers.

In 1894, Mr. Leatham, M.P., used in the House of Commons the following expressions: I was sorry to read them, being unable to deny, that instances have occurred to justify the attack. "The right hon. Member for Bradford had advocated the claims "of the Missionaries to protection, but, in his opinion, the "Missionaries exercised no public function whatever. The "Missionaries were merely religious freebooters, who filibustered "upon the territories of other people. Either we must double "our Standing Army in order to enable us to protect our "Missionaries, or we must recall those Missionaries from "exposed positions."

Even in the little island of Mauritius, where the majority of the inhabitants are non-Christians, and of the Christian minority the greater part are French-speaking Members of the Church of

Rome, I read in the English Bishop's charge of 1892 evidence, that the English Protestant Missionary is as it were trading on English prestige in the Island.

But it is the Empires of Turkey and China, the Kingdom of Persia, and East Equatorial Africa, that the Arm of the Flesh has been appealed to by Missionaries in these days in the most marked manner, and I proceed to notice them *seriatim*.

I take up the Empire of Turkey first. It was founded very much in the same way, as the British Empire, by the conquest of inferior races, and small kingdoms, by a strong martial and superior race, the Osmanli Turki. The Empire is now in its decadence, owing to the superior strength of its great Christian neighbours, and its hopelessly bad administration. I have traversed a great part of it, seeking lessons in the art of governing subject races, which was my profession in British India. The subject races are Christian: the dominant race is Mahometan: there is much sympathy felt in Europe.and North America for the oppressed Christians: is that sympathy expressed wisely?

I find in Reports of Missionary-Societies the following lines: " Thanks to the American Consul at Constantinople for efficient " service in defending the rights and liberties of American " Missionaries in the Turkish Empire." We have only to imagine the change of the word " British India" for "Turkish Empire": how should we tolerate the interference of the American Consul at Calcutta?

It has already been remarked, in Part II, that the question of Education is one of the prerogatives of the Ruling Power of each country. Imagine a Roman Catholic Sovereign, or the Sultan of Turkey, trying to interfere with the system of Public Education, secular or religious, in these islands. The Sultan of Turkey is trying to introduce the French and Russian system into his dominions; viz.: (1) that no school shall be held without a special permit from the Ottoman authorities; (2) that all schools shall be under Turkish inspection; (3) that no Mission-school shall admit Mahometan pupils. A Bill now under consideration tends to give legal sanction to the restrictions, from which the Missionary-Societies are suffering, and will prevent them, and the Bible-Societies, from selling even authorized books in all parts of Turkey. A decree was issued last year, forbidding Missionaries to use their houses as churches or schools without a special Imperial firman.

The right of the Missionaries to carry on their work in Turkey is established by different international conventions, and amongst others by the French and British Capitulations, the Treaty of Berlin, and by private agreements with the United States. Moreover, until lately, the attitude of the

Porte towards Foreign Missions had given no ground for complaint. Evidently the present Intolerance is prompted from abroad. There is ample room for a little plain speaking on the part of the English Foreign Office. As a rule the Government shows a disinclination to espouse the cause of the Foreign Missions, and possibly it may have its reasons for it; but in this instance it is plainly the duty of the authorities at home to remind the Turks of their obligations, and to appeal to the Sultan's sense of right and justice on behalf of the Missionary work.

Here again in public print the crave for the Arm of the Flesh is more distinctly put forth, 1892.

" It appears under these circumstances to be of great import-
" ance to the Bible and Missionary-Societies, that the Home-
" Governments should instruct their Diplomatic and Consular
" Agents in Turkey to intervene and remonstrate against edicts,
" laws or decrees, which set aside or restrict the long-established
" rights of these Societies. The right of protection of both the
" persons, and the establishments, of Missionaries in Turkey is
" clearly assigned to the Powers by the 62nd Article of the
" Treaty of Berlin."

The Turkish Government has been roused out of its usual passive and sleepy state by the overbearing conduct of the British and American Missionaries: Russia, Austria, and France, would not put up for an instant with such insolent conduct. It was not so formerly, but it has increased in late years, and there are signs, that the British Government will not support their subjects in acts of defiance to the municipal law of the countries, in which they carry on their operations, hitherto peaceful and in conformity with the laws of the country. The Missionary has no right to raise the question, whether a municipal law is right or wrong: he must obey or leave the country.

I have twice visited the Empire of Turkey, with a view of contrasting their system of governing conquered Provinces with the British system in India. I was sitting in the Divan with the Pasha of Damascus, when a European Consul was introduced, who hectored and bullied the Pasha while actually on the seat of Judgment. I had myself governed large Asiatic districts, and recognized the salient features of the complaint as of not uncommon character. The Turk smoked, and bore the abuse stolidly, at least to outward appearance. I felt for him, and felt also, that if any representative of any Power in the world had behaved in such a manner in my Office, I should have had him turned out forthwith, and, if he repeated such conduct, should have fined him for contempt of Court, and looked to my own Government to support me. The British Magistrate and Consul know, that the best Missionaries give them the least trouble, if, indeed, they give any at all. The argument, that the Consuls of other Nations have succeeded in compelling an unwilling Government to make concessions, is an unworthy one, and not always true. In a discussion in a British Committee-Room in my presence about troubles in China, a Secretary to an American Board of Missions, who happened to be present, was asked how it happened, that their Missionaries were always backed by their Consul. The reply was an expression of surprise on the part of the American Secretary, and the dry remark,.that his Missionaries complained, that the British Missionaries were always backed by the British Consul, while the American Consul refused to interfere. I have no love for the irrepressible Turk, and I have traversed great parts of Turkey, and studied its system, which is bad, thoroughly bad; yet I cannot excuse Missionaries of gross violation of the first principles of duty of an alien permitted to reside in a foreign country.

I visited a celebrated city in Turkey, and found that the Medical-Missionary was in great distress, because the Governor had stopped the erection of his new Hospital. I visited it: it was on a lofty hill commanding the town, and had the appearance and reality of a fort, with walls pierced for musquetry, and embrasures for guns. Any hospital built on such a site, and in such a style, in British India, at Banáras, or Amritsar, would have been dismantled at once. In the case of trouble it would have been at once occupied by rebels, and nothing but a siege would take it. And yet the Doctor abused the Turk !

A Missionary-Society bought, and got possession of, a house with a title open to objections, possibly false, and was sued for ejectment, and cast: the decision was confirmed on appeal. Letters were written to London, and a certain benevolent Nobleman was induced to write letters to the Ambassador at Constantinople: he brought a pressure on the Sublime Porte: orders were issued by the Executive to the Provincial Court to cancel the order. I have been many years a Judge in an Oriental Country, and felt ashamed of my countrymen. The humblest Native Judge in British India would decline to alter his decree to please the Executive authorities.

Let us pass on to Persia, another ill-governed Mahometan State: it is sad to think, that in this very year an ordained Missionary has put forth the following plea, distinctly appealing to the Arm of the Flesh: he knew very well, that a Swedish, a Danish, a Swiss, a Portuguese, Missionary would have to submit in silence; but he is a subject of a powerful State, the Agent of a powerful Missionary-Society, and he distinctly desires, that the British Government should coerce our friend the Shah of Persia.

"It is only right that those, who take an interest in Christian Missions, should understand, that one of the main difficulties in the way of the conversion of the Mahometans to Christianity consists in the attitude, which the English Government assumes through its representatives in Mahometan lands towards the spread of the Gospel. In China or Japan, the English Government, if it interferes at all, interferes to secure to Christian Missionaries liberty to proclaim Salvation through Christ. In Central Africa, if our Government be unable to afford any protection to Missionaries, it at least puts no obstacle in their way. But for some unknown reason there seems to exist a belief, that Islam must be treated with more consideration than other false faiths. Turkey is allowed to impose much more stringent limitations on Christian Missionary enterprise than is China or Japan. Any infringement of such restrictions is liable to bring punishment, in inflicting which our own Government directly countenances that of the Sultan. In Persia something of a similar kind is true; and an attempt is now apparently being made, under the countenance and with the support of the English Government, to prohibit altogether all attempts to bring Mahometans to the knowledge of Christ."

The Persian Government, rightly or wrongly, objects to the Missionary opening a Dispensary and a shop for selling Bibles, in the town of Ispahán: the British Minister has supported the Consul in his policy of obedience to the orders of the Persian authorities. The Persian Government now forbid the use of a Press, the attendance of Mahometans at schools, the teaching of Christianity to the Mahometans, and the selling of Bibles, and the Medical-Mission work of Christian women among Mahometan women. It is gathered from a letter of the British Minister, that the Persian Government is quite within its right, that the condition, on which Missionaries are allowed to reside in Persia, is that they do not proselytize among Mahometans, that full liberty is given to Missionaries as regards all non-Mahometan communities, but no interference with Mahometans can be tolerated. This is what in Missionary-parlance is called "the door being closed": it was so in many Roman Catholic countries; it is so in the Empire of Russia.

It is to be regretted, that the Shah of Persia should be so ill-advised as to persecute the new sect in his kingdom, the Babi, and to oppose the introduction of Christianity; we must recollect, how weak his authority is: the prejudice of the nation is against the foreign religion, and it is idle to suppose, that in these days the British Government will attempt to use the Arm of the Flesh: our Lord's distinct command was: "If they persecute you in one city, flee into another"; and such was the practice of Paul. A Missionary in 1894 desires the practices of the worst period of the Middle Ages to be brought back. The Persian Mission was forced upon the Society, which supports it, against its better judgment, and has hitherto worked chiefly among Christians of the Armenian Church at Julfa. Now that it commences real work against the Mahometans, it finds itself checked. It is just possible, that greater judiciousness, and a spirit of gentle conciliation, may enable the Missionary to carry on some of the minor work of the Mission. We may well inquire, who the fanatics are in this case: the King and his people, who wish to be left alone in the religious conviction, which they have held for a thousand years, or the impetuous foreigner, who desires the assistance of the diplomatic force of Great Britain to enable him to carry on his operations in a country, where his presence is not acceptable? Let him go elsewhere: whoever sent a Missionary into Arabia with any profit? The new British Minister to Persia is well acquainted with Afghanistan: not only does the Amir allow no Missionaries to settle in his kingdom, but he is authorized to deport at once into British territory any British Missionary, who ventures across the frontier line: Discretion is a part of Valour.

But the Empire of China is the most lamentable field of exhibition of the Arm of the Flesh in the interest of the preaching of the Gospel. The Missionaries say, that Indian opium was forced upon China: that may be a question for future historians to decide: there can be no question, that Missionaries were forced upon China: "Take away your Missionaries and your opium," said Prince Kung, but the nut was too hard for him to crack.

A late travelling M.P. remarks as follows in the *Times*: "The " political drawbacks to the Missionaries' work are no less ex- " clusively matters of their own creation. China can never " forget that, unlike the Christians in early Rome, in early Gaul, " or in early Britain, they owe their admission here to no tacit " acquiescence on her own part, much less to any expressed " desire; but solely to the coercion of a superior and victorious " strength. Each station is a sardonic reminder to them, that " they have been made to pass under the Caudine Forks. Nay, " not merely does it recall the national humiliation, but it is " also a badge of the continued ascendency of an alien power, " still maintained, as it was originally introduced, by force. " Nor is this impression diminished by the attitude of the " Missionaries themselves, many of whom, though they buckle " on their armour as the soldiers of Christ, remember only, in " times of peril, that they are citizens of this or that Empire or " Republic, and clamour for a gunboat, with which to insure " respect for the Gospel. To this too ready appeal to the " physical sanction of a national flag, there are many honourable

"exceptions: men who carry their lives in their hands, and un-
"complainingly submit to indignities, which they have undertaken
"to endure in a higher cause than that of their nationality.
"Nevertheless the presence of the Missionary-bodies as a whole
"in the country is a constant anxiety to the Legations, by
"whom in the last resort their interests, resting as they do
"upon Treaties, must be defended; and is equally distasteful to
"the Chinese Government, which frequently finds itself called
"upon to reprimand a native official, or to punish a local com-
"munity, at the cost of great odium to itself. In some districts
"the unpopularity of the Missionaries has been increased by
"the special privileges, which they are disposed to claim on
"behalf of native converts engaged in litigation or other
"disputes."

In the *Missionary Review of the World*, Boston, U.S., 1894, I read that "the Rev. John Ross, the veteran Missionary of
"Manchuria, has reached the conviction, that China will never
"be won to the Gospel by an appeal to the Secular Power to
"intervene in every little trouble we may experience. This
"appeal to Cæsar, or the Gunboat, simply deepens in the
"mind of the patriotic Chinese, the belief, that the Missionary
"is a political Agent, and this hinders Christianity more than
"any other causes combined."

The late Earl of Shaftesbury at the Annual Meeting of the China Inland Mission, 1889, made the following remarks:

"I was more struck with the paragraph, which said: 'Our
"brethren, who have been permitted to take the journeys, have
"given practical demonstration to the Church of God, that
"China is opened, that the people of China are accessible,
"that if they are treated with courtesy and kindness, and if on
"the part of the Missionary there be no assumption of National
"superiority, no undue insistence upon Treaty-Rights, but rather
"the according to the Chinese willingly and not by constraint
"the respect due to people in their own country, friendly inter-
"course is possible, and in many cases even welcomed.' Now,
"that is the very quintessence of good sense. It is one of the
"most sensible, most practical, and most true statements, that
"I have ever known. It bears on remarks, that I have heard
"made in the House of Lords, by peers, who have been at the
"Admiralty, just and good men, who, when discussing Mis-
"sionary-operations, have said, 'With the Missionary there
"always is the inevitable gunboat.' I believe that that has been
"very often the case, because Missionaries have stood too much
"upon National superiority, and there has been too much in-
"sistence upon Treaty-Rights, and they have not sought to con-
"ciliate the people by courtesy and by kindness, and by an
"immediate recognition of their equality in the sight of God.
"Well, China has for a long time been opened."

The words "bigoted and fanatic" are plentifully used as descriptive of the Chinese: what should we think in London, if the Italian Mission, backed by a foreign Power, who had defeated us in battle, were to come in swarms, settle down in our streets, abuse us in their periodicals, and under cover of Treaties, wrung from us in the hour of weakness, attack our cherished form of Religion, denounce Westminster Abbey as a place of adoration of ancestors, attempt to stop the cultivation of hops in Kent and Surrey, stop the import of Brandy and Champagne from France, and put down the Distilleries of Irish and Scotch Whiskey, and the use of Tobacco? Would not a thrill of indignation pass through the whole country, and an earnest desire to get rid of the Italian Mission at any price? Would anyone accept a religion forced upon them by rifles and guns? Such is the feeling of the Chinese.

Only imagine the Emperor of a Kingdom with a population of four hundred Millions, with an ancient civilization, receiving a letter like this from foreigners, who were barbarians at a time that the Chinese were highly civilized: I quote the *Times* of March, 1894: "The foreign Ministers at Pekin have addressed " a very strong letter to the Tsung-li Yamen, expressing their " conviction, that the Sungpu massacre and other outbreaks " against foreigners in the province of Hupeh are to a great " extent, if not entirely, due to the Chinese officials, and they " demand: (1) That full protection be given to Missionaries, " their *employés*, and native Christians; (2) that natives who " have been maltreated for their friendliness to the murdered " men be allowed to return to their homes in Sungpu in safety; " (3) that the Imperial Edict of 1891 shall be renewed, and " posted up, throughout the various districts in Hupeh."

It may be unhesitatingly stated, that all Treaties for protecting, or encouraging, the propagation of any religion are wrong "per se," and should be abrogated. It should be left to the Government of each country to allow, if they thought fit, free access and toleration, as is the case in British India. It is not asserted, that the Divinity is in the habit of protecting its own places of worship from fire, accident, or hostile attack, but it is asserted, that Great Truths can find their own road, fight their own battle, and maintain their own Empire. Their weapons are not carnal, like the Arm of the Flesh, or Treaties supported by gunboats. The first thing, that a false Religious conception, or a true conception falsely put forward, asks for, is Protection from the Arm of the Flesh: it is the last thing, that a true, absolutely true, Religious conception, as we believe that the Christian Verities are, ought to ask for. The Almighty opens doors, and closes doors: He influences the hearts of men, whether Christians, or non-Christians; and He, who sends the Preacher, knows whether the hearts of the hearers are ready to receive the Truth. Any vengeance, taken for the slaughter of a Missionary, is wrong: we cannot at the same breath talk of Martyrs, and take vengeance by the destruction of women and children in their villages with gunboats, or use diplomatic pressure to get compensation for the families: only imagine the families of Isaiah, or Stephen, or Paul, getting compensation in cash for such deaths, as have given, as it were, new life to the world. It shows want of the assurance of Faith, and a contemptible hungering after filthy lucre, to ask for a money-compensation by the Arm of the Flesh: Do we offer our martyrs gold?

The history of our Missionary-relations with Turkey and China is one shameful history of bullying: if the Mahometans had done so, great would have been the outcry: what Russia and France would not tolerate, Turkey and China must submit to. "Christianos ad leones!" was the placard in early Centuries at Rome: the Missionaries in China are more thin-skinned, and object to placards, and complain to the Foreign Office. The result of such Missionary operations will be the creation of a Church of hypocrites, hated by their own people, because they represent the humiliation of their country.

As far back as 1880 a case arose in a Missionary Society of the Church of England, in which the Missionaries, and some of the Members of the Committee, urged application to the Foreign office for the enforcement of Treaty-Rights, or in other words for the Arm of the Flesh, to support so-called spiritual endeavours to convert souls. I opposed it, and corresponded on the subject with two ex-British Ministers at Pekin, and the Secretaries of three great Nonconformist Societies, who had Missions in China: their replies are now on the table before me: they are all in one sense: I quote a few words from each.

I. "All our traditions are against resorting to State-aid for "any religious, or educational, object; and we are "thus spared many difficulties and vexatious inter-"ference."

II. "In the case of China, Treaty-Rights have at all times "involved Treaty-wrongs, which have been forced "upon an unwilling Government to the injury of "the people, and to the hindrance in the most fatal "manner of Missionary effort."

III. "It is possible, that an official remonstrance may bring "rebuke, or even dismissal, on an offending subor-"dinate, but this does not help us in the long run. "Patience is our strength, when we are in the right: "this applies with special emphasis to the Chinese "People."

Bad as the cases of Turkey and China are, that of U-Ganda is worse. I cannot plead ignorance of the details of the case, as I was for a series of years Chairman of the African sub-Committee of the Society, which is to blame, and the policy adopted contrary to my views was one of the many reasons for my resigning my seat as Member of the Committee in the fiftieth year of my Membership of the Association. More need not be said: this Mission may be described as "sitting on bayonets, and owing its day-by-day existence to Maxim-guns:" one of their most honoured worshippers is the "impure" King, who slaughtered their Bishop. The Church-Missionary-Society Report of 1893 states, that in the event of the withdrawal of the British officers, and their Sudanese Savage Mahometan Soldiers, the lives of all the Members of the Protestant Church will be sacrificed.

Sir Gerald Portal in his despatch May 24, 1893, presented to Parliament March, 1894, writes thus:

" The miserable history of U-Ganda for the last few years is
" sufficient to show, how inextricably religion and politics are
" interwoven in this country, and I fear, that the narrow fanatical
" nature of the people forbids us to hope for any great improve-
" ment for years to come. The three great parties of Islam,
" Rome, and Protestantism, though nominally divided only by
" religious tenets, are in reality adverse and jealous political
" camps, and the leadership of two of these camps is practically
" in the hands of European Missionaries.

" I am extremely unwilling to enter into a discussion of the
" dangerous subject of Missionary interference in politics, but it
" is impossible to avoid an allusion to so important a factor of
" the whole question. That the Missionaries on both sides are
" the veritable political leaders of their respective factions, there
" can be no doubt whatever. The Romish Fathers would admit
" this to be the case; on the Protestant side it would not be
" admitted, but the fact unfortunately remains: . . . there
" has grown up a sort of dual, or triple, system of government,
" which adds seriously to the difficulties of administration. It
" will from this be readily understood, that the race for converts,
" now being carried on by the Romish and Protestant Mis-
" sionaries in U-Ganda, is synonymous with a race for political
" power: . . . it is this feeling, which since the introduction
" of the forms of Christianity has cost so many hundred lives,
" and has thrown the country fifty years back in its advance
" towards prosperity. It is deeply to be regretted, that the
" avowedly great influence of the Missionaries in U-Ganda is
" not used to introduce a spirit of Tolerance, and Peace, even
" at the risk of the loss to the party of some political power,
" or a few wealthy chieftainships . . . There can be no

"doubt that, when the withdrawal of the forces of the Company
"was announced, overtures for alliance were made to the
"Mahometans simultaneously by the chiefs of the Romish and
"Protestant parties: two of these parties acting together could
"crush the third."

I can add nothing to the condemnation contained in these lines: can real Conversions of individual souls to God be carried out in such an environment? if Conversion be the sole object, would it not be better to leave U-Ganda to the nominal Christianity of Rome and go to the North and East side of the Lake?

I add a few words on the subject of Compensation, wrung from Foreign Governments by the Arm of the Flesh in favour of spiritual men, or at least those who pretend to be so, who ought to take the spoiling of their goods, and loss of their lives, joyfully in the service of their Master: I quote from the Church Missionary-Society-Report, 1892 : "Through the intervention of
"the Consul at Fu-Chow, a fine was imposed on the leader of
"the riot, and it was agreed, that the Mission should be com-
"pensated, a new site given for a hospital, the old hospital
"repaired, and that a proclamation should be issued declaring
"the right of Missionaries to rent, purchase, build, or reside in
"any part of Kien-Ning. The Committee are not aware,
"however, that any of these provisions have yet been carried
"out. An agreement has, however, been made and signed by
"the Mandarin and the Missionaries regarding a site at Sing
"Kio, about a mile further from Kien-Ning than Tai Chiu is."

Complaints are made in the United States of there being no indemnity, levied from the Spanish Government for the injuries inflicted upon American Missionaries: there is sure to be a Nemesis, when compensation is thus claimed.

The Consul-General of Sweden and Norway has secured an indemnity of forty thousand dollars to the relatives of two Missionaries killed in 1893. Will this advance the cause of the Gospel? Would the families of Peter and Paul have accepted compensation? Did the British Government claim compensation from King Mwanga for killing Bishop Hannington? Nowadays the citizens of such a petty State as Norway and Sweden are supposed to have Rights. Had these Missionaries been forbidden by King Oscar to enter China, they would have snapped their fingers at him. Had they been killed in a chance uproar at Banáras in British India, would the Indian Government have paid down rupees, and would any State have compelled them to do so? Is this a really Christian Method of preaching the Gospel? Will there not be a bitter rancour stored up in the hearts of the Chinese Nation? Is there a single passage in the New Testament, that can give the least support to such a practice?

The latest phase of the compensation system is, that the British Taxpayers are expected to pay to the French Romish Mission at U-Ganda a cash compensation for the unjustifiable injury inflicted upon them by Capt. Lugard, and the Protestant Converts headed by British Missionaries. At any rate it is more worthy of the character of a Christian Missionary to give compensation than to accept it. We may expect, that there will be more outrages, more violence used, in putting down attempts to gain power, and more compensation to be paid by the British taxpayer for wrongs inflicted on subjects of a friendly Nation by Protestant Converts.

I have dwelt thus fully on this bad Method, because I consider it to be the worst of all bad Methods, the most insidious, the most un-Christian, and the most ruinous to the cause, which lies nearest to our hearts.

2. Receiving Endowments from Taxes levied from non-Christians.

One of the grave errors of some Missions is to receive material advantages from a Sovereign: it is sure to bring a Nemesis with it: it is with pain I read of the attempts made by Protestants and the Church of Rome in U-Ganda to win the favour of that atrocious individual, King Mwanga, whose public crimes, and private vices, are of the blackest die. I asked a Missionary from the field, what was the duty of the numerous boy-pages, who attended his Court, and the so-called martyrdom of some of whom created such sensations: the reply was, that they were the victims of his lust. I read in the Report of the Church-Missionary-Society for 1893, that the attendance of this King at the Church is a source of danger to the purity of the Church, and yet his patronage is sought for, instead of his presence being shunned.

The Emperor Constantine slew several members of his own family, and delayed his own baptism till the extreme moment, and the servile Bishops praised him; and he began the system of endowment of the Church of Christ with material Revenues, which has been its misfortune even to the present day, placing in England the appointment to spiritual office in the hands of Sovereigns of the moral type of the late King George IV. In the Middle Ages the Revenue of Heathen Temples, and their buildings, were transferred to the Christian Church. The fickle Native Potentate, born a Heathen, and by turns a Protestant and a Papist, is not to be depended upon. Let the true Missionary keep clear of all such attractions.

And with regard to British Provinces, it is exceedingly undesirable, that Missions should be under the control of, or in any way connected with, Bishops, whose salaries are paid from the taxes on the Hindu and Mahometan subjects of Her Majesty. How keenly we should resent being taxed to support the Bishops of the Italian Missions in Great Britain! "we should do unto others as we should wish, that men should do unto us." The endowed Bishoprics of Calcutta, Bombay, and Madras, are an anachronism: they were well intended at the time, but they are out of date; and the intelligent non-Christian Indian has a real cause of objection in these hard times. The same may be said of the Bishopric of Mauritius, described as a Missionary-Diocese. Whatever may be said in favour of a National Church in England of a duration of many Centuries, cannot be said of stipendiary Bishops in a subject-State or a Colony inhabited by a non-Christian population. As a fact, only lately, the connection of the Bishopric of Colombo with the Government of Ceylon has been put an end to, and the next Bishop will be provided for by an endowment-fund. The Report of the Society for the Propagation of the Gospel for 1890 tells us, "that the Diocese " shows no sign of weakness in consequence of the withdrawal " of State-aid. The Bishop was able to state at the Synod, " which was held in September last, that in the four years which " had passed since the final withdrawal of State-aid, the clerical " order had increased by ten, which is nearly 20 per cent."

In W. Africa there is a Bishopric at Sierra Leone paid by the State: it should cease, and the salaries of Bishops be paid by Missionary Societies, or a special endowment fund created for the purpose.

But in Ceylon a charge is made of an opposite character. I give the exact words of the *Ceylon Diocesan Gazette*: "We " fear he will also be remembered as the Governor, who revived " Buddhism; and we have never concealed our disapproval of " the policy, which, in the name of liberality and justice, has " so needlessly patronized and fostered that religion, which " numbers among its votaries a large majority of the inhabitants " of Ceylon.

" On May 1st, about four weeks before his departure, Sir " Arthur Gordon distributed prizes to the successful students " among the priests who study Buddhism in the Vidyodaya " College. The report read on the occasion stated, that the " King of Siam had sent 250 rupees, to be given to the pupils " who should distinguish themselves in the knowledge of the " Buddhist doctrine. Sir Arthur Gordon, when he was re-" quested to speak, rose up and declared, that he was a " Christian, and wished, that all those assembled should attain " to higher truth; but he thought it was the duty of the priests " to study well the religion they professed, and to be known by " leading good lives, free from the influence of foolish super-" stition. Whilst expressing himself thankful for this testimony, "the writer regrets that the Government, which professes to be impartial and to favour no one religion before another in Ceylon, should spend its money for the promotion of Buddhism. The Vidyodaya College is a seminary, endowed by a wealthy Buddhist for the education of their priests, and provision is here made for the Sirpasa, the four necessary appendages of a Buddhist priest. The Government makes no grant to any Christian institution for the training of ministers, nor for the maintenance of Hindu or Mahometan seminaries. The 1,000 rupees given to the Buddhists by the Government is therefore regarded as an unjust and unlawful grant."

Of course the grant is most objectionable, but not more so than a grant for Christian purposes. Both are equally wrong.

Some would justify the grants in British India to support Christian Missions by alluding to the enormous grants of Revenue-free land to Mahometans and Hindus, which have been our baneful inheritance in British India: of course this means a deduction of Millions from the Treasury. Inquiries were made fifty years ago: large resumptions of such grants were made: people were let down gently by grants for one life or two lives: but still the burden remains. But the existence of a bad custom under non-Christian Governments is no warrant for a Christian Government doing the same: besides a privileged few enjoy these grants, while the taxation of the whole community is drawn upon for the salaries of the Bishops: if Army-Chaplains are required for the Army, one Chaplain-General would be sufficient for their control.

3. Intolerance of other Religions, or other forms of the same Religion.

This leads to remarks on the necessity of great tenderness to those, who differ in doctrine or in practice. It is astonishing to read remarks made by Presbyterian Missionaries against Plymouthites, as bitter as those, that were made in the last century by Episcopalians against Presbyterians, or *vice versa*. The greatest wisdom and most Christian forbearance are necessary in such cases.

Before the Reformation no Toleration was extended to any other form of Religion, and no freedom of opinion was tolerated on the most important subject to each individual soul, not only on the general principle of Christian Faith, but on the minor details of Church Government and ceremonies. In a manifesto published by the Cardinal Archbishop of Paris, 1891, occur these words: "No oppression is more grievous for a people, than that of a doctrine imposed by the State." We thank him for these words. What was the fate of the poor Pagans in Germany, the poor Jews and Mahometans in Spain, under the system of the Church of Rome from 400 A.D. to 1500 A.D., when her claws were finally clipped? Think of the treatment received by so-called Heretics (the word αἵρεσις means "a choosing") during that long period. There were no doubt worldly, antinomian, and immoral, men outside, inside, and on the skirts of the great spiritual revival of the Middle Ages: there was much one-sided teaching, much downright hypocrisy, but in the centre of the moving army of Free-thinkers (thank God for that word!) there were the very Children of God, the holy, the unselfish, the seekers after God, men endowed with the inestimable gift of self-sacrifice, of whom the world was not worthy, and who died as blessed Martyrs, and their blood has been the seed of our Christian Liberty. Lost causes, like those of the Donatist, the Arian, the Nestorian, have no chroniclers. The Librarians of the Church of Rome burnt all the books, which differed from their own narrow views, punished the copyist, or printer, and killed the writer. Thus the Church of Rome was built up in Intolerance, Persecution, and Crime, and its Annals are a scandal to the Christian name.

Lord Macaulay remarks, in his review of Ranke's History of the Popes, the strange phenomena, "that the atheistic " philosopher, while denying the Christian dogma, was loud " in asserting the right of the human race to liberty of soul " and body; on the other hand the Christian Church, while " upholding Christian dogma, did not hesitate to enforce bap-" tism at the point of the sword, the tortures of the Inquisi-" tion, massacres, persecution, and assassination, in defiance " of the first principles of Christian Mercy, and Love, to the " Sinner, to the non-Christian, and to the most degraded of " mankind."

There is a great temptation to a Missionary, when he is in the second stage of his work with a young Christian flock grouped round him, to make use of a friendly Arm of the Flesh for the purpose of advancing his views of spiritual interests, and suppressing what appears to him to be great moral and doctrinal evils. We find the word orthodoxy freely used: it merely means "my doxy," as opposed to "other people's doxy." The Church of Rome has ever been a persecutor. No one sinned more than Xavier: we judge him by his own letters to his friends; but all his predecessors, even those, whose names we honour most, erred in the same direction: it seemed to them essential to convert the Chief, or his lawful wife, or his concubine, and then to help them to put down opposition. Augustine of Canterbury was most anxious to coerce the British Church on such very unimportant matters as the date of Easter, and the shaving of the heads of Ecclesiastics. We hear the last echo of this absolute intolerant sentiment in Shakespeare's play of "The Merchant of Venice," where the Duke orders Shylock to become a Christian: in fact, in those days all idea of individual Conversion of souls had disappeared, and only an outward conformity to ritual was required, with downright persecution for any attempt to use free thought. Now the minds of men have changed: an enthusiastic Missionary would like a little help from the Civil Power: he would like to have the Brahminical, or Mahometan, schools shut up, and their preachers warned off; but they have found out, that the sword of the Civil Power cuts both ways, and might be used against the Missionary himself. The Church of Rome issue the loudest cry for Toleration, and denounces Persecution, when she is down; but, when in power, she makes use of the weapon. It has become an incontrovertible axiom of Mission-work, that the spiritual agent must depend upon his own spiritual power, and that absolute Toleration to Sects, and Religions, must be given. Rome tries to shut out the Protestant from her presence, but she will find that is of no use, even in little islands like Futuna and Uvea in Oceania.

If we lift the subject higher, we shall see how wrong Persecution is: the unseen Divinity, whom all Nations worship under different names, Jehovah, Jove or Lord, rules the world, and the hearts of His poor creatures: He suffers their follies, and is merciful to their errors, and their religious conceptions. Paul could not blame them: he rather praised the $\delta\epsilon\iota\sigma\iota\delta\alpha\iota\mu o\nu\iota\alpha$, which he witnessed at Athens. It was thought a very grand thing for Theodosius to destroy the Temple of Serapis in Egypt. Is it not a much grander thing to spare the temples of Banáras, and the Mosques of Upper India, and to suffer them to be repaired and beautified? We can see clearly, that the Epoch of Idolatry is passing away: the Idol is still in the Temple, but no longer in the heart of the worshippers, and before very long the great change will come. The Pagan Temples, upon which we come so repeatedly in Italy and Greece, in ruins, and forgotten, remind us, that like all things human religious conceptions have their season, and then fade away and fall like the dead leaves in an Autumn-Forest.

I quote this from the life of Lord Lawrence by Bosworth Smith: "When the city of Delhi fell during the Mutiny in 1858, " some of Lord Lawrence's friends wrote to him, expressing " their hope that he would destroy the great Mosque there. " In reply to this proposal he wrote: 'I will on no account " consent to it. We should carefully abstain from the destruc-" tion of religious edifices, either to favour friends or to annoy " foes.' And when some of his intimate friends pointed out, " that to destroy the finest place of worship in the world would "be felt as a blow to their religion by Mahometans everywhere, he jumped up from his seat, and, slapping the foremost of them on his back, said: 'I'll tell you what it is: there are many things you could persuade me to do, but you shall never persuade me to do this.'"

I quote the following remarks: "From the time of Christ to the epoch of the Reformation there were no Dissenters, only traitors and heretics, who were deemed unworthy to live in the same world, and breathe the same air as Emperors, Popes, and Bishops. But the Christian temperament can be traced through all the Centuries, whether the devout people of the period were martyrs or hermits, monks, nuns, or friars, pilgrims or crusaders, priests or warriors. The same aspirations, misgivings, trials, and difficulties existed then as now, though the trials and difficulties may be less. The best people of to-day may be trusted to recognise a touch of their own kindred amid all the varieties of time and place and circumstance, which make up the past."

To show the absurdity of the use of the term Heretic, it may be mentioned, that a certain Egyptian King of the Eighteenth Dynasty, Amenophis, was called the Heretic-King as a term of disapproval, because he worshipped the Sun's Disk rather than the Sun itself. Some of the so-called heresies of the early centuries of Christianity were no less ridiculous, and persecution of the disk-worshippers was very active.

It is delightful to read of the descendants of the Fathers of the Inquisition complaining of one of their schools being closed by a Turkish Pasha, or a place of worship, which they call theirs, being appropriated by a Congregation of the Greek Church. I quote the following from the Church Missionary Society's Report of 1893:

"At Kang Wong, in the same pastorate, two men, who had heard the Gospel at Lo-Ngwong, declared themselves Christians. A catechist was sent there during the year, and about thirty catechumens joined the congregation, and have courageously borne persecution. The Archdeacon writes: 'The reality of the faith of these new converts has been put to the test, and I am glad to report they have stood it nobly. The usual yearly offerings for the support of the idol temples, and idol-processions and theatricals in honour of the dumb gods, were demanded by the village elders from the Christians, who, of course, refused. This refusal created quite a sensation in the town, and was met by threats on the part of the idol worshippers. The Christians on their part declared, that they would rather die than give a cent to support Idolatry, as their doing so would offend God, and would be a denial of their Christian faith. On this the heathen assembled and attacked "them in their houses, severely beating them, and partially destroying their houses. The Magistrate issued a proclamation forbidding this persecution, but the heathen party took down the proclamation and tore it into shreds, and again attacked the Christians more severely than before. The persecution is still going on.'" The Church of Rome could hardly have done worse than this to the Protestants.

In British India all Religions and denominations enjoy the delightful "Laissez faire" of the British administration. Where good, quiet, men are at work for legitimate spiritual objects, with no political motives, they are allowed to enjoy what in equity they are entitled to, but are not allowed to worry their neighbours; a little healthy persecution, however, would sometimes give a new life to a sleepy Mission.

We are better able to understand the miserable feeling, which led the Religious parties in the Middle Ages to attack each other with carnal weapons, from the spectacle exhibited to us lately at U-Ganda. I read the accounts of both parties in the French and English languages. Each abuses the other without any show of justice; each seeks to get the better of the other. There is an utter absence of Christian nobility of character on both sides. Whichever party got into power was ready to eject, or tread down, the other party. The only difference is, that the Church of Rome openly says so, and the Protestants show by their actions that they would do so, if they had the opportunity.

To give an idea of King Mwanga, I quote the following from Carl Peter's "New Lights upon Dark Africa," 1891, p. 403: he himself visited U-Ganda just before the troubles.

"I asked Mwanga to pledge himself to make Christianity the one dominant religion of all his dominions: the religion was formally proclaimed as the religion of the State by the decree, that all Government-appointments should be filled by Christians only, that all heathens, who refused to be converted, must quit their appointments: The decree was carried out to its fullest extent. Mahometanism was simply forbidden under penalty of death: Heathens were tolerated, but Christianity alone was to be the dominant religion." So in the British sphere of influence in Africa a state of things arose, equalling the Middle Ages in Intolerance. I have dwelt on this subject, that Missionaries may look ahead, and act with caution. The Indians, Chinese, and Japanese have ever been tolerant; the Mahometan in India was never a persecuting fanatic. It must needs be, that diversity of doctrinal opinion, and of Church-organization, will come into existence: we must just let this alone; if arguments fail, the duty of the Missionary is discharged. It does not fall into his duty to attempt to save a man's soul by showing no consideration for his body.

It is the fashion sometimes to minimise the degree of persecution in Europe: so I state a fact.

Pope Nicolas wrote to the Missionaries in Bulgaria not to spare the apostates, and this rule has survived in Mahometan countries, and in the Empire of Russia, and was the practice of the Inquisition: once a Christian, always a Christian! Apostates ought to meet with no toleration, if they persist in refusing obedience to their spiritual advisers.

It is strange to read in Reports of Missionaries in British India and Ceylon such words as "persecution" applied by some Power to themselves: we recommend such a Missionary to take a turn of five years in Africa: he would return with a chastened spirit. How shocking such words as these appear in a Missionary-Report of the 19th century: "we are the English Church, and the Church of the English, the ruling Nation." Surely if the Missionaries were of the Lutheran, and French Protestant, or Danish, or even of the Romish Church, the sole object is to preach Christ, not the privileges of an establishment. A Romish Priest could not have expressed himself worse.

I quote from a modern writer a passage, that exposes to scorn the modern system of religious persecution:

"There is a Protestant Popery. The subtle spirit of Intolerance can inhabit all hearts, speak all languages, swear by, or at, all creeds; it can inspire the Pope and the man, who denounces the Pope, the persecutor and the persecuted, the Radical and the Conservative, the reformer and the enemy of reform. Faithful souls have suffered, that we may not have the power of suppressing opinion in the way men once did: we are obliged to limit ourselves to other kinds of racks and thumb-screws, to bitter words, theological nicknames, mean insinuations, back-biting, anonymous letter-writing, spiritual boycotting, to craft, cunning, vain-boasting, false-witness, pious frauds, and using the machinery of our Church and sect and religious newspaper, and our influence in a community, to injure and crush persons, whose opinions we dislike. We cannot kill bodies, but we try to kill reputations."

The Hebrew race were ever persecutors, from the time of Moses down to the day, when Paul stood by, and held the clothes of the assassins, who stoned Stephen: how different are the annals of the great people of India, tolerant to every other religious conception, or to any sectarian form of their own, so long as they themselves are left alone! On the numerous rock and pillar-Inscriptions found in widely distant parts of India, but made under orders of the same king, Asoka, 300–200 B.C., whose only recorded title is that of "Beloved of the Gods," we find sentiments of toleration and mercy, and loving-kindness: "The King prays with every variety of prayer for those, who

" differ from him in creed, that they, following his example, may
" with him attain eternal Salvation: He ordains Tolerance by
" decreeing, that all unbelievers everywhere may dwell un-
" molested, as they also wish for purity of disposition, and
" moral restraints: for men are of various passions and various
" desires."

The tolerant religions of the Brahmanical, Buddhist, and Confucianist survive in undiminished strength from a period long before Anno Domini, and comprise a very large portion of the population of the world, however much the young Missionary may gird at them, and call them the Kingdom of Satan. We can only bow our heads, for the Ruler of the Universe cannot do other than right, and in our prayers we utter the phrase, that " He hateth nothing that He has made "; and yet for countless generations He has left them to their own devices, and sent neither Prophet nor Evangelist to call them to Repentance, and a knowledge of the great plan of Salvation.

4. Destruction, or Appropriation, of Buildings belonging to another Religion.

Temples, Sacred Trees, Shrines on Hill-tops, Tombs of departed worthies, in Europe were ruthlessly destroyed, or converted by violence to Christian uses. Pope Gregory wrote to Augustine of Canterbury not to destroy the Temples, but to convert them into Christian Churches. In this off-hand way the sacred property of another religious cult was to be appropriated with a high hand by a foreign Missionary, while, when any one of the Church buildings were appropriated by Mahometans, there was a loud cry of Sacrilege. Lands, the land-tax of which was set apart for the support of Temples, with which we are so familiar in India, were at once confiscated. In Damascus to this day there is a groan over the conversion of a Christian Church to a Mosque, but it was originally a Pagan Temple converted into a Christian Church.

It is a dangerous temptation to a Missionary, by the help of the Arm of the Flesh, to appropriate a place of worship with the actual or implied consent of the people; but he forgets that it is a blow to the whole religious Society. In a paper published by the American Board of Foreign Missions, Boston, United States, I read a letter, 1878, from a Missionary in China headed " Overthrow of an Idolatrous Temple in N. China ": then follows a long story, how the inhabitants of a certain village were desirous of destroying their idols, and inviting the Missionaries to use the rear of the Temple as a Chapel, and the front as a School: six of the managers of the temple were candidates for Baptism: the remaining twelve remained passive: some esteemed the whole scheme to be a disgrace, and threatened an appeal to the Chinese Authorities: there was a gathering of a meeting in the town, and they voted away their temple, and its lands, to a foreign religion, of which most of them had never heard six months ago, and none of them until within a few years: they were not converts, and did it of their own motion: a deed was signed, and made over to the Missionary, who thinks that he has done a clever thing, and hopes to organize the beginning of a Church out of the twenty applicants on his list. I should have been glad to have heard how this annexation of a heathen temple answered: we have only to imagine the effect of the annexation in London of a Church by the Mormonites, or Theosophists, or Mahometans.

In another report I read how in China a Missionary persuaded a convert to collect his idols, which were made of paper, and on Sunday at the Christian service to burn them; we cannot be surprised that the Superintendent of the District has threatened to report the case to the Mandarin, and that the neighbours threaten to turn them out of their house; or, as the Missionary in the usual style describes it, " the Devil is busy in stirring up opposition."

In the Church-Missionary-Society's Report, 1892, I read how sometimes the zeal of the converts exceeds the discretion of peaceful Christian men, subjects of Her Majesty, the Empress of India, and becomes iconoclastic.

" A small village about a mile and a half from Poonamallie
" was visited by the members twice, and on the second day one
" of the leading men came forward and said: ' Yes, we believe
" all that you say; now tell us definitely what we have to do,
" and how we are to be saved.' The preachers happened to
" stand near an idol-temple, and one of them spoke about
" Gideon, how he and his men cast down the altar of Baal and
" cut down the grove, that was by the side of it, and asked if
" the villagers would likewise break down that idol-temple, and
" build in its place a place of worship for the true and living
" God. The villagers one and all of them said, ' Yes, we shall
" do so; come and help us.' May God help them, and make
" that a Christian village soon."

In the Church-Missionary-Society Report of 1893, I find that in Africa the poor ignorant converts allow themselves, or are allowed by their spiritual teachers, to go further and break the peace. Mr. Price mentions an instance of indiscreet zeal on the part of some of the Christian young men:

"A large procession of people passed one day on their way
" to one of their sacred places for the purpose of building a
" tiny grass hut (their apology for a temple), and make offerings
" to the gods. The young fellows came to me (one of them

" the late chief's son), saying they were going off to protest
" against this folly. I did not know exactly what they meant
" to do. However, they rushed off, and in the presence of all
" the people set fire to the temple they had just erected, and
" scattered the offerings placed therein. Of course the people
" were in a great rage, and threatened all sorts of things. At
" last they called a meeting of the head-men, and they had to
" appear and give an account of themselves. The people
" wanted them to pay a fine, but they refused to do this, so at
" last they let them go, saying, 'Well, you worship your God as
" you like, only let us alone to follow our customs and worship
" our gods in our way.' Both Christians and inquirers have
" to put up with a good deal of persecution in a small way.
" They are looked upon as fools, and told that, when people
" are baptized their hearts are taken out of their bodies, and
" they are no longer Wa-Gogo."

It speaks ill for the peace of the Church, when such acts done by converts, are reported by the Missionary with a certain amount of satisfaction, and are thought worthy of record in an Annual Report: it does not surprise me to hear, that a good deal of persecution has to be put up with by men, who deliberately set fire to the sacred buildings of their fellow-villagers: they would have been loud in their outcry, if their own place of worship had been set fire to: they do not seem to have learnt one of the fundamental principles of their Faith, to do unto others as they would wish that men should do unto them. I think that this Missionary also might have quoted the Devil as stirring up opposition on the part of Christians against the Pagans.

5. Making a Mission a handle for Political Schemes.

Nothing can be more reprehensible, or wicked, than to make Christian Missions a handle for political expansion. This has been the openly avowed, and persistent, practice of France for nearly half-a-century: they impute the same motive to the British Missions: in former years there was not the slightest ground for such a charge, but the events of U-Ganda have left a stain on the British shield. A British Mission went there without any impulse given by the Government: a Chartered Company some years later occupied the Region for its own commercial purposes, and finding that it did not answer, prepared to withdraw. The friends of the Mission collected large sums to induce the Chartered Company to remain, and have since tried to induce the British Government to occupy the Region. The French naturally impute the same motives to the British, as guide their own conduct. In all parts of Asia and Africa, the French Missions are notoriously the advance-guards of French occupation: large grants were made to the late Cardinal Lavigerie on account of his political services at Tunis. The French Missionary-Reports everywhere identify the Christian Religion with France.

In the Missionary-periodical published weekly at Lyons, called the *Missions Catholiques*, so persistently was it imputed to the Governments in England and the United States, that they made use of the Missionaries of their respective countries to advance their political interests, that in 1882 I addressed the Editor a letter of remonstrance, but it had no effect, and the generosity of Roman Catholics is still encouraged by impressing upon them, that their contributions will not only assist the spread of the Romish Religion, but check the progress of the Protestant political influences of England and America. The accounts of the French Missions to Polynesia is one long tirade against English Protestants, and appeals to French Naval officers to help them with the Arm of the Flesh. As soon as the Priests got a footing in an island, they persuaded some of the Chiefs to place themselves under the protection of France, and urged them to exclude English heretics.

II. MODES OF CONVERSION.

CAP. II.		MODES OF CONVERSION.
	1	Tribal, not Individual, Conversion.
	2	Purchase and Baptism of Slaves bought from the Slave-Dealer.
	3	Securing Conversion by offer of Material Advantages.
	4	Omitting Bible-Teaching in the Vernacular.

1. TRIBAL, NOT INDIVIDUAL, CONVERSION.

In the early ages Conversion of individuals was quite exceptional. When the Chief, for the hope of material advantage, or a desire for change, or under the influence of superstition, or the blandishments of his favourite wife, as in Kent, was persuaded to be baptized, all the Court, and the Army, followed suit, and the meaner subjects were compelled to do so. Augustine landed in Kent, converted Ethelbert by the aid of his Frank wife, and a few months afterwards ten thousand of his subjects were baptized in the River Swale without any preparation, or any knowledge of what they were doing. When by the persuasion of a wife, a mother, or mistress, a Chief relapsed into Idolatry, the Chroniclers can find no words sufficient to abuse the Chief, and the female, who influenced him. The case of Ethelbert is but a sample of many similar ones. Only imagine a Missionary in British India trying to work the Conversion of the people through the influence of the Raja of Maisûr, or Jaipúr, or the Nawab of Hyderabad, or the ladies of their Zanána.

I look with great suspicion at the so-called Conversions in U-Ganda: the Priests of Rome report, that the Bishop has limited them to a fixed number of baptisms for each month: in such converts there is no stability whatever: if a Mahometan preacher were to appear, they would flock to him.

2. Purchase and Baptism of Slaves bought from the Slave-Dealer.

In the story of Missions of the Church of Rome, that from the earliest times to the present hour, the purchase of slaves for the purpose of bringing up the males as acolytes and priests, and the females to supply wives, has been part of the system, is not denied, but justified even by those, who do not themselves practise it. Pope Gregory, A.D. 596, wrote to his Agents in Gaul to buy up Anglo-Saxon lads of the age of 17 to 20, and train them in Monasteries to become Missionaries in England. Wildibrod purchased boys to train for his Mission. Anskar purchased boys for the same purpose. John de Monte Corvino, in a letter dated 1305 A.D. from Pekin, mentions, that he had purchased Chinese boys, and baptized them, and that he had gradually got together 150 children of Pagans, varying from 7 to 11 years of age: he had baptized them all, and taught them Chinese, Greek, and Latin, to form a choir in his Church, and to copy the Psalter (Yule's Cathay, pp. 199, 206). We gather from this, that there were no Mass-books, or copy of the Scriptures, in Chinese, but only in European languages, which were taught to these unconverted Pagans to read, chant, or repeat, without comprehending a word of their meaning.

Up to this day the Missionaries of Rome do not hesitate to purchase children. Since the outcry against Slavery, it is called Redemption, or "Rachat," but it is the grossest form of child-selling on the part of the dealers, who steal the children from other tribes, and barter them, male or female, to the Romish Priests, not caring whether the girls go into Harems, or the boys are converted into Eunuchs, or worse. Tippu Tib would gladly supply enough converts for a Church at a fair price. Any reader of the *Missions Catholiques* will have seen notices of its existence in Missions on both sides of the Atlantic for the best and holiest purposes, and yet the practice has in it the germs of much evil. As long as there is a demand for children, the kidnappers and slave-dealers will find it worth their while to continue the trade. It is a question of so many dollars as purchase-money: it is not likely that Parents would sell their own children, or tribesmen children of their own tribe. The children must be stolen, and then sold. The Romish Priests make this part of their system, and glory in it. On Lake Tanganyika the Priests had purchased children: the relatives came to claim them, and on refusal killed the Priests, and it served them right; they call it "Redemption," but it is really "Slave-purchasing" of an insidious character, and it stains the character of a Mission, that such a practice should be allowed. One Protestant Society in ignorance was thinking of adopting the practice, but I denounced it, and it was dropped. Redemption of a slave is a term properly applied to the recovery in exchange for a sum of money of a wife, or child, or tribesman, kidnapped in a raid, but it is not properly applied to the deliberate purchase by strangers of children, who have been kidnapped for the purpose of sale for moral, or immoral, purposes. No Missionary should tolerate such a practice. In the *Missions Catholiques* of Lyons there are weekly entries of sums paid to the Editor for the redemption (rachat) of a little girl to be baptized under the name of Marie, or a little boy to be called Jean. Think of the indignation of the Christian world, if Christian boys were carried off, sold to Mahometan Missionaries, and circumcised with the name of Selim, or Mahomet.

3. Securing Conversions by offer of Material Advantages.

This lever was largely made use of in past Centuries, and always will be by unprincipled and short-sighted Missionaries. In an age, when all men were venal, when all public offices were put up to the highest bidder, the temptation to the Pagan, who never had, or had ceased to have, faith in his ancestral belief, must have been tremendous to accept baptism, a simple, painless, and inoffensive rite, nominally conform, and thus procure, or retain, office, or present, or obtain, lands, influence and wealth. The phrase "Rice Christians" reminds us, that the same disease prevails in many Mission-Fields: How about the Katikero in U-Ganda? The Romish Priests charge the Protestant Missionaries, and rightly charge them, with this failing, but call loudly for money for their own flocks. The *Missions Catholiques* contains one continual howl from every part of the world for money, food, clothing, for their people, which enables them to play the part of the Benevolent Friend. In the same category comes the ejection from office, or depression, of those, who decline to worship Baal, or in other words, the poorest heathen of each community.

4. Omitting Bible-Teaching in the Vernacular.

This seems to have been the peculiar sin of the early ages, as it is in Romish Missions to this day. In every country the idea was to retain the Latin liturgy, and Latin version of the Scriptures, and it is difficult to understand why, for it was not the language of our Lord and His Apostles, nor of the Missionaries, nor of the people to be converted: they shrunk as it were from the trouble of acquiring barbarous languages, or allowing them to be the vehicle of prayer and praise. As time went on, Latin became more entirely dead, and the barbarous languages more polished: still there was no change in Method. Augustine at Canterbury, 597 A.D., and Otho at Pyritz in Poland, 1124 A.D., addressed their hearers only through an ignorant interpreter. Boniface and his companions were able to address the Saxons in a dialect of their common language, but no attempt was made to translate the Scriptures, yet Centuries before it had been revealed to Ulfilas, and Cyril, and Methodius, that the most important requisite for a successful Mission was to introduce the Scriptures, and the Liturgy, in the Vernacular of each Region. Rome remonstrated, 868 A.D., against the translation of Methodius in the Slavonic languages, as it does still against the translations in the languages of the world: had the common folk had the opportunity of listening to the words of our Lord in their own vulgar tongue, the path of Conversion would have been easier, and the results more satisfactory: the so-called converted Chiefs would not have continued in their uncontrolled Immorality, if they had been acquainted with the lessons taught in the New Testament.

In modern Missions the Bible is the sword of the Missionary, and modern Science has supplied him with unlimited number of copies. The Priests of the Church of Rome, notably at Beirût, in South India, and U-Ganda, have admitted, that translations must be supplied, and this necessarily brings with it Bible-teaching.

III. DIFFICULTIES ATTENDING CONVERSION.

CAP. III.		DIFFICULTIES ATTENDING CONVERSION.
	1	Degradation, or Imperfect Teaching, of the Gospel.
	2	Pagan Notions of Nominal Converts.
	3	Imposing new conditions precedent to Baptism.
	4	Relapse of Converts into their Old, or adoption of a New, Religion.
	5	Low Culture, and extreme Intellectual Denseness, of Converts.
	6	Questions connected with the Matrimony of Converts.
	7	Credulousness of any new story.
	8	Injurious Influence of Western Education on certain Classes; is Education a necessary part of Evangelization or Civilization?
	9	Evils arising from raising the material status of Converts.
	10	Objections to little Barracks for Converts.
	11	Dwelling too strongly on the Sins of the non-Christian World.
	12	Assertion that Missionaries have *material* help from God.
	13	Treating with Contempt the Parental rights of non-Christians.
	14	Necessity of Union of Denominations into one National Church.
	15	Certainty of Opposition from Old, and New, Forms of Religion.

1. DEGRADATION, OR IMPERFECT TEACHING, OF THE GOSPEL.

The forms of this evil are manifold: 1. The Gospel-Message, as conveyed in the New Testament, may be degraded, and diluted, by the accretions of European Churches. 2. The Central Truth may be inadequately presented to the poor ignorant catechumen. 3. There may be too large a flavour of European and American denominationalism. 4. There may be a mixture of European and American National weaknesses. 5. There may be too much ritual, or too much dogma, or too much civilization, or too much intellectual Education. 6. There may be rank antinomianism. 7. There may be profitless asceticism.

It is obvious, that the Christianity of the Anglo-Saxon Kingdoms was in its early Centuries mere Ritualism: their whole Theology was the Creed and Lord's Prayer. The Eastern Church, from the first year of its freedom from Pagan superstition, occupied itself in Theology, *i.e.*, the Nature of God and the Incarnation of Christ, the results of which are embodied in the Athanasian Creed, which would not help a professing Christian far onwards on the Christian path. The Western Church occupied itself with the nature and needs of Man, the results of which are stated by Augustine of Hippo. The kind of Religion taught by Missionaries to Asia, sent out by Rome, may be exemplified by the following words of a Bishop, 640–649, in the very Century, in which Augustine landed at Canterbury. " He " is a good Christian, who

" 1. comes often to Church.
" 2. brings his offerings to be laid on the Altar.
" 3. does not taste of his produce, until he has offered some
    " to God.
" 4. as often as the holy solemnities return, keeps himself
    " pure some days before, that he may come to the
    " Altar with a safe conscience.
" 5. commits to memory the Creed and Lord's Prayer."

Here is another address, made by a Priest of that period:
" Redeem your soul from punishment, while you have it in " your power, by

" 1. presenting oblations and tithes to the Church.
" 2. bringing candles to the holy places according to your
    " means.
" 3. coming often to Church, and begging suppliantly for
    " the intercession of the Saints.
" If ye do these things, you may present yourselves with
    " confidence in the day of Judgment before the tribunal
    " of the Eternal God, and say, 'Give, Lord, for we
    " have given.'" (Mosheim, II, p. 92.)

Now when such was the absolute ignorance of the A, B, C, of Religion on the part of the Pastor, what could be expected from the sheep ? It is notorious that the majority of converts are from the most degraded and lowest classes: have they and their still more ignorant, and degraded, wives, any clear perception of the new religious conception, which they have nominally accepted ?

I quote the following from the Church Missionary-Society's Report, 1893. I knew the people of the Region referred to well:
" The need of giving careful teaching to the Christian converts
" is shown by a discovery, which was made almost by accident
" at Talwandi Rama, where the Christians bear an exceptionally
" good character. Dr. Weitbrecht says: 'Several of the men
" were being prepared for confirmation, when I paid them a
" visit with Padri Fath Masih, and the latter one evening held,
" as he often does, a *gyangudari*, literally patchwork quilt of
" religious knowledge. This is an informal meeting under a
" leader, in which the people sit round, smoking if they please,
" to discuss topics of religion, and the like. The leader allows
" each one in turn to express his opinion, and then sums up, or
" not, as he pleases, or lets the question circulate once more.
" At this special meeting it came out, quite incidentally, that
" all these people, with the exception of one, who was already a
" communicant, held the pantheistic doctrine of the Vedanta,
" *i.e.* that all religions are one in the knowledge of truth as it
" is, and that the differences between them are only for the
" world of phenomena. Can we fancy a group of English field-
" labourers discussing such a subject ? These people had been
" carefully taught, and had honestly accepted Christianity as
" the best of religions in the world of *maya* (illusion); but of
" course we were unable to bring them forward for confirmation
" then.' "

The work, the duty, of the Missionary is not over with the Baptism of converts, the number of which he complacently chronicles in his Annual Report. Great troubles may be anticipated in the neo-Christian Churches. In the first century A.D. the Gentile Churches would not coalesce with the Jewish Churches. Nothing but the destruction of Jerusalem put an end to the schism. No member of the Church at Jerusalem could share the Lord's Supper with a Gentile, and retain his ceremonial purity. We may expect the same phenomena in the neo-Christian Churches in India, and the denominational system of Missions will accentuate the tendency. Men of Caste will not associate, as far as Matrimony and commensality go, with men of low Caste. Ask the Secretary of a Missionary Association to give his daughter in marriage to, or share the evening meal of, a pious Christian ticket-porter, or dustman, and he would decline: why place a burden on the Indian convert, which an Englishman would not touch with his finger ? Every Indian

Reformer from the time of Buddha, and Kabír, down to the present Epoch, have tried to do away with Caste, and have failed.

The other evils speak for themselves: there may be signs of them all, but emphatically they are not signs of the Kingdom.

I quote the following from the *Indian Churchman*: "Bishops "Smythies and Hornby are asking for Indian Christians to "be sent over to Zanzibár to work among the Indians there "as Mission-agents. There seems little chance of the Bombay "diocese being able to help them, as there is a dearth of "really able men here, and with the exception of the Church- "Missionary-Society there is no provision for training such "men. Christianity in some parts of this diocese is, I fear, "a very nominal thing, and until this is recognised we cannot "hope, that the necessary means will be taken to remedy this "state of things. As a rule our Missionaries, instead of being "concentrated in centres, where personal influence would be "brought to bear on those amongst whom they dwell, are "scattered units, wearing out their lives in travelling as quickly "as possible from village to village, and paying a visit which "can never be sufficiently long enough to really influence the "people. A seven days' or ten days' Mission in some of the "larger villages might do good, if there were hope of steady "work being carried on afterwards, but this is in most cases "impossible, owing to the Mission-agent having to itinerate "through some fifteen or eighteen villages in a month. The "only resident person is a schoolmaster, who, having had "no training as a teacher of any sort, is useless for the work we "refer to. I do not wish to imply, that the present generation "of Missionaries is responsible for this state of things. Many "of them regret it as much as I do, and would change the "system of work entirely; but it is not always the case, that "those who see the defects of a system have the power to "remedy them."

The difficulty of language is very great: in China Missionaries talk complacently of the Chinese language, as if that vast population spoke one language instead of several scores. In India people do not talk of the Indian language, because it is notorious, that there are at least one hundred: but, strange to say, the necessity of having one Church is alluded to, when it is obvious that, if people do not understand the same language, common worship is impossible. One congregation must wait outside the Church-door until the service of the other is completed.

2. PAGAN NOTIONS OF NOMINAL CONVERTS.

We have only to look under the surface, and mark the amount of Paganism, which still clings to Religion in Christian countries.

When Europe was converted, it was not done in a spirit of love to the people, but in a spirit of hatred to the Pagan Priesthood, hatred to the Pagan idols, which were supposed to be Devils. They did not try to convert by reason, or by advice, but by slaughter of Priests, and destruction of Temples. They knew nothing of, and cared nothing for, the history of the human race, as we know it, of the deep religious feelings, that seem to be part of the furniture of uncivilized or civilized man. They had not read Paul's address at Athens and Lystra: how the poor heathen felt for God, if haply they could find Him, and when the heathen consented to be baptized, as at Canterbury, they brought Paganism with them, not in outward form, but in inward reality, for there had been no Conversion of the Soul, no creating, as it were, a new man.

It will be no matter of surprise, if under the influence of political causes, or on a wave of religious novelty, a whole Nation of nominal Christians turn away from the Christianity, which was only skin-deep, and adopt some sensational form of their old Religion, or some new religious conception. We may fairly expect this in U-Ganda: the story of their conversion by hundreds and thousands, some to Protestantism, some to Romanism, is not pleasant reading. There must be a great deal of Paganism just covered over with a liturgical vaneer, and a surface-education, and a smattering of Bible-knowledge, accompanied by an absolute certainty, that there are two forms of Christianity so deeply opposed to each other, that whichever gets the upper hand will shoot the opposite party down with Maxim-guns.

3. Imposing New Conditions Precedent to Baptism.

I read how in one Mission-Station Baptisms are performed in secret, and the neo-Christian has not the grace, or strength, to confess his Saviour before the world; that is his affair, but the duty of the Missionary is not to perform the rite in secret: if the catechumen be not prepared for the consequences, the rite cannot be performed. There must be no mystery, or secret, in such matters. I am glad to find from the following extract from the Church-Missionary-Society Report of 1891–2, that the Missionary in Persia is now of the same opinion:

"One, who escaped imprisonment by a timely warning from
" some one, who knew what was impending, left off coming to
" me for instruction, but still visited us occasionally, and ex-
" pressed his conviction of the truth of Christianity. A few
" weeks ago, before returning to Persia, he consulted with me
" whether, as religion was a mere personal affair, he might not
" be baptized privately, without any strangers knowing about it,

" so that afterwards he could remain in his social position as
" before. But bearing in mind that 'baptism doth represent
" unto us our profession,' I did not feel justified to administer
" it upon such an understanding, and counselled him to seek
" more grace by prayer and the reading of God's Word, till
" either religious liberty could be enjoyed in his country, or he
" was prepared to profess Christ at any risk. In the same way
" I had to decline the application for baptism of an aged
" Persian trader, who, for more than a year, had been coming
" to our Mission-house for religious discussion, because I could
" not discern in him evidences of that spiritual awakening,
" which seeks Jesus the Saviour of sinners, but rather feared
" that he might be chiefly actuated by secular motives."

And another case from the same Report:

" He is convinced of the truth of Christianity, and has ex-
" pressed his desire to be baptized. I believe him to be sincere,
" but as yet he is not strong in Faith. He asks for private
" baptism. I tell him, he must wait until he has courage to
" receive it publicly."

And again:

" A wealthy Brahmin told him, that he trusted Christ as his
" Saviour, and that he read the Bible, and prayed to Jesus every
" day, but could not see the necessity of being baptized, and
" confessing Christ before men."

Another form of difficulty is the hasty baptism of a passing traveller, who does not intend to form part of the congregation of the Missionary, who admits him to the fold. I state the case:

" In the month of February a Mahometan of Turkish origin
" was brought to me, who expressed a strong desire for baptism.
" The peculiarity of the case was, that the man wished to be
" baptized at once, as he was returning immediately to Ceylon,
" where he carried on a small business, as a confectioner and
" shopkeeper. He had come to Bombay partly on business, to
" purchase various kinds of stores for his shop, and partly
" to obtain Christian books, and get further instruction in the
" Christian religion. He was willing to have remained for a
" time so as to be more fully instructed, but he had a partner,
" who declined to remain longer, and therefore he asked for
" immediate baptism. If we had had no other knowledge of
" the man, I should probably have declined such a hasty
" baptism, for, as a rule, I have found such baptisms to be
" eventually unwise; but fortunately there was a Persian
" Christian here, a very trustworthy man, who knew him well,
" and spoke highly of him. I therefore baptized him on
" February 24, and he at once returned to Ceylon. The reason
" he gave for not wishing to wait till after his return to Ceylon
" was, that there was no Missionary there (in Kandy) who knew

" either Urdu, Arabic, or Turkish, and he did not know English
" or any vernacular of the place. I have heard from him since
" his arrival there."

I knew a Missionary in India, who started a separate Mission of his own, and his practice was to go into a village, preach the Gospel, and, if on the hearing of his words anyone came forward, and expressed belief, he would then and there baptize him: he justified his conduct by citing the practice described in the Acts of the Apostles. I think, that I have seen signs of this tendency elsewhere.

Another form of difficulty arises. A Missionary, who has adopted a peculiar fad, declines to baptize anyone, who will not accept his fad as a condition precedent: this is indeed a limitation of the Lord's free gift. Sometimes a vow of total abstinence from liquor or opium is required. Tertullian tells us, that the Marcionist admitted no married man to Baptism: he must divorce his wife: he was not permitted to enter his new Christian life before he had directly contravened his Lord's express command. Such is the folly of mankind, especially of those who are exceedingly religious. In China I read of an inveterate opium-smoker, after hearing the Word, resolving to give up his pipe, and be baptized, and try to influence others to do the same. So far so well, and his conduct is highly commendable; but if, owing to the infirmity of the flesh, he had been unable to give up his pipe, and yet had a firm belief in his Saviour, was he to be excluded from the Church? Is everyone, who drinks Whiskey and Port Wine, to be excluded from the Lord's Table?

A great deal is said about Caste in India: is everyone before baptism to be compelled to break his family-Caste, as regards Marriage and Commensality. How did the Early Christians behave to those, who failed in morals, or differed in some detail of dogma? They cut them off from the Church, and denied them all social intercourse: "with such a one do not eat." Was not this Caste in private life?

I read in the Report of the Church-Missionary-Society for 1893 the following additional condition precedent to Baptism, which Missionaries with other fads impose upon converts:
" She is most anxious to receive baptism, and will, I hope,
" before long, in her own city, as I shall, if possible, go up
" there. One matter, which was of some difficulty to her, she
" overcame in the best of all ways, by simply obeying what she
" believed to be God's will. The question was as to unbinding
" her own and her two children's feet. She at first told me,
" that she was sure it would only hinder the spread of the
"·Gospel, were she to do so, as other women would fear to come
" to the church in case that should be required of them. I

"must tell you that her husband, too, had given his eldest girl strict injunctions not to unbind her feet, when he brought her to school a year ago. However, his evident fear, that he would lose on the price received when his daughters are betrothed has evidently been overruled by their mother's conviction, that the thing should be done, for shortly before returning to her home she said to me, ' I don't mind what the people will say or think; I am sure it is pleasing to God, that I should do this,' and the new shoes and stockings were purchased before she returned home, as the girl is still with us."

Have we not heard of European women wearing tight-laced stays much to their injury, painting their faces, dyeing their hair after the manner of Jezebel? but are these poor fools, if they have by God's grace a saving Faith, to be excluded from Baptism, unless they buy new stays, and leave off the painting?

I quote another instance from the Church-Missionary-Society-Report, 1893: "When Mansabdar began to show an eager desire for baptism, the great difficulty about polygamy (for he had three wives) blocked the way. He was privately told, that he would have to put away two of them, and only could keep one. To this he after some time agreed, and in church at Narowal, before the congregation, Mr. Bateman interpolated among the usual pre-Baptismal questions the following: 'Art thou prepared to call two of the wives thou now hast thy *mother*'? [To call one's wife 'mother' is among Mahometans tantamount to divorcing her.] To this he replied, 'I hereby call them mother.' After his baptism he returned to Dhrag. There was a terrible commotion in his household. He declared, that he had taken refuge in Jesus from the wrath, which his sins deserved, and told the third wife, that as he was a Christian, she too was free by Mahometan Law to leave him if she pleased. He was not less plain-spoken to the villagers, and now he lives a bold soldier and servant of Christ, and urges his neighbours to accept the Saviour. One day, as we were walking along a street in his village, he said: ' 'I know that these people will all become followers of Christ, but oh! that I might see it before I die.'"

Mr. Bateman's words on the subject of indiscriminate baptism are too important to be passed over. He, or rather the joint report, says: "When we received these people, together with a certificate of their baptism, there were not five in a hundred of them, who knew anything distinctively Christian, though several hundreds of them were registered as communicants. Many would tell you, that they had become Christians *mukti de waste* (to obtain Salvation), but if you asked them what *mukti* meant, they could give you no answer at all.

" There was many a village with a Christian community in it,
" wherein nobody, man, woman, or child, had ever bowed the
" knee in Christian prayer, or knew that there was such a book
" as the Bible. And when we began to work amongst them,
" they would resent the invitation to worship or to learn, as a
" novel burden, for which they had not bargained. At first we
" tried to teach and to work through the men, who had been
" paid agents of the American Mission, and who were pre-
" sumably the best of their class. We have been obliged to
" discharge every one of these, not generally for mere incom-
" petence, but for worse. They were most of them men, who
" had brought their brethren forward for baptism in order that
" they themselves might gain employment and prestige, which
" would be profitable and useful to themselves at any rate.
" My own conviction is, that the result of the baptism of
" masses of uninstructed people is downright bad; bad for the
" baptized, bad for the heathen, and bad for the Mahometans;
" and that we could have employed our time and strength to
" much better purpose on behalf of all, had these baptisms not
" been administered."

4. Relapse of Converts into their Old, or adoption of a New, Religion.

At one time it was not thought good form in a Report to allude to the lapses back into old beliefs, or the adoption of new ones. In those days perhaps there were not many converts, but now each Annual Report of each Mission tells us of this great feature in the progress of Evangelization. When a man has changed his Faith once, there is always a risk, that he will do it again, and something more: he will become a bitter enemy of his late friends. In the future decennial Census of British India this feature will be recorded, for this is an era of spiritual disturbance. The ice of cold centuries has been broken.

I give some instances : " The Missionaries at Tunis and
" Algeria have lately been much tried by the apostasy or
" deliberate hypocrisy of professed converts. This is, perhaps,
" the heaviest trial in the life of a Missionary. He lives
" if the converts stand fast in the Lord. They are his
" glory and joy, the one reward for the labour, to win which
" he is content to endure all things, and for which he counts
" no labour and no suffering too great. But when they fail,
" when they prove false, reprobate, how bitter is the sorrow,
" how keen the disappointment! To have marked what seems
" to be the dawn of spiritual life in a soul, and then to have
" watched for months, or even years, its seemingly gradual
" development; to have rejoiced with a joy too deep for words

" over a soul, that seemed really to have been won for Christ;
" and then to find, that the whole profession from first to last
" had been merely a clever counterfeit, is indeed a bitter sorrow,
" such as none but they who have at least in a measure tasted
" it can fully understand. Yet one thing is perfectly plain, that
" this has been the lot of the faithful ministers of Christ from
" the very beginning."

In the Church-Missionary-Society-Report of 1893 I read:
" Another cause of anxiety is the apparent number of defections.
" Many Christians disappear unaccounted for. The total number
" of baptisms during the last five years was 26,574, which, added
" to the number of Christians at the close of 1887, would give a
" total of 45,863. If from this number an estimated loss of
" 5 per cent. through deaths be deducted for each year, the de-
" fections must have been 3,000, or say 600 a year, at least."

And again in the Church-Missionary-Society-Report of 1892:
" The spirit of the congregation, which has been referred to in
" former Reports, shows no improvement, and the lack of unity,
" which resulted, renders it less a matter of surprise that no
" baptisms occurred, but that, on the contrary, several left the
" communion, and some of the catechumens, relapsed to
" heathenism for a time, discontinued all intercourse with the
" Missionary, and do not seem to have returned to membership
" in the Protestant congregation. The reason of the other
" three leaving is not known."

In the mercurial population of the Empire of Japan the most extreme oscillation may be expected. My own feeling is, that the danger is greater from the attacks of the newly-formed sensational and quasi-spiritual forms of belief, represented by many names, than from the old-fashioned Book-Religions, which have settled down to meaningless ritual. In the *Indian Churchman* is noticed a book on the Problem of Christianity and Scepticism, or Lessons from twenty years experience in the field of Christian Evidence, from which I quote the following:

" We ought to be very careful not to encourage seekers to
" profess more than they believe; and equally careful not to
" reject those, who believe, at any given point in their career,
" less than we wish. I am afraid we are to blame here. The
" principle, that you must grasp Christianity in its entirety, or
" not touch it at all, is, I think, unjustifiable. Our Lord plainly
" recognised the fact, that there were certain things in His teach-
" ing which even His Apostles *could* not receive at the then
" stage of their culture. It is my profound conviction, that our
" forgetfulness of this has greatly contributed to the increase of
" unbelief, and that our remembrance of it, if embodied in our
" conduct, would do more than anything else to bring sceptics
" back to Christ."

My own attention has been drawn to the subject, and my views are given in my book entitled "Clouds on the Horizon," 1891, or "Essay on the various forms of Error, which stand in the way of the acceptance of Christian Truth."

Dr. Weitbrecht of the Panjab, in the Church-Missionary-Society-Report, states as follows:

" The Brahmin lad, Kunj Lal, an account of whose baptism
" was given in last year's Annual Report, has, to Dr. Weitbrecht's
" great surprise and sorrow, joined the Arya Samáj. On the
" other hand, a former catechist at Fathgarh, Narayan Prashad,
" who apostatized in 1887 to Mahometanism, although previous
" to his baptism he had been a Hindu, together with his family
" of seven persons, has publicly abjured Mahometanism, and
" they have been re-admitted to the Church as penitents. The
" apostacy of this man arose upon a question regarding his
" son's marriage, and such questions are of continual recurrence.

" At Osomare, which Mr. Bennett visited, he found that nearly
" all the professing Christians had relapsed into Polygamy, and
" some into Idolatry, and one into Mahometanism. He con-
" sidered the place to be diminishing in importance, and to
" present no openings for aggressive work towards the interior.
" One of our converts was talked over by his friends, and
" consented to do as they wished, and, in spite of all our efforts,
" expressed his determination to return to heathenism. One of
" the arguments used by his friends was, that his sickness was
" owing to the anger of the gods, and that on renouncing
" Christianity he would at once recover. The next day he had
" a relapse, and two days afterwards he died."

The Bishop of Blomfontein in his Charge, 1893, writes: " He
" would have (1) a class of Hearers, (2) a Catechuminate for
" three years: that the responsibility of remitting sins by Baptism
" is at least as great as that of retaining them by withholding
" Baptism, for nothing had done more to weaken the Army of
" Christ than the failure or desertion of those, who had been
" hurriedly converted." He alludes to the painfully large number of (so-called) Christians, who had fallen away, or been cast out, but he orders a list of them to be kept, and prayers to be offered for them.

Excommunication should not be too rigidly enforced. " Un-
" due severity, even in case of moral offences, is to be deprecated,
" bearing in mind the low standard of the environment of
" the neo-Christians, and the examples supplied in the Old
" Testament of nearly universal moral lapses, and laxness of
" conduct. What will become of the man put out of the
" Church for either cause? It entails the loss of the soul of an
" individual or a family, and of children yet unborn."

5. Low Culture, and Extreme Intellectual Density, of Converts.

No idea can be formed of the gross ignorance of all, but the Priesthood, of the simplest elements of Divine Truth, and of the Bible, at the time of the Conversion of Europe. The introduction so conspicuously of the names of deified mortals, local martyrs, and saints, so darkened the vision of the laity, that the figure and name of Christ seem removed to a distant obscurity. A great, principal, and all-powerful, Deity was accepted as a fact, and a certainty of a day of Judgment and Hell-fire, but the Holy Spirit was ignored, or his place occupied by the Mother of our Lord, and heart-prayer, and real penitence, were crushed out by an unintelligible ritual in an unknown tongue. It may be doubted, whether the people of India are more ignorant, and less receptive of Divine Truth, than were the Teutons and Slavs of that period, but it is beyond the power of imagination to suppose, that a Protestant Missionary would pretend to teach such flocks in a dead European language, and read to them the Scripture in that tongue. This is, of course, what a Missionary of Rome does to this very day, and the results are known.

There can be no question, that many undergo the process of so-called Conversion without understanding all, and some cannot be made to understand anything, and to remain unconverted. In the Acts of the Apostles we read of many Conversions, which seem to have been hasty, and wonder how such Methods would work. I quote from the report of a Missionary given in the Church-Missionary-Society-Report, 1893: " The heathen in Lucknow and in the district around have for " ages been in such thick darkness and superstition, that they " have fallen into a very deep sleep, and nothing but the power " of the Holy Ghost can awaken these dead souls and say to " them, 'Awake, thou that sleepest, and arise from the dead, " and Christ shall give thee light.' It does not lessen our " responsibility, it rather urges us to come to their rescue. " They are like men in a burning house, heedless of their " danger. These poor people seem to have no concern about a " future life, so taken up are they with their pice and cowries. " May the Holy Ghost be so given to each one of us, that we " may be instant in season and out of season to turn their " attention to the unsearchable riches of Christ!"

Here is the opinion of a Missionary, quoted in the same Report: " From impressions, that had been made on me at " the five Annual Meetings of the Society at Exeter, I had the

" privilege of attending, and elsewhere, I had the opinion, that
" the heathen were eagerly crying out for the Gospel of Jesus
" Christ. I had heard of crowds of people in Japan and China
" coming, so I thought the virgin soil of heathen-lands would
" be much easier to work with than the much-trodden and
" beaten track of South London.

" The close of my first year in India brings me to a different
" conclusion. This is the verdict: that wherever we go the
" human heart is the same. The carnal mind is at enmity
" against God. Men do not naturally like the terms of the
" Gospel of Jesus Christ. It is not until they are really aroused
" to think about their souls, and whither they are going, that
" they see and acknowledge the nature of the offer made to
" them." In fact their hearts are encased in a thick rind of the
cares of this world, and it seems impossible to pierce through it.

Some more sanguine Missionary writes as follows from a
five-year-old Mission in the Kongo-basin: "When I came away,
" there was a church of united devoted followers of Christ.
" Many at home may think, that Christians so recently gathered
" from among the heathen must be of a very low type.
" Ignorant they are and must be on many points; neither
" would they be well up in Bible-history, nor have very clear
" ideas on many matters of doctrine. But they have an under-
" standing of the main essential points, and the miracle of the
" new birth has been wrought in them, and Christ is a living
" personal Saviour to them."

The Bishop of Calcutta at a Meeting of the Oxford-Mission
thus expressed himself: " It is, I think, universally true, that the
" uneducated embrace what they are attracted towards; and
" they get to understand it afterwards. But when you have
" an intellectual and educated class of people to deal with,
" the operation must be reversed. They must to a very great
" extent be dealt with intellectually, and get to understand
" what you put before them, before they can accept it. I have
" reason to feel, that this is the point, which must be very con-
" stantly kept in mind, as regards our work in India. You are
" aware, that some of our Missions are amongst the Kôl and
" the Santál. There you have people, who are attracted by
" the character of the Mission, by the way that the Missionary
" deals with them, and by all that illustrates Christianity to
" them, and they accept it and welcome it; and afterwards
" Education follows, and they are taught to understand and
" know about it. To a great extent this is equally true as
" regards our Missions in Tinnevelly. But it is perfectly true,
" that such a presentation of Christianity is quite incapable of
" having any very strong influence on the highly educated
" classes of Hindus or Mahometans. The fact is, that for the

"intellectual and educated men, you must adopt the other
"principle. There has to be a great deal of intercourse with
"them; there must be much argument; there must be a long
"process, which the mind must go through, before they are
"prepared to accept the truth. And this explains the condition
"of things in India in this respect. Our converts, wherever
"they are in any number, are converts from the less intelligent
"races. And as regards the higher classes and the more
"educated races, the work is much more slow, very much
"more difficult, and the results cannot be shown so imme-
"diately."

Hear the words of a Missionary in Eastern Equatorial Africa:
"Our Sunday-services have been lately very well attended. I
"occasionally get our teacher. (Mugimbwa) to follow me in
"preaching, in order to make the truth plainer to them, for it is
"a humbling fact, that these people will sit under you for some
"time, apparently taking it all in, and yet not understanding
"a word said. I know many, who have not the slightest
"knowledge of Swahíli, and yet who listen to the language,
"and assent as though they were coast-men."

Bishop Patterson of Melanesia remarked, "that the second
"stage of a Mission was more difficult than the first. We have,
"as it were, drawn these poor heathen into the Christian net,
"and we have now to make them worthy of their great name."
The greatest self-control, gentleness, self-abnegation, is required
by a Missionary during the critical years of religious training,
when the soul is expanding to the divine light, and the baser
elements in man are contending against the new power of the
Holy Spirit, working on the awakened conscience.

It is a fallacy, demonstrated by hard facts, that the human
race can be so degraded as not to be able to understand,
appreciate, and by divine grace accept the promises of the
Gospel, and undergo its transforming power. The personal
witness, the object-lesson, found, exhibited, and wondered
at, in the self-denying, consecrated, life of the Messenger of
Salvation, is as necessary as the witness of the inspired Message:
one is the Gospel in the letter, the other is the Gospel in the
flesh: one is abstract Science, the other applied Science: it is
the Ἡ ἁγία Σοφια made manifest in the Ὁ ἅγιος ἀνηρ. Words
may fail, but the gracious example of the "Man of God"
cannot fail.

6. QUESTIONS CONNECTED WITH MATRIMONY OF CONVERTS.

In all discussions about the marriage of Natives of any
country it must be recollected, that at the time of the introduction
of a new Religion the mode, in which the mysterious union of

the two sexes is dealt with, is the highest test of the moral evolution: the laxer the marriage-tie, the lower the form of Religion developed.

I will quote an abstract from the Report of the Church-Missionary-Society, 1891, regarding a congregation in the Delta of the River Niger, W. Africa: " The moral and spiritual tone " in the church is far from satisfactory. The class and minute-" books in the station declare and show this lamentable fact. " Many of the young men have become Polygamists. Many " have put out their first wives, and taken others in their stead ; " and this changing of wives is due not to the wives' " unfaithfulness, but to the inconstancy of affection on the part " of the husbands. The men foolishly allege as a reason, that " they never married their wives in the Church. The sin of " impurity is, I am sorry to say, common."

And the following in the Panjáb, N. India, from Dr. Weitbrecht's Annual Letter: "I believe we may say, that the " congregations are gradually making progress in Christian " knowledge. That the process is gradual cannot surprise us, " when we consider the religious and moral state of the low " Castes (and not the low Castes only) in this country. In one " of our Christian villages there was a man, professing to be an " inquirer, who migrated for a time to another village in search " of work, and there made friends with a sweeper of the place. " One of this man's female relatives lost her husband, and the " immigrant being single, his friend pressed him to marry the " widow; but the stranger steadily refused, much to the " annoyance of his host. At last the host said, 'You are very " obstinate; but as you won't be persuaded, what do you say to " taking my wife ? I am ready to make her and her family over " to you, only I want to keep one of my girls, and then I'll " marry the widow.' The exchange was duly made, and in " course of time our villager returned to his home provided with " a wife and young family. On being asked how he had come " by them, he told his story, and was severely blamed by the " community for being married without the help of a padri."

Dr. Weitbrecht in the same Report states another case, showing the extreme difficulty of the problem before us: " In this same village a quiet, respectable man had been living " with his married brother. The brother died, and, according " to custom, the man 'spread his skirt' over the widow, or 'cast " his blanket over her,' in a case of this kind no regular marriage " ceremony being necessary. I found out casually, that they " were living together as man and wife, and represented, that " this was contrary to Christian law, adding that, if the man " would leave his sister-in-law, the Church would be responsible " for her maintenance, till she could be married again. This,

" however, he refused to do, and for the present he stands
" excluded. The congregation has upheld the decision of the
" pastor, after some discussion; but the difficulty in such a
" case is, that the former moral code of the community actually
" demanded this kind of marriage as an act of duty, analogous
" to the Levirate marriage of the Mosaic law, though not
" identical with it, because here the question of raising up seed
" unto his brother does not come into consideration."

The table of affinity is another difficulty: it is of no use declaring, that the marriage of a Native to his wife's sister is illegal, when it is notorious, that in British India it is legal to European British subjects. The problem of Divorce, and Legal Separation, will be exceedingly difficult. An attempt has been made to substitute in Christian marriage a necklace for the ring, but it should be resisted, and the Society for Promoting Christian Knowledge has lately refused to sanction translations of the Book of Common Prayer, where that substitution has been made.

But the real difficulty attends the conversion, when the neo-Christian has to give up his wife for his Faith. Till within a few years ago it was the practice of Jewish converts in London on being baptized to divorce their Jewish wives, and take a new Christian wife: it came to my knowledge in the Committee of London-Jews-Society, and the practice was forbidden. As regards British India, I subjoin the remarks of the Bishop of Lahore in 1892:

" Dealing with the question of the remarriage of converts,
" the Bishop said that they knew, that Conversion often meant
" for the newly baptized the loss of home, and of a wife's
" society. The most distressing cases were those of converts
" from Mahometanism. According to the law recognised in
" India, the baptism of either Mahometan consort *ipso facto*
" dissolved the previously existing marriage. If the parties
" continued to live together as husband and wife without any
" break whatever, their status before the law was at least
" doubtful. Should the question be raised as to the legitimacy
" of children born after the husband or wife had been baptized,
" it was at present an open question what the Courts would rule.
" The marriage had been dissolved, and no new marriage con-
" tracted. Yet the *bonâ fides* of the parties was unquestionable,
" and, as in the supposed case, only one of them had become
" Christian, no marriage with the benediction, which the Church
" pronounced upon Christian marriage, was possible. Moreover,
" they had the ruling of the chief Court in the Punjáb, that the
" children of a Mahometan convert were dealt with under
" Mahometan law, and that consequently the father was
" deprived of the custody of children of both sexes of tender

" age, and of that of his daughters until they were marriageable.
" So that the convert from Islam, through the simple profession
" of Christianity under a Christian Government, forfeited all his
" rights as husband, and as father too. Was there not there some
" claim to relief by legislation? In the case of the Hindu
" provision had been made in the Native Converts-Divorce-Act
" for the recognition of the continuance of the marriage-tie,
" until certain prescribed steps had been taken to dissolve it.
" Ought not the Mahometan to be protected in the same way?"

It will be remarked that the Mahometan, who abandons Islam, at once loses his wife: the contract is dissolved. In the case of the Hindu the marriage-tie is indissoluble. In the first Mission-Congress at Lahore, 1862, I protested against any facility being given to the convert to marry again, and when the Native Converts-Divorce-Act was brought before the Legislative Council of India in 1864, I again, as a member of that Council, opposed it, but it was carried, and is now the law. The convert has to cite the wife to come and live with him: if she does not do so within a certain time, he may marry again. This seems a bad beginning of a new life: *pari passu* a man might get rid of a lunatic wife, or a bedridden wife, or any other wife, who from incompatability of temper refused to live with her husband.

All these are difficulties, through which the nascent Churches all over the heathen-world will have to steer: it is idle to suppose, that they will adopt the practices of Great Britain.

7. Credulousness of any new Story.

It is clear, that in the first Century of the Christian era a strong conviction was entertained, that the end of the world was at hand. It has been the trade of heated enthusiasts in all countries to promulgate such rumours. Quite lately in South India a large number of Christian converts fell into the delusion, that the world was coming to an end on a certain day. When all reasoning failed, the prudent Missionary adopted the policy of waiting, and when the day passed by, and all things went on as before, the humbled enthusiasts returned to their Pastor, and admitted their error.

Within the last few years, in the tribe of the Sioux Redskins, west of the River Mississippi, a man stood forth, claiming to be the Messiah, and credited with the power of speaking to each tribe in their own language. There is short shrift to a Prophet in this generation: the newspaper-reporters are too many for him: he proved to be a harmless fanatic, named Hopkins or Johnson, but the danger always is, lest designing men should make use of such fanatics for their own seditious purposes.

Since in Europe such notions still survive, that the Jews kidnap, and kill, a Christian child at their Passover, what can be expected among the grossly ignorant races of Asia and Africa, ready to believe anything?

The reason is obvious: when a man lives in the midst of all the comfortable environments of civilized life, with ready access to the Doctor and the Policeman; when the events of life are prosaic, and the great event of Death always subject to a Coroner's Inquest, if the Medical authority cannot certify ordinary causes; when the Newspapers come in daily: under such circumstances the mind becomes more reflective, and ceases to impute every trouble or peril, every blessing or joy, to some Divinity: it is not, that the pious man does not recognise the presence of God everywhere, but his environment deadens the feelings of Divine interference.

But at the present epoch in Asia and Africa, where a man dwells in a solitude, or a forest, or a secluded valley, cut off from contact with his fellows, liable to the intrusion of robbers or wild beasts, liable to death without help, with companions as helpless as himself; where the elements are great hostile realities to him, the thunder, and the tempest; it is no wonder, that such a man is liable to greater fear: he fears the unknown Divinity, is full of credulity, and ready to believe any fancy. The stories are magnified in repetition: secrets of Nature, still only partially revealed, supply a boundless variety of actual lies: and the wildest rumours agitate the minds of thousands.

Only last August, 1893, a middle-aged Negro at Kingston in Jamaica, belonging to the labouring class, declared, that he was a Prophet of God, and offered prayers every Wednesday on the banks of the Hope, the waters of which were endowed with the power of healing disease. The attendance on such evenings amounted to thousands: the Prophet did not ask for money, and cures were certified: the Bishop of the Church of Rome stoutly exposed the fallacy of his claim to be a Prophet, and the truth of his cures, as the man was a Wesleyan: had he been of the Church of Rome, his reception might have been different, as the circumstances very much resemble what happened at Lourdes in S. France.

8. INJURIOUS INFLUENCE OF WESTERN EDUCATION ON CERTAIN CLASSES: IS EDUCATION A NECESSARY FEATURE OF EVANGELIZATION, OR CIVILIZATION?

There is great objection to any form of Education, however elementary, or training of boys and girls, which alters "per se" their social status, *i.e.*, the state of life, in which God has placed them. It is false kindness to turn out of the Mission-Schools, pupils, who have been elevated above the social rank of their own people, and lost their means of existence: this applies to the labourer's child in Europe, and with double force in Asia and Africa. What is to become of the nicely educated girls in certain orphanages, who have become young gentlewomen with a future surrounded with perils and disappointments? Soberer views would restrict the degree of culture to what is absolutely required: there must be poor and humble Christians in all flocks.

I quote from the Report of the Church-Missionary-Society, 1893, with regard to the spiritual state of the Christians in N. India:

" That they are a rising community there can be no doubt, and
" this makes them eager to push themselves and their children
" forward even at the expense of a Missionary-Society. Any
" post, which gives them importance, is immediately made use
" of to improve their position in life, and raise their family in
" the scale of society. All these things are signs of progress,
" but they may, or may not, be signs of life. The Native
" Christians are passing through a crisis, and gradually be-
" coming more like ourselves. Their habits are becoming
" more expensive, and their wants more imperative. All these
" things must tell upon the spiritual life of a Church in one
" way or another. There is a greater demand for good educated
" pastors as a consequence, but no more money is forthcoming
" in the midst of their own increasing wants to meet the
" demand. The pastors are many of them overworked; there
" are not many of them men of ability, and work becomes a
" routine to them. There are no clerical meetings, or con-
" ferences, to stir up their spiritual life, and the probability is,
" they have little to encourage them, and very much to depress
" them, in their spiritual life, surrounded as they are on all sides
" with heathenism. We want conferences for our pastors and
" Native Christians, and a brotherly hand to lead them on in
" the midst of discouragements."

This opens out for the sake of argument the question, whether the converts should be educated beyond the status of their heathen-neighbours. If Education be a necessary accompaniment of Christianity, how about the Millions of uneducated Christians in the last eighteen centuries? Francis of Assisi, the founder of the order of Franciscan friars, not only turned away his thoughts from wealth, and comfort, but from Education also: "for what is learning," said he, "but a kind of intellectual wealth?" Have we a single word in the Gospels, or Epistles, to show that any greater value was placed on Education than money? Is it right to spend the money subscribed for the Conversion of the heathen in the Education of the children of converts, as I remark is sometimes done? Surely Christian communities should pay for their own Pastors and Schoolmasters.

Admitting, as I entirely do, the gross ignorance of the great majority of the lower strata of the population in Asia or Africa, the question arises, "are they in a lower state than they were at any period since the Christian era"? From the Church-Missionary-Society-Report, 1893, we quote the opinion of an Archdeacon:

" One great difficulty with us here is *how* to teach our people,
" the vast majority of whom are not able to read a word, and
" probably never will be able. This inability arises from the
" almost insurmountable difficulties of their written language.
" It is useless to try to convey to English people at home any
" clear idea of this difficulty, and of the extent of the ignorance,
" which prevails among this people generally, when it takes
" twenty years or more of hard and continuous study before a
" Chinaman can master his own written language, and even
" then can only partially understand it. It is useless to expect
" poor villagers, many of whom embrace Christianity long after
" middle age, to make very much progress, even if they had
" leisure, in the knowledge of either reading or writing Chinese.
" *Vivâ voce* teaching, therefore, is the principal means here of
" conveying Christian instruction, and the Church must depend
" almost entirely upon the living voice in conveying Christian
" truth to those, who have placed themselves under her fostering
" care."

And will not *vivâ voce* teaching suffice to meet the requirements of our converts? is it absolutely necessary, that every middle-aged convert, every old woman, every all but beggar-child, should be brought up to the standard of reading the Bible? Is not this importing our nineteenth Century English notions into the houses of populations living under very different social circumstances? Let an Educational Society of all the unlettered races be started, and do this duty. The duty of Missionary-Societies is to preach the Gospel, and convert souls.

Hear what General Booth says: "But it is said: 'We must
" educate the people, in order that they may read their Bibles.'
" But alas! in teaching them to read their Bibles you have
" enabled them to read the works of unbelievers and doubters,
" which you meet in so-called Christian literature. I have an
" impression, that for every one, who through his boasted
" education is to-day reading his Bible, a hundred are lost to
" all regard of God and Religion.

" I believe thoroughly, and say deliberately, that so far as the
" Salvation of souls is concerned, the Christian Church in India
" has by her Colleges and Schools done more harm than good.

"Did the Apostles go about teaching the people to read and write, and that by the help of the literature of the Pagans themselves, as modern Christians do in their Schools? I am tolerably certain, that the majority of those ancient Saints were unable to read themselves, and moreover there were no books, that were accessible to the few who could.

"How, then, did they succeed so wonderfully in spreading the Salvation of God? We have certainly not a scrap of evidence to show, that it was by educating the people, or by civilizing them, while we have every reason to believe that it was by *converting* them. And what is our business as their successors? I contend that it is to follow in their track. The business of a true Missionary is to seek to lead as directly as he possibly can, these ignorant, sinful, and wretched, people to that Christ, who can reconcile them to the Father, and regenerate them by the power of the Holy Ghost. This once done, they will clothe, and house, and educate themselves."

I fear that there is much truth in the remarks of General Booth. He then remarks on Civilization: "What has Civilization done for the Heathen-races apart from the small handful, who have been converted? I should think that they had better never have known our Civilization. What has Civilization done for the native races of America? Improved them? Yes, off the face of the earth, or nearly so! What has it done for the Aborigines of Australia? And is it not on the highway to do the same thing for that magnificent race, the Zulu of South Africa? And if they don't look out, it will do the like for the whole of the native populations of the Dark Continent. What has European Civilization done for the people of India? My own impression is, that the Millions of India would be very glad to see our backs to-morrow, even if we took our boasted Civilization with us, and a great many other things into the bargain; and I am not sure, whether in such case they would be sufferers to the extent some of us are apt to imagine."

Europeans in this nineteenth Century place too high a value in the scale of Salvation of Souls on Education, Civilization, and even Cleanliness: they are excellent things in themselves, but they are only incidents in the Christian life, and often deadly antagonists to the onward course.

9. EVILS ARISING FROM RAISING THE MATERIAL STATUS OF CONVERTS.

With regard to the status of Native converts, whose political situation is in no way changed by their change of religion, let me

quote the words of a Chinese Missionary: "It is true that all
" British subjects resident in China are required to obtain an
" annual certificate of registry at a Consulate by payment of a
" fee to Her Majesty of five dollars each, or one dollar each for
" artizans and labourers. But no Native Christian whatever is
" eligible for such registry, nor would the British Government
" on any pretext whatever admit *the claim of a Native Christian*
" *to be regarded as otherwise than a subject of the Chinese Empire.*

" In cases of actual Persecution the British Minister has on
" certain occasions interposed, basing his remonstrances, not
" on the ex-territoriality of the victims of persecution, but on
" the Treaty-stipulations with regard to liberty of conscience.
" The same remark applies to the American Representative.

" With regard to the French and Russian Ministers, I cannot
" speak with certainty; but my impression is, that, although they
" are possibly more ready to intervene on behalf of converts
" than are the British and American Ambassadors, they make no
" pretence to exert anything but a benevolent influence in favour
" of Toleration, relying upon Treaty-stipulations."

In the Church-Missionary-Society-Report, 1891, I find the following ominous notice with regard to " Rice-Christians":
" Mr. Deimler of the Mahometan Mission writes, that he had
" several enquirers on his list, but it transpired, that they all
" expected to be supported, at least till they should find em-
" ployment. Mr. Deimler says there is a class of these men, who
" go from one Missionary to another, and allow themselves to be
" baptized by whoever offers the best prospect of support! The
" attendants at the Urdu service were few in number, those, who
" formerly attended, having left Bombay."

Another form of trouble arises, when the convert expects, that he is to be supported by the Missionary in his criminal, or civil, contests with his neighbours. A Missionary's wife once wrote to me to beg to have the wife of her Christian servant sent back to her, who had been carried away by a non-Christian: I inquired, and found that the woman in question was the wife of the person, who had carried her off. I gather, that there is a movement in some quarters in favour of providing for Native Christians: I implore those, who advocate those views, to hold back, if they care for *bonâ fide* Christianity in any land.

I give from the Church-Missionary-Society-Report, 1891, an extract: Mr. Perkins was holding a high civil appointment before he resigned the Service, and became a Missionary: he has thus seen both sides of the shield, and his opinion is valuable: " During Mr. Perkins' absence some of the Christians
" suffered much trouble and expense by being charged in the
" Native Magistrate's Court with certain offences. Mr. Perkins,
" rightly believing, that it is no part of a Missionary's duty to

7

"undertake the defence of Native Christians, even against un-
"founded charges, took advantage of this opportunity to assert
"and act upon his conviction, and declined to espouse the
"people's cause in litigation. To this cause largely he attributes
"the fact, that there were fewer baptisms and several apostasies;
"the number of baptized Christians is returned at 200, less by
"twenty than last year. Mr. Perkins says: We must face the
"fact that, as a Missionary-brother of wide experience in such
"work said to me, 'the movement amongst these low-Caste folk
"is a social one, to which we Missionaries are trying to give a
"spiritual direction. I do not think it is a religious one in the
"first instance, and we must look most narrowly, lest the poor
"people should practise on our inexperience, and deceive them-
"selves too, by seeking Christianity for mere loaves and fishes,
"under whatever specious guise.'"

The subject presents itself from another point of view in Labrádor, in the Dominion of Canada. The introduction of new habits, new kinds of food, and clothing, not suited to the climate, and habits, is dangerous. Nature has adapted the food to the particular animals: the Eskimó, unnecessarily fed on coffee, cannot work as they did on a diet of train-oil.

We shall prove the enemies, and not benefactors, of the poor non-Christian races, if we mix up with our spiritual teaching material advantages: "You have made me a Christian," said a poor convert to a Missionary; "give me food to support my own and my family's life: I did very well before I made your acquaintance; give me back my old life."

Among the many sombre, and anxious, features, which surround the future of the people of U-Ganda none is more charged with anxiety than the material welfare of this mercurial race. Even the Committee of the Church-Missionary-Society in the general blindness of their Arm of the Flesh-policy seem to realize this. I quote from the *Intelligencer* of May, 1894:

"But from a Missionary-point of view, the introduction of
"the political and commercial influence of England into
"U-Ganda is not of unmixed advantage. The converts will be
"subjected to temptation and trial more severe in a spiritual
"sense than the fire and sword of Persecution. They will need
"our prayers more than ever. It is an especial cause of
"thankfulness, that there should come just at this time the
"tidings of remarkable spiritual blessing upon the Christian
"leaders and people at Mengo. Three days of solemn meetings
"for consecration in December last were a time of very great
"blessing. The power of the Holy Ghost was realized by
"many as never before."

The transcendental style of the last lines show, how far removed the writer is from the hard unsympathizing wheel of human events of the nineteenth Century. These neo-Christians have been ready to shed the blood of their tribesmen; very little of the Gospel-practice has reached them.

10. OBJECTIONS TO CONSTRUCTING BARRACKS FOR CONVERTS, AND ERECTING EXPENSIVE CHURCHES.

The Christian village has its dangers: such was the commencement of Monachism: the thought was a good and pure one, isolating those, who wished to serve God, from the evil around them, and so to preserve their integrity: but the whole history of the Church shows, that it was a mistake, and has worked evil to the converts, evil to the Foreign Missions, and evil to the Heathen. The isolation was so much Christian power lost to the work of Evangelization; nor was the individual benefited by being sheltered from the rude struggle, and temptation, and Persecution: their example was lost to the Heathen, their leaven to the lump, and their own Faith became less strong, because not nerved to the test.

All who have seen the Christian barracks, springing up round the Mission, must admit this: let the converts live amidst the Heathen and Mahometans, among them, not of them; not changed in external habits, but changed internally. They should not be denationalized by false kindness: the living water of the Gospel is able to strengthen the fibre, and develop into beauty any form, of civilization with which it comes into contact: above all, let the danger be avoided of accustoming races of lower culture to the luxuries and wants of a highly civilized life.

Hear what the Indian Missionary Manual says on this subject: "There is a great fault in collecting Converts in little houses round the Mission, a kind of Native Cantonment: each person there finds his whole outward, and inner, life changed. He is removed from contact with his countrymen, and his idea of an honest life, and a decent home, altered; himself and his wife are placed, as it were, in a foreign garden, in little glass hot-houses. A feeble dependent spirit is produced: the Missionary is of course expected to find him employment, and he is never satisfied."

My memory recalls many such little hot-houses, and I always disapproved of them: even the large Christian village has its objections: it will certainly be attacked and destroyed in the first political trouble against the British Government. Our object is to Christianize India, not to make portions of the population British, or American, or French, as unhappily has been the case in U-Ganda.

Another most dangerous feature is the erection of expensive Churches in European style, or hospitals, or schools: who will be able to repair them, or rebuild them, when in course of time they undergo decay? What false kindness, what want of judgment, what ostentation, there is in this? Some Societies are firm in not contributing to such expenditure. In the early days of Christianity in Europe the Church was in the house of some Christian: gradually modest buildings in the Native style grew up. Imagine in a village of semi-barbarians a temple built in European style, with altar-cloths, etc., forgetting that the first thing to be impressed upon idolaters is, that God dwelleth not in temples made with hands: if buildings must be erected, let them be arranged to combine all requirements of worship, school, and hospital, all paid for by the people. It should be as good as, but not better than, the best house in the locality, and not attempt to rival the Hindu Temple, or Mahometan Mosque. I was pained to read in one Missionary Periodical an application for a supply of Crucifixes for the use of the members of an African Protestant Native Church; they are the very last things, which should be placed in the hands of the African. On the West of Africa there used to be flourishing Missions of the Church of Rome: being erected on the foundation of the Arm of the Flesh they perished, and the converts relapsed into Idolatry, but their crucifixes still remained as fetiches of the first quality.

I read a remark of a Missionary, which showed his extreme want of judgment: a Hindu temple caught fire, and was burned to the ground; he went to see the ruins, and chaffed the Priests on the subject of the impotence of the Deity, to whom the temple was consecrated, inasmuch as he could not save his own house from destruction. Was not the Temple on Mount Moriah twice burnt to the ground? are Christian Churches never burnt, or struck with lightning?

11. Dwelling too Strongly on the Sins of the non-Christian World.

Judging from the exaggerated statements in some Reports, the religious world at home often thinks, that the non-Christian world is living in the practice of shameless and abominable sins: this is not the case. I have lived among the people in the villages of India, and found rude and patriarchal virtues, and evidence of great nobility of character, and kindly disposition, dutiful conduct of parents to children, purity of home-circles, loving meetings of relatives, neighbourly friendships, and gentle manners. It is the act of a partizan, not of a faithful Chronicler, to be so severe on the Heathen and Mahometan, and overlook the sad failings of a European population, and the avowed vices of nominal Christians. God has not left Himself without a witness, in that He does good, and gives them rain from Heaven, and fruitful seasons, filling men's hearts with food and gladness. Missionaries should abstain from sweeping assertions, and excessive statements : it is enough, that they are not Christians, and must be made so by the Grace of God.

Hear what Dr. Benson, Archbishop of Canterbury, says : "It is not true, that they are ordinarily wicked, except by contrast. We know, that there may be wickedness in and among them, promoted even by their ministers. But we know, it has been so in Christianity too. We know, that in the Christian Church itself there have been veins and seams of wickedness which have gone far to make the society they pervaded unpalatable to earnest minds. I deprecate very much our setting to work, I do not believe we shall ever succeed if we set to work, believing that the religion of any nation, which God has allowed to grow up in it, and to be its teacher up to this point until Christianity is ready to approach it, I do not believe we should succeed, if we held, that the religion itself ministered to pride, to lust, and cruelty. It would be as reasonable, if we were to impute to the Gospel the sins of London. We know what the sins of Mahometanism are, but do we not know what the sins of Europe and of London are ? Do we not know what the sins are of other places, where the Gospel is preached most earnestly and sedulously ? We mistake, if we do not look at the root of the evils ; you must look into the region of human nature, and first accept a religion as having done what it could for the moral and spiritual welfare of its followers ; having done that, and in that spirit, you can move forward, and offer yourselves as those, who have a more excellent way to present to the Nations, living in the faith of these old religions."

I read in the Report of the Society for the Propagation of the Gospel, remarks on the painfully low standard of the Burmese Christians, which are at once wise and kind, that "as far as their gifts, and opportunities, and environment permit, they abstain from the grosser vices, and are perhaps as good Christians as the majority of those so-called in England." I recognize here the ring of the true Missionary: it was not angels that He sent forth to convert, but poor weak, ignorant, men : "it is the poor, the illiterate, whom God has chosen, because they have chosen Him." Let us get rid of the notion, that in the sight of God the high-Caste Orientals, or the comfortable self-satisfied middle classes in England, are dearer to Him, who hateth nothing that He has made, than the poor Pariah : he brings his soul as an offering to God, and the conventionally pious in the home-Churches can do no more. Remember the Pharisee and the Publican.

Think of such expressions as the following, issued by a Society in 1890: I should be sorry to have written them: "There must be something wrong, when a Church of God can "look out on one thousand Millions of souls under the almost "undisputed sway of Satan, and going down in darkness to the "grave, without definite sympathy and definite effort on their "behalf."

I have been Magistrate in the Cities of Banáras, Allahabad, Amritsár and Lahór, as well as a resident, and Magistrate, many years in the city of London, and can safely say that, if the sale of intoxicating drinks, and the abundance of what are technically called disorderly houses, are part of the apparatus of Satan, London bears off the palm from any Indian city, or any city in the world.

A Missionary was at Lokója, on the Niger, for two years, and he is reported to have thus expressed himself at Harley House, June 1892, as reported in *Regions Beyond:* "What is in Africa? lying, hypocrisy, abominable and shameless immorality." Has he ever walked after dark the streets of London near the Haymarket, or read the reports of the Divorce-Courts in the Daily Papers? Moreover, he had only brief experience of one corner of Africa, and knew no vernacular language; why does he attribute such sins to the whole Continent of Africa? Is Europe, or even Great Britain, responsible for the vices and immoralities of London?

Not long ago a young Indian from Calcutta was beguiled into a disorderly house, and robbed: his case in the Police-Court made one ashamed of a Christian country: can we, who live in glass houses, throw stones?

Hear what General Booth says:

"Take any intelligent Heathen, for instance, who comes "from India to this country, and hears us talk about him, as "a Heathen, or an Idolator, or the like, which indicate that "we regard him as though he were a sort of respectable "two-legged animal. Now, when such an one comes to "travel about this country, he must find considerable diffi- "culty in discovering wherein the boasted superiority of the "Christian over the Heathen lies, and wherein the Heathen is "inferior to the Christian. If he goes out late at night, and "walks our West-End streets, and sees the crowd of harlots "processioning through them; or if he goes to the slums, and "sees the poverty and wretchedness, the filth, and devilry, and "riot, that runs wild there; if he lingers round the doors of "the gin-palaces, and listens to the blasphemies belched forth "from those hell-houses; if he makes inquiries about the "brutal wife-beating, and savage treatment of women and "children in general, that is becoming quite an institution

" with us; or if he happens to see a prize-fight, or marks the
" growing sympathy in the public papers with this kind of
" muscular Christianity, he must find it difficult to guess,
" wherein the people of this so-called Christian land are in any
" way superior to the people he has left behind him in his own
" country."

Whatever may be the weaknesses, and want of wisdom, of the Salvation-Army, at least they know the ways of the submerged population of London.

The description of the non-Christian World, as given by Missionaries, and as circulated in Reports of Missionary-Societies, is shocking to read: if even the truth were proved in a Court of Justice, it would be wrong to circulate it: as it is, it is the raving of the young man, or young woman, from a town in Great Britain, who is ignorant of the sins of Christian Europe, and is brought face to face with manifest forms of human vice in Oriental countries, which are all cloked, and concealed from the public gaze, in Occidental countries.

I have been struck by the words of the Bishop of Southwell:
" At home men sit dissatisfied with Centuries of Christianity.
" The world is worldly still, the flesh is fleshly, and the devil
" devilish. Crime, ignorance, and misery, baffle reform by their
" insuperable mass, and the Religion in possession seems re-
" sponsible. It takes a second thought to ask, which Religion
" is in possession and responsible: is it the Religion of
" obedience to Christ, or disobedience? of unity in Christ, or
" of division? of Faith in Christ, or of doubt?"

Besides of what advantage is such abuse? to take the lowest view it is unmanly; to take the highest it is un-Christian. I wonder for what purpose the compilers make such quotations: I conclude, that there is a stratum in the body of their supporters, which expect this form of abuse, that with Pharisaic pride they may say: We thank God, that we of the comfortable middle class of England are not like the Indian, the Chinese, the Melanesian, or African, or "even as this Publican."

These Missionary-denouncers of the poor ignorant Natives of Asia and Africa forget that a religious paper of London, not long ago, informed its readers, that Religion and the Church were entirely out of possession of certain parts of London. I heard Dr. Benson, Archbishop of Canterbury, say at a public Meeting, that we had two duties before us, one to make Christians out of the Heathen, and another still more important, to prevent nominal Christians becoming Heathen. I do not wish to palliate, or ignore, the sins and weaknesses of a non-Christian people. I have lived twenty-five years of my life in their midst, ruling them, loving them, and loved by them: their first, last, and great fault, or misfortune, is that they are not Christians, and we must try to make them so with Love, Pity, and Sweet Reasonableness, following the example of the first Christian Missionary, Paul.

Hear an indignant remonstrance from the educated Negro Editor of a Newspaper, in the English language, at Sierra Leone, March 1890: " Europe is now tottering under the burden " of its own social problems and complications, to which ours " is the mote as compared to the beam."

In *The Christian World*, March 1, 1894, we find the following:

"*Manufacturing Heathens.*—An article, which is really terrible " in the state of things it discloses, appears in the number of " *The Humanitarian*, by the Rev. Arthur Robins, M.A., entitled, "'Our Home-made Heathen.' Mr. Robins is familiar with " English slums, and his indictment of the Church and of the " social system generally, which permits the existence of the " moral cesspools he describes, is almost prophetic in its " intensity. He says that 'in London only there are at the " present time 50,000 families, who have amongst them all but " one room to each family.' The following is a typical example " of one-room morality: Within, when I went that day, there " dwelt a family of eight; husband and wife and six children, " of all ages, the eldest a girl of twenty, and they slept four in " a bed in one cramped, cupboard-like room. The next week " this household had increased, not quite legitimately, to ten. " The wife had at her breast her new-born babe, whilst her " eldest daughter unabashed showed me her bastard-boy. " There, in a foul and filthy area, where no one would have put " a brute-beast with a pedigree, had been a double birth, with " all the family assembled. There were five in a bed that day. " I could multiply such examples, but there is no need. I asked " myself, as I looked upon this very representative human home " of Christian England's poor, does not the sty make the pig, " does not the hovel help to make the harlot? How does this " gross demoralization work? That mother, who looked upon " her child of sin without a blush, has long since relieved the " congestion in that little upper room by joining, outright, the " *forces of the fallen.* I asked the superintendent of Police in " a profoundly polluting district of a great city, where the slums " have degraded human life down to the deepest depths of " defilement and depravity, what, in his opinion, was the chief " factor in filling the public-houses, and he answered, 'The " dreadful dens they dwell in. It is the slum that does it.'

" The English papers and reviews are constantly full of illus- " trations of the evils, which afflict the social system of Europe; " and no one can read the above without feeling the intense " inconsistency on the part of those, who leave behind them such " a state of things to come to a distant land among an entirely

"different race, to endeavour to upset the social and domestic
"customs of the people without being able to give them any-
"thing half as good. This kind of Crusade did very well in
"the early days, when the people could not read, and when
"Newspapers were difficult to obtain, and they were dependent
"for all their information, whether secular or religious, upon
"the Missionaries, and when there had not been sufficient time
"to test the results of the foreign social system upon the
"natives. But times have changed. When the people read
"the papers, and compare what is going on in Europe with
"what the Missionaries tell them, the first thing that occurs
"to their mind is, 'Physician, heal thyself;' and they are
"led to doubt the sincerity of their teachers, when they
"remember the words of the Apostle, 'If any man provide
"not for his own household, he hath denied the Faith, and
"is worse than an infidel.'

"The Newspapers on the one hand, and the Liquor-traffic on
"the other, both European in origin, are raising and, from all
"appearance, will continue to raise, insuperable obstacles in the
"way of the Christian Missionary from Europe, as long as he
"will insist upon interfering with that, with which he has no
"authority to meddle. Missionary-Societies will be obliged to
"change their Methods and their tactics. The plan of ignoring
"facts, and shutting their eyes to circumstances is a policy, that
"seems wise only to the ostrich."

12. Asserting that Missionaries have Material Help from God.

Every good gift and every perfect gift is from above, and we cannot be too thankful at the close of each day for travelling mercies, staying mercies, sick-bed mercies, death-bed mercies: but are the quotations, which I propose to make, mere "gush," mere pious phraseology, or does the writer mean what he says, and, if he does mean it, is it judicious on the part of the Editor of a serious Publication to put it forth? will it commend itself to the devoted champion of Missions? will it conciliate the much larger army of downright antagonists? will it tempt the indifferent class to read a Missionary-Publication?

I quote from the Church-Missionary-Society-Report of 1893:
"Occasionally our Sundays have been days of real blessing,
"very sweet to us, because we have seen God's hand 'silently
"planning' for us about them. Feeling that we ought not to
"travel on Sunday, Mr. Horsburgh offered to give the skipper
"fifty cash a man for each Sunday, if he would stop. He was
"not very willing, and, although he assented, we did not know
"whether he really would. On the first Saturday he hinted,

"that, if there were a good wind, he should go on. We prayed much about it, and, when Sunday came, it was raining heavily. No Chinaman cares to go out in the rain, so we rested 'according to the good hand of our God upon us.' Each Sabbath has been more blessed than the last, and God has arranged, that we should never travel on His day. More than once He has used the rain to keep us quiet, and to disperse crowds."

I quote from *Regions Beyond*, 1892: "Often at our summer gatherings the Lord seemed to favour us with specially pleasant weather." Alas! we all know how at Missionary-Garden-Meetings in England it often rains: is it pretended that the Almighty exerted his Sovereign power over the elements specially to secure a fine day for a North London Missionary gathering?

Again, in the Church-Missionary-Society-Report of 1890: "The Hospital-Missionary declined in a station in China to give any money for heathen processions. The Natives returned to what both they and we feared would be trying Persecution and insult; the surgical instruments and other valuable things were got together, so as to be easily preserved in event of a disturbance, and the fixed day drew on. We, in Nang Wa, were daily in prayer, and, when the day came, we recognised in the heavy drenching rain the protecting care of God, for through the heavy rain no crowd gathered and all was quiet. But, in addition, the owner of the house having heard there was a likelihood of his property being injured, went to the leaders of the idolatrous arrangements, and said, 'I know those Hospital people won't give you any money, and it is a pity my house should be injured; I will pay their subscription if you are willing.' To this they agreed, but our people made it known to everyone, that the owner of the house had paid the money of his own will, and that we would on no account countenance Idolatry, but, if there were a road or bridge to be mended, we would subscribe to that."

It appears also that Pentecostal gifts of tongues are still made. In the Church-Missionary-Society-Reports of 1891 and 1892 I read: "Up to the time I went to Muya I always read my addresses to audiences of non-Christians, but I had been feeling more and more strongly, that I ought to speak to the people, and not read to them, and here God gave me grace to open my mouth and speak with freedom, and every night for a week I was preaching (not reading) in different places. I have not *read* a sermon or an address since that time. It is wonderful, how the Lord helps with a language, when we commit ourselves to Him to be His mouthpieces. I cannot speak fluently at all on any other subjects, but when preaching the power comes." We have yet to learn, whether this Missionary was understood by his audience, and many good Missionaries have failed after years of test to gain the power of making oral addresses.

The wonderful way, in which money is supplied in some Missions, surprises me. In *China's Millions*, 1892, I read:

"While this has been the case, there has not been a "corresponding increase of income, but the reverse; moreover, "exchange in China has been seriously against us, requiring a "guinea or more to purchase as much silver as a pound would "formerly have bought. It has, however, been wonderful and "beautiful to see, how God has helped us; timely gifts from "members of our own Mission, some of them meaning much "self-denial; and contributions from foreign residents and "visitors have not infrequently in the day answered the prayers "for the day, so that every need has been met. On one "occasion a party preparing to go to a distant station had their "packing completed, and the hour of departure was drawing "nigh before the funds came to hand to take them forward. "Repeatedly we have been without any funds for the general "requirements of the whole Mission, though for particular "objects there have been balances of unexpected donations, "which, of course, could not be touched. Our hearts have been "kept in peace, knowing that God's promises cannot fail; and "to the question 'Lacked ye anything?' we can only reply, as "did the Disciples of old, 'Nothing, Lord.'"

Faith-healing comes into the same category. A few years ago a party of American Missionaries landed at Sierra Leone: two of their main principles were Faith-healing, and Pentecostal gifts of tongues; no medicines were to be taken, no grammars or dictionaries made use of; the party was attacked by malignant fever; two died, refusing quinine. As the disease was highly infectious, the Garrison-Surgeon called on the survivors, and found their minds fixed not to take medicine, as they were ready to obey the divine behest. The astute Surgeon pointed out, that there were many in Sierra Leone, who were not ready, and who would catch the infection, unless they allowed themselves to be healed. So they submitted, and were healed. Here Faith-healing signally broke down. On the Niger a little Heathen boy met with an accident of a serious character: the Medical-Missionary applied his surgical skill to the case, and then he and his brethen prayed over the child, and "claimed him of God." The boy recovered, and ran back to his dirt and heathendom; and this was reported home as "Faith-healing."

Let such enthusiasts read the story of the Conversion of Europe. Trials of strength in those days took place between the Heathen and Christian God about Rain, or Healing, or casting lots, or success in battle, or rescue from shipwreck. The mendacious Chronicler always reports in favour of the Church.

Such objectionable features should be sternly rejected by the modern Missionary. He should be cautious in his language, be still, and know, that there is a God. The Romish Mission to this day in E. Africa records visions, dreams, the active co-operation of dead Missionaries, who prepare the field in a mysterious way for their surviving brethren: all this is to be deplored at any epoch, but should be laughed out of Court in the Nineteenth Century.

The great Missionary Anskar, who died in 865 A.D., is reported to have said: "One Miracle I would ask the Lord to grant me, and that is, that by His Grace He would make me a good man." O! that all were like Anskar!

I do not wish to be hard on the Monastic Annals of the ninth Century any more than on the Missionary-Reports of the nineteenth: they both have the monopoly of Missionary-literature of their time. Secular organs pass by the subject in disdain. The Missionaries allow their feelings, and their profession, to unduly influence them: devoid of critical spirit, the compiler of the Report writes to a still more uncritical class of readers: a Secretary writes about his Missionaries very much, as a Mother would about her Sons, "Bona verba quæso." Stories are told in past times in Europe, of famines and pestilences. Heathen Deities are invoked in vain; at length the Church of Christ intervenes; the grievance ceases. Would any modern Missionary dare to make such assertions now? and yet it is the same God, who rules the world with unceasing and unvarying order: Lies do not live in a literary age.

I wonder, that it never occurs to Missionaries writing their Annual letter, and the compiler of the Annual Report of the Society, that afflictions, and disappointments, and calamities, such as the murder of good Bishop Hannington, and the death of good Bishop Parker, are blessings in disguise sent by the Fatherly hand, who does all things well. Why are there such triumphant Pœans at the success of some little undertaking, or the recovery from some sickness? There have been deaths of agents to the Societies, which have been very much to the advancement of the cause of Missions: there have been prolongation of long, and no longer useful, lives, which have been prejudicial. Short-sighted Committees have striven, and striven in vain, to keep doors open, which He in His wisdom intends to be closed, and on the other hand, doors have been thrown open beyond all human dreams of possibility. Individual Missionaries, and Compilers of Reports, should not lay claim to such familiarity with the hidden counsels of the Almighty. In no other department of Human affairs is this pretence put forward: it is a most striking feature of Missionary-literature: it may impose on the emotional and uneducated: it is repellant to the conscience of those, who leave all their affairs with Him, and accept with thankfulness what He in His wisdom, Life or Death, Success or Failure, pleases to send.

It is well written that

"Material miracles may have ceased, but who can say that "spiritual miracles have ceased? May not God's gracious σημεῖα "be traced in

"(1) the transformation of personal characters of individuals
"and communities? was not the Conversion of Paul a
"miracle, and is not that miracle repeated from generation
"to generation?
"(2) the voluntary consecration of individuals to the work?
"They did not choose the work; God chose them,
"sometimes against their will.
"(3) the reflex blessings of the Missions on the Church
"which supports them? Is not this evident to the
"eye?"

13. TREATING WITH CONTEMPT THE PARENTAL RIGHTS OF NON-CHRISTIANS.

Hear the words of an Indian Statesman, a true friend of Missions, from whose published works I extract the following: let Missionaries lay it to their hearts: "The natural right of "a Hindu parent to direct the religious education of his child, "while under years of discretion, is as sacred, *as that of the* "*Christian Parent.* It cannot be interfered with by the State "without a breach of the first principles of Christian Liberty, to "which we ourselves should appeal, were we the subject party. "The spirit of Christian Equity enjoins us to do unto others as "we would, that we should be done by."

A Bombay-Missionary, 1892, writes as follows: "One enquirer "has an old father, who is under medical treatment, and whom "he is supporting: there is nothing whatever keeping him from "confessing Christ in baptism but this, that he believes his "father's heart would break, if he did so. No one without "Indian experience can understand the depth of a father's "affection for a son, or the unspeakable disgrace he would "experience, if that son were baptized. Let him die, but let "him not bring this curse upon his family! Another inquirer "of long standing is kept back because a wife, to whom he is "devoted, will not hear the suggestion even of learning about "Christianity: if he were baptized, she and her children would "go at once to her father's home. These are typical cases. "Only Divine Grace can so order, that such men shall be enabled, "either by a modification of their circumstances, or by standing "alone, to testify to the Lord in whom they really believe."

The agony of the parent, when he contemplates the idea of his son or daughter leaving his ancestral Faith, which from his point of view is the only Path of Salvation, cannot be described, or realized, except by those unhappy Christians, whose children have lapsed into Mormonism, Theosophism, or some form of unbelief, which denies the Divinity of our Lord. The young Missionary, who has no children, or only children in their childhood, should write gently on such subjects: Can we wish to destroy all those sentiments of Humanity, which underlie all Religion? Among the heap of heavy sins, piled up by Paul in the first Chapter of the Epistles to the Romans, is "disobedience to Parents." The dilemma is awful: in the course of nature the son may expect to outlive the father: at any rate he must tarry the Lord's leisure. I do not forget the Lord's words, Matt. x, 37, but the application of them must be gentle, and the allusion made to the struggle by outsiders must be merciful. The centurion remarked, that with a great price he had purchased his Roman citizenship; Paul replied that he was free-born. We should all think of this, and feel sympathy for the sufferers, and not hold the old parents, or female relations, to contempt, as the manner of some Missionaries is.

In the Church-Missionary-Society-Report of 1890 I read as follows: I regret, that a Missionary should have made such a charge against a brother, sent it home to England, and that the Editor should have published it: if true, was it the part of a Christian to publish it far and wide? A Christian Father, in his agony at his son or daughter becoming Mahometan, might have used such hasty words.

" Some time ago there was a young Mahometan, the son of a
" great Mahometan saint and doctor, who had great anxiety
" of soul because of sin. He read the Koran through and
" through without finding light, when he found in it an ex-
" pression referring to the Old Testament and the New Testa-
" ment. The thought came into this young man's heart, 'If I
" can only get possession of a Bible, I might get what I need.'
" Two Missionaries happened to be in the district, and he got
" what he wanted. He began with the Gospel of St. John, and
" by the time he got to the third chapter he was a free man, and
" desirous of throwing off Mahometanism. When his father
" heard of it, he offered a reward of 500 rupees, to anyone,
" who would kill his son, and 200 to anyone, who would bring
" him the good news. For two years I had to watch over
" that young man, and then his father found him, and with
" much difficulty we managed to keep him safe. At last the
" old man went back with a New Testament. A year afterwards
" he came again, and said, that he had brought together other
" mullahs, and read it to them. He also said, 'We have noticed

"that this is the New Testament; that shows me, that there must be an Old Testament, and they have sent me to get the Old Testament.' I had the pleasure of giving him one, and just before I left he came with his son and said, 'The God of my son, whom I wished to murder, is now my God; baptize me, too, into the Faith of Christ.'"

14. Necessity of Union of Denominations into one National Church.

The *Quarterly Review* of January, 1894, remarks as follows: "At the present rate of progress in India it is calculated, that the Protestant Faith will absorb the entire population by the middle of the twenty-first Century. Such a thought suggests deep searchings of heart about the form of Church-Order, which is to prevail there, and in the other lands, which our divided, and sometimes competing, Missions are conquering. No reasonable Churchman would wish to see a mere slavish reproduction of Anglican ceremonial or standards; but are the miserable divisions of Protestantism to split up Christianity the wide world over, as they are weakening it at home?"

Whoever uttered the above prophecy about the 287 Millions of British India becoming Christian within a century and a half, cannot have studied the Census-Returns of that country of 1891, where it is clearly shown, that the actual annual increase of population by the ordinary process of generation exceeds three Millions: on the other hand the work of Conversion of the Syrian, Romish, and Protestant Churches during eight centuries has barely reached to two Million and three-quarters. A more sober writer states the acknowledged fact, that there are more heathen on the earth to-day unreached by the Gospel than there were 100 years ago, notwithstanding the glorious work, done in the intervening period, speaks volumes for the need of making the present Missionary-Income accomplish much more than it does.

The sound policy seems to be, that a Missionary-band should do its best to convert the non-Christians of a Region, organize a Church, appoint officers, as Paul did, and then pass on to Regions Beyond: that would not suit the dominant spirit of modern Committees: they do not trust the people, and wish to keep the neo-Christians under their control, and, as each Committee has a different ideal of Church-Government, the prospect of the future is gloomy. The question of the union of such Native Churches, belonging to different denominations, is however gaining ground; and it will be a great blessing to them to find some simple Organization, based on the Asiatic usages of the New Testament, not on the overbearing, unsympathetic, and

unintelligible, American and Anglican model. Progress has been made in Japan so far as to unite in one Church all the multiform Presbyterian bodies; it is to be hoped, that the Episcopal Churches of Great Britain and America will coalesce. The different forms of Methodism have found a common shibboleth: so far so well, but something more is required for great Regions, occupied by populations differing in race and language. Bishop Evington thus expressed himself in 1894:
" In the second division of his speech he referred, in illustration
" of the difficulties, to the spirit of patriotism, which was
" growing in Japan. It was a perfectly right spirit, that they
" should desire to be masters of their own country, and that
" they should not like to have a foreigner over them, but this
" spirit brought with it its difficulties to the Church. What
" happened at the recent Synod was an illustration of it. The
" native Christians said, 'We are not going to have all the
" details of your English Church-Service forced upon us'; and
" one felt, that they were entitled to some freedom in these
" matters. Another difficulty the Church had to face was due
" to the fact, that they went into the Field in force rather late,
" and even then did not establish schools, with the result that
" they could not now get Catechists and fellow-workers in the
" proportion in which they were needed. But if there were
" difficulties, there were also many things to encourage them."

I heard Bishop Bickersteth of Japan express himself at the Society for the Propagation of the Gospel, that there were only necessary four points of uniformity of the Japanese Church with the Anglican: the two Sacraments, the Inspiration of the Scriptures, Episcopacy, and the Nicene Creed.

Bishop Bickersteth thus expressed himself at a Church Congress: " And further, in Japan, above all lands, if we can only
" advance towards it slowly, we are bound from the beginning
" to have an eye to the day, which may or may not be distant,
" when the Church shall be wholly independent of ourselves.
" The few thousand Christians, who are attached to our Missions,
" are members of a nation numbering forty Million souls, a
" nation, where patriotism is almost too universal to be counted
" a virtue, and whose ideal it is to take its place as an equal
" among the great civilized nations of the world. Such a nation
" must of course have a Church of its own. Even now, though
" an Indian Christian, if a Churchman, not seldom counts him-
" self a member of the Church of England, of the Church, that
" is, of the conquering race, to a Japanese, the idea of belong-
" ing to the Church of a foreign land would seem too ridiculous
" to be worth growing indignant at. We have tried to meet
" this feeling, surely a right and worthy feeling, on the whole,
" to the utmost extent that prudence, not to say the slow move-

"ment of the complicated machinery, by which our Anglican communion does its work, have permitted us. We have to-day a genuine native Church in Japan, with its own constitutions and canons, drawn up in 1887, not 1603, and Synod, and Vestries, and Missionary-Society, etc. All, it is true, in their initial stage of working, still, all mainly carried on by Japanese themselves, and on, I believe, such primitive and Catholic lines, as will only need expansion and development, not change, till the day of Independence is reached."

Archbishop Benson of Canterbury thus expressed himself at St. Bride's Church: "The growth of great Churches in the Greater England will involve the recognition, that not every syllable of our formulas, which is essential as against those, who on our own ground contend with us, is equally essential to the Catholic Faith at large. That not every word of our dearest liturgies can be as full of meaning to those, who have not lived our theological life, as it is to us. That for their liturgies of the future they may yet again fall back upon the primeval quarries, out of which our own were hewn, but which contain magnificent stores, that we never could appreciate as Easterns can. Only under a total misapprehension of the conditions of the problem, of the enormous multitudes, of the extreme diversities of customs, of the vast number of languages and races, can the idea be entertained, that our own limited ministries will suffice to spread living Christianity even in India alone. Conversion will not remain a function of the Clergy only. The converts must convert. They must be trained to make the first use of their Conversion orderly and enthusiastically. There are some kinds of elasticity, which must be active in many countries, if the Church is to win the world to Christ."

Bishop Westcott of Durham thus expressed himself: "India is our special charge, as a Christian nation. India is our hardest problem, as a Missionary-Church. Hitherto we have kept too exclusively to beaten paths. Our mode of dealing with the Indian has been too conventional, too English. Indian Christianity can never be cast in the same mould as English Christianity. We must make up our minds to this. The stamp of teaching, the mode of life, which experience has justified as the best possible for an English parish, may be very unfit when transplanted into an Indian soil. We must become as Indians to the Indian, if we would win India to Christ."

The late Sir Bartle Frere, an experienced Statesman, and staunch friend of Missions, wrote thus: "We may hope, and at no distant period, to see a great Christian Church in India, with distinct national characteristics of its own, but with "features, which may be recognised by all Catholic Christians, as betokening true Catholic unity with the Great Head of our Faith. It would be vain to speculate on what are likely to be the distinctive features of such an Indian Church, but we may be confident, that they will be no mere copy of the Churches, which have grown up in and around Europe; and that, holding the truths which are to be gathered from the teaching of our Lord and His Apostles, the framers of the Church-constitution of India will find no necessity for copying peculiarities, which have been impressed on so many of the older Churches of Christendom by the circumstances, under which they were originally organized, in communities at that time quite as barbarous as the least civilized portions of India now are."

The case is thus fairly stated: "There are about sixty different Church-Organizations working at present in this country; and, though the success of each of these Organizations has been considerable, still those, who wish to see Christianity have a firmer footing in India, cannot help regretting the absence of a complete working harmony between them all. The various Mission-bodies working in India have taken good care to reproduce in their converts the distinct denominational peculiarities, that unfortunately keep them asunder at home. 'It is, indeed, a lamentable and even a melancholy thing,' remarked the *Quarterly Review*, 'to force upon native converts the evil inheritance of the divisions, which sever Church from Church, sect from sect, in the lands of the Reformation; divisions, which have mainly grown out of peculiar historical circumstances, and have little intelligible meaning for the races now being won over to Christianity.' There is a desire, an anxious desire, amongst many of the generous and active-minded Christians everywhere, at this period, for some compromise."

Dr. Pulney Andy published at Madras, in 1893, a collection of papers connected with this patriotic movement. A National Church for India is out of all reason, but a Church for the different Regions, united by race and language, is a reasonable aspiration. He was one of the first Hindu, who visited England, and he was deeply struck by the Sectarianism in the Christian Churches: He became a Christian in 1863: he desires a National Church without the aid of European funds, or the curse of European supervision: one friend objected: "what are we to do for our livelihood, if we sever our connection with the Mission, which provide us with the means of existence?" Here we hit the nail on the head: our converts are rice-Christians: the Indian Christian is entirely dependent for his earthly existence on the Foreign Mission, which moulds the new Society too much on a European pattern, for Missionaries are anxious to perpetuate their own Church-peculiarities, instead of preaching the broad, simple truth of New Testament-Christianity, and allowing the Indian Church to develop, and amalgamate, on a comprehensive basis with other clusters of neo-Christians, now divided by party-differences. Christianity was of Asiatic origin, but it has donned a European garb, both in thought, practice, moral, social, and political aspects: it will make no progress in Oriental Nations until it gets rid of its European externals. Moreover, the Missionaries are paid members of an arrogant, dominant, race, and their avowed object is to break up the social system of the country, more for purposes of political ascendancy than for the sake of real Christian Doctrine.

Dr. Andy thus expresses himself: "Now look at the evils
" resulting from the Sectarian Churches in this land. A member
" of one Church gets discontented with the managers of that
" Church. He leaves it, and joins another Church, where he is
" heartily welcomed. Is this not an encouragement held out
" to malcontents? An Agent of a Mission is often tempted
" away to join another sect by the offer of a higher salary,
" a mere proof that worldly motives have greater influence
" than sectarianism, or the conviction of the doctrines of any
" particular sect. And with reference to the self-support of the
" Churches, say, for instance, that there are about one hundred
" Christians in a certain parish. By having three or four
" Sectarian Churches in that locality there will be, if equally
" divided, twenty-five members for each of those Churches.
" Even if each member be able to contribute a rupee a month,
" there will be about twenty-five rupees collected; will this
" sum be sufficient to maintain a Minister, and meet other
" demands of the Church? If there be only one Church for
" the hundred Christian inhabitants of that parish, there will
" be one hundred rupees collected monthly, which may in a
" great way be found sufficient for the management of that
" Church. Again, when a Native Christian finds, that he is
" prohibited by the Church to which he belongs from marrying
" his deceased wife's sister, he goes to another, where that
" ceremony could be easily performed, and he immediately
" afterwards returns to his former Church, where he is again
" received with his new bride by the Minister, who refused to
" marry the party in his Church. These and other irregularities
" of the Christian Church are carefully watched and criticized
" by the non-Christian public, to the detriment of our religion,
" and of the further extension of Christ's kingdom in this land.
" Thus man-made Sectarianism is proving itself a stumbling-
" block to the spread of the noble religion of Christ."

I quote from the Church-Missionary-Society's Report, 1891:
" Mr. Hutchinson in his Annual Letter dwells upon a special

"danger, which arises from the intense national feeling of the
"Japanese Christians, and to other dangers of a still more
"serious kind. 'I remember that twelve years ago, when
"spending a few days in Tokio, there was a meeting of Japanese
"representatives from the different Churches, at which was
"mooted the desirability of bidding foreign teachers adieu, and
"setting out on the Christian course on Japanese lines with
"the Scriptures as the sole guide. That proposal was then
"negatived, owing to the good sense of some, who recognised
"the gravity of such a step, and their own want of preparation
"for it. But the idea has never been abandoned, and it is now
"both widely spread and deeply felt, that the forms and cere-
"monies and institutions of Christianity generally must be
"overhauled and re-shaped by Japanese minds and hands,
"apart from foreign interference, the reason being, not that
"our present forms and regulations are unsuitable, but simply
"that they have been made by foreigners, therefore something
"different must be set up by Japanese alone. Let us not call
"this childish, but sympathetically recognise it as the outcome
"of an intense national feeling, more than a wave of passion
"sweeping over the land, rather the welling forth of an irre-
"sistible stream of long pent-up patriotism. How to meet this,
"and, whilst avoiding the semblance of opposition, which
"would be futile, to guide in a safe, because Scriptural,
"direction, is the serious problem which is before us.'"

At the first of the Indian Missionary-Conferences held at Lahór, December 1862, at which I was present, the Rev. John Newton, of the American Presbyterian Mission, read a paper on the subject of an Indian Catholic Church. He proposed a Mission on the following bases: (1) a Creed; (2) Rites and mode of worship left to each congregation; (3) a Collegiate Presbyterian Pastorate in each Church; (4) a body of Evangelists, or Bishops, superior to Pastors; (5) general Councils or Synods as a bond of union for all the Churches of India.

Short of this he suggested separate Church-Organizations, separate creeds, but the uniting work of confederation, providing for (1) interchange of ministerial service, (2) intercommunion of the people, and (3) councils to regulate the affairs of the entire body in its relation to the outer world.

He remarked with truth, that there would be no difficulty with the Natives, as they have acquired as yet no great partiality for one phase over another. They have not as yet passed through the furnace of affliction, and would readily adopt any mode of worship, any form of government, any system of doctrine, based on the Bible. The difficulty would be from the European and American Missionaries. In his opinion a present Union of the Churches was not to be thought of: the time, however, was near at hand, when Natives Churches must be independent of foreign support and foreign control.

He then suggested by way of preparation for such future Union: (1) Joint itinerancies; (2) Interchange of pulpits; (3) Union-prayer-meetings; (4) Joint Communions; (5) Common religious Periodicals; (6) Periodical Conferences.

Thirty years have elapsed, and the dear good man, who uttered these words, has passed away, dying at his post. When I glance my eyes down the list of speakers in that Conference, I find few, who now survive, and the prospect of Union, while a single white Missionary remains, is distant. But after all some of the Churches are in the fifth generation of Christians, and they ought to have some degree of independence: if Episcopal, their own Native Bishop; if Presbyterian, their own organization: the real struggle between the white and the dark coloured man has still to come. The true policy of a Missionary-Society is to efface itself, as soon as the Lord's work is done.

15. CERTAINTY OF OPPOSITION FROM OLD, AND NEW, FORMS OF RELIGION.

I remark with great satisfaction notices of organized opposition to the Missionaries. I read in one report, that an active Hindu Propaganda is at work in S. India; lectures are given in defence of the ancient Faith, and tracts distributed against Christianity. This is as it should be. Anything is better than passive stupidity, or scornful contempt. If the Missionary be, as he ought to be, confident in the Truth, he will rejoice, that the hour of contest has arrived. The National Indian Association of London has started a school for girls, in which purely Secular Education is given: in fact attempts are being made to buttress up Hinduism, and a period of great intellectual, and spiritual, struggle has been entered upon, not without social and domestic pressure upon converts, which can hardly be called Persecution in the sense usually applied to those words.

I read again of the Press being vigorously employed to counteract Missionaries, and scurrilous tracts upon Gospel-history being circulated. How old Missionaries must ponder upon their practice forty years ago in grossly abusing, and holding up to scorn, the Hindu Deities, and Mahomet, while the crowd, scarcely understanding the question, only laughed. Things are changed now. The Gospel is as true as ever, but it must be preached in a spirit of love not dogmatism, sympathy not abuse, sweet reasonableness, as Paul used to preach at Athens and Lystra. I read of a Society for the Propagation of Hinduism, and it is wisely remarked, that such hostility proves the attention, which Christianity is compelling. The

Agents of the Madras-Hindu-Tract-Society meet the Missionary at nearly every station, abuse Christianity, and circulate anti-Christian literature, but their opposition only brought larger audiences. The Mahárája of Travancór appears to entertain a lecturer in his College in defence of his Faith.

In Calcutta the Missionary is met by the agents of the Arya Somaj: the increased spontaneous evangelical activity of converts is noticed: many educated natives listen patiently to the Missionary, who a few years ago would have reviled the holy Name. Sometimes, but not often, stone-throwing is mentioned: the British rule over subject Provinces is tighter than was that of the Roman Procurator at Jerusalem: we allow free speech, free assembly, and free Press, but no violence or uproar. The Hindu places himself close to the Mission-School, and urges the children to leave the School; and implores their parents to save them from the jaws of the English wolf: endeavours are made to keep wives and daughters from contact with the female agents, but the conduct of the latter is so gentle and judicious, that the feeling of their own sex is in their favour. The Buddhists of Japan summoned the aid of the American Colonel Olcott, a Theosophist, to help them to oppose Christianity: he went on a preaching tour, and had numbers to listen. The Unitarians are also very influential. A Missionary from Japan in the Church-Missionary-Society-Report, 1891, writes:

" Unhappily Unitarianism has been presented lately in a most
" fascinating guise, promising all that is good in Christianity
" without the essential, the foundation-truths concerning sin
" and atonement and regeneration and sanctification. This
" has laid hold of the Native mind, and is doing untold harm
" to the infant Churches. Besides this, owing to the spread
" of un-Christian teaching generally, there is great danger, lest
" the minds of our people be turned aside from the Faith by
" specious doctrines of a materialistic and speculative philosophy,
" which is being warmly welcomed even by many Native
" Christian teachers."

In the Church-Missionary-Society-Report of 1891, I find the following:

" At one place, indeed, where we had been staying several
" days, the schoolmaster (schoolmasters in South China are
" often our worst enemies) wrote a warning notice about us,
" and fixed it on the trunk of a tree by the roadside near to the
" place where our boat was moored. Our native helper on
" seeing it took it down and brought it to me. I have it now
" before me. Translated into English it reads as follows:
" ' Beware! Whereas barbarian demons have for many years
" clandestinely entered the Flowery Land, be it known, that two
" of these demons. possessing cunning eyes, have presumed to

" come into our neighbourhood, and have brought with them a
" dog, which also possesses cunning eyes. Now, when these said
" barbarians arrived at Tai Ting May, they were forthwith com-
" pelled to leave, because the people of the eighteen provinces
" of China have been commanded indeed to stab to the heart
" any barbarian demon they may meet, with faces as smooth as
" oil, but with hearts like swords. Consider what these demons
" are about. By day they beguile simple folk by giving away
" medicine; whilst at night, under the cover of darkness, they
" sally forth, accompanied by the dog, and dig into the hills
" of our pure country (China) and take out precious stones.
" Nor is this the only evil. They thereby cause the baneful
" influences to escape, which will certainly injure us. Why do
" we remain heedless? Dated the year of Kwong Sii, the fifth
" month and the first day.' The dog referred to is a very
" harmless terrier. This idea of our coming to seek for precious
" stones is very prevalent. Along this river it is hardly possible
" to go on shore near towns or villages without being watched,
" and questioned as to the whereabouts of silver and precious
" stones. However emphatic may be our denial of having
" come for such a purpose, they generally hold fast to their
" opinion of us. We are supposed to possess seven eyes, by
" means of which we can see into the depths of the earth."

This is almost as foolish as what the Missionaries say about the non-Christian people, but not so wicked.

In the Church-Missionary-Society-Report, 1891, a Madras Missionary writes thus:

" Brahmoism and Theosophism are not now making that
" progress, which those, who introduced them into this country,
" hoped that they would do. The adherents of the above
" Associations are but few, and these do not succeed in attracting
" the attention and in enlisting the sympathies of their fellow-
" Hindus in reference to their peculiar line of thought and
" action. As a matter of fact, materialists, secularists, and
" indifferentists are increasing in the educated Hindu com-
" munity. This state of things is not to be wondered at, for
" the very nature of the Education given in this country cannot
" but produce the above results. It is an undeniable fact, that
" the more the Hindus of this country imbibe Western scientific
" and literary truths, the more they are led to look upon their
" religion (Hinduism) as fabulous and fictitious. At the same
" time they entertain the erroneous, as well as unhappy, idea
" that all religions, including Christianity, are equally false and
" so incredible. This is invariably urged by the Hindu as their
" main difficulty in accepting Christianity."

This opens out the great question of high-class Education, to which I have already alluded among "Methods not recommended:"

let Missionaries and Christian Teachers remember, that, if they sweep the human intellect clear of all belief in the Supernatural, the result must follow described above.

The danger of opposition is not so much from the Old-World Religions: they are in their nature tolerant, but from the new religious conceptions, which English Education has produced. I quote from the Church-Missionary-Society-Report, 1891:

" Opposition from the heathen has been bitter in some cases.
" Attacks on the Bible, and on the character of Christ, were
" made by lecturers, particularly by an Arya Samajist. At the
" end of January we had a visit from Padri-Kharak Sing, who
" continued for several days to give addresses to Aryans, and all
" who cared to come and hear him. Carpets were spread in
" our hospital-compound, and forms provided for the audience.
" But none are so deaf as those, who will not hear, and those
" present were chiefly Aryans, of whom it may be truly said,
" 'They enter not in themselves, and those who are entering in
" they hinder.' One youth was, however, greatly drawn to us,
" but the Aryans got hold of him, and he eventually returned to
" his home in a native State. Anyone, wishing to become a
" Christian, is immediately attacked by these Aryans, who entice
" him by offers of place or salary; or, if he will not listen, they
" dog his steps wherever he goes, threaten him, nay, shut him
" up, steal his clothes, and in some cases even poison those,
" who are firm in their wish to join us."

It is a pity, that a Missionary should condescend to write the closing lines: no doubt, when a Hindu is persuaded to be baptized, the same ungenerous remarks, and with equal truth, are made as regards the Missionary. There should be no abuse.

I have alluded above to the Hindu-Madras-Tract-Society: it is interesting to quote from their first Report, for they follow after European models: we have taught them the art of fence, and attack, in our own language: " The chief causes, that con-
" tributed to the establishment of this Society, are to be found
" in the various spiritual influences, that are at work amongst us
" in these days of religious revival. After a long sleep of many
" Centuries, during which, owing to many political convulsions,
" we did not pay due attention to our religion, literature, and
" other things, that distinguished us as a nation, or that gave
" us national individuality, we have now awakened to the
" grandeur and perfection of our ancient religion. . . .
" We owe more to the activity of antagonistic foreign in-
" fluences in our midst than to any other cause, for the for-
" mation of this Tract-Society. We have painfully witnessed
" the injustice done to our religion by foreign and native
" Christian Missionaries. Baseless charges were trumped up
" against it; and, relying on the poverty of the masses, and

"the ignorance, that generally prevails amongst them regard-
"ing their own religion and their own traditions, those apostles
"of foreign creeds have, by means fair or foul, attempted, and
"even succeeded to some extent, in leading our poor brethren
"astray. This aroused in us the instinct of self-preservation,
"and made us see the need of some Organization like the
"present one; and, since the Christian Propaganda could
"only thrive by destroying the better religion bequeathed to
"us by our ancestors, we were obliged to use against the
"Missionaries their own weapons."

There is much dignity, and a high tone of feeling, in the above remarks: they are foemen worthy of our steel. We doubt nothing of the strength of our cause. "Magna est Veritas, et prævalebit." But we have no precedent for such an environment of circumstances in past centuries. The lists are kept open by a strong British Government: the combatants must fight no longer by empty abuse, but by the power of the Spirit, and the deep convictions of the Soul.

I quote from the *Mission of the World*, No. 1, of 1894, the following passage: "A universal Hindu Conference was "lately held at Banáras: the practical conclusions were to "appoint a day of united prayer, to employ evangelists to "circulate Tracts and Scriptures, and to establish a Hindu-"Mission-School: this is the Brahmanical revival."

I remark, that all the Christian Methods, even that of approaching the Almighty in prayer, are adopted by the non-Christian.

In Africa I read of actual opposition by force: I quote from the Church-Missionary-Society-Report of 1891: "In Abeokúta "some of the chiefs have repeated the effort, which was made "in January, 1891, to expel the Missionaries, and, failing in "this, have sought to hinder their work in other ways. They "have prohibited the refugees from Iberekoda from attend-"ing the services. One of the most powerful of the heathen "chiefs, however, has not approved these acts. Ikeriku, one "of the townships of Abeokúta, still continues alone to be the "heathen centre of Human Sacrifices."

I notice symptoms of the same opposition to the Missionary among the Maori in New Zealand. New religious conceptions, quite unconnected with Animism, or Idolatry, have gained an entrance, and are known by the names of Te Kooti, Te Whiti, or Hau-Hau: they are indigenous. Mormonism is brought from America:

I quote the remarks of the Archdeacon from the Church-Missionary-Society-Report of 1892: "With regard to the work "in Waikato, and amongst the Hau-Hau generally, there are "many hopeful signs. Tawhiao, the religious as well as civil

" head of his followers, has formally renounced his makeshift,
" childish, religion, and discourages its practice, so that there
" is no profession of any kind, excepting amongst the followers
" of Te Kooti and Te Whiti. This has been succeeded in
" most instances by absolute indifference. Of them it may
" truly be said, that their last state is worse than their first. I
" was present at a large gathering of upwards of a thousand
" in May last, and spent a week with them. I thus had abun-
" dant opportunity of talking with them. When asked what
" religion they intend to embrace next, there was great difference
" of opinion, but very few had any idea of returning to the form
" of Christianity they once professed. So deep-rooted is their
" alienation, that it will take much patient and faithful working
" before they will return as a body. The work of bringing
" their fathers to Christ in their early days of Cannibalism and
" gross superstition was easy, as compared to that, which now
" lies before us. We have to contend not only with the original
" natural man, but also with the vices and infidel teachings
" derived from Civilization."

And again in the Report of 1891 : "The defection of a large
" number of Maori in the Whanganui district to Te Kooti
" was mentioned in last year's Report. Altogether, it appears,
" that about one hundred adherents, including twenty who were
" communicants, have gone over. These were on the Whan-
" ganui River, under the pastoral care of the Rev. Eruera H. Te
" Ngara, who has been much disheartened in consequence of
" their desertion."

Efforts have been made to bring them back into the Christian fold, but without much success. Sometimes the Civil power has to interfere. Mr. Maunsell, and the local constable, had much difficulty in preventing a resort to arms on the part of a loyal tribe in the neighbourhood, who resolved to intercept Te Kooti by force. Troops from Auckland to Gisborne arrived opportunely on the scene, and most of Te Kooti's followers were put under arrest. He himself, after making his escape, was secured and conveyed to Auckland, but was subsequently released on bail.

It is not clear, why the Missionary called the tribe, who were prepared to use force against Te Kooti "loyal" : it was a matter of Religion, not of obedience to the Ruling Power. The Arm of the Flesh should under no circumstances be resorted to : there is always this tendency in the followers of a dominant Religion to coerce all, who dissent from their views, and it is unworthy of our Great Cause.

The Mormons are described in the following extract from the same Report:

" In the Otaki district also a sad secession has occurred, the "majority of the inhabitants of a small village near Porirua having gone over to the Mormons. Mr. McWilliams says: I am glad to say, however, that those who were really, and not merely nominally, Christians and Churchmen, have remained faithful to the Church, and will no doubt in time, by their consistent example and arguments, win the more intelligent and spiritually-minded of their brethren back again. When I was last there, I was shown a copy of the 'Book of Mormon,' which has just been published in the Maori language, and which had been lent to our lay-reader, in hopes that it would turn him to Mormonism. But it had no such effect. Fortunately he is very intelligent, thoughtful, and, for a Maori, well-read man. He characterized the book as 'a jumble of platitudes and nonsense, intermixed plentifully with cribbings from our Holy Scriptures with the sense altered and the names of persons and places changed.' He said, that had it come to them before the Bible, it might have been some improvement on their former condition of heathenism and constant strife to have followed its teaching, but to attempt to introduce it now, as an advance upon the teaching of the Bible, was like trying to make them believe that fern-root was better food than bread and mutton." The Hindu-Tract-Society writes in the same style about the Bible, and the Jew speaks thus of the New Testament.

I quote the remarks of a writer from China to show the degree of opposition to the Missionary: I can in no way support his appeal to the Arm of the Flesh: Supposing that we substitute the word Russia for China, and suggest, that the Western Powers should compel Russia to admit Protestant Missionaries, how ridiculous it would sound! and China has as much right to manage her own affairs as Russia.

"Unless the European Powers insist, that China shall fulfil the elementary duties of a civilized State, and protect residents, who have due passports, these riots will grow more numerous and dangerous, and eventually there will be national embroilments. This is no mere Swedish question. The rowdy mobs make no distinction; Missionaries and merchants of any other nationality are in equal danger. It is a question for the united firmness of all Western nations dealing with a Power, which will issue high-sounding proclamations by the acre and do nothing. We should insist, that it shall be made harder for a mandarin to do wrong than to do his duty."

What a low idea the writer has of a Missionary, the Ambassador of Christ, when he classes him with Merchants of Opium, Liquor, Lancashire Cottons, and Incense brought by Christian men for the use of Pagan Worship.

IV. MISSIONARY HOME-AGENCY.

CAP. IV.		The Missionary Home-Agency.
	1	The Board of Missions.
	2	The Association, sub-Sections A and B.
	3	The Deputations.
	4	The Financial Department.
	5	The Publications.
	6	Sensationalism.

1. THE BOARD OF MISSIONS.

1. For Administrative Purposes.
2. For Consultative, and Controlling, Purposes.

This subject cannot be left without remark, yet it does not require detailed description. It used to be one of those fond visions, which rose before the minds of old Clergy, who knew nothing about the actual work of the Missions of the Church of England all over the world. It was not a question of shades of Ecclesiastical thought, for the Society for the Propagation of the Gospel, and Church-Missionary-Society, were equally opposed to it, and I denounced the original plan in the Committee of both Societies, and at the Society for Promoting Christian Knowledge. The Church of Rome is too wise to entertain such an idea: she has twelve, or more, Congregations in Great Britain, or France, or Germany, or Spain, or Italy, or elsewhere, to whom she entrusts the work of particular Geographical Areas. At Rome the Council "De Propagandâ Fide" controls, but does not interfere with, the Organization of these powerful Congregations: of course Rome controls their doctrine, arranges their Geographical limits, and as they are totally outside all Old-World territorial Episcopal jurisdiction, settles their hierarchy. Twenty years ago I called at the De Propagandâ, at Rome, and asked for a Report of the different Missions of the Church of Rome. No report was to be had: so I waited on an Ecclesiastic, and asked him, whether I could have a copy of any Annual Report:

he replied, that it was possible, but not probable. However, time has gone on, and we have now annually an admirable Report in Latin, "Missiones Catholicæ," with Maps and Statistics. Nothing could be better. The windows of the Church of Rome are opening to the Light of Reason, and Public opinion

" Fas est et ab hoste doceri : " this is just what the Church of England ought to do, and is doing : all wild attempts at administrative interference have been placed aside, but an excellent Organization has come into existence for consultative, and controlling purposes, such as a Church, which places in the Field a larger number of Missionaries than any other Church in times past or present, ought to have. I had no hesitation in accepting a seat on such a Board : it moves slowly, but perhaps that is a merit : there is one for the Province of Canterbury, and another for York, but they meet, and very much act together, and there is the germ of good things in the movement. Their Reports throw together the work of all Associations : this is a great advance : I happen individually to know what each Association is doing, but the general public have no means of information, and to the old country-Clergy it must have been a great mystery : the greatest glory of our Church from the time of Patrick, Columba, Aidan, and Boniface, has been her Missions to the non-Christian World. So be it always!

2. THE ASSOCIATION.

I divide this Section into two sub-Sections :

- A. The relation, which the Association through its representatives bears to the Church and the outside public.
- B. The relation, which it bears to Missionaries in the Mission-Field.

I quite understand, that I am playing the part of a fiend in rushing into sacred regions, where Angels dare not tread, but I have no "arriére pensée," no personal predilections, or antipathies. I am well acquainted with the principles of administration, and have an eye to perceive the merits and demerits of a System, which has grown, as it were, by the influence of its environment. I feel convinced, that Reform is necessary. I proceed now to discuss

Sub-Section A. .

A voluntary Association, composed to a great degree of simpleminded and unworldly persons, male and female, contributes funds to create and carry on the affairs of a great Spiritual Empire in Foreign parts. I confine myself solely to the Church of England: I am well acquainted with the practices of the Church of Rome, and our Nonconformist Protestant brethren in England, and the independent Churches in Scotland, Ireland, the Continent of Europe, and the United States, but I have no space for such details.

The Church of England is represented by the following Associations, self-supporting and self-governing, owing Ecclesiastical obedience to the Archbishops and Bishops, but entirely independent of the State:

1. Society for the Propagation of the Gospel.
2. Church-Missionary-Society.
3. London-Jews.
4. South American.
5. Melanesian.
6. Universities' Missions to E. E. Africa, Calcutta, and Dehli.
7. Society for the Promotion of Christian Knowledge.
8. Rio Pongas, W. Africa.
9. Zulu-land, and possibly others, who will forgive me for not mentioning them.
10. Female Associations. (God bless them!)

I omit all notice of (1) attempts to proselytize other denominations of Christianity, (2) all Colonial Church-enterprises, (3) all sporadic efforts of good, but often very unwise, individuals, (4) all purely Educational and Training Institutions, (5) all Associations, in which Members of the Church of England act in concert with their Nonconformist brethren, of which blessed union I highly approve.

I did not hesitate, when the idea was put forth of superseding Associations by an administrative Board of Missions, representing the Church in its central entirety, to put forth a pamphlet against any such policy: my words were quoted at a subsequent Church-Congress, and the idea was dropped. I do not hesitate, however, to quote, what other persons put forth as their opinions on the merits of the Association, or Society.

Some very pregnant remarks occur in the *Missionary Review of all the World*, Jan. 1894, p. 119. I am not informed as to the name of the author.

" The 'Society' has become rich, tyrannical, never was very " spiritual, and was always unscriptural; it has a tendency to " Ecclesiasticism, and to spend *the largest reasonable amount of the* " *Church gifts on the smallest reasonable amount of service due.*

" The 'Society' has a standard different from that of the " Church. It has certain test-questions, which, if not directly " put to the Missionary, is answered by some inquisitor to the " satisfaction of the 'Society.' Qualification in heart and head " have little force here, if one of the questions is not answered " satisfactorily.

"It would be more economical for Congregations, or clusters of Congregations, to send out their Missionaries; it takes not less than 7 or 8 per cent. of the Society's receipts to manage the concern.

"The existence of the 'Society' is an obstacle in the way of the spread of the Kingdom. The native helpers, and workers, become dependent upon the various 'Societies'; the growth to self-support is very slow indeed. If the Missionary came to the people unsalaried, and representing nothing but the Cross of Christ, he could with more power, and grace, exhort the native believers to labour for themselves, that they may be a burden to no man. Very few Missionaries can explain with a clear countenance the words of Paul, that he worked with his own hand, that he might not be a burden.

"The 'Society' is a positive hindrance to self-support among the Native Churches. The 'Society' prohibits workers from acting without orders from headquarters, as that would be destruction of the rights, and the authority, of the 'Society.'

"I do not forget to make the distinction between the 'Society' and the 'Society'-brethren. I can easily conceive, how good brethren might be led away by the 'Society,' and by virtue of the relation they sustain to it, fall into error and injustice, to which they would not condescend if acting as individual brethren. This of itself exposes a danger not to be passed over lightly."

I wish to treat the subject impartially and judicially. The Association is represented (1) by a Committee of Managers, which will be commented upon in this Section; (2) by Deputations, to get in Subscriptions; (3) by a Financial Department, to record the income and expenditure; (4) by its Publications, to report progress and rouse interest. These three subjects will be commented upon in the three following Sections.

The Committee consists of Members and Secretaries. The Members receive absolutely nothing, no salary, and no fees, as in Insurance-Companies, no advantage whatever, except free copies of Publications, against which I entirely protest, as an abuse. They are elected, or rather co-opted, on which I shall have remarks to make. The Secretaries, as a rule, are paid Salaries not exceeding £500 per annum; the Honorary Secretary has no salary, and is of course a Member of the Committee, like any other Member.

I wish to make some preliminary remarks before I go into detail. In these days of self-laudation, and the easy building up of a transitory reputation, I would warn all friends of Missions to "Beware of setting up your own Society in the place of Christ, and doing worship and sacrifice to your own net, and bringing incense to your own drag: if the Lord's work be accomplished,

" what matter by whom it is done? If the Lord's work can
" only be accomplished by the death of a Missionary, and the
" destruction of a Society, be it so: it was a means to an end:
" let that end be accomplished."

Next comes the difficulty felt in State-Offices, and in Secular and Scientific Societies, to repress the inordinate power, claimed by the permanent salaried officials against the Members of Council, who go out by rotation. I quote the following from the pages of the *Times* regarding Secular Associations: "This
" arrangement only adds to the power, which naturally accrues
" to the permanent officers. No matter how able and honest
" they may be, and I have not said one word in derogation of
" the ability and honesty of any one of them, they naturally and
" inevitably use that excessive power in accordance with their
" personal idiosyncrasies, from which no man can escape, and
" under the influence of motives, which, when in long and
" persistent operation, deflect the course of the best men.

" The President, after discussing possible ways of giving
" ordinary councillors greater power as against permanent
" officials, declined to commit himself to any definite proposition,
" and added : ' But the great confidence, which the Society has,
" especially of late years, placed in its more permanent officers,
" and the power, which naturally accrues to them from the
" comparatively short tenure of office by the other members of
" council, appear to me to be points, of which the Society should
" not lose sight.' This is just about as strong a pronouncement,
" as could be made in the circumstances upon any matter
" affecting the management of the Society."

The next danger is illustrated by another passage culled from the *Times* with regard to the management of Hospitals.

" A strong objection to the constitution of the proposed
" Board might be made to rest upon the extent, to which it
" would provide a happy hunting-ground for faddists, a class of
" people, who cluster thickly about every kind of charitable
" work, and of whom it may be said, generally speaking, that
" they neither do good themselves, nor suffer it to be done
" by others." Secretaries are famous for Fads.

The constitution of all Missionary-Committees is not the same: the same feature is exhibited in Hospital-Committees. I again quote the *Times*: "Some donors contribute to St.
" George's, because they approve of the weekly Board, open to
" all Governors, by which the affairs of the hospital are managed,
" and to which committees can only report. Others approve
" of, and support, an almost absolute personal government, such
" as that, which exists at St. Bartholomew's, at Guy's, or at
" St. Thomas's. Others approve of a plan, which prevails at
" many hospitals, under which the general body of subscribers

" submit themselves to a ruling Committee, and which combines
" all the weaknesses of a despotism with all the weaknesses of
" a democracy. Out of these main differences in modes of
" government, many minor differences in organization become
" developed."

I also quote from the *Times* the account of an investigation into a most unsatisfactory case, which seems to describe in its salient features the mode of procedure of at least one Missionary-Committee, with whose mode of conducting business I am very familiar. I have only made slight changes to bring out the resemblance.

" What did the Committee do?: It used to sit every Monday
" morning, and receive reports from the Secretary, the Solicitor,
" and the Accountant. Their statements were considered, and
" discussed, and the officers were instructed to act according to
" the terms ordered by the Committee after having heard the
" reports.

" The Committee consists of all the members of the Board?:
" Yes.

" Over 40?: Sixty members, including myself.

" And the attendance is often as numerous as 50?: Very often.

" Does it strike you, that that is hardly the kind of body suited
" to deal with such a matter as the management of a great
" concern, and the details connected with it?: The officers
" report to the Committee.

" Does not that necessarily leave the matter in the hands of
" the officers?: I do not think so. They make their report to
" the Committee. Their reports receive the greatest possible care.

" But surely a body of 50 persons cannot go into the details
" in the same way as a small body would do?: There was a
" difference of opinion. Some of my colleagues preferred a
" smaller body, but the majority the larger body.

" The result seems to show, that the matter was left in the
" hands of the officers of the Board, who did very much what
" they liked?: I do not think so.

" Perhaps 'did what they liked' is too strong an expression,
" but at all events they did a good many things, that the Board
" was totally unconscious of?: I am sorry to say, that this
" investigation shows that they did.

" Do you think that a body of 50 people selected the best
" machinery for managing?: The attendance of the Board is
" very good, but there are not always 50 members present at
" 11 o'clock, when the Committee sits.

" But sometimes there would be one set of members, and on
" other occasions another set?: No. Some members, as at the
" House of Commons, attend to their duties thoroughly, and
" others do not.

"Still there were usually 30 or 40 members present, as far as I can gather?: Generally."

In the smaller Church-Societies there is no trouble: in the Melanesian and Universities' Missions the Bishop is, in fact, the autocrat-ruler. It is in the Society for the Propagation of the Gospel, and the Church-Missionary-Society, only that the action of the Committee is felt. For the first time in its history this year there has been a contest for seats on the Executive Committee of the Society for the Propagation of the Gospel, which has all the power: the General Committee, which all Members can attend, are mere dummies, and often doddering old men: it is not even reported to them, what the Executive has done, or proposes to do: here we have a Committee reduced to the very lowest level of mere existence: clearly this is an error in one direction: no doubt the affairs are conducted wisely by the Venetian Council, which sits with closed doors, but a breath of popular opinion ought to be allowed to fan the cheeks of that august body. The Secretary, and his Assistants, act with great reserve, and take no forward part; the latter neither vote, nor open their mouths: all that the subscribers can do is to ventilate any possible grievance, and submit their resolution to the kind consideration of the Venetian Council. The *Church-Times* remarks, that the two outsiders were pledged to Reform, and that it is a healthy sign, that there is an increased interest outside in the concerns of the Society.

Not many miles off, in another street, you can enter the Committee-Room of another Society, the Church-Missionary-Society. The Committee of Correspondence consists of scores of members, lay and clerical: the Secretaries, every one of whom has votes, do not fall short of eight. The qualification of a clerical member of the Committee is an annual subscription of half-a-guinea. Every measure relating to the Mission-Field goes in the first instance to a small elected sub-Committee for each large geographical area: there the subject is thrashed out without the forms of regular debate, and a resolution arrived at: this is submitted to the Correspondence-Committee, the majority of whom, though not so well qualified as the sub-Committee, are still capable of forming an opinion: the matter then for the third time is submitted to a kind of $\delta\hat{\eta}\mu o\varsigma$, called the General Committee, consisting of scores of ten-and-sixpenny parsons, country-clergymen, who have dropped in for a few hours at a kind of Ecclesiastical Club, and doddering old lay members, who crawl in for a short time, and it is in their power to cancel, or modify, the careful decision of competent men. Nothing can be more unwise than this arrangement. I have repeatedly protested. "Magna est vis inertiæ."

Then comes the question as between the Members of the

Committee, and the paid Secretaries. These last choose to usurp the status of a "Secretariat," or a corporate body: of course Mr. Venn, Mr. Wright, and the present Honorary Secretary, are as much members of the Committee as any other member: I have been for a very long term of years Honorary Secretary of the Royal Asiatic Society, and no one would dispute my right; but the paid Secretaries, neither in Scientific Societies, nor any Religious Society, have a right to vote, or debate: their duty is to make statements, and answer questions, and it is a mere usurpation on their part to do more than that. The Secretaries of Hospital-Committees, of the Boards of Guardians, of the Bench of Magistrates, are Medical Men or Solicitors, yet none of them ever intervene in the debate, or presume to vote: the fact, that they are paid servants, bars them. This is a fundamental error, and should at once be corrected.

To a letter of Mr. Venn, the honoured Honorary Secretary of the Society, when it was a comparatively small concern, this error must be traced.

"It is more than half a century since I first took my seat in
" the Committee. Perhaps I may, then, be allowed a few words
" at the close of so long a period, which comprises nearly two
" generations of men. In such a work as this it is absolutely
" necessary, that a large and generous confidence should be
" reposed in the Secretaries. There can be no practical danger
" of their confidence being disappointed, as long as the Com-
" mittee shall uphold the principle of equality of responsibility
" among the Secretaries, and the practice of forming their
" decisions by general agreement rather than by casting votes.
" The relation of Secretaries to the Committee is not that of
" Secretaries, or Clerks to a Parochial Board, or an ordinary Com-
" pany, but rather that of Secretaries to a Scientific Institution,
" or of Secretaries of State to a Cabinet Council. The Secre-
" taries of our Society are the originators of the measures to be
" passed, the chief authorities on its principles and practice,
" and must often act upon their own discretion in cases of
" emergency, and in confidential interviews with Church, or
" State authorities. At the same time I must bear my testimony,
" that this large confidence reposed in the Secretaries is not
" inconsistent with the independence of judgment and ultimate
" supremacy on the part of the Committee. I could give
" innumerable instances to show, that the Committee never
" resign their opinions in any important point without a frank
" discussion of the difference, and that great principles are
" never sacrificed in deference to the authority, age, or ex-
" perience of others."

Mr. Venn had been the nursing-father of the Society for many years, and was an able administrator: it is recorded of him, that he never voted himself: of course he had become a benevolent despot, but the Committee, which used to consist of a few persons gathering round him, had grown into a strong, independent body. As a sample of the pupillage, in which they were held, no Agenda-paper was laid before the Committee: the Secretaries brought forward such business as they thought fit: the correspondence of the Missionary was only accessible to the Secretary: it was only by a struggle that these elementary reforms were gradually arrived at.

Another feature of the Committee is, that it is composed of men with their sons, and sons-in-law, and their brothers, in the Mission-Field: it is difficult to raise the voice against an agent without offending a Secretary or a Member: the Committee itself is a great-family-preserve of brothers-in-law: I have sometimes looked round the room to work out the relationship of each member. I have sat on many Boards and Councils for the settling of affairs of the greatest magnitude, but no secular work could be properly conducted under the conditions of such a Missionary-Committee: it lasts sometimes eight hours: part of the time there is a crowd, and a dozen sub-Committees talking in each corner of the Room: after luncheon it is difficult to maintain a quorum: the persons the least qualified make the longest speeches, and are heard the most frequently: while scores sit on, and utter no words: (Bless them for their silence!): perhaps one of the Secretaries gives a kind of lecture, as from a Professor's chair: it must be recollected, that this Committee is not, like the House of Commons, a deliberative body, but like a Board of Education, or Guardians of the Poor, an executive body.

I must in justice throw in a little colour on the other side. I have been for more than forty years a witness, and a student, of the conduct of human affairs, but I never realized such purity of motive, such simplicity of conduct, and on the whole such practical wisdom, as is found in such a body. There is always a feeling of tenderness, almost too sentimental, on the part of a Committee towards their Missionaries: on the other hand, the wild complaints, and often unreasonable requests, of the Missionary, which would distress a Director, roll up like the waves of the Atlantic against the impersonal Committee, and go off in noise. The Missionary would no doubt prefer leaving the direction of his affairs in the hands of a Committee rather than be at the mercy of a Director. Committees ought to consist both of ordained and lay members, and their duties should be divided: the control of the Finance should be left exclusively to the lay members, while the selection of candidates for employment should be reserved to the ordained members.

There are always two alternatives open to an Association. An influential moderate-sized Committee is decidedly the best machinery, as it never dies, and is composed of such a diversity of experiences and talents, as conduce to good Government. If again there exists in the Association men of independent means, and good capacity, able and willing to be unpaid Secretaries, and as it were Prime Ministers of the Committee, nothing could be better. But sometimes the material fails for an efficient Committee, and paid Secretaries have to be secured. It is then quite open to the Association to entrust the Executive to high-minded and efficient paid Directors, responsible only to the Association, or they can appoint the same calibre of men to be paid Secretaries to carry out the decisions of the Committee. Both these Methods have their advantages, and corresponding disadvantages. Under a Directorship is a more defined policy, a greater control, greater economy of time, but Death, Decay of Faculties, and the human infirmities of Arrogance, and Egoism, have to be reckoned upon. A Committee leaves no room for such faults, but there is a terrible waste of time in useless talk of ill-informed members, vacillation of purpose, laxity of control, and then the Secretaries, or *one or two pushing ones*, attempt, and succeed in their attempt, to wield the power of the Director without the responsibility, and this has none of the advantages, and all the disadvantages, of both systems.

For the last fifteen years my life has been from week to week a daily tramp from the Church-Missionary-Society to the Bible-House, from the Society for Promoting Christian Knowledge to the Society for the Propagation of the Gospel, from the Bench of Magistrates to the Board of Guardians, from the Council of the Royal Geographical Society to the Council of the Royal Asiatic Society, from the Local Political Committee to the Anti-Slavery-Society-Committee, in addition to innumerable temporary or smaller ones, such as Organizing Committees, General Purposes-Committees, Subject-Committees of Missionary Conferences, etc., Committees of the Spanish and Portuguese Church, or Rio Pongas-Mission in W. Africa; yet in none have I found the position of the paid Secretaries so markedly, and really objectionably, prominent as in the Church-Missionary-Society. A Secretary is appointed on a salary to do a particular duty, hold his tongue, edit the Periodicals, keep the accounts, but not to get up and speak without being called upon by the Chair on every possible subject, just because he is a self-asserting individual. Those Secretaries, who remain quiet and mind their own business, have greater personal influence, as the trusted, experienced, and honoured, friends of the Committee. There is no peculiarity in the work of the Church-Missionary-Society to justify it. It would not be well to fill a Committee with dummies to vote the decision, previously settled upon, of a paid Secretariat. This is a stage lower than the Venetian Council of the Society for the Propagation of the Gospel.

I have remarked with freedom on the features of the Committees of the two great Societies, both of which I honour, and I do so in the interest of those Societies. The constitution of one requires expansion, of the other contraction. One perhaps is too staid and cold, the other too sensational and warm. Of the Church-Missionary-Society it may be remarked with extreme gratitude, that it is quite ready to surrender, if necessary, some portion of the Church-Order, which we inherit from the Mediæval Centuries, but will not surrender anything, that leads to the saving of souls, which is the very object, and hope, and joy, of its existence. Moreover it has no Ecclesiastical bandage over its eyes, and recognises great facts, and extends the right hand of friendship and sympathy to all Protestant Societies, whether British or Foreign, without reference to Denomination, remembering the words of our Lord: "Other sheep I have, who are not of this fold."

Another difficulty, which will press more each decade, is that the Church-Missionary-Society is getting too large to be managed by one Committee: there are two remedies: (1) decentralize; (see sub-Section B) (2) have two Associations and two Committees. When Secretaries are multiplied to a dozen, one of two things will certainly happen: either the work of the Society will be sub-divided, and a difference of practice will arise, or in the strain of each Secretary and a certain number of the Members, to keep themselves informed of the whole, the work will be scamped: there will be a continuous unhappy struggle to keep abreast of the work, and no time for quiet counsel, and unofficial exchange of views.

I have often reflected on what should be the model-constitution of a Missionary-Society-Committee: it differs from a Secular Society in this: if I had had to deal with an official environment, such as that of the Church-Missionary-Society, and the Society for the Propagation of the Gospel, in the Boards of Hospitals, Guardians, or Magistrates, I should have formed a party, and fought; replaced the Secretaries, got rid at the next Election of the opposing Members, or have been got rid of myself. But in doing the Lord's work, such as Missions, Religious Conferences, etc., etc., we cannot use carnal weapons: In old days in the Church-Missionary-Society I have witnessed stand-up fights between the Prime Minister and Chancellor of the Exchequer, and some Members of the Committee were notoriously on the subject of their own fads combative and intolerant: "Non tali auxilio:" We may be thankful, that that phase has passed away: if the Opposition had succeeded in outvoting the Honorary

Prime Minister, he would have resigned: who would take his office ? as to turning out the paid Secretaries, it could not be thought of: ten years ago a paid Secretary was dismissed, and individual Members of the Committee had to support him out of their own pockets for two years till he was got off to America, for he was entirely without resources: his eyes were blind to his own untenable position till the day came, when he was got rid of to the great relief of all.

I proceed now to discuss

Sub-Section B.

Still more difficult is the relationship of the Home-Committee to the Local Conference-Committee, or Council, and the Missionaries, who compose it in the Field. In some Missionary-Societies the Home-Committee exercises a despotic, and often injudicious, rule; on the other hand, I have met Missionaries in the Field, who stated, that they allowed the Home-Committee no power of interference: Their duty, according to my informant, was to supply Money and Men, and leave everything else to those, who being out in the Field knew best. Thus in some cases the Bishop in his Diocese, the Presbytery, or the Mission-Conference settle everything, and, if attempts were made to draw the reins tight, would break away into separate Organizations. No doubt there is the greatest safety in the middle course: those, who hold the Purse-strings, sooner or later must have the control. But a wise policy suggests great liberty to the local bodies within certain rules. The necessity of preparing an annual budget of expenditure will always remind the local Committee of their helplessness in a death-struggle, unless they have a strong home-party behind them. I cannot think it wise in a Home-Committee deputing a Secretary, or Inspector, to visit the Mission-Field: it creates a bad feeling: if any particular information be required, it is better to ask the brethren in the Field to depute one of their number as a delegate to the Home-Committee. In some desperate contingency, such as, when in South Africa misguided Missionaries took away the life of an African, it might be justifiable to send men of weight from home. The Missionaries have experience, the Inspector has none. In Secular Matters, such as the administration of India, the high officials, who manage the great Provinces and Districts, would not tolerate the appearance of a Jack-in-office from the India-House in London, and the Secretary of State is too wise to have recourse to such an expedient. The Opium-Commission of 1893 was merely a snare of the Fowler to put a stop to an unhealthy, and ridiculous, agitation.

The fact is, that a much larger delegation of authority must be made by the Home-Committee to the Local Committees.

Nothing is so dangerous and injurious as over-strained centralization: the little men, and busybodies, who compose the Home-Committee are jealous of surrendering to an old-established Mission that degree of independence, to which they are entitled: it is not proposed to confer the same, or similar, powers on all Mission-Fields, but to class the Fields according to their peculiarities and degree of progress, as the Colonial Office has classed the Colonies. I have seen the work in the Field: I say to the Home-Committee, "Trust your men": remember that they are all spiritual men: there is no danger with them of peculation or dishonesty: Mission-work has got to a level far above such possibilities: what the Local men lack is often Wisdom, and a wider knowledge than their environment supplies, and many of them are babes in Finance. There are signs of murmuring in the camp, while there is a congestion of work in the Home-Committee: the great motto is, "Divide et Impera." As I described a few pages back, the cakes are baked three times over, and burnt, in the Committee: the Local Authorities are crying out for fresh bread of their own baking.

The conditions of graduated Home Rule in the Mission-Field must be, that

(1) They do not exceed their Budget-allowance.
(2) They undertake of their own volition no new work, which entails a recurring expenditure, for which they cannot provide in the Field, for they have large local resources in some Fields.
(3) They make the Native Church feel the dignity of independence, and become self-supporting. Anything short of this is mere playing with the great duty of Evangelization: a village of rice-Christians is a disgrace, not a glory. Paul the Apostle is quite clear on this subject.
(4) Grants for salaries must not be diverted to other purposes. They must keep clear of the epidemic of brick and mortar, which attacks weak emotional minds of those, who have the Church architectural tastes of an old rich country. The souls of the congregation compose the Church of Christ, not the brick and mortar-walls.
(5) They must be prepared to share in the years of tightness, as well as of abundance, of the Home-Committee.
(6) They must make a proper rendition of accounts: frightful deficiencies are sometimes disclosed on the death, or withdrawal, of a spiritual agent: but it is the same in Great Britain. It is not sufficient to be honest, but so to act, that the world may be convinced of your honesty. There was trouble some years ago about a Secretary in the Church-Missionary-Society, and I

was conversing with our late President, the Earl of Chichester, on the subject, and he remarked, that the same thing had happened in another case twenty years before.

(7) If high-handed individuals on the Local Committee defy the Home-authorities, their delegated powers must be withdrawn, and they themselves invited to withdraw, for the Home-Committee is the sole Trustee of the funds collected in Great Britain, and has the sole responsibility of accounting to its supporters, who know the Members of the Committee, but are entirely ignorant of the local Agents.

But in the Field, in addition to the Local Committee, which is a creature of the Home-Committee, there exists the Bishop of the Diocese. Now there are Dioceses *and* Dioceses; there are Bishops *and* Bishops. The purely-Missionary-Dioceses, such as Melanesia, Falkland-Islands, East Equatorial Africa, and such, have free hands. Here the Bishop must know better than the Committee, for all things are new. Another group of Bishops are very improperly paid by the State from taxation of the non-Christian subjects of Her Majesty. A third group is paid partially by contributions from the Missionary-Societies; a fourth group is paid entirely by the Society, which has a voice in recommending. The Society for the Propagation of the Gospel invariably works through the Bishop as a matter of course; the Church-Missionary-Society appoints the Bishop to be the Chairman of the Local Committee at its own pleasure. With great and wise Bishops, to whichever school of thought they belong, there is no difficulty: it is the ignorant, egoistic, self-willed man, that gives trouble: and such persons, to the great injury of Mission-work, do exist.

The reorganization of the Constitution of the two great Societies is a " sine quâ non " of future progress. Secretaries receiving salary must be reduced to their proper position: if it be asked how this can be managed, go to the Bible-House, and see: nothing can be better than the practice there. Theirs is a worldwide Empire, and purely Missionary: they disburse more than two hundred thousand pounds per annum. No ordained Clergymen, or Minister, is admitted to the elected Committee, but those, who are elected, attend, and insensibly each group attends to that portion of the work, for which his professional or acquired gifts qualify him. Thus, some look after the Finance, others after the Administration abroad by the numerous agents of the Society: some attend to the details of paper, printing, and binding: a fourth set throw themselves into the great question of the languages, to which the Word of God is to be entrusted. The Secretaries, men of great ability, occupy their proper position: there are no tedious speeches from Members or Secretaries. The work done is done in a spiritual way, and business-habits, and specialities of acquired knowledge, are sanctified by consecration to the greatest Manufactory, and Commerce, that the world has ever known. Old worn-out members of the Committee, lay or clerical, should not be re-elected. I made my bow at the age of seventy, set a good example, and withdrew, and was content with my sixteen other Committees, Councils, and Boards: it is not edifying to see decaying remnants of vitality on the benches of a Committee, which administers the affairs of a spiritual Kingdom: let there be an infusion of new blood every year by a stern enforcement of the number-of-attendances rule, and let no attendance count, which commences after midday and ends before four P.M.: let the number of three great Geographical sub-Committees be maintained, and their hands strengthened: let the number of the Correspondence-Committee be reduced, and be annually refreshed by striking out of worn-out, or incompetent, members, or the fathers, or fathers-in-law, or brothers, of Missionaries in that particular Field, and the introduction of fresh and mature zeal and ability: let the General Committee, or Assembly of Dummies, be merely a Court of Record, and Appeal, resembling the General Committee of the Society for Promoting Christian Knowledge, where the work of the sub-Committees passes under review, and can be challenged, and new Motions introduced: the third baking of the Committee-cake under the present system, before an audience almost entirely ignorant of the principles of Missions in general, or the details of the particular case, is a miserable folly. In the Society for the Propagation of the Gospel the General Committee has fallen to a still lower platform of degradation, and is not even informed of the work done in the previous month. Old Clergy come in, sit round, and grin, while idle forms are gone through, followed, however, by an admirable address by a Missionary from the Field, which is most enjoyable, and worth the trouble of a long walk. In the Society for Promoting Christian Knowledge, and the Church-Missionary-Society, the General Committee is at least informed of what has been done: the Society for the Propagation of the Gospel throws a veil over its proceedings. In the Committee of the Bible-Society every Member is acquainted with what has previously occurred for the simple reason, that he took part in what has taken place at a previous meeting. I wish finally to point out, that a badly-constructed Committee is merely a mask, behind which high-handed Secretaries, who pull the strings, can do just what they like. We require something real: not a Venetian Council of Nine, as the Society for the

Propagation of the Gospel, not an ignorant δῆμος in the Agora, as the Church-Missionary-Society, with a fluctuating body of hearers, like the Members of a Club who are here, and are gone, while someone is talking, and finally the Chairman should have a Bell: the "Kakoethes loquendi" is largely developed in a Missionary-gathering: few have the grace given to them to store up their thoughts among the things not said: or, if they have nothing to say, to leave it unsaid, or if they have only the conventional two words to utter, to remember, that "Brevity is the Soul of Wit." The Clerical Members are so uncontrolled in their Pulpits, that they carry the bad habit of saying the same thing twice over into the Committee-Room.

The aspirations of the Local Committee of a Mission-Field have been voiced by one, who is singularly competent. Henry Perkins, the son of a Missionary of the Society for the Propagation of the Gospel at Cawnpore, and born in the Mission, gained his post in the Indian Civil-Service by competition, and held the highest posts: he was at one time my personal assistant, and I feel indebted to him for the example of consistent love for Missions, which he evinced thirty-five years ago: when he retired from Office on his Pension, he had the grace vouchsafed to him to join the Church-Missionary-Society's Mission at Amritsar at his own charge: in 1889, he printed remarks on the subject above discussed: his experiences were from the Field, mine were from the Committee-Room, and we agreed. He remarks, that the supervision of the Home-Committee was too minute; that an army in the field cannot be governed by a general in an armchair in Salisbury Square; that the Home-Committee is hindering the Lord's work with the sincerest wish to help it. He suggests a scheme of decentralization, which will give more autonomy in the Field, for it is impossible for a Committee 8,000 miles off (even if an efficient body, which the Church-Missionary-Society-Committee certainly is not), to keep itself acquainted with the details of each one of its Missions in the wide world. The Home-Committee, (of which in 1881 he himself was a member,) has no full knowledge, on which to found a judgment. Members come in, when the matter is half discussed, and vote.

In his opinion final power of decision should be given to the Geographical sub-Committees, with only a power of appeal or challenge in one of the superior Committees, whichever survives, and one or other ought to be got rid of. He then tells us of the difficulty of getting together a Local Committee in the Field, owing to the distances, and the press of business of every man in India: he makes a suggestion for a new Constitution, and points out the danger of the appearance "of a strong man with a Fad": and they are the peculiar fungi, which come into existence on the branches and trunk of great "Religious

Societies." "Goodness without wisdom" is the name of those fungi. Such men are misfortunes in every part of the world. Strange to say he is not opposed to a Missionary being on a Secular Committee, whose chief duty is to look to the drains of a great city, where he dwells: in this I can see, that the odour of his past official life, when he had to do such work, still clings to the old human vessel: and he expresses this opinion on the same page, in which he deplores, that the hard-worked Missionary has not "more time for a quiet retirement with God": we all feel in middle, and old, age how sad life would be without that rich blessing, and yet how distressing it would be to be interrupted in the study of the Bible by a summons to inspect the Parish-Sewers. He sums up his really noble paper (and he has left India in his old age) with the suggestion, that a freer system of administration on a few broad principles, carefully applied to details, would relieve everyone of useless correspondence, and profitless discussion, facilitate true work, and minimize friction. Oh that we were wise, and considered these things! but there is a blindness in Associations of men, secular and spiritual, until a shaking of dry bones takes place, till a Bishop is killed, or a promising Mission, like that in the Niger-Delta, is destroyed by the blind, and wayward, folly of an uninstructed Committee, driven on by impulsive Secretaries, determined to have their own way.

Perhaps the writer of these remarks may be asked: why did not you during the long years of your Committee-life urge Reform on your Committee? It was throwing words away, and I gave up the attempt.

My last proposition in Committee was, that experienced women should be eligible, if proposed, to a seat in Committee, which, considering the evidenced capacity of numerous women, the vast number of female Agents, exceeding that of the male, in the service of the Church-Missionary-Society, and the great fact, that half the population of the world consists of females, was not wholly unreasonable. It was met by a fat old clergyman, who knew as much about Mission-work as he did of Astronomy or Chemistry, and who evidently had more of the conventional old woman in him than the thoughtful male, moving the previous question, which was carried by a forty-parson power of ten-and-sixpenny clergymen. And yet we all know, that this measure must very soon be carried. I rose from my seat, and have never darkened the door of Salisbury Square since. I had twice published confidential pamphlets suggesting reforms: one in 1880, "Thoughts on our mode of conducting business"; a second in 1887, "Suggestions for four organic changes." My first thought was, that the Secretaries should be reduced to be *Ministers*, not *Rectors*, of the Committee, and I think so still: they should have no vote, and no license to debate: no Reform has been made. I suggested and pressed the subject of Geographical sub-Committees, in order that documents from the Field might be read: this Reform was made. The other suggestions were more or less attended to, but of the suggestions made in 1887 most are incorporated in this Essay, as none have been attended to; indeed, one Member suggested a vote of censure upon me for having ventured to criticize so perfect an administration. A Missionary-Committee is the last refuge of old Tories, and being so, it will not long escape the scorching light of Public opinion thrown upon it by the Devotion, Faith, and Intelligence, of this Progressive Age: old things must pass away, and sweep the old fogies with them.

3. THE DEPUTATIONS.

I must now allude to the accepted machinery for raising Funds, and the scientific organization spread over Great Britain and Ireland, making the whole transaction very secular, very formal, very business-like, and very unlike Spirituality. The Ministers of the Churches are to blame. The *duty* of conveying the Gospel to Regions Beyond should be preached systematically week by week from the Pulpit, and enforced from the Platform periodically, by accurate information of the progress of the Work. Every member of the Church should supply himself with Missionary-Publications: they need the food, supplied by the Committee, quite as much as the Committee needs their subscriptions. A spiritual stimulus, and uplifting of flagging hearts, are wanted. Men will never care about matters, of which they know nothing: they cannot know unless they are informed. It gives Life, and Love, to a Church to know, and desire to know, how the Lord's work progresses among the Heathen: if the workers are in trouble, it melts the heart in sympathy; if in triumph, it rouses a Spirit of thankfulness: both circumstances are remembered in private and family-prayer. We read with long-drawn breath the fortunes of the Queen's soldiers, because we are good citizens: why not have similar feelings for the Lord's soldiers, if we are good Christians? Missions to the Heathen are a component part of the Whole Duty of Man, and should not be treated as a fancy, a fad, a something extraneous from the necessities of a good life. How much more interesting would be a stirring picture of Missionary Progress, than the conventional drone, which has reduced the power of the Pulpit so low? When the great Societies spend respectively £8,000 and £10,000 per annum on Deputations, there should be some result. Now one-half of the Annual Income comes in without reference to Preacher, or Deputation.

Established friends of the Society send their contribution as a matter of duty: of the remaining moiety, one half would come in on receipt of a half-penny reminder by post: it is for the remaining half moiety, or quarter, of the whole, that the whole struggle and expenditure takes place, and the percentage should be thrown upon that quarter only.

Many of the Deputations unite the arguments of the Gospel with the manner of the Water-Rate-Collector: it is the daughter of the horse-leech, that we seem to be listening to, " Give, Give!" Instead of giving the information, expounding the motives, interesting the hearers with the magnificent story, and leaving the duty of collecting to the Local Committee, ridiculous comparisons are made betwixt the vast sums spent in Liquor, Tobacco, Milliners' Bills, Foreign Wars, and the cost of living, and the small amount contributed to Missionary-objects. Such arguments are more calculated to offend than to conciliate. What shall be said of the frightful statistical tables, pinned to the walls in white, black, and red, colours, showing the preponderant number of Heathens, and the paucity of Christians? tall stately columns represent the non-Christian world, and a mere ninepin the Christian. The danger is, lest the sceptic should turn the argument round, and say, " Here we are in the " Nineteenth Century of the Christian era, and not only have " we gained no ground, but we have lost, and the Mahometan " Religion is seven hundred years later in date, and so much " more successful, and a whole family of new Religions has " come into existence, as a direct consequence of the contact " of the Morality of the Gospel, with the Traditions and " Religious Conceptions of the Old-World-Faiths."

Then stupid calculations are made of the amount of people's income and their subscriptions, holding them up to a kind of obloquy. What becomes of the right hand not knowing what the left has given, when the Deputation wants accurate information of what each man does ? And of what profit is the late onslaught on the so-called "Titled Classes" ? It is nothing new (I Cor. i, 26). It is a miserable alliance with Radical snobbism.

Quiet, undemonstrative Christians are vexed by the perpetual calls on them: they give the miserable shilling to get rid of the trouble; the people, who go about with cards, are a nuisance: it is a bad phase of religious life: all, who are in earnest, set apart a portion of their income; no blessing can accompany money given without any heart, just to get out of the door of the church, or assembly-room, respectably. It turns to dross in the Treasury of the Society, and, having no enduring blessing in it, it is got rid of in the pay of an extra Clerk, in the Railway-fares of the Deputations, or the first-class steamer-passage of a Negro. It might just as well have been left in the purses of the contributors, as far as having the remotest influence on Evangelization. The list of subscribers, given in such detail in the Report, doubling its bulk, is a reproach to the Christian Churches, and to the Christian character of the donors. What can they want to see their names in print for? It is like the trumpet sounded before the hypocrite, when he gave his alms, condemned by our Lord.

Above all things it is desirable to keep the actual Pounds, Shillings, and Pence-view in the background. What can be more depressing, or opposed to spirituality, than the cries from the Platform, as at a gathering in Cumberland: "Another Ten Pound Note; another Five Pound"; and so on. And where is boasting? It is excluded. From the East, and the West, and the South, come up tidings of terrible failures, fearful blots. If the enemy knew our shortcomings, as well as our friends, where should we be? I am afraid to express my own feelings. I substitute those of an aged friend of the Church-Missionary-Society: " It is not easy to exaggerate the grandeur of the opportunity, " or the power of unfaithfulness. To-day we must do the work; " to-morrow will be too late. Let us realize this very great " opportunity, and so go forward. God grant, that these things " may be brought home to us to-day, and that we may go forth " from this hall as from the presence of the Lord himself, " touched with the flame of the Holy Spirit; not boasting of " what we have done; not in the spirit of the Ephesians of old, " crying aloud, " Great is the Church-Missionary-Society "; not " boasting of our crowded platforms, our large meetings, our " bountiful subscriptions, but impressed more and more with " the thought, that very much more yet remaineth to be possessed, " that the Fields are everywhere white unto the harvest, and " praying that God will quicken our halting steps, will accept " our offerings, and arise and do great things by our humble " means to the glory of His Holy Name."

The exposure of the idols of the poor Heathen to be laughed at, of curios brought from foreign countries, of children dressed up as natives of the East, of blind old men brought on the platform to interest; such things are thoroughly wrong, and a secular lecture on foreign cities, nations, and customs, is a serious mistake. The object of Deputation-Addresses is to warm up the feelings of supporters, educate a Missionary-spirit, correct mistaken impressions as to policy, inform those interested of progress, evidence sympathy with the fallen races, and to do what Paul and Barnabas did eighteen centuries ago: " Rehearse all that God had done, and how he had opened the door of Faith to the Gentiles."

Great restraint should be maintained on the Platform, and in the Pulpit, not only not to say what is not true, but to abstain from uttering sheer nonsense. There may be said to be three objects: (1) To stimulate. (2) To inform. (3) To take counsel. But in no possible case to talk twaddle, repeat common-place expressions, or air Quixotic notions. And how culpable are those, who encourage their relations, or friends in a country-town, to pass frothy resolutions calling for Expeditions, and Annexations, and Protectorates, and "Jingo" generally! Is the Gospel of Christ to be preached by such methods? We are a great, strong, self-asserting, arrogant, Nation; let us restrict those qualities to our Commercial, and Political, trans-actions, and conduct our Mission-work as simple Christians: we can expect no blessing on Gospel-teaching, when in close contact with Calico-bales, and Rifles, not to say tuns of Liquor, cases of firearms, barrels of gunpowder, and Maxim-guns, as at U-Ganda.

No subject can be more pregnant, more susceptible of varied treatment, with wider scope, furnishing room for every kind of eloquence, and full of such romantic Poetry. What Epic Poem of ancient or modern days could be more full of moving scenes, and varying fortunes, if the speaker were only worthy of the subject? A spiritual tone should dominate. If a smile be raised, it should be one of sympathy and love towards the Missionary, and the poor Heathen people. There should be no rude jokes, or depreciatory remarks, or condemnation of great Governments, denunciation of a great Commerce, or sneers at rival denominations. The heart should indeed go forth towards the poor Heathen. Their rude conceptions of a Power greater than themselves show, that God has not left Himself without witness in their hearts. They recognise an environment of supernatural agencies, because something tells them, that God is very near them. They see Him in their blessings and their troubles, and they try to propitiate Him. In some things they are better than we are.

Some Deputation-speakers try to get up a Church-party-feeling, or to make a hit against the Nonconformists: how unwise and un-Christian it is to do so on such an occasion as converting the Jew, the Mahometan, or the Pagan. Hear what the Bishop of Bombay says:

"Beware, again, of that miserable so-called humour, which
" finds in the conventionalities of a religious party material for
" a most invidious kind of sneering. Suppose that it be ever so
" true, that the phraseology of a particular school of goodness
" has shown a tendency to become uninvitingly stereotyped;
" that we have acquired certain associations with certain phrases,
" which prejudice us against those who make use of them; it is
" still true that, to the members of those circles, they embody

"experiences and aspirations among the noblest, that ever
"thrilled human bosoms. In the training of those whom we
"love, and in the expression of our own deepest feelings, let us,
"by all means, employ words and phrases, which are free from
"the savour of conventionality. But let us treat with the most
"reverent respect the honoured phrases, which helped to save
"the Church of England from being smothered in a worse con-
"ventionality, the conventionality of sheer deadness and in-
"difference. If you associate Missionary-effort with such
"conventions, then ask yourself what this really means. It
"means, that Evangelicals did the work, when others stood
"still, or attempted little. If it be associated with evangelical
"conventionality, it was at least done by evangelical fervour.
"Let us respect it then with shame for our own shortcomings."

Hear what a Nonconformist writer says on this subject:

"Much also depends on those, who speak and preach on
"behalf of Missions. The sermons should be far more what
"they profess to be, an exposition of Missionary-principles, a
"narration of Missionary-facts and incidents, or an enforcement
"of Missionary-motives and aspirations. So with speeches
"great care should be taken to ascertain what kind of
"information is most useful; and the trivial, absurd, and
"sensational, should be altogether eschewed. Ministers should
"give Missions a very prominent place in their public and
"private teaching. The claims of God to universal love and
"obedience; the power of the Gospel to give eternal life to the
"Heathen; the loving desire of the Saviour for a larger Empire
"of redeemed and happy souls; the grandeur of prophetic
"hopes and anticipations; the sad state of the Heathen, and
"the duty of Christians to do their utmost to bring the whole
"world nearer to God, all justify and demand a large share of
"attention in the pulpit. The great cause is worthy of:

"1. A Missionary-sermon preached once a quarter by every
"minister.

"2. A Missionary-Anniversary in every place of worship.

"3. A monthly Missionary-Prayer-meeting in every Con-
"gregation.

"4. A Missionary-magazine taken by every family.

"5. A weekly, monthly, quarterly, or annual subscription
"from every Christian.

"6. A Missionary-box in every house.

"7. And more vigour and earnestness thrown into all that
"is done.

"It is lamentable, that there should be so many places of
"worship, where the duty of sending the Gospel to the Heathen
"is in no way recognised, either by sermon, anniversary, or
"subscription. I believe there are thousands of such places,

"hundreds belonging to each denomination, where no annual meeting is held and no sermon preached. Books relating to Missions and to Heathen countries should be more read.

" Great responsibility rests on Missionary-Societies. The degree of wisdom, nobleness, thrift, and efficiency, with which they manage their affairs, has much to do with the fervour or langour of what is called the Missionary-spirit.

" Still more does an interest in Missions depend on Missionaries themselves. If they are able, wise, zealous, disinterested, and successful, attention and admiration will be drawn towards their work as well as towards themselves."

The Church-Missionary-Society in 1888 made the following suggestions: " With respect to *Sermons*: Is it not possible still more frequently than is at present the case, either by an exchange of neighbouring pulpits, or by Incumbents very kindly pleading for the cause themselves, to lighten the call on Salisbury Square? The Committee feel assured, that they will carry with them the opinion of many of their supporters, when they express the confident belief, that nothing tends, under the Divine blessing, more effectually to evoke hearty sympathy from a congregation than by the Vicar being prepared from time to time *himself* to plead the cause of Foreign Missions.

" With reference to *Meetings*: In conjunction with their Association-Secretaries, the Committee feel, that more might be done to encourage Clergy and Laity carefully to prepare Lectures on Missionary subjects of their own selection, which could be delivered by them in various neighbouring parishes in co-operation with the local Clergy."

I have been for the last fifteen years constantly on deputations at my own charges in every part of England, and in Dublin, for different Societies: it has always suited me best to put up at hotels on account of the state of my health, and my custom of taking my work and books with me so as not to lose time in a strange house as a guest. I cannot imagine any employment more dear to the heart than speaking for a Missionary-Society, or the Bible-Society. I have certainly heard much, of which I did not approve, and sometimes what I thoroughly condemned, such as abuse of the poor Heathen races, their religious beliefs spoken of in terms of derision, and perhaps their objects of worship exposed to be laughed at: how a Mahometan audience would laugh, and poke fun at the Reredos of St. Paul's, or the mitre of a Bishop! All this is most unworthy. The principles of Missions, and the Duty, can be inculcated by the Incumbent from his pulpit, but how is he to supply his audience with interesting facts, or accounts of the progress of the movement? A Missionary, a skilled Deputation-Secretary, or some one, who has studied the subject, is required. I have published Essays on certain views of the subject, and have received the thanks of (to me) unknown Clergy, as they have been able from those pages to prepare themselves for the pulpit; so really volumes of Normal addresses, or reprints of esteemed addresses by good speakers, are what is absolutely required by the country-clergy. I have listened to addresses from Missionaries, Deputations, and local friends, which were simply admirable in tone and style, and holy fervour. Nothing has surprised me more than the strong feeling exhibited in the Public Press, and at Meetings, against Deputations: many unkind things have been said on both sides, and clearly the matter requires looking into. The expense, incurred by the Society, is indeed enormous, in addition to the kind hospitality offered in the locality: the attendance at some meetings, when the room is filled with children of the village-schools, is disheartening. The whole subject is an anxious one. I heard last week of a meeting held in a lady's house, who had invited the audience, on behalf of the China-Inland-Mission: The whole tone of the speaker, a returned Missionary, was reprehensible: he began by describing in ridiculous terms the dress worn by the Bible-Society's agent, whose only fault was, that he wore the English dress of his country, while the Missionary and his friends were got up with pig-tails as Chinese. He then enlarged on the Opium-Traffic, with which he had no concern, as he worked in a Province, in which the Poppy was grown to a great extent, and at any rate there was no demand for the foreign drug: he then abused the Chinese Government, and the Chinese people: if that kind of person is a sample, can we wonder that there is a restlessness in the Empire of China, which may some day eventuate in the expulsion of all Missionaries from China? Great Britain is not likely to go to war on such a subject.

4. THE FINANCIAL DEPARTMENT.

"Trust in the Lord, and keep your powder dry," were the marching orders of the Puritan soldier: it is the same with us now. The Treasury of the Lord is always overflowing, but, as there is a principle of divine Economy in the supply of good things to God's poor children, so a human Economy should be exerted in the disbursements: that is the blot of the great Missionary-Associations. I have taken a share in the control of the Income and Expenditure of vast Provinces far exceeding those of a Missionary-Association: I call the present system extravagant, and I mean what I say, and I know what I mean.

The Annual Reports of the great Societies speak for themselves. There is no insinuation of carelessness, or absence of a proper system of accounts, or any possible malversation. There is a continuous audit by professional auditors from the outside, and a Committee of Inquiry would have very little to discover, as all is above-board, and unpaid lay Committees are very much in earnest, and have great experience of human affairs, and are terribly outspoken; but everything is done in much too expensive a style, just like a Government-Office, which has the purse of the British taxpayers behind it. Anything more ridiculous than paying first-class-steamer-passages for Negro Missionaries, the sons of redeemed Slaves, and for Englishmen in extremely humble positions of life, cannot be imagined. In my travels, I have often found the Italian, or Spanish, or French, Romish Priest stretched out on the deck, as a third-class passenger, but the *Protestant Negro must go first-class*: this is a fair sample. The expenses with regard to the wives and children of the Missionaries are enormous: the country-clergyman with a large family must feel surprise, and a certain amount of envy. The luxuriousness, and indulgence, of the nineteenth Century have caused this, and I am bound to say, that signs of the same evil are not wanting in all secular establishments, where the funds are provided by the State, or the County, or the Parish, and *not by the person himself*. What is required is not the Faith-Mission, or the Brotherhood, or the Common Fund, or the Haphazard, or the " Root, Hog, or die " systems, but a stern, economic, and fearless, administration of our sacred funds, reminding the Missionaries, that the Committee will not tolerate luxuries, or indulgences, or pride, or waste, *and expects self-sacrifice, and self-consecration, and self-control, on their part*. This would set free large sums for the entertainment of additional Agents.

I am glad to chronicle symptoms of this feeling in the Field. Instances occur, where the Missionary has, in the presence of the Home-Committee, offered to share his subsistence-allowance with another, assuring us, that his expenses fell short of his supply: invitations have come home to send out men on sixty Rupees per mensem, or £70 per annum: all Missionaries should contribute as much as they can from their private means to their own support, and draw as little as possible on the sacred funds.

Still more discouraging is the lavish expenditure on Clerks, and offices. Anyone, who thinks, that a Missionary-Society can work by an automatic process, without Secretaries, or, in other words, an Executive, might believe, that a cart would move along the road without wheels; but there ought to be found men in Great Britain, of independent circumstances, and good training, whose health would not permit them to venture on the foreign Field, and yet who could do the work of Secretary gratuitously, and *men of that stamp are found*, and more should be looked for.

If we believe anything, we must believe the words contained in the opening pages of the Church-Missionary-Society-Committee-Meetings, that "the Silver and Gold is of the Lord": I follow this out logically: When the Lord assigns to a Society a certain income, it is because that it is all, that He deems, that the Society can properly spend. He speaks by years of Drought as well as years of Plenty: by Seasons of Abundance as well as by Seasons of Retrenchment. Both are blessings in disguise. He is often quoted as sending "open doors," but, unless He sends the means also, the message is not clear, and, when he sends "a closed door," the Committee should accept it, without appealing to the Arm of the Flesh. He sent ravens to Elijah, but He also filled their *beaks with food* to feed the Prophet. The cruse of oil did not fail, but the supply was limited to the legitimate expenditure of the widow, not to encourage her *to increased outlay beyond her actual wants*. He expects us to serve Him to the utmost of our Talents, whatever He may have lent to us, but *not beyond our Talents*. It is unwisdom, as well as a want of appreciation of the teaching of His Government of the World, to be sending out repeated special appeals for funds, and calling for fresh supplies, instead of making the most economical possible use of funds already supplied. Sums collected in pennies are heedlessly wasted. Those, who support Missions, have a right to insist upon the most rigid economy. It is not because a Society is large and rich, that it should waste its resources.

The Society should treat its Missionaries, as a wise Government treats its soldiers in a foreign campaign, and something more. In these days of heroic Missions care should be taken to alleviate the danger, and the risk, and the hardship, and the suffering, by every human appliance of Art and Science. Nothing is so useless as a sick Missionary: nothing so sad as a dead one, if his precious life could have been preserved by human forethought. It is false economy, it is wickedness, not to make provision, which will anticipate sufferings. There is much sense in Henry Stanley's remarks, the comments on which in a religious Periodical I quote:

"We trust the Committee will give due attention to the sug-
" gestions of Mr. Stanley, and warn and instruct the young men
" they send out to temper zeal with discretion, and to work
" prudently, that they may live to work for many years. Mis-
" sionaries are commissioned to evangelize the world, and *to do*
" *this they must live*. We think a Missionary in his grave is
" worth more than Mr. Stanley apparently imagined; but he is
" unquestionably worth much more to the world alive than dead,
" and, therefore, we trust, that all possible care will be taken to
" preserve the precious lives of the young brethren."

The question of subsistence-allowances, pensions, provision for children and widows, should be approached in a wise and fatherly spirit. The Missionary-Agent should be freed from worldly anxiety: he does not desire profit, or savings like a worldling, but he must be made to feel, that those, whom he loves, will be provided for: he is ready to undergo peril by land and by sea, to suffer hardship like a good soldier, but he should not be cut off from proper sustenance of every kind. Many have sunk under rude trials, which might have been avoided, or have had to fly for their lives. The Home-Committee is to blame, when any precaution is neglected. Those, who take out a large party of men, women, and children, into a foreign country, without a certain provision of money, and reasonable comforts, are to be heavily condemned. Just as the Missionary receives no salary, properly so called, but only enough to sustain his physical wants, and enable him to apply his intellectual and spiritual gifts to the Lord's work, so there should be found at home in this rich country, men ready to consecrate their time and talents for the glory of God without seeking profit, without necessity of maintenance. In some Societies there is a very cheap administration, owing to the amount of voluntary Service supplied: all the Committee-men's work is voluntary, and gratuitous, but the Executive should be supplied by Volunteers also. The only remedy is to rule, that every shilling collected for Mission-purposes should go to *Missionary-work out of the country, without any deduction.* A separate Fund should be raised from the Friends of the Mission, for the office-expenses, or rather to supplement what cannot be supplied by voluntary labour. The time may be near at hand, when contributors of money to convert the Heathen will label their contributions:

"Not a sixpence of mine to go to maintain a Children's "Home, or the outfit of the wife of a Missionary under ten "years' service, or the first-class passage of a Negro Missionary, "or an office-Clerk's extra pay."

The laxness of expenditure in the Home-Committee leads to laxness of expenditure in the Field. The foolish attempt is made to elevate the Asiatic, African, or South Sea Islander to a platform, socially above his Heathen relations, *because he is a Christian.* We have no Apostolic sanction for this, and it is a deadly mistake. The Religion of Christ has no relation whatever to the social culture, or civilization, of the convert. In the early Missions of Christianity there was comparatively little difference in respect of culture and civilization, betwixt the preacher of the Gospel, and those, to whom he preached. They ate and drank the same food, and were clothed in a similar manner. Paul worked among men not inferior to himself, and he moved among them as an equal. In the Middle

Ages and the time of Columba of Iona, as regards all things, that represented Civilization, there was little difference betwixt the Missionary and his convert. But the modern Missionary has to work among races undoubtedly inferior, and lower in culture. This is owing to the enormous advance of European culture, and it often proves a great snare to the Missionary, and generates pride, arrogance, and self-assertion. He is led on to another snare, the attempt to introduce a higher social Civilization among his converts. This may come in its own time, and probably will come, but Conversion should be his object, and he should be cautious not to introduce new and expensive habits and wants.

The most depressing thought is, that of the vast sums spent in Secretaries, Clerks, Warehouses, postage, and parcels, Stationery, Printing, Rent, first-class Steamer and Railway-fares, and the needlessly liberal way, in which such charges are incurred, *because a great Society pays for them*. My thoughts go back to the sums collected at Corinth for the poor Saints at Jerusalem, and Paul, the poor prisoner of the Lord, conveying it in the undecked vessel of that period. I remember his tender advice to have the collections made in advance, and fancy conjures up the image of the earthen pot, or wooden casket, filled with denarii and sestertia, bearing the image of one of the early Cæsars, which was reverently consigned to him, and my heart sinks within me at the thought of the frightfully complicated Organizations forced upon us by the 19th Century, the flogging of the congregations to get at their money, and the men, like Judas, going about holding the bag. Happy are those, whose admitted Poverty enables them to laugh at the plate, pushed under their nose, and happier still are those, who have, at the beginning of each year, set apart the proper proportion of their Income, and been cheerful givers to the Lord, who bought them, and made their contribution in advance. My remarks may seem cynical, but they are offered in good faith, and with a large experience, and long reflection.

Benevolent men outside Missionary-circles indulge in the same liberal thoughts, and spend beyond their means on purposes beyond the scope of the Constitution of their Association: I quote one instance:

"As regards the past action of the Board we find evidence,
" that some questionable work has been done, and that ex-
" penses have been incurred on schemes not strictly within
" the Board's statutable powers. The matter has been forced
" on the attention of the members in the most unpleasant way
" possible. Some items in the Board's accounts have been
" disallowed by the Government-Auditor, and the sums so dealt
" with have been surcharged on the members, by whose authority

"they were paid. The Board, it appears, has established six cookery-centres, at which instruction has been given not only to children at the Board-Schools, but to assistant cookery-teachers and ex-pupil teachers. The cost of these centres has therefore been legitimate in part, as far, that is to say, as it has been on account of instruction to school-children. The Auditor's objection has been to the remaining portion."

Here the blot is hit: there has been no misappropriation, no vulgar jobbery or stealing: spiritual men are not liable to such frailties: at least I have never detected the least sign of such tendencies in Missionary-circles, though I have seen them very clearly in Secular Boards: The money is voted by competent authority, and reaches the proper quarter, but

"Qui custodiet ipsos custodes?"

The proper Authority under the influence of Faith, Emotion, Enthusiasm, spends more money than it has, spends it on objects outside the one sole object to "bring souls to Christ," erects a palace for the Home of Missionary-children, who really ought never to have come into existence; trains at considerable expense men for the Field, who, when the health of their wives fails, or something better offers, turn their back on the plough; gives life-pensions, not to veterans, who well deserve it, but to those, who do not deserve it at all, or have never been in the Field. What is wanted is some one analogous to the Government-Auditor, who, in the case quoted above, disallows the expenditure of the Secular Board, some one who will disallow the heedless, improper votes of a Missionary-Committee, constituted as in previous Sections I have described, and worked, or rather coerced, by an overweening Secretary.

We hear in Committee the cuckoo-cry, "Never refuse the offer of services of a candidate": get the money, if you can, to support him: if not, make a dark Prophecy about Faith. I give the following from the pages of the *Rock*, 1894:

"The *Intelligencer* has the following reminder and warning: It should be distinctly understood, and we hope it will be fully realized, that the Society has literally no money to send out the great majority of these new Missionaries. That is to say, supposing not one of them went out, there is no reason whatever, judging in the only way man can judge, by God's dealings with us in the past few years, to expect, that the contributions of the year would even then cover the expenditure of the year. The *Intelligencer* will not be suspected of forgetting how God honours Faith. It has for some years taken a line on this subject, which many of our friends have regarded as in advance of their convictions. And if we could see any signs that the Church-Missionary-Society-circle as a whole, or any large part of it, were deliberately facing the position in a spirit

" of unfaltering Faith, we should not have a moment's apprehen-
" sion. But it seems to us, that only a small minority are thinking
" of it at all, and that the tendency is to drift along listlessly and
" expect, that the Society will get through all right somehow.
" But that is not Faith. It is a fatalism, which may almost be said
" to challenge God to give it a sharp awakening. We said 'the
" great majority.' We did not say 'all.' For (1) a few are
" honorary, and (2) some of our friends, who really are awake,
" are adopting the suggestions made by us in July, and in the
" official appeal that accompanied our August number, and are
" either undertaking themselves, or getting their local circles
" to undertake, the entire maintenance of a particular Missionary.
" A few of the new recruits are already provided for in this
" way."

Could the great Societies but break with the past, there is a better way. Hear the practice of the Universities' Mission to E. Africa: " The Bishop is quite unable to offer any induce-
" ment in the way of salary, or periodical holidays, or ultimate
" pension, or temporal advantage of any kind: it is necessary,
" that those, who join the Mission, should do so with the sole
" desire to live for, and willingness to die, for their work, because
" it is Christ's. He offers to those, who may need it, the help of
" Board, Lodging, and necessaries during their stay in Africa."

In the life of Bishop Steere, I read: " At the present time not
" one of the Members of the Bishop's staff in Africa is receiving
" any stipend beyond the moderate allowance of £20 per annum,
" for clothes, etc.; all other necessaries are provided from the
" common fund of the Mission." Thus, rich and poor live and work together on equal terms. All the Missionaries are celibates: women Missionaries are not admitted below the age of thirty. . This Mission belongs to the High-Church party, and is doing good work.

The China-Inland-Mission is in the Antipodes to the above as regards Church-Government and Doctrine. Hudson Taylor thus formulates his principles: " Some have gone out at their
" own expense: the rest have gone out under a clear under-
" standing, that the Mission does not guarantee any income
" whatever, and knowing, that as the Mission does not run into
" debt, it can only minister to those connected with it as far as
" the funds allow: in other words, they have gone out in
" dependence upon God for their temporal supplies."

Again: " The China-Inland-Mission accepts suitable can-
" didates, whether possessed of private means, or not: those,
" who need it, are assisted in their outfits, have their passage-
" money provided them, and have funds remitted to them from
" time to time, as the supplies come in. God, in a very special
" way, is the Treasurer of the Missionary, and *to Him they look*,

" *not to the Mission.* Hitherto He has supplied, and henceforth
" He will do the same. 1888."

The North-African-Mission, and the East London-Institute, are conducted on similar principles; the latter makes the following appeal, 1888: " This state of things would make us
" anxious, but that we gratefully and trustfully remember the
" long years, during which our large households, though like the
" birds without storehouse or barn, have been fed day by day,
" and had every need supplied."

Again I read: " The Mission-Board of the Free Methodists
" show much interest in Foreign Missions, and the Church
" is increasing its contributions, but the Board *guarantees no*
" *salary to anyone,* only a portion to the different Missions,
" which the Church contributes; so that each Missionary is
" independent, using what comes as the Providence of God,
" and planning for self-support as soon as possible."

A Member of the Universities' Mission to Calcutta puts the matter very bluntly: " A Hindu asked me, how we lived, as we
" had no ' talab ' (the well-known Urdu word for ' salary '): I
" told him, that we lived chiefly by begging : from a professional
" beggar no apology was needed. The very object of a Native
" Catechist, or Teacher, or Pastor, is to get a 'talab.' "

I shall notice the Organization of such Missions in Cap. V, but I look at the question now financially in this chapter. None of these Missions have yet had the experience of fifty years: in due course there will be a survival of aged men, and women, who cannot be allowed to starve, when there is no more work in them. Staunch as I am (see Cap. VI) against the premature Marriage of Missionaries below the age of 33 or thereabouts, I cannot give my adhesion to Missionary-celibacy for life, and therefore there must be widows and orphans. No Mercantile Association, no Government, can live from hand to mouth without running the risk of great disaster, and exposing innocent persons to tremendous suffering. Though a rigid economist, I have still the feelings of a Statesman, or even of a lower type " Genus Homo." The alternative is, that there must be forethought and provision for the survivors of the Lord's battles. The lives of these veterans must be insured.

The Committees are always putting forth appeals, drawing on the Bank of Faith and Hope, suggesting, as in a paper now on my table, that the Members of the Committee should make up the deficiency of £15,000: certainly one or two of the Secretaries, and one or two of the Members, and the careless voters, who voted without knowing what they were voting for, might be expected to contribute freely to fill up the hole, which their own recklessness had made : one extremely transcendental Member whispered once in my ear: " why make such a fuss about getting in filthy money? Go into your closet, and pray to God to send it." I agree with him, but add the condition, that the Committee should be satisfied with the amount, which the Lord has provided, and make use of its talents, but not beyond its talents. " Quo plus habeant eo plus cupiunt."

Think of such a notice as this being sent from Harley-House, Bow : "Accept our heartiest gratitude, dear Friends and "fellow-helpers in this work, for all the valued sympathy and " confidence you have given us these many years, and we would " very earnestly add, under the present pressure of heavy " financial strain as regards our *general* work, do continue to us " the kind and liberal co-operation, without which our efforts " must needs be sadly crippled ! With more work in hand, and " with a larger number of students than we ever had before, we " have not at this moment the means to meet a single week's " expenses, but have to look up for daily bread. You will not " wonder when I say, that we trust that you will be able to respond " to this letter with even more than your customary liberality ! "

I once had a letter telling me, that the members of an Institution had, for want of funds, left off eating meat, and taken to vegetables : and another sent a brief Postcard, "Nothing in the locker." Why not send a cart round, as in Italy, into which householders may fling old clothes, food, and jewellery out of fashion, or go round like Buddha in India with a bowl, and collect daily scraps ? All such carelessness of Finance is out of touch with the spirit, the honest healthy spirit, of the nineteenth Century. Spend what you have, and neither accumulate, nor forestall. A Missionary-Institution should be conducted with the same propriety, forethought, and restraint, as the families of the Members of that Committee : I cannot help thinking, that the next generation will take a different view of this subject, and pass a severe and not undeserved censure on the conduct of this generation. Members of the Committee would be ashamed to adopt the course in their own affairs, which they abet in the affairs of the Association.

It is the same sanguine, reckless spirit, which ruins secular companies. It is true, that the Lord can make jewels at His pleasure out of common stones : He could in past ages sanctify the labour of the Shepherd-Boy, the Fisherman, and the Collector of Taxes, and in these times the labour of the Cobbler, the Gardener, the Shopkeeper, the Domestic Servant, and bless with success enterprises commenced in defiance of the precepts of worldly wisdom : " Not by might, not by power, but My spirit : " yet none the less are we bound to offer our best, our talents, our experience, our careful thoughts, our words boldly expressed, our writings fearlessly indited, our zeal controlled by prudence, following the example of Paul, Columba, Columbanus, and

Boniface, and many a Saint of the Protestant Church, and of the great Church of Rome, who rise before us as an example of entire self-sacrifice.

There is an objection to large overgrown Associations: there is a vaunting spirit, as of all rich people, a desire to appear well before the world: "a great Committee must do so." It is well for a wealthy British Noble, or an American Millionaire, to be lavish out of his own resources, but it is not well for a Committee to be lavish out of the sacred store, collected in pennies from little children under the influence of prayer. Each contributor hopes, that his obolus will do something better in the cause of Christ's Kingdom than make up the extra pay of a clerk in the Mission-House, the salary of an additional Secretary, or the pay of a Deputation, or the postage and printing of thousands of unnecessary circulars, the outcome of the brains of a busybody. There is a certain amount of degradation of the religious and charitable conscience by the constant appeals for money. I have enough waste-paper for the lighting of the fires of my household from this single source. "Ecce iterum Crispinus" is the cry: something pleasant was expected to emerge from the envelope, but it proves to be only an appeal from the Church-Missionary-Society to make up a deficit, which ought never to have existed. The Missionary-spirit has spread over a wider surface of the population, but it is very thin indeed, because it is presented to the Public with some of the attributes of the prospectus of a great Company, or the allurements of an advertizing speciality.

It is singular, that in no Missionary-Report is there a direct allusion to the extraordinary windfall, that has come to all Missionary-Societies, which have Missions in India, by the depreciation of Silver, vulgarly called the Fall of the value of the Rupee. The Church-Missionary-Society has its collection made in Great Britain in gold, but has to provide certain sums in silver in India, say 800,000 Rupees annually, which are purchased for £50,000, leaving a profit of £30,000. On careful examination of the accounts, and the price of the Bills of Sale, it is clear, that the amount is duly credited, but while thanks are offered for so many trifles, thanks to the Dispenser of all human blessings might be expected for such a windfall: how long will it last? the password has been, "Do not allude to it."

I think, that it may be asserted, that, of the amounts collected from the supporters of Missionary-Societies, a far too great a percentage never gets beyond the shores of England. Speaking roughly the Church-Missionary-Society retains £30,000 annually, the Society for the Propagation of the Gospel £8,000, the London Missionary-Society about £17,000, and so on. This is dreadful to think of. In 1888 a special sub-Committee of seven Clergymen and Laymen were appointed to examine into the Home-Expenditure of the Church-Missionary-Society: they were undoubtedly all strong, earnest, and well-informed men; they made their Report April, 1888, and nothing came of it, except the withdrawal of an old Editorial Secretary since deceased. Of course this was a point gained, but much more might have been done, if it had not been the interest of so many to retain the old system. I am afraid to give figures, because, if an Angel from Heaven were to state figures, another Angel from another place would challenge their correctness: The totals of the Annual Report of that time were something like this:

	£
Cost of children of Missionaries, with their Parents, or at home	9,000
Deputation Staff	10,000
Administrative Staff at Head-Quarters.	4,900
Training of young Missionaries	5,000
Pensions of old Missionaries and widows	7,000

The Recording Angel making use of his notes taken from the Reports writes the above figures: if the Criticizing Angel says that they are wrong, let him substitute the actuals: I confess my errors before they are proved, but I adhere to my thesis, that these things should not be, that they are symptoms of the dropsy of the great Association, and that a new broom is required. If a Board of Guardians were to attempt unnecessary expenditure, the Local Government-Board would come down upon them, and the Government-Auditor would disallow the items: In a Bank, or a Mercantile House, motives of self-interest, and the intelligence of the Manager, secure this supervision: for the Missionary-Association to spend a quarter of a Million annually there is no check whatever.

The great object of the Society should be to secure men of the same social status, and the same stamp of Education, as the Clergy at home. The profession of the Missionary is the noblest and the holiest, the most courageous, and the most blessed: but by becoming Missionaries they should not divest themselves of the feelings and duties of their class: they should not allow themselves from zeal or carelessness, or contempt of worldly wisdom, to do what honest gentlemen would shun to do, *e.g.* spend money, which is not at their disposal to spend, or upon purposes, to which the money is not allocated, let their accounts get into confusion, and set a bad example to their flock. This has occurred. A good steward is faithful in little things. It is exceedingly unadvisable on the part of a Missionary-Society to make a permanent endowment of a College, or Bishopric, unless the entire control of the former, and the selection of the latter, be reserved to the Committee: and even then it had better be avoided.

The income of the Society should be jealously guarded against

    I. Undue tenderness to favourites.
    II. Waste.
    III. Muddling.
    IV. The evils of delay in rendition of accounts.

It is no derogation to a good minister of Spiritual things to be a good steward of things, necessary for maintenance of life, efficiency, and good order. It is shocking to read of defalcations of money on the death of a Secretary of a Religious Society. Professional auditors should always be employed, not three old gentlemen without experience. The Committee should retain unfettered control of every shilling in its coffers, and not allow its supporters to force its hands by conditional contributions: it may accept distinct Trusts for approved purposes. Every shilling collected by its agents, whether at Home or in the Field, should be brought to book, and spent with due economy.

I quote the following from an Agenda of a Missionary-Society, as a sample of the comfortable aspirations of a female Missionary in 1894. We all know how miserable and precarious are the emoluments of well-educated women in Great Britain, and that men are content with £70 a year: this lady evinces very little Missionary-spirit: " Finds that the salary of £100 " allowed her is not sufficient. After paying for board and " putting aside a sum for charity, she only has £30 per annum " available for all other expenses. This is an expensive place. " Asks that during the summer-months the salary may be paid " in advance, to enable her to pay travelling-expenses for a " change."

Charity begins at home: she wishes to be charitable at the charges of the Society: what need is there for a change? Do the Nuns of the neighbouring Romish Convent take it?

No amount of Income will meet the ever-increasing desire evidenced in the following: " Resolutions of Finance Com- " mittee, containing proposals for increases in salaries of House- " Staff not exceeding £200, and for increased accommodation " in the House at a cost exceeding £100."

This happens not once in a term of five years, but "toties quoties" in the same year. Decentralize, trust the Local Committees, and the plethora of work would diminish: British India could not be governed, if the Viceroy in Calcutta, or the Secretary of State for India in Whitehall, trusted none of their subordinates.

5. THE PUBLICATIONS.

When some Leckie, or Froude, or Buckle, passes the Literature of the Nineteenth Century under review, the Missionary-Literature of the last half Century will indeed astonish him. I have been a steady reader for the first half of that period, and an omnivorous reader for the last twenty-five years. I can quite understand, that many would criticize my taste, as I, being a non-smoker, criticize the smell of tobacco, but the subject fascinates me, and I must keep up my touch with what is going on in every part of the world in the only way, that is available. I confess, that there is much to be desired, and much which would repel anyone, who in middle life began the study. Certainly there is no parallel to it in the literature of this Century, and no precedent in the past Centuries. No doubt, it is conducted on both sides of the Atlantic with ability. It consists no longer of goody-goody stories, or dry facts, but kaleidoscopic pictures of the manners, and customs, the material and Spiritual thoughts of all the non-Christian Nations in the world. Such a disclosure of the mysteries of Human Life was never made before; but these Publications should be made self-supporting, and could be made so. The narrow-mindedness of the different Sections of the religious world should be corrected by each Society devoting two pages of every issue to Notes of the Wide Field, as well as their own Little Vineyard. Many good souls believe, that their petty denomination is the only one, that has Missions at all, for, as they naïvely remark, *they never heard of any other*; but our Heavenly Father is glorified by the work of *all* His children, and more especially the Missionaries of each denomination should be informed up to date of the work of their dear brethren scattered over the world. What a poor conception they must have of the Communion of the Saints, when they shut their eyes to every ray of light, but the one which comes through their particular lens!

Of course, the Report of each individual Missionary is the basis of the general Report of the Association: these are printed and circulated to selected persons, and I have read them by the scores: if the writer but knew, how these letters expose the weakness of his character, and the limitations of his knowledge, he would refrain; he should take pains with his Annual Letter, and have no gush; he should abstain from Scripture-quotations, and stock-phrases of piety, which are expressions of common form, and neither calculated to instruct, inform, or edify. Many read Missionary-Reports by the yard, or the furlong, and such conventional expressions pall very much on the taste, and most readers skip them. Sometimes there is a most indecorous, and unjustifiable, familiarity with the plans of the Almighty. I have sometimes remonstrated against the vain repetition of the Divine Name in every page, but have been told, that liberal supporters of the Society expect it: they should be taught better things: the compiler of the Report should try to elevate the taste of his readers, not lower himself to their vulgar level. The allusion to birth or death of children of the Missionaries is really quite unnecessary. I sometimes seem to detect in a good Report the marks of a second hand, which has inserted pious tags, or hits against the Roman Catholic, or a tilt against Caste, or the Opium-Trade, as if some one on a perusal of the draft had said, "Mrs. ——, or Dr. ——, who are good supporters, lay great stress on such remarks to flavour the Report." Many Reports, however, contain no such blemishes, or conventionalities, and yet from the first to the last line breathe a holy and devoted spirit. The Bible is not textually quoted, but the whole Report is, as it were, steeped in the very essence of the Scriptures. If subordinates in secular employ in India had garnished their Reports with such platitudes, and quotations, they would have been checked by the remark, that old hands knew them better than they did. The Home-Committee can say the same, as it has to read them from year to year. Sensational stories of death-bed-scenes are not wanted: a narrative of the consistent walk of a redeemed community is more acceptable. A thoughtful and earnest labourer can so bring his joys and sorrows, his successes and failures, his hopes and his fears, before his friends at home, in a humble and subdued tone, as will secure their love and esteem. Above all,. let there be no abuse of the Powers that be, no railing against men in authority, no sneers at Missionaries of other denominations. Such phrases do not speak well for the Christian spirit of the writer. He can state his facts truthfully, and leave it to the Home-Committee to form a judgment on those facts. Stereotyped abuse of the Romish Missionaries should be avoided. Any case of *illegal* aggression should be the subject of a separate letter.

In the Church-Missionary-Society-Report I read as follows: " Mr. Perkins thinks, but many will differ from him, that Missionary-Reports and speeches are far too roseate." I quite agree with him.

I quote another writer: " How hard it is for the Missionary
" to be patient, when his friends at home are so impatient, and
" how great is the temptation to embellish the account of his
" annual labours! I fear there are grave scandals connected
" with Missionary-Reports, but the fault lies rather with the sub-
" scribers to Missions than with Missionary-Agents. For the
" pious, simple folk, who take great interest in Missionary-enter-
" prise, but who are entirely ignorant of the circumstances of

"Missionary-work, the sun must always shine; a cloud on the
"horizon is intolerable; this is, as it were, the condition of
"their support; the result is the issue of Reports positively
"grotesque in their optimism, in which Scripture-texts jostle
"strangely with palpably exaggerated retrospects and fore-
"casts."

Here another writer remarks on the roseate hue of Reports:
"What is the present state of the case? Many people are
"quietly assuming, that Christianity is making a yearly en-
"croachment upon Heathenism and Mahometanism, and upon
"the corrupt Christian Systems of Continental Europe; in other
"words, that at each year's close there has been such a dis-
"placement of Error and Idolatry, that we may reckon on a
"relative increase of vital Christianity in the world. No greater
"delusion could be fostered. Every year the excess of births
"into this world of sin, above the number carried away by
"death, is estimated at twelve Millions of souls: is anyone
"sanguine enough to suppose, that even five Millions of true
"believers are added annually to the sum of converted men and
"women in the world? And yet, unless some such result as
"this or more than this is attained, there is an obvious loss of
"ground, and a prodigious increase to the ranks of the foes of
"Christ. The normal increase of the tens of thousands in
"Protestant countries of Christendom sinks into insignificance
"when compared with the hundreds of thousands, the millions,
"who form the normal increase to the numbers of heathen
"peoples, of Mahometans, of the Greek and Roman Churches,
"to say nothing of the dead mass of professing Christians in
"more favoured lands."

These false statements should really cease to be made, and the late works of esteemed authors be consulted: it is of no use acting on the Middle-Age-practice of the Church of Rome.

"Populus vult decipi, et decipiatur."

I quote the following from a religious newspaper of Nov., 1893: "Sir, I have observed with deep sorrow, that for the last year
"or two the Church-Missionary Society has been in danger of
"losing its character for sobriety, and there does seem to be a
"special need at the present time of earnest prayer, that the
"increased zeal, at which we all rejoice, may be 'according to
"knowledge.' November 4, 1893. N. A. A."

The books of Joshua and Judges are freely quoted by writers, who forget, that the quotations only applied to the commencement of the occupation of the tiny Province of Palestine, which small as it was, was never fully occupied. We in the Nineteenth Century have to deal with the great round world, and 2,000 languages. The comparison is ridiculous, and is mere pious rodomontade.

Considering the matter judicially, I find the following objections to the style of Missionary-Literature:

A. There is a tendency to advise the general public as to the mode, in which they should spend their income.
B. A denunciation of all other Religious Conceptions, and the races, who have held them for two or three thousand years.
C. An unjust description of their moral state, forgetting the moral state of the people of England.
D. A wide indulgence in Prophecy, and use of the Divine Name.
E. A loud assertion, that the Almighty is on their side, and consequently they must succeed, forgetting that, had it been the Divine Will, the world might long ago have been converted.
F. Some Societies using an Evangelical Patois, others a High-Church-Word-store: both equally unpleasant to read.
G. In many cases evidencing an intimate acquaintance with the Divine Plans, which is most presumptuous.
H. Phrases from the Old Testament made use of in a non-natural sense, and applied to circumstances, for which they were never intended.
I. Unreal, or exaggerated, statements as to numerical success.
J. Hero-worship of the most audacious kind.
K. Puffing up particular Methods, "worshipping their own drag."
L. Interfering with worldly politics.

I quote from the *Catholic Missions* of Manchester, Jan., 1891, p. 136, the following statement:

"We put up in a village in the Sunderbunds (India) and there "constructed an altar, and under the roof of the hut there came "down from Heaven our Lord Jesus Christ in shrouded majesty."

To a Protestant these are terrible expressions to read, but the Romish Priests meant what they wrote: it would have been more judicious on the part of the Missionary not to have written it, and of the Compiler of the Journal not to have published it: the same remark applies to the countless anecdotes, pious thoughts, moral ejaculations, emotional gush, with which a Protestant-Missionary-Report is padded. It makes one sick to read it.

The ministration of the Gospel was not committed to Angels, but to very weak and erring men, yet strange to say year after year no failure, no misconduct, is reported amidst a staff of so many agents: occasionally a dark-coloured agent, such as a

Negro Pastor in the Niger-Delta, catches it, but the white men are all impeccable, so far as the Report tells us: such a Report would obviously have light and shade, but here all is "couleur de rose," and this gives to all readers an unreal character to the Narrative. Paul concealed nothing: he published to the Church of Corinth of his time, and to the Church of Christ for all ages to come, the shocking misconduct of some of his early converts: why should Missionary-Reports pass over errors, mistakes, and sins? Had the Committee no occasion to groan in spirit, and hang their heads at no misconduct on the part of their agents? it is well-known, that in Africa they had reason. Then we find in these Reports too many common form-expressions: all, who died early, had evinced remarkable progress: all, who died late, had done good work: were there no bad bargains, no hasty and injudicious selections of incompetent men, who were cheerfully got rid of? what is the history of the "returned empties," whom we meet with everywhere? Profuse thanks are offered for what appears to the narrow human vision as a blessing, or a mercy, but no thanks are offered for the chastisements, which are blessings in disguise, and which clear away so much self-complacency. An account is given of some strong opposition to the Missionary, and a great deal made of it, as an Englishman always does make a great deal of the least opposition to his will; yet at the end we find complacent remarks, that the opposition had done no good, and "the people hear us gladly."

The great thing would be to have a shorter Report: it requires great determination, and a strong stomach, to get through the present bulky volume, and a considerable knowledge of the subject to make the reading profitable and intelligible: a great many of the extracts should be omitted altogether, and the remainder relegated to an appendix, or foot-note, as is the case with some Associations: The device of putting words in inverted commas as quotations should be abandoned, such as "they listened most attentively"; "as full of fun as little kittens"; "say that name again"; "seemed to drink in our words": all this savours of the penny-a-liner, and the special correspondent, who wishes to attract. There are not many, who can say, that they read the Reports both of the Society for the Propagation of the Gospel, and the Church-Missionary-Society: as a literary work the Society for the Propagation of the Gospel-Report is far superior, and is much more pleasant reading. The printing by the Church-Missionary-Society of the Sermon preached at St. Bride's Church is quite unnecessary. As a rule, it is not worth much as a contribution to knowledge. I wonder, how many even of the Church-Missionary-Society-Committee read it. It is a survival of old practice. Many persons only read the Reports of their own Society: that is well, for many do not even do that: but it is better to read the Reports of others, both of the Protestant, and Romish, Missions.

I quote from a Report of the Established Church of Scotland, 1878: " Missionaries in the Field are discouraged by the notion, " that their friends crave exciting and novel narratives; that " the plain record of daily duties, petty disappointments, and " serious hindrances, would be unacceptable. The fact is " otherwise: what is wanted is such a setting out of common- " place-details, as will bring their life vividly before the eyes " of their friends, who feel a deep concern in the trials, as " well as the successes, of their representatives. Let them not " shrink from telling of all kinds of opposition, and apostacy, " no less than Conversions."

The ignorance, evinced by the Missionary of all the lessons, taught by the history of the Conversion of Europe, of Ethnology, Geography, Linguistic Science, and the ancient Religious Conceptions of the people, is calculated to alienate the mind of the ordinary reader: it is idle to say, that such knowledge of the civilized races of Asia is unnecessary, or unattainable.

What shall be said of the following quotation from the Church-Missionary-Society-Report on Japan? "The leading family " there are very earnest Christians, and I seldom have seen " faces, which bear more plainly the marks of the Lord Jesus " Christ's ownership. The husband, Tobikawa San, has the " true shepherd-spirit, and is always trying to bring others, his " own farm-labourers, ignorant old women, little children, any " whom he comes across through the day, into the fold."

I could have wished, that the Missionary had told us more particularly of these marks, coupled with a remark, which I shall quote further on, of the Satanic appearance of a man, who declined to be converted: such expressions are unworthy of a serious Report. I remember one of my subordinate Magistrates summing up the case against a malefactor by stating, that the man had a squint in the right eye, which satisfied the Magistrate of his guilt: I need hardly say, that a severe reprimand was the result of this improper remark: do we not know excellent Christians all round us with most forbidding expressions of the facial organs? Do no rogues have most innocent and holy features? I read with surprise the word "lady" in a Missionary Report: A few days ago the word "gentleman" also caught my eye, but on only one occasion, which will be alluded to further on. From the Church-Missionary-Society-Report I remark, that a sick person is described "as a half-breed lady": this is a most singular expression on the part of a Missionary, and how it got into the Report is not obvious: at any rate the term "lady" should never be used: our Lord called His Mother "Woman," and no higher title can be desired.

I rise with an intellect wearied, and a failing Faith, and a nausea as of something unpleasant in my mouth, from the perusal of some Reports and Publications: I do not venture to say which. I have for many years read the Reports of six great Societies, and a half-a-dozen smaller ones, such as the Universities' Mission, the Melanesian, the American Board, the Moravian, Rio Pongas, and the Reports of the three branches of the Presbyterian Church in Scotland, besides French, German, and Latin Reports.

Every page in some Reports has the Divine Name unnecessarily brought in: it is in our thoughts always, and everywhere: why bring it into vulgar use? In a Circular of the Church-Missionary-Society, lately issued, of about thirty to forty lines, I found the Divine Name seven times; and the supporters of the particular Society styled "God's people." Every page of some Reports announces the marriage of a Missionary, the birth or death of a baby: in one French Report the Missionary tells us in his full gush of the birth of his ninth child, gives us her baptismal name, and adds the information, that the little stranger resembles her elder brother, and that the mother has a copious supply of milk to rear her. Then in another Report we have abuse of a poor heathen, who would not let his son, his only son, be baptized, which meant social death: we have full accounts of the immorality of the Heathen: we hear of a Missionary, trained at the expense of the Society from his boyhood, throwing up his work, and coming home, because the climate does not suit his wife. Nothing is so humiliating as the perusal of such a Report in the last decade of the Nineteenth Century: pious tags, hackneyed quotations from Holy Writ are inserted in inverted commas, attacks on the Opium-Trade, the Liquor-Traffic, the Church of Rome, and the non-Christian world in general. A kind of finishing up with a parody of the Mahometan formula of Belief: "There is no Society like this Society, and this is the Report," with a final call for more money, and more men and women.

If this description be doubted, I ask the doubters to read Reports all round for a cycle of five years, as I have done.

But ever and anon in the wilderness of quotations and Editorial platitudes, unkind stories of the Mahometan, and Hindu, and Buddhist, and Confucianist, who are after all also, as well as us, the poor children of the same Father, the reader comes suddenly on a spark of light, which illumines the pages: I find in my copies the words "most interesting!" or "beautiful!" scored in pencil in the margin: little indications of a simple belief, which had come no one knew how: the story of some one, whom the Spirit of God had gone out to meet, and made him a new man ere he returned home: the story of the catechist, who was found stretched on the ground, under the trees of the forest, reading the translation into his own language of a Gospel, which the ship had brought to him the previous day: we find little traces of the natural goodness, which still survives in unconverted men, which will develop itself under the gracious touch of the Holy Spirit, for God has not left Himself without a witness. Such words as these are worthy of record, "it was worth a lifetime in the Mission-Field to see this soul saved." Every part of the world has its message of Love, for we are all men: in one Report I read touching incidents of a party of Redskins waiting several days, in inclement weather, on the shores of a great river, hoping to stop the Missionary's boat, as it was proceeding down stream, that they might have their little children, whom they had brought with them, baptized.

We read with interest the long-continued contest between an experienced Missionary, and a young Brahmin, which after many days of struggle on the part of the latter ended in his surrender: he lives to this day, though his converter has long ago received his reward: we read with thankfulness of the Cannibal Chief, who spared a victim to please the wife of a Missionary, and himself became a convert, and a lay-reader to his subjects: all such affecting facts (for I care not for speculations, or visions) teach us the lesson, expressed by Galileo in his famous utterance with regard to the rotation of the globe in spite of Popes and Cardinals,

"E púr si muove."

There is a movement, and the Truth of the Message, and the very present aid of the Divine Power, are evidenced by the progress made in spite of the feebleness, and unwisdom, of the poor human agents employed, and the fact, that so much remains to be desired in the Modes, in which the work is reported. The Lord does make Himself manifest by His Works: it is not the dogma, or the creed, the hackneyed prayer, that marks those, whom He has chosen. He reads the heart. In spite of the presumptuous Boasting, the Faith-healing, the Self-laudation, the complacent Euphemism, the suppression of all facts, that are unpleasant, there is sufficient evidence to show that "Great Pan is dead." There may be worse forms of Religious Conceptions coming into existence, but the old ones will not hold out before the attack of Education, Civilization, and contact with other Nations, and the light of the simple Gospel.

The additional Publications, monthly Periodicals of all kinds, fugitive pieces for distribution, tracts, and leaflets, leave much to be desired. Many of them are distinctly goody-goody, and as such to be deplored: it is difficult to say what class of the community, from the working-man's family to the Noble's, such productions are calculated to impress favourably in favour of Missions, and that ought to be the only object.

6. SENSATIONALISM.

Too much time and money should not be wasted in sensational gatherings under domes of Cathedrals, or in great Assembly-Halls, listening to Visions and Rhetorical figures of excited Preachers, or still more excited Platform-orators. Such vain demonstrations will soon develop into processions, and other eccentricities, for the passion or rage is advancing year by year. The work of conducting Missions is a very serious one, and the words "Ora et labora" seem to cover the whole ground: this was the Method adopted by the founders of our great Societies: it is not, that they had less piety, or love for prayer, but they wore it less on their sleeve: it was well said by an old friend of Missions, that: " If the walls of some Committee-Rooms could
" speak, they would tell, how discussions were often stopped,
" while the Committee knelt down and prayed over difficulties,
" that were perplexing them. All their deliberations were
" conducted in a spirit of weighty and dependent prayer."
This spreading out the letter full of anxiety before the Lord, and praying over it in the Room, where His work was being carried on, was something very different from the issue of thousands of tickets, and the setting in motion of hundreds of vehicles, and the bringing together crowds of women and men, who would have been more profitably employed, working in their own homes, or worshipping in their own Churches.

Sensationalism is not confined to Missionary objects. I quote from a religious paper: " It would seem, that our Ecclesiastical
" authorities have definitely adopted a policy of what may be
" called euphemistically impulsive movement. There are two
" modes of progression, the one by steady and regular motion,
" the other by successive impulses. The Church has hitherto
" gone on the former plan. 'Next to a sound rule of Faith, a
" sober standard of feeling in matters of Religion' was the
" object even of the enthusiastic party, which created the great
" Ecclesiastical movement of the last forty years. But this very
" party, or, at least, its most advanced representatives, are now
" the chief advocates, though not perhaps the originators, of a
" system, which subordinates sobriety to more impulsive qualities.
" Yesterday, for instance, a precedent set last year was renewed,
" and the day was set apart for special services and intercessions
" on behalf of Missions in Foreign Parts. Such a plan, no
" doubt, has its advantages. On the strictly religious aspect of
" the question, indeed, it does not become us to speak. That,
" which is ostensibly the main object of the movement, is to
" unite the members of the Church in one act of Intercession

"on behalf of Missions; and we do not know, whether it is
"supposed, that the louder voice of a united Intercession is
"more likely to command a hearing than the less obtrusive
"supplications of individuals and scattered congregations, or
"whether it is simply thought, that the appointment of a given
"day will rouse people to a duty, which they would otherwise
"neglect, and that a deeper interest will be excited by the
"consciousness of common action. In this respect the move-
"ment is of the same character as that for the Hospital-Sunday.
"It is found by experience, that the wave of sympathy rises
"higher and rolls over a wider area, when it is set in motion
"over all parts of the surface of society simultaneously. Men
"are swept within its reach, who ordinarily stand aloof in easy
"security on the shore. Whether it is altogether a good sign,
"that these supreme efforts should be annually needed, and
"whether the greater the flood the greater may not also be the
"ebb, may, perhaps, in all such cases be questioned."

We may fairly ask: will a united voice obtain a more certain hearing of the Giver of all good things? Does not over-excitement produce a reaction? We implore the popular speaker, or preacher, not to dilate upon Visions, which he describes poetically as having seen, as we know that the Epoch for young men seeing visions, and old men dreaming dreams, is past: we are living in a material unromantic age, when flights of oratory have no effect, but when words of Divine Wisdom fall very deep in the heart. Of what profit is the working out of analogies with Joseph and Queen Esther, or other Old Testament characters? they are mere verbiage: they have no relation to the subject of Evangelization: it is not necessary to go behind the example, and words, of the Master Himself, and Paul. Let him tell the audience the old, very old, and yet new, ever new, story, how Science has revealed every corner of the round world, and that in the Victorian age we are brought into contact with Nations, and tribes, and tongues, of whom our Fathers knew nothing, the white, the black, the red, the yellow races, differing from each other in colour of skin, in the skull, the skeleton, the temperament, and environment, yet all recognising the existence of a Great Spirit, and of a Life beyond the decay of the poor body, all waiting, waiting to be instructed: "if," as the Northumbrian Chief said to the Missionary from Canterbury, "ye have anything to tell us, let us hear." He might then tell his audience, how the Holy Spirit has been poured out with exceeding abundance on this generation, bidding us, enabling us, sustaining us in the wondrous desire to carry the Gospel to every Nation, on which the Sun shines in its daily course. If he be a Missionary, or one, who has lived among Missionaries, he can tell them with glistening eye, but in the simplest possible words, how the War goes on: words steeped in Love with no single expression of hatred to, contempt for, abuse of, the poor benighted heathen: Words of Love and Pity, such as Paul uses, when he speaks of God's chosen people: if the preacher be not a Missionary, he may have read, or he ought to have read, the narratives that come in from the East and the West, the North and the South, not of one Nation, or one Church, or one denomination: let the story be written with an iron pen on the tablets of the hearts of the hearers, but let him remember, that by his gleaming words he may conciliate new allies, or alienate by egotistical, boastful, unjust, expressions, hitherto faithful supporters. The twentieth Century may see the work in greater completeness: the present Century has only paved the way, and much of its work is only wood, hay, and stubble: there will be something then to record, though our eyes may never see it.

This is not sensationalism, but fact. But what shall we say of cries from Westmoreland for one thousand men, echoed by a cry from Shanghai for one thousand for China only? when the Armies of Nations are increased in this hasty way, the standard of height and fitness has to be reduced? If a thousand be called for, why not ten thousand? It is a mere election-cry. Can the average of capacity of the men and women now sent out safely be reduced? The exaggerations, and sensationalism, and emotional transcendentalism, have grown up, since Mr. Venn, a calm and practical Statesman-secretary, laid down his pen. A historian remarked, that there were two classes of Nations in Europe, the robust like the Russian, the Teuton, and the Frank, who are masculine, and the Greek, Latin, and Iberian races, who are feminine in their emotional want of control, and their sanguine temperament: can we not detect a large diffusion of the feminine element in the proceedings of the Home-Committees, and the labourers in the Field? but it is not the brave, dauntless element of the Female Evangelist, but the ill-considered utterances of the ignorant emotionalist.

V. THE MISSION IN THE FIELD.

CAP. V.		The Mission in the Field.
	1	The Very Small Mission without Resources.
	2	The Solitary Mission-Station: the Pioneer-Mission.
	3	The Self-supporting Mission.
	4	*a.* The Native Agent. *b.* Independent Native Church.
	5	The Unpaid Agent.

Prefatory Remarks.

I. The simplest expression of a Missionary is, that of a person of either sex, or accompanied by one or more fellow-labourers, who goes out at his, or her, own charge, subject to no external control, to preach the Gospel to a non-Christian population. Should funds be collected by friends, in aid, there are no accounts published. This is what some call a "Faith-Mission."

II. When several such individuals unite, and have all things in common, and bind themselves by certain Rules, they form a "Sisterhood" or "Brotherhood." Should accounts be kept, they are not published, as the concern is a private one.

III. The next stage is an organized Association of contributors to a Fund, controlled by a Committee, which is annually elected out of the body, and is empowered by the Rules of the Association to select Agents, send them out, support them while out, and recall them at pleasure. This is a "Missionary-Society." In its fullest development, such a Committee trains Students, selects suitable Mission-Fields, provides for sick and disabled Agents, and the children of all Agents, and is responsible to no one, but its constituents, duly assembled in General Meetings, to whom it renders accounts, and full reports of work done, and whose order it must obey on penalty of being superseded.

IV. When the Association comprises the whole body of Christians of a particular denomination, who have formed themselves into a corporation of a so-called "Church," Missionary work is then said to be conducted by the Church. This is only possible, when there is a fixed confession of Faith, without diverging shades of theological opinion within the Church. In the case of a National Church, like the Church of England, it is impossible.

V. Missionary-Societies have satellites, independent in organization, but formed solely to co-operate. Such Societies are called Home-Aids, or Foreign-Aids, according to the work, which they undertake: "Special-Aids," if they are satellites to several Societies. Some of these Aid-Societies have exceptionally a double position, as satellites to other Societies, and doing independent foreign work of their own. These Societies do the Women's Work, Medical Work, Training Work, Miscellaneous Work, and Publishing Work, of other Societies, and are of exceedingly great importance.

VI. Associations, which admit members of all Protestant Denominations, are called Catholic or Undenominational.

1. The Very Small Mission without Resources.

There is an objection to small Societies, and the smaller they are the greater the objection. The Heathen must be conquered by great battalions, not by Knights-Errant, and romantic and ill-considered attempts made by misdirected enthusiasm: I have known too many of such mushrooms. They fade away, or die with their founders. Consider then the waste of time and money, the vacillation, the delay from want of funds and men, the nullity of effect. Many names rise to my pen, but my remarks are to be colourless. A wise governing Committee, an Agency for collecting funds, and preparing Agents, are necessary. Such skirmishers do mischief, and impede the progress of the main army, and sometimes cause scandals: I make this remark with knowledge. In the case of a small Society the charges for the Home-Office have an unduly large average. I do not despise the day of small things, but that day in most Fields has passed away, and greater progress will be made by strengthening great Societies. I know of one Society, whose efficacy is injured by parasitical growths, or extraneous grafts, which have become suckers rather than feeders. A Society, which is to continue and flourish, must be based on a Church, or a Section of a Church, or a Denomination, and must not depend on the life and energy of one individual, one family, or a body of friends; if it has no root, it will fade away, and die, as many have done. The starting of a personal Mission does a mischief to the cause: Missionaries must have the gift of obedience to some one, Church, or Society: if they have not, and go in for simple Egoism, they had better leave it alone.

The noble army of Keltic Missionaries, whom we love and honour so much, worked in a sporadic way, without system, or tap-root on their mother country, and they passed away like a Stormy Cloud. The Anglo-Saxon Mission of Boniface made an oath of obedience to Rome, and with organized support lasted on till Europe, by means fair and foul, as above described, was converted.

One who has tried it and failed, in a letter to my address now on my table, dated 1888, writes that " a free-lance Method of " Mission, unless under exceptional circumstances, and by " Agents of unusual good sense, is very injurious to the Christian " cause."

I refrain from mentioning names: they rise up before me in Asia and Africa: the enterprisers are worthy of all love and esteem for personal qualities: what they are entirely deficient in is sanctified common-sense: what abounds in them is " Egoism."

2. THE SOLITARY MISSION-STATION.

Next comes the objection to solitary and single-handed Missions. Our Lord sent out His disciples two and two. The Romish Church makes it a rule absolute, that no Agent ordained or lay should be alone. There is comfort and support in fellowship, and there is the check imposed by the presence of a Brother against the first temptations to Sin. We should try to paint to ourselves the Missionary left many months quite alone: I have known it as a public officer, and in my youth I enjoyed it, while ruling a people, whom I loved, with all the surroundings of Anglo-Indian comfort, in a Climate, which during the winter season is very delightful; but during the hot season I dwelt in houses in the midst of my fellow-men. But the Missionary is often in a deadly climate, for a very long time, in a rudimentary kind of habitation, without medical advice, without a friend to sustain his parting spirit. Many holy men have made their solitary moan, and no one, but their God, has known how they died. It does sometimes happen, and within my knowledge, that a particular Missionary is of such a disposition, that he cannot get on with his colleagues, and has to be consigned to an isolated spot: such instances of infirmity should be the exception: the Missionary, who has failed to convert himself, will scarcely be an efficient agent to convert others. "Better is he that ruleth his spirit than he who taketh a city." There are many men fit to be Missionaries, but not fit for Holy Orders. The French Romish Priests divide their Agents into Pères and Frères, both celibate, and both receiving the same stipend, *i.e.* food, raiment, and home-roof.

Men should not be left alone ; the Church-Missionary-Society have had to disconnect several men, lay and ordained, for sexual profligacy. Solitude and a hot climate are hostile to morality, and to spiritual advancement. Early marriages are destructive of all real devotion to Missionary-work. Many men, after receiving gratuitous education at a College, steal home because of a sick wife. It is a waste of our sacred funds. Two Missionaries living together, or a Brotherhood, are comforted by society, discussion, and in case of illness being looked after.

But we must learn to distinguish the Solitary Mission-Station of a permanent character from the Pioneer-Mission, which may perhaps consist of one man feeling his way : all things must have their beginning. I quote the words of a Missionary, Mr. Blackett: "The Pioneer-Missionary is a comparatively inex-
" pensive worker. He needs but to be planted in or near the
" district, which he has to open up, and to be furnished with the
" means of travelling through it. He goes with a tent, and two
" or three helpers, and attendants, or he travels and lives in a
" palki, which serves him as a carriage by day and as a house by
" night. He preaches in village after village, until an interest
" is roused, and the people in some convenient centre begin to
" ask for a teacher to reside among them. Then a Catechist must
" be placed there, and his house-rent and support form additional
" expenditure number one. As the interest deepens, the Catechist
" wants a place to preach in, and though a mud-hut with open
" sides may not cost much, it yet forms a second fresh demand.
" It seems a pity not to utilize the place in the daytime, as well
" as in the evening, especially as there are plenty of children
" needing to be taught. So the Society is called upon for a
" Schoolmaster. The work in that centre outgrows the capabili-
" ties of the Catechist, and he tries sundry experiments by
" placing two or more native workers together, all which involves
" definite increase of cost. He finds the women hard to approach,
" and asks for a Bible-woman at least to help in this direction.
" This may not involve any very heavy expense, and yet it is
" an addition to the Mission-Budget. Christians are gathered,
" and a simple Church is required, which entails periodical
" repair: then comes the necessity of a Native Pastor, whom
" the people are too poor to support." Here we part from Apostolical Methods. Nobody asked, how Titus or Timothy meant to support themselves, but the Englishman of the Nineteenth Century writes, *they cannot provide a stipend, on which a man with Education would be able to live.* This pre-supposes the existence of rich extravagant Missionary-Societies during the last eighteen Centuries.

" However the Missionary being set free extends his work
" to the Regions Beyond. Fresh villages are opened, more

" Teachers are called for, and the necessity of a Training-College
" for Teachers is felt. The Catechist must be taught in a
" Divinity-School: all this means money.

" The Missionary is always asking for more. It would be
" easy to indicate the number of steps in this sketch by going
" more fully into innumerable details, which arise in the actual
" working of a Mission. Meanwhile, there is another quarter
" from which urgent demands arise. We have supposed but
" one Missionary pushing on the Evangelization of this opening
" region. What if he break down? We may take it as certain,
" that he will within a few years. If his work has been un-
" successful, or has only reached the initial stages of success
" and of expenditure, his place may as well be left vacant for
" awhile. But if something has been accomplished, if the Word
" has begun to take root, we dare not leave it untended. A
" new man must be found, and if possible an Apollos, suitable
" for the work of watering, where a Paul has planted. Where is
" he to come from? No work in an unhealthy climate can be
" considered properly provided for, unless it be doubly manned,
" so as not to be forsaken in case of a break-down. And yet
" this is an ideal state of things, which is hardly ever attainable.
" The fresh man must be drawn from somewhere, and the least
" raw of the recruits must be put in to fill the gap thus made."

3. THE SELF-SUPPORTING MISSION.

This is also called the Faith-Mission: it is clear, that this idea has arisen as a protest against the extravagance, the want of self-sacrifice, the worldliness, attributed rightly or wrongly to the snug and comfortable Agents, who draw salaries from the great Societies, which have so far obtained the characteristic of an endowed Church-Establishment.

I give some extracts to exhibit this new departure: " We
" believe that, if we do the work, which God has called us to,
" He will move the heart of His children to supply the money.
" If God sends out workers, He will also send supplies. There
" is no limit to the measure, in which God can work on Christian
" hearts to move His children to give for those, who have gone
" forth to seek the Kingdom of God. We need 8000 Dollars to
" keep our accounts balanced, and we ask all to pray, that these
" things may be added to us. Has any Pastor forgotten to take
" the collection? 1888."

And again: " God never intended His heralds to be hirelings
" at all; or men with fixed assured salaries, as secular Servants,
" and Commercial employés. The Christian world has begotten
" a Missionary-system, unknown to the Lord, and His Apostles.
" We look in vain in the New Testament for any authority for
" what we see on every side. 1887.

"India has fifty unsalaried Faith-Missionaries. I can count over two hundred in the world, whom God feeds, as he does the birds, and they have all things, and abound. We are praying for the means to build a suitable home for three thousand Rupees. God is with our Mission."

And again: "I have been without money since Saturday, but truly the Lord never has failed, nor will fail. It is good to be without funds, as it is quite a luxury to stand still, and see the Salvation of the Lord. I feel less anxiety in having no money than in looking forward with but little. 1887."

Another report says: "Nothing in the locker." A third notifies, that they have left off eating meat, and are content with vegetables. Again: "A brother in Christ sent word, that he wished me to come, and see him. I went. He informed me, that God had impressed him, that he should send out a Missionary. As I was consecrated to India, he was satisfied, that God would have him send me. Accordingly he put the money to cover all expenses to India in my hands. It now became a matter of conscience between me and God. I felt, that God would have me go to India, inasmuch as He had provided the necessary funds unsolicited. I praise God, that I am here. I mean by His Grace to do His will. He sanctifies me through and through. Glory to God! 1887."

Again: "I am glad you feel as I do about paid Home-Agents. I believe, that God wants a larger number of His children to have a part in the work, and in this way each can do his part without pay.

"I have now finished the second year of self-support: it seems to me, that the support of my work comes under the head of Faith in God, and His dear children."

The writer, a woman-Missionary in Africa, enumerates every kind of present received by her: dollars, barrels, clothes, corned meat, etc., etc.: she adds: "The dear Heavenly Father has many good children, and their number is rapidly increasing: they are planning for the conquest of the world to Him, whom we adore."

And again, from Liberia, W. Africa: "I want ten acres of land in the city. I believe, that I shall get it: the King tells me, that he will build me a house to live in, and give me a farm to make a living from, and a boy (a slave) to wait upon me. I am going to take out six or seven Missionaries from America. I will need money, of course, to pay their way, and give them a start, and then I believe the work will be self-supporting."

Bishop William Taylor's name, both in South India and West Africa, is so connected with this elastic word Self-Support, that it is but just to quote his very words: "Jesus forbade His Disciples

" to take purse, or scrip, or extra coat: the labourer is worthy
" of his meat: those, who preach the Gospel, shall live by the
" Gospel. And they lacked nothing. The Master's Method is
" literally practicable, and adequate, now. The dividing-line
" betwixt a Missionary-Charity, and adequate, and reproductive,
" indigenous support for God's Ambassador is, (1) To depend
" entirely on native resources for the support of all ministers,
" school-teachers, and their families; (2) to welcome the co-
" operation of God's stewards in Christian countries for providing
" money for our Transit and Building Fund. 1886."

Another feature of an agricultural enterprise is thus recorded:
" The Government allowed the Missionaries to take land for a
" plantation, employ the natives, and teach and preach to their
" own employés. Agriculture was thus undertaken, not for the
" purpose of supporting the Mission, but to be able to evangelize:
" no profit anticipated. 1885."

In spite of all these brave words I look upon the system, or rather want of system, as dangerous and bad, and what is most important to me, as likely to retard the Evangelization of the world. One of Bishop Taylor's Missionaries, a Swiss, who had several years of work in W. Africa, called on me in London: he would not say one word against his leader, or his system, but he had given it up, and he handed to me for perusal a bundle of American newspapers. I there read of constant appeals for money: large piles of dollars made up: great liberality of supporters at home. I had to think it out, and I perceived, that the only difference was, that there was no Home-Committee, and no Organization to maintain a certain annual supply, and with that exception these so-called self-supporting Missions were supported by money and goods of all kinds; these so-called Faith-Missions rested a good deal on Works: I gathered, that some of the Missionaries kept the Post-Office, or a Grocers' Store, or taught the Portuguese language: this was the Nineteenth-Century analogue of Paul's tent-making.

I quote from an American Presbyterian paper the following:
" Nowhere have we found so clear and comprehensive a state-
" ment of Bishop Taylor's work, and its method, as the following
" from the *Presbyterian Observer:* One of the most remarkable
" men of the Century is William Taylor, the Methodist 'Bishop
" for Africa.' He has begun two chains of Missions across Africa,
" and hopes to start two more during the year. His Missions
" are founded upon principles, novel, but sound. He enters
" into agreement with chief and people, agreeing on his part to
" import good preachers and teachers from the New World, free
" of expense to the tribe, and to purchase tools and machinery
" for industrial schools. The chief and his people, on their
" part, are required to give a thousand acres of land for each

"school-farm; to clear and plant, immediately, a few acres
"of the farm, to provide subsistence for the preachers and
"teachers; to build houses for the workers, and to pay a small
"monthly fee for the tuition of day-scholars. Boys and girls
"may work for their tuition. Those wishing a full course, must
"be allowed to remain in the school at least five years. By
"this agreement the natives are made to feel, that they have
"made a valuable acquisition, and the Mission is at once put
"upon a permanent, self-supporting basis."

Formerly the Bishop had a Committee in New York, but now the Bishop says, if he wished a Committee for Africa, he would, by all means, have the same Committee as before; but, seeing the necessity for a change, he does not want even the semblance of a Committee, and will not have even a Treasurer, as such, but has selected a banker to receive funds, and pay them out on his order; and for this office he has a most efficient man, and for Secretary he has a many-good-sided man. The two men could and would be a Committee if they did the work of a Committee; but the Bishop will personally select and commission all Missionaries, returning every two years if necessary, and he has arranged with the Missionaries in the Field needing food supplies, so that they will make a careful list of a year's needs, and these, when approved by him, will be filled in Liverpool, or New York, or partly in each. Thus the Missionaries will look direct to the Bishop for the help they need, and to him they will report. Then comes the moral in the following lines:
"Do Missions pay? Does it pay to send men and women to
"Africa to sicken, and maybe die? At best, they can't do much,
"and then 'it costs so much money!' Friends, the results
"are with God. It is for us to have rather more of the mind,
"that was in Christ, 'who went about doing good,' and sought
"not His own comfort. Let us give good support to those, who
"are willing to go."

Bishop Taylor, of the Episcopal Methodist Mission, in the United States, is not the only holder of such theories. I quote from the Church-Missionary-Society-*Intelligencer*: "Interest has
"lately been aroused, in the large circle, who are readers of *The*
"*Christian*, by a series of articles, that appeared in that paper,
"signed 'A Missionary.' The writer was Mr. E. F. Baldwin,
"who was for three or four years a Missionary of the 'North
"Africa Mission,' but is now entirely a 'free-lance' on his own
"account. Mr. Baldwin's articles were forcibly written, and
"appealed to the fervent, and very independent, spirit now so
"widely prevailing, which rebels against all systematic method
"and organization, which very often produces the most disas-
"trous results. The gist of the series of eighteen articles may
"be thus summarily expressed: (1) Modern Missions are a

" failure, as compared with the Missions of the Early Church;
" (2) this is because New Testament-principles and practice
" have been departed from by modern Societies; (3) that the
" Divine order of Missionary-work is laid down in the instruc-
" tions of our Lord to the twelve, recorded in Matt. x; (4) that
" therefore Missionaries should go forth without purse, scrip,
" change of raiment, staves (*i.e.* convenient appointments of
" travel), and salutations by the way (*i.e.* the engrossments
" of human friendship); (5) that our Lord's own life was the
" typical example of this, and should be followed, not only in
" its spirit, but in its external features, such as 'not having
" where to lay the head,' etc.; (6) that after Pentecost the
" Apostles and early Christians strictly followed Matt. x;
" (7) that thousands of them spread themselves over the earth,
" their Faith giving them miraculous power, and their life of
" asceticism winning multitudes to their cause; (8) that similar
" Faith and similar asceticism can now produce similar results
" (including miracles); (9) that 'the average Missionary' ruins
" his influence by his unscriptural worldliness; (10) that no
" money collections for Missions were made in the Early
" Church, and that the prominence of Money in our Modern
" Missions is fatal to their success; (11) that the only Mis-
" sionaries, whom God blesses, are the 'free-lances,' who 'live
" on the Lord.'"

It seems scarcely necessary to go into detail to reply to such transparent absurdities; however, this task has been done, and done well, in the *Intelligencer*. I presume, that it is the narrowness of vision, the absence of study of the world in its present and past social relations, that prevents the intellect of good men from piercing the vast gulf fixed between the first and the nineteenth Century. Had it been the Divine Will, that our Lord should have appeared at this epoch, how different would have been His environment: the same difference applies to the environment of His Disciples.

But worse things remained behind. Mr. Baldwin, who had made these bold assertions as to the success of his Mission in Mogadór, N. Africa, left that country to start in Syria a Mission on the so-called Matthew x principles: his successor admitted, that it was " not possible to carry out the instructions of
" Matthew x in connection with Gospel-work in Morocco on
" an extensive scale, or for any considerable period, and that
" consequently they did not offer a sufficient basis, on which to
" found the future permanent procedure of the Mission."

The Editor of the *Reaper*, a Periodical, which principally recorded the work of this Mission, with regard to the asserted power of Faith-healing sadly admits that "the injunction, 'Heal
" the sick,' is still conjoined with the command, 'Preach the

"Gospel,' and *since we have not received supernatural power, in this Mission at least, to perform miracles of healing*, as the Apostles did, we believe, that it is incumbent upon us to do what we can by medical skill, and the use of *natural means*, to relieve the distress of the people, and to give them evidence, which they can appreciate, that in coming to them in the name of Jesus we seek their good.

"The discontinuance of the title (Matthew x Missionaries) leaves us free to take action in this direction, and we are now making arrangements, whereby Messrs. Geddes and Badger will at once begin a course of medical training, and probably other members of the Mission will, at a later date, follow a similar course. The medical department will, however, be made strictly subordinate, and accessary, to the one great and all-important work of the Mission in preaching Christ Jesus, as the Son of God and only Saviour, to Moors and Jews alike."

In his report of the present actual condition of the work, as he observed it on his visit to Mogadór, and according to the evidence he was able to collect, the Editor states:

"We have sorrowfully to admit, that there is grave reason to fear, that the Reports of a great work in the interior have been greatly exaggerated, if not in part entirely false. These Reports were sent to us in all good faith; but Abraham, upon whose testimony they mainly rest, has proved unfaithful.

"Of those known to our Missionaries personally, who professed Conversion, very few have remained faithful: . . . The work, in one sense, may be said practically to have yet to commence, and the difficulties are many and great."

Hence it would seem that, instead of more than a hundred converts, there were few or none, and that the glowing reports were fiction, and not fact.

The remarks, which I quote, are taken from the pages of *Regions Beyond*, and a paper on the Mogadór Mission by Mrs. Grattan Guinness. I should not have ventured to make them on my own authority, though I certainly agree with them, and I have visited Morocco.

The same writer contributes a paper to *Regions Beyond*, 1891, on Self-supporting Missions in Central Africa, a portion of which I quote:

"The subject of Self-supporting Missions has been brought to the front a good deal of late, in connection with certain work in Africa. It is an exceedingly important one to all, who are interested in the spread of the Gospel in the Dark Continent, and we propose, therefore, briefly to consider it in these pages.

"The unspeakable needs and claims of Heathendom; the miserably small financial resources available for its Evangeliza-

"tion; the short remainder of this Gospel-age; and the con-
"siderable number of volunteers for Missionary-work, all
"naturally conspire to make many ask, Is there no possibility
"of Self-supporting Missions? The question we propose to
"consider is, Are such Missions practicable in Central Africa?
"Bishop Taylor and some others think so, and have attempted
"to establish such in Liberia, and at other points on the West
"Coast, in the Congo region, and in Loango and Angola. It
"is now several years, since this attempt was commenced; and
"though those, who have made it, would probably say, not long
"enough fairly to judge of the experiment, we are inclined to
"think the period is quite sufficient to afford at any rate fair
"grounds for a comparison between this special plan of evan-
"gelizing the Heathen and other plans.

"We, of course, sympathize deeply with the end in view, and,
"as regards Bishop Taylor's Missions especially, admire the
"self-denying labours of their founder. We love and esteem
"him personally, though we cannot but believe, that he and
"some others have adopted a very seriously mistaken Mis-
"sionary policy, causing their efforts to be more costly and less
"effective than ordinary Missions."

The arguments to prove this thesis are overwhelming, and, brought from experience of the Ba-Lolo Mission on the Congo. It is remarked, that "there are a few spheres, in which Self-
"supporting Missions may be carried on, but they are not to
"be found in tropical countries, and least of all in Central
"Africa. In sparsely populated regions, where the soil and
"climate admit of colonization, and where many of the re-
"sources of Civilization, such as roads, carts, and beasts of
"burden, are available, Christian emigrants may find time and
"opportunity to sustain themselves, and yet do some amount
"of Missionary-work. This is the case in South Africa, in
"Natal, and in our Australian and Canadian Colonies. But
"such workers ought no more to be called Missionaries, than
"men, who give some of their time on Sundays to Gospel-work
"at home should be called Ministers. It only confuses the
"subject to confound such with Missionaries to the Heathen in
"Central Africa. In China and in India Self-support is scarcely
"possible, unless Englishmen care to compete with natives, who
"can live on two or three pence a day. Missionaries must
"either be supported by the natives, or from home; but in
"Central Africa the thing is simply impossible, if rapid and
"effective Evangelization of the Dark Continent is to be
"attempted."

The writer then carries the war into Bishop Taylor's own Mission. I longed myself to express similar opinions, but refrained. The head of a great Missionary-Association with

Missions in W. Africa has stepped down into the lists to do battle for my views. "The Liberian mission of Bishop Taylor
" is an illustration of this. It is situated on the coast, where
" steamers call regularly, and among professedly Christian
" negroes, a very much easier sphere consequently than the
" wholly unevangelized interior, a thousand miles from the
" coast. Between fifty and sixty Missionaries have, at very
" heavy expense, been sent out since 1887 in connection with
" this Mission, mostly from America. Six of the party died,
" twenty-seven (including families) withdrew, and nineteen
" remained last year. These were distributed in sixteen stations;
" so that a 'station' was for the most part a solitary man,
" without any helpers or resources. What has been the
" Missionary result of this effort? Some houses have been
" built by the Missionaries' own hands, and some vegetable
" gardens cleared and planted, and some coffee-plantations in
" the same way. But no attempt has been made to learn the
" native language, to translate the Gospel into it, or to evan-
" gelize the Kru people. The Missionaries were instructed to
" preach as they could in 'pigeon English' (which some of the
" Kru understand), and to try and teach the children English!
" No heathen congregations were gathered, no itinerating
" attempted, and no preaching to the Heathen. One, who
" worked three years in this Mission, and whose heart was
" burning to evangelize the Kru people, found it impossible to
" get time for the study of the language. He had to build his
" house, clear and cultivate his garden, to light his fire and
" cook his food, and even to wash his clothes, for of course he
" had no means of paying a servant; he had no time for linguistic
" study, or even Gospel-preaching among the Heathen, which
" might have been imagined to have been the sole object for
" which he left his country."

The writer concludes with the following remark: "We trust
" that all, who have been led to attempt from right desires this
" wrong plan, will do as we did ourselves, for we once tried it.
" There are diversities of gifts. The labourer is worthy of his
" hire. Do not employ your war-horse to draw a cart of sand
" and hay."

4 (*a*) NATIVE AGENTS. (*b*) INDEPENDENT NATIVE CHURCH.

Up to this time we have only been dealing with means to an end; we now have to consider that *end*. The white Agents must in time disappear: the native Agents will remain for all time, and consolidate into a Native Church, an entirely independent Native Church: I propose to treat the two subjects separately.

(a) *Native Agents.*

When the Missionary himself exhibits the character of Self-consecration, and Self-sacrifice, he can enforce those characteristics on his flock; but not otherwise. For the welfare of the Native Church, and for the spread of the Gospel by the agency of Native Evangelists to the Regions Beyond, it is most desirable to maintain the greatest simplicity of life, and the great grace of gratuitous ministration, the consecration of body and soul, with a mere provision for the humblest human wants. I rejoice to see the steady opposition to the entertainment of paid Native Agents in China; or, in other words, providing with a salary a crowd of hungry converts, well deserving the name of "Rice-Christians."

" The injurious effects of the Paid-Agent system on the mass " of the Chinese population, outside of the Church, are perhaps " still greater. The *à priori* judgment of the Chinaman, as to " the motive of one of his countrymen in propagating a foreign " Religion, is, that he is hired or bribed to do it. When he " learns, that the native preacher is in fact paid by foreigners, " he is confirmed in his judgment. What the motive is, which " actuates the foreign Missionary, a motive so strong, that he is " willing to waste life, and money, in what seems a fruitless " enterprise, he is left to imagine. The most common expla-" nation is, that it is a covert scheme for buying adherents with " a view to political movements inimical to the State. Of " course it is supposed, that no loyal native will have anything " to do with such a movement. If the Chinaman be told, that " this enterprise is prompted by disinterested motives, and " intended for the good of his people, he is incredulous. The " result is, that many well-disposed Chinamen of the better " classes, who might be brought under Christian influences, are " repelled, and those, who actually find their way into the " Church, are composed largely of two opposite classes: those " whose honest convictions are so strong, that they outweigh " and overcome all obstacles; and unworthy persons, to whom " that feature in Mission-work which we are controverting is its " chief attraction."

So much for Asia: here speaks a Missionary from Africa: " I am " still of opinion, that the policy of paying Africans for spiritual " work with European money is a false one. The Native Agents " do not feel as they should towards the Society. Self-denial " scarcely ever enters their minds. While it is not easy to " introduce new measures for existing Agents, might not a better " policy be introduced with regard to new ones?"

This is the message from Oceania: " The Polynesian Evange-" lists received clothing, and laboured with their own hands.

"The principles of most Societies point to the policy of raising
"up an establishment of Native Pastors, upon a self-supporting,
"self-governing, and self-extending, system. The more these
"are enforced, the better."

The necessity of Native Teachers is admitted by all, but has not been encouraged by all as much as it ought to be. The black net to catch souls must be let down, but held in its place by white corks. Hear what Missionaries, who do employ Teachers with marvellous success, write: "The necessity for
"careful European supervision becomes the more urgent as the
"number of Natives, who become teachers, increases. It is a
"wonderful evidence of the hold, which the Gospel takes on the
"natures of these people, that, at so early a period in the history
"of the Mission, so many are found willing to be trained, and
"fit to be trained, as Evangelists to their fellow-countrymen.
"The rapid progress of the Gospel is assured, if this responsive
"spirit continues to be manifested. At the same time, it must
"be borne in mind, that at present, there are at best but young
"converts to Christianity. Though their knowledge of the
"truths of the Gospel, after a course of training at one of the
"Mission-Institutions, may be such as amply to qualify them
"for the duties of teachers, strength of principle, and that fine
"Christian spirit, which can discern and maintain the right
"course in times of temptation and difficulty, cannot be acquired
"with equal facility. To leave such men to stand entirely alone
"for any length of time among their own Heathen countrymen,
"without the moral support, stimulus, and counsel, afforded by
"frequent visits from a European superintendent, would not be
"wise or kind."

I quote further: "The Missionary should utilize to a greater
"degree and more suitable manner than has hitherto been done
"all available native piety and talent for Mission-service, till
"Indian Churches are able to appoint their own Missionaries.
"When such is the case, (may that happy day soon come)!
"England's responsibility will cease. But till then let all
"vacancies, as they occur, be filled up by qualified natives of
"the country. Two, probably three, Indian Missionaries could
"always be engaged for the pay and allowances of one European
"Missionary. This will greatly multiply Missionary-power. If
"there be increased Missionary-power at work, greater results
"may be expected, with God's blessing. The true solution of
"the Missionary-problem in India does not lie in the direction
"of encouraging large numbers of European Missionaries to go
"out, as celibates and ascetics, but in earnest efforts to multiply
"an efficient and consecrated Native Ministry. This is the key-
"note. Let such efforts be honestly made, and I am sure
"qualified native Missionaries will be forthcoming. But they

" must be treated as brethren, and not as servants; as accredited
" agents, like the European Missionaries, and not as their sub-
" ordinates and helpers, as at present. Formerly qualified
" converted natives used to offer their services to Missions, and
" their services were gladly entertained. Some of these men
" have gone to their rest, some have left the Mission-service,
" and others, though still in the field, are not much pleased
" with the treatment they receive. If a more liberal policy were
" pursued, that is to say, if native Missionaries were regarded
" by Missionary-Societies as their Agents in the same sense as
" European Missionaries were, made the members of Mission-
" committees, and allowed independent charge of stations, men
" of education and parts would be willing to become Mission-
" aries. Everybody knows that such men, as a rule, do not at
" present offer their services to Missions. Here is evidently
" much room for improvement, and if Missionary-Societies are
" really anxious to satisfy their constituents, to secure greater
" Missionary-power and to economize Mission-expenditure, they
" should inaugurate the policy above adverted to. The sooner
" it is done the better. 1889."

But there is a limitation. The Native ordained Evangelist and Pastor will, under any form of Church Organization, claim to be on an equality with the Missionary; but there must always be one exception, and the control of the expenditure of the funds, supplied by the Home-Committee, must be reserved to the Missionary only; while the Native Church has control over its own funds.

The Native Agent must be trained: hear what Mackye says:
" Men say, 'The blood of the martyrs is the seed of the
" Church,' but one dozen live Missionaries are worth vastly
" more to Africa than hundreds of dead ones, who never got
" even a fair start at work. The agency by which, and
" probably by which alone, we can Christianize Africa, is
" the African itself. But he must first be trained for that
" work, and trained, too, by the European in Africa. Just
" as the mountains of ironstone in the Continent are perfectly
" useless, until first quarried, smelted, and forged by European
" tools, which were also once nothing but ore, but by means
" of which alone it is possible to convert the raw African
" ore into implements exactly similar to themselves, and
" capable of replacing them in future work of the kind, so
" the untrained African mind is absolutely powerless to effect
" any beneficent results, unless first thoroughly trained by those
" of European tempering. This, too, must be done in Africa
" itself, for if the European in Africa has proved a difficulty,
" the African educated in Europe has proved a still more
" unsuitable instrument for his country's good. It behoves us,

"therefore, to select with the greatest care a few centres, to which Europeans shall have easy access, and where they shall be able to live under comparatively healthy conditions, centres within easy reach of Natives within a wide area. Mombása has proved a failure as to health, while the introduction of the freed-slave-element would alone ensure the ruin of an Institution for the training of freemen. I have seen hosts of specimens of the men turned out at the Institutions of Nassick, Mombása, and Zanzibár, where freed slaves are educated, but the best I have yet met was bad. Modern Educationalists have come to recognise the fact, that it is not enough to cram into the student a certain amount of book-knowledge; the eye must be trained to see, and the hand to reproduce, just as much as the mind must be trained to reason. Hence none but teachers, born teachers, need ever expect to be able to train Africans to be teachers in their turn. Unless this point be carefully guarded, it will ever prove the weak link in the chain. It has too often been supposed, that because a man is a University-graduate, or has taken Holy Orders, that, therefore, he knows how to teach. Few greater delusions have prevailed, and Africa has suffered in consequence.

"The staff at each educational centre must never be allowed to fall below a minimum of four. The scheme I have drafted is by no means new. It is much the same, as that adopted by the Monks for the Christianization of Europe, and which is pursued in Africa by the Romish Church to the present day. Only their strength lay in the Papal sanction, and in the possession of relics, and a pretended power for miracles. Our strength will lie in the dissemination of Truth, and careful preparation of Native minds, first to absorb and then to impart to others this knowledge. In this way the students from our central seminaries will become a connecting-link between the very un-African European, and the mass of their fellow-countrymen. Such connecting-links are in accordance with all analogy, both in nature and in art. We do not propel our ships by setting the piston to beat and thump at the water direct. To bring the piston into direct contact with the sea would be to cool the piston, condense the steam, and thus entail much loss of power. But we keep the piston in its place, dry and hot, and make it turn a crank-shaft, which has at its cold seaward end an arrangement of blades admirably contrived for pushing against the liquid element.

"It seems to be overlooked by many apparently zealous advocates of Missions, that in the command to go and Christianize the Nations, we are expressly told the Method by which we are to achieve success, viz., by Teaching them."

The necessity of a Staff of Native Teachers, Native Preachers, Native Medical practitioners, Native itinerants, Native colporteurs of the Scriptures, and Religious Books, and of Native Church Officers, has been universally recognised. The health and life of the white man is precarious, and he can neither speak, nor act, nor travel about, nor get access to the people, as one of their countrymen can. There is no necessity for hard and fast rules, with the one exception, that care should be taken not to make it a salaried Profession, paid by Funds from alien Associations: we find no trace of anything of that kind in the New Testament, and the mediæval Missionaries gave nothing but food and raiment. Training Institutions are a necessity to keep up the supply. But all that is done is but a prelude to the establishment of an Independent Native Church, as described in the next sub-Section.

(b) *Independent Native Churches.*

This heading presupposes some kind of Organization, differing according to the idiosyncrasy of the Church, which sent out the Mission. However much denominationalists may be sure in their own minds, that their system is the best, and the only one, the wide observer can read their remarks with a smile. There are many forms of Organization, possessing each their special weakness, and compensating advantages, and no arrangements of the men of this generation will prevent future generations altering and refashioning the human frame, or introducing an entirely new one. May God in His mercy grant, that they will not refashion the doctrines, re-interpret the Scriptures, or assert new Revelations! It looks very like it.

Lord Northbrook remarked in 1879: "What precise form of "Church-Government, or even of dogmatic theology, the Indian "Church may assume, I believe no man can see, and I, for one, "by no means consider, that it is a thing to be desired, that the "Native Church should take upon itself any particular form of "Christianity, which at present prevails in this country or in "Europe. Our dogmatic differences, as it seems to me, have "arisen from the history of Europe and of England, and it "seems to me, that it is some advantage to the Christians of "India that they may go, if they please, to the first Truths of the "Gospel without guarding themselves at every point against "what people are pleased to call the heresy of their neigh-"bours."

After all, the formation of Christian communities, and the creation of Christian life, is the object of Missions. I make this quotation as a warning and an encouragement: "In "estimating the advance, which has been made in developing "a higher type of Christian life, I fully recognise the difficulty

"of obtaining reliable data for observation, and I do not forget,
"how misleading it often is, to apply a standard in calculating
"the growth of moral perceptions and spiritual instinct. The
"Natives have been nominal Christians for more than fifty years.
"The time has been long enough to effect a great change, but
"let our demands be reasonable. It is unreasonable to expect
"from a people, who had sunk so low, a type of exceptional
"holiness, or to complain, because they are not paragons of
"virtue, and superior to the grosser forms of vice. I have no
"hesitation in saying, that a very great change has been wrought,
"and a change as great as I have a right to expect. I have met
"and addressed large assemblies of Native Christians; I have
"met in conference more than two hundred Native Pastors. I
"have attended meetings at the college, where more than one
"hundred students were present. I have had quiet talks with
"individuals. I have talked with Missionaries and foreigners
"about the converts, and unhesitatingly I affirm, that a great and
"unmistakably Christian work has been accomplished. Native
"Christians have not yet conquered their characteristic National
"and social weaknesses, but the force of new Christian principles
"is felt, and the Divine Truths of the Gospel are transforming,
"by a sure process, the character of the people. It is possible,
"to throw over Paganism a Christian dress without changing
"the old Pagan heart or eradicating the Pagan nature. I am
"persuaded, that more than this has been done. The Pagan
"nature has, in many cases, been brought into subjection to the
"mind of Christ, and the subjection has advanced as rapidly as
"the circumstances surrounding these people would permit. I
"place no bounds on the power of the Spirit of God, but I do
"not forget, that the effects of human environment is still seen
"in those, who are manifestly the subjects of the Spirit's power."

A voice from Melanesia tells us that: "One hindrance to the
"spiritual advancement of the people is to be found in the in-
"fluence of a certain class of foreigners, who have settled in
"the Islands. I gladly recognise the fact, that there are credit-
"able exceptions; but my Report would not be complete, if I
"did not refer to the foreign elements being in too many cases
"a distinct obstacle to the Christian life of the Native churches."

We must not expect to find Angels, but we may hope not to find surface Christians or downright hypocrites, or dull formalists, or, as may be said of the Romish converts, the same men using different fetishes, and repeating different, but still unintelligible, formulæ.

Hear the thoughts of another speculating on the possibilities of the future Native Church : "By what Organization governed,
"to what precise creeds affiliated, I for my part do not pretend
"to foresee. It is being hewn out now by many hands,

"furnished from many countries. But the main burden of the growing work must ere long be taken up by the children of the Indian soil. It is not beyond the bounds of possibility, that the native Church may in time produce its own Apostle, destined to lead his countrymen in myriads to the feet of Christ. The story of Buddha may renew itself within its pale."

Every Native Community, even before a Church had come into existence, should be taught and compelled to be self-supporting, providing for the modest stipend of its own Pastor, the Church-expenses, and the education of the children. No material inducement should be held out to a catechumen to accept the new Religion. In one Mission the rule is, that no Church should be organized before the Community has selected a man for their Pastor, and provided the means of his support: this principle ought to be universally accepted, and no progress of a permanent character can be anticipated if it be neglected.

I quote another writer from India: "Many of the Christians are very poor, but not a few are fairly well-to-do, and the Missionary expresses disappointment, that no advance is perceptible in the matter of liberality. He rightly regards this as one of the indications of the feebleness of spiritual life. 'When self-denial for Christ is an unknown quality, there never can be much real life.' And he strongly emphasizes his conviction, founded upon observation and experience, that 'from the very first, converts should be taught that nothing whatever will be done for them, that they can possibly do for themselves.'"

So far for the duty of the converts; now what is the duty of the Committee and the Missionary? Mr. Venn said to an African Merchant, who visited him in London: "You are spending your money in travelling for your own pleasure; why do you not contribute to the support of your own clergy?" The answer was: "Treat us as men, and we will behave like men; but so long as you treat us as children, we shall behave like children: let us manage our own Church-affairs, and we shall then pay our own clergy." This conversation led to the partial, only partial, emancipation of the Church of Sierra Leone: it is still under a white Bishop, paid from the taxation of the Colony: Mr. Venn was a Statesman, and took the hint; he went as far as at that date he could venture, and appointed a Negro to be Bishop of the Niger-Delta: narrow-minded views have now prevailed, and the Committee has decided, that a Negro, however educated and godly, is not fit to be an independent Bishop. The Negro would turn out all the white men, if he had the chance, as some day he will have.

It is still a great scandal, and reproach, that after a Century of Mission-work, and with native Christians in the fifth generation, we have not a single Native Independent Church with its own Independent Native Bishop, and self-supporting Pastorate. It is an instance of the Egoism, and Albocracy, of the English character: there is one Negro Bishop of the American Church at Cape Palmas, and one Negro Bishop in the West Indies, but the approved plan is, when a See falls vacant, to hunt up and down for an English Curate, ready to risk his life, leave his wife at home, and go out: those, who leave their wives, are constantly coming home to visit them, under the specious pretence of consulting the Committee. I have seen Bishop after Bishop go out, and die: I have written so fully on this subject in a separate Essay, that I will say no more here. The Churches in Asia and Africa have survived to our time, simply because they had a native Organization: My remarks apply chiefly to Bishops of organized Churches, such as West Africa, and South India: Suitable men are available, and two assistant Bishops have lately been appointed, but why could they not be trusted as independent Bishops? We do not hear of white men going out as assistant Bishops: the difference of treatment is only skin-deep, and the reason only extends to the skin.

As regards Africa we have had a Negro-Bishop for a generation, a good man, and he died beloved: there were competent men to succeed him: one a member of the Council of the Governor at Lagos, two Archdeacons on the Niger: why were they passed over, except from feelings of un-Christian contempt of so-called inferior races, just as a Pagan Roman of the time of Trajan would have passed over a Gaul, or a Briton, as something below contempt, as indeed in scale of education they then were: but these Negroes are highly educated and accomplished men, whose conversation in the dark might have been mistaken for that of an Englishman. Still more glaring is the presumptuous contempt of Englishmen of the middle classes for the ancient races in India, who were educated at a time, when Britons and Anglo-Saxons wore skins, and were savages. The only idea of a Bishop for the Pastorates in S. India is a white man, a Curate picked up in England, or a Missionary: at any rate the latter will know the language and the people. The people of India are not barbarians: in the contests for the Civil-Service they are known to outstrip the very flower of English candidates: they hold the highest Offices under the State: in one instance a Native commands a Regiment: yet no one in the eyes of the white Ecclesiastic, or the lay Committee of a Missionary-Society, is fit to be a Bishop, and yet in the eyes of the laity, with rare exceptions, the Bishops at Home, or the Colonies, are not men of high calibre, or Scholars, or men of Science, or Administrators, or Authors: on the contrary, any younger son of a Peer, or Head-Master of a Public School, is supposed to make a good Bishop: at any rate they know the language of the English people, and can speak to their flock without an interpreter, and this is just what they do not know in Asia, Africa, Oceania, and America.

Hear what Sir William Hunter writes in the *Times*, April 1894:
" In every department of the Government there is a tendency to
" incorporate the native element more largely, and upon more
" liberal terms. Thus the Covenanted-Civil-Service, which
" forms the controlling body in India, has been reduced by
" 22 per cent. since 1874, with the prospect of a further
" reduction of 12 per cent. In January, 1892, it contained,
" including the statutory appointments, 941 members, of whom
" 73 were natives of India. Of these Indian gentlemen 15 were
" admitted by open competition in England, and 58 were
" appointed in India under the Act of 1870. Without entering
" into contentious matter, we may remark, that they show what
" steps have been taken to give effect to the Queen's Procla-
" mation of 1858, which opened official employment in India to
" all races of Her Majesty's service competent for the work.
" They also suggest reflections as to the danger of further
" reducing the small British nucleus of control. In regard to
" emoluments, it is stated 'that out of 114,150 appointments in
" the Civil departments, carrying an annual salary of Rs. 1,000
" and over, 97 per cent. are now held by natives of India, and
" the remaining 3 per cent. by others.' It should be borne in
" mind, that a salary of Rs. 1,000 means a much better income
" to a native of India than £100 a year to an official in this
" country."

If the arm of Great Britain were shortened, all our Missions would be driven out of India, China and West Africa, and the Christian Churches having no backbone of Organization, with power to renew itself from generation to generation, would disappear as the Jesuit Missions disappeared in South America and West Africa.

In non-Episcopal Churches the same remarks would apply to the necessity of organizing a system of Church-Government, and Native office-holders, according to their particular constitution: with this precaution, when the time comes, and the English take to their ships, or are cut down by an invading force, like the poor Ma-Tabéle in South Africa, the Kingdom of Christ will not be uprooted, and perish with the alien Bishop and white clergy.

5. THE UNPAID AGENT.

I confess that I feel objections to unpaid Agents, those free-lances, who do just what they like, go where they like, and make the fact of their warring at their own charges an excuse for conducting the war on their own Method, and flinging it up at their own fancy. I would insist on all Agents being on the same footing as regards discipline: if anyone has abundance, he can find plenty of opportunity of advancing the Mission-work by his bounty, but he must not arrogate to himself a status differing from that of his fellows, because he has a few hundreds of Pounds per annum at his disposal. In some Missionary-Societies we hear of the boast, that their Agents receive no sort of remuneration: if this implies, that they war at their own charges, the objections stated above apply to the system; but generally the point is different. In some Missions all the Missionaries in each Station dwell together, as in a College, and the necessity of a separate establishment for each does not arise: allowances are made for their clothes, if wanted. Now, where subsistence money is provided, the amount is calculated on the necessity of a bare subsistence only, and such decent comforts, as will preserve the Missionary's health, and calm of mind. It is difficult to see the difference. Besides, the real question is, Has the man the Missionary-Spirit? If he has, it matters not how he is maintained, whether by a common or a separate fund. If he has no private resources, he must be supported in some way or other. It is impossible at this period, that he should maintain his life by a trade, as Paul did, though he did not enforce this practice on others. And in Mission-life there must be a great scattering of the Agents: perhaps two or three will be grouped together, and they must be sustained, and it seems far better, that they should have fixed subsistence allowances paid from the Common Fund: if they are wealthy, they can throw their gifts into that fund. They should abstain from mixing up their personal expenditure with the accounts of the Society, and should make no promiscuous drawings on the General Fund.

Then again it may be an unpleasant truth, but the conviction forces itself upon me, that the life of the modern Missionary is very easy-going compared with what it was fifty years ago. Take the life of Bishop Gobat, and see what he suffered in Abyssinia: privation, want, long delays in unhealthy places, tedious voyages, hope deferred, absence of success. What were the perils, and sufferings, of Selwyn, Patteson, Williams, Allen Gardiner? They had Faith, and Love, and Patience, and were real Apostles. One Missionary of that period mentions, that his boxes arrived after having been despatched more than two years. On being opened everything was as rotten as tinder.

Two or three packets of letters were in the middle of one box, but, when touched, they crumbled to dust. It was most trying, said the Missionary. It was the only time, that he saw his wife give way to sorrow and tears. In this luxurious age we find some Missionaries quite out of thoughts, if they do not get their post regularly, complaining bitterly if their things are not sent out to them as they like, and neither enduring hardships like good soldiers, nor exhibiting the external attributes of Servants of the Cross. I remember one unpaid Missionary persuading the Committee to cut him out a little Province of his own, like a German Duchy in the middle of the German Empire, where he could have his own sweet way : he soon threw it up, and came home. The only sound rule is not to have two orders of Missionaries, but both on the same footing : if anyone has wealth let him contribute to the Society's funds ; that is the rule of the Romish Church, that is the rule of the Cowley Fathers : there is no independent property of individuals.

I once urged in Committee, but as usual urged in vain, that something should be done for the Native Indian and Chinese, who flock to England, and sojourn a few years, and then return to their home. We send Missions to the Jew, and the Mahometan ; why not also to the enfranchised and enlightened Indian, who has learnt to despise the Religion of his forefathers, and has to be taught the better way ? Let a beginning be made with the small, yet intelligent, company of Indian law-students in this city. Amiable, gentle, and social, they might be impressed with the friendliness of Christian people during their temporary exile from their country, instead of being left quite to themselves. They frequent the meetings of learned Societies, and are able to address audiences in the English language ; and I have heard a Mahometan of Bangál with singular simplicity speak up for the purity of his Religion, and, with startling paradox, for the happiness of Mahometan women. A society called the London Mahometan Mission has been formed to look after the Arab and Turkish visitors to this city, but the natives of India are unnoticed, and yet some of them might, if brought under proper Christian influence, be powerful auxiliaries to the cause of Christian Missions on their return to India.

VI. THE MISSIONARY-AGENT.

CAP. VI.		THE MISSIONARY-AGENT.
	1	The Untrained Agent.
	2	Not Gifted with the Grace of Winning Souls.
	3	Failing to Master the Vernacular Language.
	4	Losing Heart and Desponding.
	5	Quarrelsome.
	6	Puffed-up by Undue Praise: Declamation.
	7	Meddlers and Busybodies, "Allotrio-Episcopos."
	8	Marrying early.
	9	Arrogant to the Natives.
	10	Deficient in Sympathy and Love, and Justice, to the Natives.
	11	Disloyal to Employer.
	12	Defying Laws and Customs of the Country.
	13	Tilting against Legal Native Customs.
	14	Throwing up the Vocation for Private Convenience.
	15	Holding Secular Offices, or Honours.
	16	Living in Society of Secular white men, and keeping away from touch of the people.
	17	Offending against Mission-Comity, Protestant or Romish.
	18	Ridiculing, and speaking ill, of non-Christian Religions.
	19	Immoral.
	20	Importing Western Ideas.
	21	Undertaking Work not belonging to his Duty.
	22	Intruding new Fads, such as Total Abstinence, etc.
	23	Insulting, or making use of, non-Christian Places of Worship.
	24	Preaching to Prisoners in Public Gaols.
	25	Taking up New Work to the neglect of old.

I make some general remarks : here are the attributes of the Missionary:

1. He must count the cost, before he begins to build.
2. He must be a man of sanctified common-sense.
3. An unworldly spirit, and unselfish aim.
4. Thoroughly intent on his work.
5. A man of Peace, with the Spirit of Peace in his house, heart, speech, and environment.
6. Simple habits and contented spirit.
7. Personal holiness.
8. Inexhaustible patience.
9. Unshakeable faith.
10. Full of prayer, and a reader of the Bible.
11. Dauntless, but quiet; courage of deeds, rather than of words.
12. A sound judgment, a chastened spirit, a man of soft answer.
13. Loyal to his Church, his Society, and his God.

Missionaries should ask themselves, why Missionaries, and Missions, are so exceedingly unpopular among their own countrymen, both sojourners in different parts of the World, and in their own Native land. Yet it is so undoubtedly. And it is not the irreligious and unbelievers, that speak ill of them, but persons, who are given to benevolence, but have a deep-rooted aversion to Religious Missions. There are certain individuals, families, and classes, who enthusiastically support Missions, but the great majority ignore the work, the men, and their Publications. I remark this Phenomenon with regret, but I do remark it, and see clearly the cause. Missionaries are narrow in vision. Cannot they correct this by reading systematically the Periodicals, and Reports, of other Societies, of other Denominations, and the Home-Committee should supply them. Each Society should publish Biographical notices of esteemed deceased Missionaries, and collective narratives of each Mission, so that the traditions of the past may be maintained. The Missionary will then find that the difficulties, which press on him in some remote corner of the world, have been disposed of elsewhere: he will find Methods, and machinery, at work, which will admirably meet his wants, but of which he had never heard: he will gather wisdom from the failures of others, as well as his own. The Lawyer, the Statesman, the Merchant, in their secular avocations, do this with advantage. The human side of Mission-work is an Art, and a Science, and is progressive from age to age. The Grace of God upon the imperfect labours of his Servants is unchanged.

Two errors in the selection of men should be avoided: if the standard be lowered and less well-educated men are admitted, there is danger ahead: the history of the Mission in Eastern Equatorial Africa during the last twenty years will prove this: on the other hand the Missionary must not be an enthusiast, feeding as it were on the "Pilgrim's Progress," and the "Holy War" of Bunyan: he must not picture himself as addressing an assembly of holy picturesque Brahmans under a wide-spreading pipal tree, and fancying, that his feeble words would destroy the prejudices, the legends, the practices, the hopes, the fears, of an ancient race: he may reflect, that if he were able to make in a short time such a change, as with the stroke of a wand, the Mormonite, or Theosophist, or the neo-Mahometan of Sayad Ahmed Ali's school, might come in a few months, and carry off his converts to their views. The duty of the Missionary is long, tedious, and prosaic, and the more, that Education and Civilization spread, the more difficult it will become.

1. Untrained Agents.

It does not answer to send out an untrained Army to the Field, composed of inferior, incompact, and ill-supplied, troops. A Mission should be composed of the best material, and care taken to adapt that material. It is not enough for a young man, or woman, to think, that they are called by the Spirit: their capacity from a human point of view must be tested, and the amount of self-sacrifice, which they are prepared to make, must be found out. Undeveloped powers must by teaching be developed. The very best materials, the choicest trees of Lebanon, were requisitioned for the Lord's Temple at Jerusalem, and then fashioned without any noise or excitement by the most skilled artificers. To send out foolish boys and girls, engaged perhaps to marry, who wish to do something, somewhere, somehow, without the manifestation of any gift, even of humility, or spiritual call, is sheer folly, and unworthy of a Society: yet we hear the voice of a Secretary shouting out at public meetings "More Men!" when there is not enough money to pay the workmen already in the vineyard. We have to guard in certain quarters against gush, romance, platform-demonstrations, mock heroics. We have to seek for a mind after long reflection made up, a quiet determination, an unostentatious laying oneself on the Altar, a placing aside absolutely for a certain term of years all human affections; we seek also an absence of a vaunting spirit, of a presumptuous, sanctimonious, Pharisaical, demeanour. "I have counted the cost," wrote Paul for himself and for all ages. Paul supplies us with an excellent word, $\dot{\epsilon}\theta\epsilon\lambda o\theta\rho\eta\sigma\kappa\epsilon\dot{\iota}a$, "will-worship," Colossians, ii, 23. The goodness of some is like a morning cloud: the wife falls ill, and home they come.

Hear what Livingstone said: we all know what he did. "The sort of men, who are wanted for Missionaries, are men of "education, standing, enterprise, zeal, and piety. It is a "mistake to suppose, that *anyone*, so long as he is pious, will do "for this office. Pioneers in everything should be the ablest "qualified men, not those of small ability and education. This "remark especially applies to the first teachers of Christian "Truth in regions, which may never have before been blessed "with the name and Gospel of Jesus Christ. In the early ages "the Monasteries were the schools of Europe, and the monks "were not ashamed to hold the plough. The Missionaries now "take the place of those able men, and we should not hesitate "to give up the small luxuries of life, in order to carry knowledge "and truth to them, that are in darkness."

Hear what Lord Northbrook, the Viceroy, said: "I believe, "that this Society has been wise and right in encouraging the "sending of learned Missionaries to India. In India the "Missionary has to deal with old Religions; he has to deal with "educated men, men of a very high order of intellect, and subtle "in reasoning. The Hindu is accustomed to a Philosophy "more accurate, I believe, than the Greek Philosophy; and in "dealing with Mahometans the Missionary has to deal with "men, who have strong faith in their Religion, and possess "a considerable extent of Arabic learning. Therefore I think, "if I may venture to say so, that you cannot send too good men "to India; and that by sending the best men you have—I know "that this Society has taken great pains in the education of its "Missionaries—by sending the best men you have you will "command respect, and you will probably be able to educate "and train, what it is your anxious desire to secure, an able and "powerful class of native ministers of the Gospel."

Hear what Sir J. Kennaway, President of the Church-Missionary-Society, said: "It is all-important, that the right "men should be selected, and trained, for the responsible "work they have to carry on. There is work for all, who are "animated with the Christ-like Love, and burning desire to "save souls. The training must vary with the class of men, "and the work which they are called upon to do. There "must be leaders to direct and govern, scholars for linguistic "and translation-work, schoolmasters, mechanics; indeed, "every Missionary must be ready with his hand, as well as his "head. He must have fertility of resources and self-reliance, "the better to grapple with difficulties. He may have to build "his house, make his furniture, work a printing-press, till his "garden, cook his food, and some training should be given "him, with some special medical instruction of an elementary "and practical character, such as is required for a voluntary

" ambulance-corps. It is not possible to generalize; particulars
" must be worked out by those conducting the Training-Insti-
" tutions."

Of what use is a party of untrained, and partially educated, enthusiasts, full of wild schemes, adopting the Native dress, upsetting all existing practices, dismissing all Native Agents, making a solitude of a great Mission, as has lately happened on the Upper Niger. I could specify name and place, but for the sake of the dead I forbear. We have had instances of hare-brained excited young men and women, full of so-called zeal, empty of all experience, ready to adopt the last new hallucination, such as Faith-healing, Pentecostal gift of vernacular languages, *claiming* a sick person of God, and talking of their work being *owned by God*.

The contest is between Christianity, other Religious Conceptions, and of actual Unbelief: of Sceptics the name is legion, and Missionaries should be men of culture and sweet reasonableness, something of the type of Paul, capable of arguing with such men, not in an arrogant, dogmatic, and angry manner, but with all the stately sobriety of Socrates. Some such men have gone out in times past and times present, and in order to secure a succession courses of lectures should begin to Missionaries under training, instead of leaving each man to try and discover for himself the best methods of arguing, and of general administration.

Stress must not be laid on numbers, but on qualifications: any youth or young girl will not do: Missionaries must be weighed, not counted. The following statement of qualification has been laid down: "Spiritual men for spiritual work. No
" candidate is accepted, who does not give clear evidence of
" having yielded his heart to God, and of his personal realization
" of the work of Christ for him, and of the work of the Holy
" Spirit in him. With this there must be soundness in the
" Faith, an intelligent and unfeigned acceptance of the Creeds
" of the Reformed Churches.

"*Intellectual.* There is room in the Mission-Field for various
" degrees of mental capacity and attainment; but those, who
" are to teach others, should be well-taught themselves, and at
" least there must be good reason to expect, that the candidate
" will succeed in mastering a foreign language.

" *Physical.* A sound constitution and good bodily health are
" essential for work in a foreign climate.

" *Practical.* Practical qualifications are of three kinds: First,
" the candidate should be of a cheerful, unselfish, amiable,
" character; diligent and self-denying; ready to obey, and able
" if necessary to command; without 'fads.' Secondly, he
" should have had experience in actual Christian work, especially

"such as has given opportunity for faithful and fearless witnessing for Christ, and practice in teaching the ignorant and seeking the lost. Thirdly, he should be a handy man, able to put up with the inconveniences, and sometimes privations, of life and travel in uncivilized or partially-civilized countries, ready of resource, able (if need be) to mend his own clothes, to put up his own tent or hut, to sail his own boat, to tend his sick or wounded comrade."

Let me here lay before my readers the account of a totally untrained party arriving at Shanghai, Feb. 1891: "'Why, there they are! the American party must have arrived.'

"We turned to see, and, sure enough, there were two Scandinavian strangers, unmistakable somehow in their pleasant, simple appearance and manner, standing at the door, and waiting a welcome. We hastened to greet them, glad that they could speak some English at any rate, and proceeded to enquire as to the number of the party they represented.

"To this very leading question, Mr. Pilquist promptly and cheerfully replied, 'We are thirty-five, seventeen men, and eighteen sisters, and there are ten more on the way, who will be here next week perhaps!' We could hardly believe it. But the faces of the dear brethren were so happy about it, and they seemed so glad to be here, and so anxious to start off immediately to bring all the others up to share their own warm welcome, that there was no possibility of doubt, and the only thing to do was to make preparation for them all as quickly as possible.

"Away they went to fetch their friends, leaving us to realize the blessed fact, that the largest Missionary-party, that has ever been known to arrive in China, was given to us that day, and that without our having done anything in the matter, either written a word, or spent a penny, or made one single effort to bring them, just given of God in answer to prayer, part of the coming thousand!

"Before very long the two brethren reappeared with such a company of pleasant-looking strangers; all able to speak English, and evidently happy in the welcome they received. A musical party too, evidently, for amongst the things they carried were several guitars, and kindred instruments, in interesting-looking cases. By degrees, after the first greetings were over, and we had found out all their names, and that amongst them were five from Norway, the remaining thirty being all from Sweden, we began to learn a little of their history as a Missionary-band, and most interesting it proved to be."

It is indeed overpowering to think of such a party arriving, including a man with the banjo, not a trained man or woman among them. I remember the five Moravian wives arriving at Calcutta, each with a ticket allotting them to an unknown Moravian brother in Tibet; but that incident of forty years ago is as nothing compared to this: they were trained Missionaries.

How were they got together: "Mr. Franson began in
" Brooklyn, by inviting, through the Swedish religious papers,
" any young persons desirous of giving their lives to foreign
" Missionary-work to meet him in that city for a fortnight's
" Bible-study. Hospitality was offered to all, who came in
" Christian homes.

" At the end of the fortnight, sixteen out of the fifty were
" accepted for China, their support being guaranteed by the
" Churches which had recommended them, and sent them up
" followed by their earnest prayers.

" The accepted candidates were then sent away to spend the
" remaining weeks before they could sail for China in making a
" tour of the Churches, going in little companies, some who
" could sing, and some who could talk, to deepen interest for
" China in a wide circle, and to quicken the spiritual life of the
" various gatherings that received them.

" From Brooklyn Mr. Franson went on to Chicago, and in
" November opened another Bible-School with seventy members.
" Of these also, sixteen were chosen for China, and sent out in
" like manner to stir up interest, and to be a blessing in the
" Churches, while he went on himself to open a third Bible-
" School in Minneapolis. Of this latter effort we have not yet
" heard so much, for the Minneapolis party are only on their
" way, having sailed twelve days after the first band, the
" support of each one lovingly guaranteed by those, who sent
" them forth; and more than this, he had 5,000 dollars in hand
" towards the general expenses of the work."

Now, if this kind of thing answers for the purpose of converting China, a great change will come over the Missionary-system: untrained young men and women caught up at random, Scandinavian settlers in the United States started off in a few weeks after they had answered the Newspaper-advertisement. One thing only is certain, that there will be a large number of marriages, and a great deal of distress some years hence to maintain them, and their prolific families, in China.

The late Reverend George Percy Badger many years ago wrote to me as follows: " There is one point, which ought to
" engage the serious attention of Committees, and that is the
" importance of sending out learned men. I mean learned in
" the books and tenets of the people, to whom they are sent: such
" men would secure respect. An ignorant Missionary has no
" chance with the Mahometans: he will do no good, and may

"do much harm. Possessed of knowledge he may be instru-
"mental in creating inquiry, which may lead to Conversion."

Another writer thus expresses himself: "Quite as important
"is it, that the Missionary should enter on his great Crusade
"with some definite conception of the Superstition, which he
"wishes to overthrow. That it is heathenish, erroneous, and
"immoral, is usually all he does know; but he is hardly likely
"to become an able Missionary, or a successful one, unless he
"knows a great deal more.

"Even African and Polynesian Superstitions need to be
"understood; and each of the stupendous systems of the East
"require the closest study. It is in the East, and during the
"years of active toil, that this may best be accomplished; and
"so much is there to be learned, and so interesting is the study,
"that the ablest and oldest Missionaries pursue it the most
"ardently; but a beginning should be made at home, and some
"book or books on the subject be carefully mastered.

"Since much is now written and spoken in commendation of
"Comparative Religion, it is necessary to point out that, im-
"portant and interesting as it is, that, which the prospective
"Missionary should aim at, is a study for practical purposes of
"the particular Religion he is about to assail. May I also be
"allowed to point out, that Comparative Religion, as usually
"taught, fails to deal adequately with the social and moral
"tendencies of various Religions. It seeks mainly to show their
"common origin; how far they agree, and in what they re-
"semble each other; it emphasizes their philosophical aspects,
"but fails to take adequate account of their practical defective-
"ness in the moral, and social, life. It is this, which more
"than justifies the Christian war waged against all forms of
"heathenism, and its study is worthy of far more attention than
"it generally receives."

Ignorance by itself is bad, but in the young men, who go out as Missionaries, and whose education is limited, it is accompanied by a contemptuous overlooking of the motive, which underlies all Religions however erroneous. Take your Atheist of modern times, and he will smile at the idea of God: the ancient races have never failed to affirm, that there is a Divine Power, which controls man: the Missionary's duty is to explain to them the nature of that Power.

To my amazement I read from a cutting from a religious journal, which lies on my table, that the person selected to be a Missionary "must be a gentleman," and of course this applies to the other sex, that she should be "a lady." In one Society I heard a discussion as to the line to be drawn betwixt the "women" and the "ladies." Merciful Heavens! and the Secretary found a dividing-line betwixt women and ladies by the latter having nicknacks on their tables in the Training-College. Will there be a place set apart in the next world for gentlemen and ladies? Were the son of the Carpenter, or the Fishermen on the Sea of Galilee, "gentlemen?" Were the sweet women, who attended on our Lord, and those others immortalized by Paul in the last chapter of the Epistle to the Romans, "ladies"? they were something infinitely better. The practice of the Churches of Christ, both Protestant and Romish, has been against this harsh and ridiculous suggestion. We have had Missionary Bishops sons of tradesmen, sons of menial servants, and a whole army of Missionaries, who do not lay claim to such a title.

Mark the care taken in the Romish Church to secure a proper training for their Missionaries: they go out for life; they have unconditionally given up everything: father, mother, wife, country, for Christ's sake, and are worthy of Him. I cannot approve of their Methods, or their Dogmas, or their Practices, but I love them for their devotion: they evince the great and inestimable gift of self-sacrifice, which is so often found wanting in Protestant circles.

2. NOT GIFTED WITH THE GRACE OF WINNING SOULS.

Every good gift, every perfect gift, is from on high, and cometh down from the Father of Light. A Missionary should not be cast down, if he finds, that the great Grace of power of converting souls be not given to him, or rather that he thinks, that it has not been given in the way, in which he expected. Others have been aware of the gift having been denied them: to some the power of the brain, to some the charisma of utterance, has not been conceded; some have humbly admitted, that "they thought, that they had not the power of bringing " souls one after another to Christ, of showing them their sins, of " breaking down the barriers, that gird the heart against religious " influence, and of creating in them a sense of their true need." Perhaps they may have failed in words, but the attracting and converting light shone out of their deeds, their modes of expression, their earnest countenances, and the vision of their lives: there are diversities of gifts, but the same Spirit. Of the Missionary, who uttered the above holy and humble opinion of himself, the natives, among whom he worked, had formed another estimate, and described him as "*the man, who prayed for the African, and tried in every way to do them good*": of another Missionary his people still speak tenderly, as "*the man, who after Christ's example died for us, black fellows!*"

And the spirituality, which once existed, may die: In the elder Weitbrecht's Journal appears the following: " Had a conversa-

" tion with Lacroix on the sad fact, that many of us Missionaries
" lose our spirituality while engaged in our work: it is necessary to
" warm the heart afresh by intercourse with Christians *at home*:"
here sounds the note of "*νοσταλγια*," which marks the man not
entirely devoted to his Master: at any rate Weitbrecht died at
his post, preaching from the text "Even so, come, Lord Jesus."

And of those, who humbly thought, that they had not the gift,
some really had it; and some glib smart talkers utterly failed,
and had no conception of the nature of the gift.

3. Failing to Master the Language.

The difficulty of mastering the language is always to be
reckoned with, and this, in fact, fixes the Field of each Missionary for life. It has amused me to hear from a Missionary
confidentially, that the language, which he has acquired, is the
most difficult of all languages. This assertion is sometimes
made with regard to the great literary language of Arabic,
sometimes with regard to the multiform, yet cultivated, languages
of China, and sometimes with regard to the wholly illiterate and
uncultured languages of Africa. As no living man has tried to
master all three, the degree of difficulty may be hard to determine; but it may be laid down, that in one year with ordinary
application any language can be acquired; and, unless it be
acquired, the Missionary is a dumb dog: the idea of preaching
the Gospel through an interpreter, or in a mongrel Coast-Patois,
such as the low class of traders use, is revolting. It is impossible for me to acquiesce in the practice of teaching in
Schools and Colleges in any other than the Vernacular of the
Students. The policy of throwing upon the Students the burden
of acquiring a new language, which the Professors avoid, is
questionable. I mistrust those Societies, in which the Agents
are not compelled to acquire the Vernaculars: any departure
from this absolute rule is not to the permanent advantage of
the Mission. No Secular Government would tolerate any
breach of this Rule in its servants, if it cared for the weal of
the people. It is a mere burlesque of a Mission, where this
step is not taken. A man or woman can care but little for the
Souls of the Heathen, when they will not trouble themselves to
understand their words, and let them understand theirs. All
Missionaries go out young, and the greater portion have that
Educational training, which implies the study of one or more
foreign languages. I think poorly of the man, who shirks this
obvious duty. It shows a want of self-consecration. I heard
the other day a Bishop, who did not choose to acquire the
Vernacular, dilate on the advantage of speaking through an
Interpreter, and the English Clergy, who went out on a winter's

tour to India, talk in the same way: they were satisfied, but how about the people? There is an old story of a dog, which had lost its tail, abusing tails generally, and recommending other dogs to cut theirs off. On the other hand, I heard Bishop Milman, of Calcutta, preach in India, in Urdu, which he had acquired when past 40 years of age.

I have been shocked to attend Services and Meetings, where Missionaries even of seven years standing could not preach in their Vernacular. I speak as one, who for the best part of a quarter of a Century, had to conduct intricate business of the State in more than one Vernacular: any public servant, who did not acquire his Vernacular, was put on board ship to go home. This applies to every kind of Missionary without exception, and to both sexes: if it be not idleness, but incapacity, the Missionary had better go home. "If he does not get over the " difficulty after living among the people one whole year, there is " little likelihood of his getting over it at all: those, who defer " the study and the practice of talking, generally neglect it alto- " gether." I quote this last from the "Missionary Manual." My own experience is, that the majority of Missionaries do not fail in this particular: some are admirable, and vastly superior in their style of speaking to the officers of Government.

4. Losing Heart and Desponding.

Missionaries should not be down-hearted, if their labours are not crowned by immediate visible success. Nothing is more remarkable in Missionary-Annals than the uncertainty of results. "I planted, Apollos watered, but God gave the increase." We read in the biographies of Missionaries, how in some cases a harvest suddenly sprung up, and then all faded away: in other cases no harvest at all appeared in the lifetime of the laborious founder, but soon after his departure, there has come a change, and his successor has entered into his labours. To few has it been conceded to do what is recorded, on the tombstone of a Missionary in one of the Islands of Polynesia: "When he came there were no Christians; when he left there were no Heathen." After all, if the Missionary has preached the Gospel faithfully, and intelligently, as far as he is concerned, his work is done.

There is a streak of Egoism underlying this despondency: if he recognised himself as only a cog-wheel in the great machine of Evangelization, he would be satisfied, that he had done his best, and no one can do more. Public opinion is in every field of human life unjust: certain men and women are unduly puffed up, while the silent labourer, faithful to the end, leaves no name behind him: what matters? His works will follow him. It is the case in all professions.

There are grounds for despondency both for the European, and the Native, Missionary, more for the latter than the former. I give one specimen: "All the life and work of the place are "shadowed by an immense temple. The Evangelist is alone. "Amid the constant din of pipes and horns and tom-toms in "the daily processions, that one man is but an insignificant "presence, and his voice is well-nigh drowned. Alone he "proclaims, that God is One and a Spirit, and gets back for "answer a flourish of horns. Alone he insists, that He is a "God of purity, and then sees Nauteh-girls dance defiance to "his words around the idol. As far as possible this painful "solitude is relieved by visits from the European and Native "ministers, and by tours which are taken by several Evangelists "in company. Such tours are generally arranged, so as to give "the preachers an opportunity of speaking at the markets, fairs, "and festivals, which are so numerous in this country."

It seems wrong to leave a Native Missionary exposed to such trials, especially when we read the following: "Their wives have "most of them enjoyed the sheltering influences of our boarding- "schools, until in early womanhood they were called out to the "Lord's work in towns and villages, where they have no "Christian neighbours and no religious helps. Most of the "people, who surround them, either despise or abuse them, not "infrequently avoiding their presence as if the mere shadow of "a Christian might bring an epidemic."

The early Christians in Europe must have gone through the same trials, or worse; and this shows, that boarding-schools are not an unmixed blessing: they lift the tender plant into a kind of preserve out of the forest, and, when the time comes to return to the forest, they are not equal to the fight with the hardy plants. We must think of Apostolic and sub-Apostolic times. My old friend and teacher Bishop Daniel Wilson once remarked from the pulpit in Calcutta; that "there was no going to Heaven in velvet slippers." Each of us must take up our cross.

5. QUARRELSOME.

The following is a Bishop's advice: "Each Missionary "should pray for mutual love and concord among themselves; "that they may learn to think more of the graces of their "fellow-workers than of their defects; that they may never "intrude their own opinions, and practices, into the works of "another; that they may be very slow to take offence, and "always answer unkindliness, and injustice, by special kindness, "and mutual acts of self-denial, and self-forgetfulness, that "they may all be helpful one to another, and with or without "them God may be glorified."

Laymen in Committee look with astonishment on the quarrels, and the consequence of quarrels, of ordained Missionaries. Everyone in official life knows, how often he is yoked with an uncongenial fellow-labourer, yet he gets on by mutual concession, and the Government, which he serves, would not think well of him, if he complained. As to asking, that a Colleague might be removed, so as to make oneself more comfortable, I never heard of such a thing: when this state of affairs transpires, a move is often made, so as to oil the working of the machine: but I have known Missionaries *ask for men to be removed*, regardless of the deep injury done to the man removed, the serious expense to the Society, the injury to the work of the Mission, and, if he could look forward, the entire discredit to the judgment of the applicant.

In India I have known the Magistrate having to interfere to prevent a breach of the peace betwixt two Missionaries quarrelling about their dwelling-house: I have found Members of the same Mission, all noble and God-fearing men, living in total estrangement, with no possible hope of reconciliation. I can point out Stations with only two Missionaries, unable to live together, and as hostile as dogs and cats. Public servants of the State do not act like this, and are spiritual men made of baser clay? Under the Statue of King Henry V of England at All Souls' College, Oxford, is inscribed: "Conqueror of his Enemies, and of Himself." Under the photograph of each Missionary let these blessed words be recorded: "Converter of the Heathen, and of Himself."

I now quote from a Manual, composed by a Missionary: " Quarrels are specially rife at small stations: Missionaries, " accustomed *to command* natives, become very dogmatic, and " desirous to have their own way; thus a Mission ceases to be " a model of Apostolic zeal, and self-denial, and becomes a " hot-bed of jealousy; small men contending bitterly with " each other for the exercise of a feeble power. Missionaries " are notorious for littleness, narrowness, and puny mental " character; a record of their disputes would form a humiliat-" ing chapter in the history of Missions: these quarrels are " always, according to themselves, *on principle*: if they are " reminded of the course laid down in the New Testament they " reply, 'Oh! that does not apply to this case.' Through the " deceitfulness of the human heart the working of self-esteem, " and jealousy, are regarded as zeal for the Truth, and the " advancement of Christ's Kingdom."

Perhaps their wives fall out: some brood over the imaginary injury in silence; some write to their friends; some send to the Committee a formal complaint, without letting the other side know; some write to the offending party: half a sentence in a letter misunderstood gives rise to a correspondence, which would fill a volume. The proper course for us all would be: "if our brother has ought against us, to go and tell him his fault alone."

6. PUFFED UP BY UNDUE PRAISE: DECLAMATION.

The Missionary should abstain from frothy Declamation and Egoism. Where is boasting? it is excluded: yet that such are the failings of inferior Missionaries, there is no doubt. Hear what that aged and experienced Christian Lord Shaftesbury said at a public meeting in my hearing a few years ago: " I notice, " that the Reports of the Missionary-Societies show a great " deal more sense than they used to do. They are not so full " of magnificent declamation, or great promises. They state " things more accurately, telling their obstacles and difficulties, " and they are beginning to come round to this great truth, and " the sooner it is known the better, that certainly Missionary- " Societies are not the great instruments, by which God will " convert this world. This is reserved for One higher. It is " because Missionary-Societies had held out such prodigious " expectations, and made such large promises, that the infidels " can turn upon us and say, 'After all you have said, what have " you done?' If we had told them that our Mission was to " carry the Gospel to every creature, and spread it over the face " of the earth, leaving the issue to God, we should have stood a " better chance in argument with infidels and gainsayers. I " know that Missionary-Societies do not like to be told this, and, " when to-night I said at a Meeting, that we must look chiefly for " the grand final consummation of the Second Advent, it was " not denied, but was not well received. It will be asked of " your Society, What can it do? Well, if it depended on your " intellectual and physical strength, very little could be done; " but you must remember, that you are engaged in raising up a " Native Agency, and, if you establish the nucleus of that, it is " impossible to predict the issue. Our duty is perfectly clear. " We are to do our best, and leave the issue with God. He will " superintend such a work as this, and carry it to a right issue. " Our duty is to sow the knowledge of Christ, and do everything " we can, so that, when the people of India become an adult " Nation capable of governing themselves, or desiring to do it, " or taking it into their own hands, whether we desire it or not, " we may prepare for that day by sowing broadcast the Word of " God. Whenever we shall retire from India, do not let it be said, " that we have left only in India the traces of Western vice and " oppression, but let it be known, that we have sown the seed " of Gospel-Truth, and done all we can to fix that in the hearts,

" of the people, without which no Nation can subsist in peace
" and honour; and in sowing the seed of the Gospel, be sure
" of this: that we have sown the seed of political morality and
" domestic virtue."

Hear also what another aged Christian, with a still more intimate knowledge of the idiosyncrasies of men, remarked at a dismissal of Missionaries of his own Society: "Mr. Venn was
" so infirm (1872) that he could not stand up, but he read an
" address to the Missionaries: he remarked, that Selfishness, and
" Self-seeking, were the bane of Missionary-life and work. *My*
" work, *my* catechists, *my* teachers, *my* converts, *my* pupils, was
" a language, that always pained him. One of his hearers, an
" old Missionary, now at rest, adds, that he could not acquit
" himself of the charge. Yes, it is the tyrant *Self*, that must
" decrease, before Christ can increase."

I can confirm the truth of Mr. Venn's complaint from my own experience. Whence come wars and fightings among you? Come they not from *Self?* In all my experience I never knew men so opiniated, so thoroughly perverse, and unreasonable, so harsh in their judgment of others, and so wilfully disobedient to orders, as some Missionaries. I speak as a Public Officer, who has had to obey, and thus learnt how to command.

The cause is the puffing up of the Missionary-Platform in Exeter Hall, and elsewhere: it is not surprising, that many men of moderate self-control lose their balance, and fancy, that they have done wonders: it depends on the temperament of the man, for some, who have really done wonders, are scarcely aware of it.

I now quote the words of one, who is dead, and from whose pen I never expected to read such lines, with which I heartily agree, though I ever entirely disapproved of the policy, practice, and utterances, on other occasions of the writer: This paper is entitled "Warnings not generally given."

" *Farewell-Meetings.* Here we find ourselves surrounded by
" scores, perhaps hundreds, of kind, sympathetic friends in a
" most uncritical mood, ready to applaud us enthusiastically,
" whether we talk sense or nonsense. Every speech, every
" prayer, reminds us of the things we are giving up, while no
" warning voice tells us of the fame or popularity, that we are
" likely to get in exchange; no one points out to the audience,
" that in almost every part of the world white traders press in
" more rapidly than the Missionaries, and face equal hardships
" for the same, or in many cases even less rates of pay; yet no
" one ever speaks of their devotion. If, then, we listen to all,
" that is told us at these farewell-meetings, and forget the things
" that are not told us, we very soon form most exaggerated
" notions of our own devotion and hardihood, while the con-

"tinual note of praise sows the seeds of that impatience of "criticism, to which foreign Missionaries, as a class, are so "subject."

As an instance of declamation, I quote the utterances of an itinerant American Pioneer: "God has declared His decree to "the effect, that Heathendom, and all princes and people, and "all the powers of this world, must either surrender to the "Living Christ, or be dashed to pieces like a potter's vessel. "We can see, how all the heathen Empires of the world, which "have resisted Jesus Christ, have gone down under appalling "calamities, and how all Nations which, having once received "the Gospel, subsequently closed the Bible, have, as by an "irreversible decree, fallen steadily away from their former "greatness, and sunk into second and third-class powers. I "appeal to my Indian hearers not to put themselves in "opposition to the Lord and His Anointed, and I read the "Second Psalm as the basis of my closing appeal to them."

Fortunately the preacher knew nothing but English: so none could understand him but educated Collegians, who would consider the subject academically. I cannot imagine a line of reasoning more foolish, and more unsuited to the great Problem of the Conversion of India, than this.

7. Meddlers and Busybodies.

In reading my Greek Testament I came to I Peter, iv, 15, "Let none of you suffer as a murderer, or a thief, or an evildoer, or as a busybody in other men's matters": the word used for "busybody" is "$\dot{\alpha}\lambda\lambda o\tau\rho\iota o\epsilon\pi\iota\sigma\kappa o\pi os$," rendered by Tertullian "alieni speculator": Bishop Wordsworth renders it: "one who sets himself as an overseer and censor of what belongs to others; a judge of other men's servants": It might have been supposed, that the Missionary, being tolerated in a non-Christian Empire, would behave himself cautiously, and keep to his sacred duties of preaching the Gospel, and building up Churches: It is much to be regretted, that in China more particularly, and in India to a certain extent, the British Missionary has departed from the line traced out for him by the Bible, and meddles with Politics.

The Missionary is sent out to preach the Gospel, and he will find, that to do that properly will require all his time, strength, and ability. He should not meddle with matters, lying out of the orbit of his chosen and blessed duty. Paul is his great example. At Corinth, or at Rome, he saw "Nothing but Christ crucified." Missionaries should not take up fads, and give way to crazes, and join Crusades against the evils of this wicked world. Many practices, which seem strange to them, have the sanction of Centuries, such as child-marriages, and will only be abandoned under the gradual enlightenment of Christian Education, or give way to civilized customs of a much worse type.

Most objectionable is his interference with the customs of the people, such as are not obviously contrary to Law, Human and Divine, or his denouncing particular branches of Commerce. The Home-Society should forbid all such extravagances, and insist upon their Agents rendering unto Cæsar the things that are Cæsar's, and fixing their thoughts upon the things of God.

The Jesuits last Century made themselves Priests and Kings, and were detested, and exterminated : I quote the following with regard to China :

"In regard to the Missionary-question the Yamen's views are
" sound, and excellent: it recognises the fact, that by Treaty
" the Missionaries are to be allowed to teach, and protection is
" guaranteed to them, and their converts: but it will not submit
" to Missionaries arrogating to themselves an official status,
" and transacting business, which can only be profitably dealt
" with by the Chinese local authorities, nor will it tolerate their
" converts making Christianity a cloak, to protect them from
" the consequences of breaking the laws of China."

The subjects of interference by Missionaries in China are connected with the Opium-Traffic, and the binding of women's feet : in India they attempt to interfere in matters connected with the manufacture of Opium, the Drink-Traffic, and the morals of the British Soldiers in their Cantonments. It is not to the credit of the Missionaries, who thus play the part of busybodies, which the Apostle Peter classes in the same category with Murderers, Thieves, and Evildoers. How different was the attitude assumed by Paul, who had to face the much greater sins of the Empire of Rome! There is an extensive literature on the subject, so I say no more.

My opinion is, that the Missionary should mind his own business, and, following the example of Paul, keep on good terms with the Powers that rule, whether in British India, China, Japan, or Turkey: he should abstain from writing complaints home, but get access to the local authorities, and get them over to his side by the pleasantness of his bearing, and conversation. Missionaries very rarely quarrel with the Authorities in British India, as they are highly valued, and as a rule are reasonable men. The elder Missionaries never think of complaining: they put up with little inconveniences, and get their way in the long run, when their wishes are reasonable. The difference is well-known between the real Gospel-preacher, the simple-hearted Missionary, and the grievance-monger, the spy, who introduces himself into the Military Cantonments, to watch the sad weaknesses of the brave, but thoughtless, British Soldier, the frothy declaimer against the Liquor-Shop, and the man, who is always at war with the Education-Department. The former are loved, honoured, and always welcome. The latter are a disgrace to the name of Missionary.

8. Marrying Early.

This is one of the greatest errors in our present Missionary-system. Some Societies have broken away from the old practices, and adopted a wiser course; but the evil is still one of the greatest. It will be remarked, that public opinion is gradually coming round: I remember the time, when a certain Missionary was ordained, and married, on the same day, and thought, that he had done a good stroke of business: when I met him last, his wife was dead, and he had been dismissed by his Society.

It is mere waste of time to discuss the comparative advantage of the Roman Catholic and Protestant Systems, and to answer the sneers on the great expense of widows and children, which their System obviates. I am not one, who does not admit the great devotion of the celibates of the Church of Rome, both male and female; and the great simplicity and economy, as well as purity, of their lives. The answer is sufficient, that the Protestant Church will not allow any restriction on natural liberty not based on Scripture. Still, early marriages are to be deprecated. The young public servant in India does not marry directly he lands in the country, and yet lives a holy life: he waits until he has learnt his duty, and mastered the language by living among the people. Why should not young Missionaries exert the same measure of self-denial? An engagement to marry, made before even the Missionary is accepted, throws a doubt upon his motives. It shows an absence of self-consecration. In Africa the Missionary must return home at short and stated periods, as the best chance of preserving his life: in India, China, and other places, this is not necessary, but he should return after more than ten years: these intervals should be utilized by the Missionary to perfect his knowledge on particular subjects. Ill-health may compel earlier return, but the health of a Missionary's wife or child should never be allowed to be a reason for his leaving his post. The servants of the State habitually send home their wives and children under suitable escort, and widows in bad health are constantly coming home: the Committee should sternly resist the tendency of men to place the health of their wives above their sacred duties. Our Lord, and Paul, have spoken clearly on this subject. That a Missionary should resign his high office, because his wife is unable to go back with him, is a lamentable instance of the decay of fibre in the Missionaries of modern times. How many Governors, and Generals, go out alone to serve an Earthly Sovereign? Is the Soldier of Christ not to endure hardship?

On the other hand, the sending out of young women to Africa, merely to die, is a cruelty, which cannot be too severely condemned. How many young wives lie buried in Africa, valuable lives needlessly thrown away! The African Mission is a Campaign, and Soldiers do not take their wives on a Campaign. I have steadily, but fruitlessly, resisted this weakness for many years, and have seen a succession of young wives pass from the Committee-Room into African graves. The really offensive suggestion, that a Missionary in Africa must be married, should not be entertained. Those, who have made moral lapses, have all been widowers, or married men. We must look this matter firmly in the face, and the example of Missions in Africa, where all the Agents are single, should be followed, except in those Stations, where a Christian community requires the care of a Female Missionary. I have letters from a Missionary in the Field, supporting my views, and stating distinctly, that, until a Mission has attained a certain stage of advance, the presence of married women is a decided drawback to the Lord's work. I earnestly hope, that Committees will give this subject careful consideration.

Some Missionary-Societies, and Training-Colleges, have become mere Matrimonial Agencies: still there is a marked tendency to recognise the evil, and to try to cope with it. This is the argument of one Society, the most devoted to Matrimony:
" It is doubtless wise, that both parties should spend a few years
" in the Field before marriage, to acquire the language, get accli-
" matized, and approve themselves by doing some good work.
" Missionaries should not marry too early, and should choose
" only Missionaries, for no more fatal hindrance to a man could
" well be imagined than an unmissionary-spirited wife. It is to
" be feared that some have forgotten, that a worldly woman,
" or even an unspiritual Christian, can never be a helpmeet
" for one, who wishes to serve God among the Heathen.
" The Bible knows nothing of monks and nuns, and the Heathen
" distrust unmarried men and women. Marriage is God's
" ordinance, and a pastor is to be the husband of one wife.
" A resident Missionary is a pastor, and according to universal
" testimony, a good wife is the best colleague he can have.
" With itinerants the case is different; but few itinerate all their
" lives. Undoubtedly in the Mission-Field, as at home, the
" married will have trouble in the flesh, trouble which the single
" escape. The principle, which the Apostle laid down, that
" celibacy is good for the present distress has its application

" in the case of pioneers in dangerous climates. But as soon
" as Stations are planted, and regular work begun, women are
" wanted, unless precious opportunities are to be lost. The
" well-being of the Missionary himself demands, that he have a
" home. Domestic duties must be attended to, with care and
" skill in uncivilized countries and dangerous climates, yet they
" only waste the time of a man. Heathen women and girls
" must be sought, taught, and cared for, and men cannot
" do this."

Hear what the Romish Priests think of this : " Il n'est pas
" rare d'apprendre le marriage d'un Missionaire avec une
" Missionaire : la nouvelle dame est invitée à conserver son
" emploi, mais si son rôle de mère lui suffit, elle reçoit un
" subside pour elle, *et pour chacun de ses enfants*. Peu-a-peu le
" jour vient, ou l'apôtre fatiguée change de vigne, et va ex-
" ploiter pour sa famille un nouveau champ. Pour le Missionaire
" Catholique c'est sans esprit de retourner qu'il est venu : C'est
" pour la vie." *Missions Catholiques*, 1891, p. 93.

Allusion is made to the Missionary giving up his vocation to suit his wife's health : this will be discussed later on : there are incidents in Missionary-Marriages, which precede this final turning the back on the plough of the Missionary, and manifesting his own unworthiness; that is to say, the deserting his colours, and leaving the Field on account of his wife's health : In the Bible-House one Member openly stated, that every man was bound to come home once a year to comfort his wife : In Missionary-circles a greater interval is required, as evidenced by the Church-Missionary-Society *Intelligencer* of Dec., 1893 : " In
" returning to England at the Committee's request, Bishop
" Tucker is doing a wise thing. His presence here for a few
" months will be of great value, for consultation, for influencing
" the country on the question of the future of U-Ganda, and for
" obtaining fresh recruits. It would be short-sighted indeed to
" question this. Another visit home would be reasonable and
" right, even if it had no other object than to see the wife and
" son from whom (at present) Africa separates him. But in
" existing circumstances, even if they were in Africa, it would
" be right for him to leave them, and come to England in the
" interests of the Mission. Financially, of course, such a visit
" pays itself twenty times over."

The Editor of the *Intelligencer*, having thus intruded into the family-secrets of a Bishop, I have broken my rule, and given his name.

As regards the Missionaries, I classify their cases. The Marriage-Bell sounds cheerily through every page of the Reports, the Agenda of the sub-Committees, and the Agenda of every Committee, Corresponding, or General. Weddings and

Births are the conspicuous feature, and every death of an infant is recorded with proper terms of sympathy. The Report assumes the characteristics of the Matrimonial and Family News.

1. The Missionary leaves his Field for England to get married; he names the woman to the Committee, and asks leave.
2. The Husband leaves his Field to take his sick wife home, and is not ashamed to leave his flock, his school, and his work.
3. The son leaves his Field on account of his Mother's serious illness; he comes home again soon afterwards in consequence of her death to wind up her affairs.
4. The loss of little children is reported repeatedly.
5. Two Missionaries proposed by telegram to their friends, but both died soon after "re infectâ."
6. A Missionary summoned home by telegram from the Panjáb, and another from Egypt, to visit his sick wife at the expense of the Society.
7. The husband is unable to return to his Field, because his wife is too ill to accompany him.
8. The husband throws up his Vocation, because his wife is sick, and takes a living in England: their *consecrated* labours thus come to an untimely end, and all the expense of their long training in a Missionary-College is lost to the Society, for they have neither the wish, nor the means, to pay the forfeit.
9. The Missionary on the Upper Niger conducts his wife to the Canary Islands for her confinement, and takes the Medical-Missionary of the Mission from his hospital, and sacred duties, with him to assist at the event. The Missionary is recorded to be an "unpaid" Agent, paying his own expenses, but he sends in and receives £80 from the Society for the *unexpected* expenditure of the confinement; surely Marriage implies such possibilities.

The Report of the Church-Missionary-Society generally informs the readers of the parentage of the woman married: In another report I read, that white children are an *object-lesson* of Christianity: In my hearing the present Bishop of Calcutta at a Meeting in London stated, that the exhibition of a white Baby was favourable to Conversion: as a matter of surprise the exhibition of a spaniel, or a ferret, would have had more effect. In Bishop Taylor's Self-supporting Mission in W. Africa, South of the Equator, the children and babies are all counted in the effective staff of the Mission. The American Missionaries continually describe the contemplation of American Family-life as one of the Christianizing influences on the Heathen; the Romish Priest uses exactly the contrary argument, and with some force.

I heard one Secretary to a Society state, that it was important, that Missionaries should have wives; but this will not prevent their being widowers, and it is the widowers, who have given such great cause for scandal: I heard another Secretary say, that the Missionaries came chiefly from a class, which always married at puberty: I have witnessed a case of a man being engaged as a Missionary, who had already four children: then sometimes the Committee has to send out a Governess to educate children of a widower, or a grown-up daughter, not as a Missionary, but merely to join her parents: sometimes the wife of a Missionary, the so-called mother of the Mission, is absent from the Field many years to look after her own children in England: sometimes widows get pensions, who have never been out in the Field at all. In other walks of life the young engaged couple wait, and, when they marry, they do so at their own cost and risks: in the Missionary-Society the practice is just the reverse.

A Bishop writes as follows, and his words are entered in the Report: "We had to part with six of our seven children, a larger " proportion than we have ever before had to forsake for Christ: " we found our dear brother with his six round his table every " day: this excited our envy." All these exhibitions of parental affection are charming, but it is not Evangelization; it is more suitable for the *Matrimonial News*, and these few lines give an idea, though only a faint one, of the heavy burden imposed on the Society, which has to clothe, feed, and educate, these children till they are sixteen.

I wonder, that the subject is not looked at from another point of view: the burden of domestic cares in a foreign country thrown upon both husband and wife, the constant anxieties, the repeated losses of children, the miserable economies, which are necessary, the sufferings of the mother, the separation, and the uncertain prospects in life of a pack of children thrown on the hands of the Society: the woes of the parochial clergy are now brought to notice: why are ordained men more reckless in such matters than laymen?

In this respect the Missionary resembles the people, to convert whom he is sent: Sir W. Hunter writes thus about the people of India: " I deal with the ever-present problem of " India, a population which marries *as a religious duty*, and " produces new mouths to be fed, without concerning itself as " to the increased means of subsistence."

A Correspondent in the *Record* Newspaper stated the Case Fairly in 1891.

"*Married Missionaries.* Sir, Your correspondent 'A Vicar' on the above subject has been taken to task very rightly by your correspondents in your issue of July 3 for censuring an absent brother, without being familiar with all the facts of the case. The subject, which has been raised is, notwithstanding, extremely important, and vital to the interest of Foreign Missions. As a bachelor and a Missionary, I should like to point out what seems the obvious lesson to be learnt from the case in point, or from the frequent cases, where a Missionary has been compelled to leave the Field on account of his wife's health. Surely any of us, who are young and unmarried, should think very seriously before we enter into such a relationship. In most parts of Africa, and in other countries, where the climate is malarious, the conditions seem to me very much unsuited for married women, and, if two Missionaries on the field unite in marriage, the possibility of their being able to stay in the country is diminished twofold, or in the case of a family even more; and can it be said, that either of them can give so much attention to our primary work, for, as Paul says 'He that is married careth for the things of this world, how he may please his wife.' We might well, all of us, take earnest heed to the rest of that seventh chapter of I Corinthians, which most people seem to explain away, or else say, that it is only Paul's advice, as he had 'no commandment of the Lord.' In any case, I should prefer Paul's judgment to that of any living man. Dr. Cust, in 'Four Essays on Missionary Subjects,' gives us some very common-sense remarks on Matrimony, which would carry all the greater weight, were it not combined with some rather sarcastic allusions to some individual cases. I am no advocate of enforced Celibacy, but, if we Missionaries would put the Lord's work first, before considering such a step, there would be fewer instances of abandonment of posts in a foreign Field for family-reasons. At any rate I think no Missionary has a right to marry without very carefully, as in God's sight, counting the cost, and believing, that it is truly for the good of work. I have no desire to criticize the conduct of anyone, but only wish to give my testimony for the sake of those, who are in the same state as I am, or as an additional testimony to those, who have the examination of Missionary-candidates.

July 3. S.M."

But on the other side of the Atlantic, we are met by wonderful utterances of Bishop Taylor of the "Self-supporting Mission," the same leader of Mission-bands, who counts every baby as an additional Missionary. " He is a very hard worker on his " Mission-farm, and is probably the healthiest Missionary we " have on the West Coast. His great need is the same felt so " keenly by the first man, when 'no helpmeet was found for " him.' Every good Missionary-man should have a good Mis- " sionary-wife by the will of God. Dear fellow, he ought to have " a good Missionary-wife. If I had such a steward as Abraham " had, I would send him to Mesopotamia to find Rebekahs for " my faithful Isaacs, who need young women of God, who are " on the self-supporting line, and ready to run and draw water " for the camels. Most of my Missionary young *ladies* are so " united to Jesus, and so absorbed in His soul-saving work, that " they prefer to take the sole charge of Mission-Stations. They " are God's heroines, and we hold them in highest esteem, and " afford them every facility we can to work on the line of their " own preferences and convictions."

Ill-judging fanatical enthusiasts have at all periods of Church-history made themselves ridiculous. Tertullian mentions, that the Marcionist admitted no married person even to Baptism, unless he divorced his wife; and in the early Church the Marriage of Bishops, Priests, and Deacons, was forbidden, and those, who were married before Ordination, were compelled to separate. It is an equal departure from common-sense, and a just view of human affairs, to encourage Matrimony as a necessity, or to forbid it as a sin. It is clear, that in the early days of a Missionary's career in a foreign country it is an impediment, a weakening of strength required in the Lord's service, and, when the Missionary lives on the alms of the Churches, an unjustifiable extravagance, or even worse, a misapplication of consecrated funds. Every additional child, which a Missionary has, is an additional burden to the Treasury of the Society, and a large family prevents the Committees from sending out an additional Missionary to the same Field.

A serious aspect of this great evil is the financial one. In the Report of the Church-Missionary-Society for the year 1889 I find hundreds of children of Missionaries clothed, fed, and educated, for secular occupation, at the cost of thousands of pounds, collected under the influence of prayer for the purpose of converting the Heathen : additional hundreds might be converted by the expansion of our Missions, if our funds were not absorbed, wasted, misapplied, in the support of children, who ought never to have come into existence. Many of these children are the grandchildren of, or connected with, well-to-do people, India, or Ceylon, Pensioners : we meet the children smart and well-dressed: and it is painful to think, that the pennies collected in Missionary-boxes from little poor children in hundreds of Churches are thus devoted.

A Romish layman, Sir C. Clifford, writes thus: "The reason, "why the Romish Missionary has so great an advantage over "the Protestant Missionary, of course, will strike everyone. "The Protestant Missionary has a double duty to perform. "They will all tell you, that it is necessary for the proper "carrying out of their Mission, that they should have wives. "The natural consequence of that is, that they have families. "They cannot, therefore, go and stand the brunt of the pitiless "storm. They cannot go, as I have seen Romish Missionaries "do, and stand between two sets of savages in the act of "fighting. They have to think of the little ones at home. They "have to think, moreover, how, when those little ones grow up, "they shall be supported. The consequence is, that, with the "best intentions in the world on their part, the savages, among "whom they dwell, see that they are collecting property about "them, that they are dealing in land, that the spiritual welfare "of the people, although it is one great object with them, "is not their sole object. Until you send from England men, "whose sole object is the Spiritual Welfare of those, among "whom they dwell, you will not have performed the duty, which "you owe to those countries, that are enabling you to be a "great Nation."

A thoughtful critic cannot but agree with this stricture: the first, last, sole, object of a Missionary-Society is to bring souls to God, and this cannot be done, if the Agents employed live in comfortable homes, and send home half-a-dozen boys and girls to intercept the alms of the Church: they had better not have been born. Shades of Columba, Columbanus, Aidan, Willibrod, Boniface, and Gall, the early Missionaries of the British and Anglo-Saxon race, who gave up all things for Christ, and suffered hardship like good soldiers, who had not the advantages and comforts of the Nineteenth Century, and, in the case of Boniface, died a blessed Martyr, what would they have thought of degenerate English Christians, spending a few years in a foreign land, making a great pretence of consecration, and sacrifice, and devotion, more in words than deeds, and then for their own convenience, or because a wife, or one of their numerous children, are sick, leave the field, the flock, the labours blessed by God, and go home, and hide themselves in some obscure parsonage. And yet the words of the Lord are very clear, and good Bishop Steere drew attention to them: "He, "that loveth Father or Mother more than Me, is not worthy of "Me." "No man, having put his hand to the plough, and "looking back, is fit for the Kingdom of God."

It may seem harsh, but it is necessary to speak out: Bishop Caldwell, and Bishop Sargent, and John Newton of Lahore, have set the great example of continuous service even to old age, even to the grave: The late Bishop of Nova Scotia, in the Dominion of Canada, at a meeting in St. James's Hall, in my hearing said: "God deal with me so, and more also, if I do not die amidst my people." The Missionaries of Rome have set the example: why cannot English Colonial Bishops and Missionaries act in the same way? The old Missionaries from these Islands of our own race went out in celibacy, in poverty, in suffering, to work with their hands to sustain life, with no hope to see England again. Some portion of the grace of these great Apostles has clung to the modern Religious Orders of Rome: the Protestant Missionary has fallen from the ideal: he must have a wife at puberty, and a family supported by the alms of the Churches: he must have salaries, houses, comforts, conveyances: he is educated at the expense of the Society, but throws up his Vocation whenever it suits him. An English Peer, well-known in religious circles, openly stated on his return from India, that the most comfortable houses were those of the Missionaries: we have all heard of the controversy among the Missionaries of the Wesleyan-Society on this very subject.

I quote the following from a printed article: "What is it that " floods the Mission-Field with men, who have no pretence to " the Missionary-spirit? The prospect of salaries, and houses, " and wives, and children, and comforts. I have seen Mis-" sionaries abroad living in a style far superior to that to which, " from their evident social status, they could have been accus-" tomed at home. I am firmly convinced, and my conviction is " founded on actual experience, that the Mission, which offers " least to its Agents, and spends least on them, gets the best " men, the educated, the pious, the devoted. Happy, in my " judgment, is that Mission, which is in a position to say: 'We " want a new labourer in this corner of the Lord's vineyard: we " offer you nothing; will you come, dear friend, in poverty, in " celibacy, in self-surrender; for the love of God and His " Church?' Through this net the little fishes will escape, the " great ones will remain."

Let us consider the Children's Home, lately erected by the Church-Missionary-Society: a letter from one of the Secretaries lies on my table, stating, "that he repeatedly and consistently " protested against it; that he implored those, who pressed on " the measure, to stay their hand": he calls it a scandal. One of the Vice-Presidents suggested to me, that we should sell the building as soon as we could: it is justly described as a great scandal. Money collected to convert the Heathen is squandered on maintaining children, chiefly the result of early, improvident, and thoughtless, marriages. If these children, or at least a large portion, became Missionaries, there would be some reason in trying to secure a constant supply of trained Agents, but the maintenance ends at the age of sixteen. Many of the families brought up there belong to a lower stratum of social life, and are thus educated above their natural position: Missionaries, who come from the Universities, decline to send their children, and try to get separate allowances paid for home-training. Every child born to a Church-Missionary-Society-Missionary receives a stipend, so from that point of view Bishop Taylor's assertion, that every baby is part of the Missionary-staff, is true: as these allowances are distributed over the whole Field it takes some time and care to find out the total cost of the Nursery, and School-Room, of the Church-Missionary-Society, but it seems to reach £10,000 per annum. In another Missionary-Society I find a scheme to start a school for the children of the Missionaries in China at Chefu: there appear to be about 172 already: as time goes on this number must be increased. This Society admits, that "the expense of Home-"Education in a Mission like theirs, where a small income has "to cover a large work, would be a serious difficulty: the mere "passage-money to get the children from China to England "would be £2,460, and the expense of bringing them up in "England would be heavy." The Church-Missionary-Society has no such scruples, and does not spare its rich constituency, or rather diverts sums, intended for Evangelization, to the maintenance of the children of the Agents employed in Evangelization. The Chefu-scheme is fraught with peril: a class of "Creole" Europeans and Americans will be brought up in China with all the arrogance of the white man, without the counteracting influence of English and American Society. The Sandwich Islands are stated to be overrun with the progeny of the first American Missionaries, whose families settled in the Islands: even the Queen herself is stated to be descended from a Missionary.

What is the alternative?

Under different names the two Sections of the Church of England have adopted, or proposed to adopt, the same remedy:

(*a*) Missionary-Brotherhoods and Sisterhoods.
(*b*) Bands of Associated Evangelists.

No pretence is made, that Celibacy in itself has any merit: it is merely a question of economy, and good administration for about ten years after entering the Field: if the heart of the Brother, or Associate, fails, he can withdraw, and fall to the lower level. No attempt is made to limit the age, at which a

Sister should be allowed to leave her Sisterhood: this matter is too high for me to enter into, but she has some form of contract with those, who sent her into the Field, and she should carefully read I Corinthians, chap. vii. I was much exercised on this subject, and went over to Herrnhut, in Saxony, to talk it out with the Moravians: when a helpmate is required for a Moravian Missionary, she is chosen by the Church, in all ways suitable to the one object in view. I had a long talk with Frau Jäeskhe, the widow of a Missionary in N. India: I asked, whether she regretted her choice of the Mission-Field, and could have wished to have chosen her helpmate for herself: she replied, that all had been ordered well: the Lord had chosen the best of men for her: she had laboured in the vineyard with him, while he lived, and treasured his memory after his departure. I read in a Report of the London-Missionary-Society of a Missionary pleading for the appointment of three or four unmarried colleagues, who will be prepared to endure hardship as a Soldier of Christ. This reveals the fact, that the evils of early and thoughtless marriages is being felt, and that the Missionary-fibre requires strengthening.

I ask no more than that, which was demanded from the Fellows of Colleges in former years, that for a stipulated term of years, say ten, from the date of their Ordination they should not marry. After the age of thirty-three they should be free to do as they wish. I wish to impress upon the young Missionary, that in undertaking family-cares in extreme youth he is doing what is manifestly wrong, and unworthy of his high calling. Nobody forced him to come out of the ranks of his relatives, and the stratum of life, in which God had placed him at his birth, respectable but humble, for the purpose of undertaking the glorious profession of preaching the Gospel, and doing something for his Lord, who had done so much for him: he chose it, or in many cases the Lord unmistakably chose him: in the presence of his fellows he avowed, that he had been called to the work, that he had given his whole heart to his Vocation. Now the work requires self-consecration, self-denial, an entire crucifying of the carnal man, a readiness to go where he is ordered, to live out in tents or huts, to bear hardship like a good soldier, to spend and be spent, to be content with a little; to set an example to native acquaintances, native converts, and native catechists, and Pastors, of the great and inestimable gift of Self-Sacrifice; dwelling in their midst, sometimes wearing their dress, sharing their simple joys and simple fare with them on the road, on the river, in the hut, in the tent; speaking their language as one of them, and being all things to them.

It is true, that the young Soldier, the young Magistrate, and the young Merchant, by the necessity of their position, keep clear of family-entanglements, and give their hearts to the service of their earthly employer, with a view to get themselves forward in the world, to put by economies for middle life, and declining years. They would deem it madness to encumber themselves with a family, until they see a way to support them; is the Missionary to fall to a lower level, not only to cramp his means of usefulness, and his power to discharge his duties, but to be a burden to the great Society, that sends him out?

Sir W. Hunter remarks that "without some show of self-"sacrifice, the Hindu will not believe in the sincerity of the "Messenger, or the truth of the Message. A man with a wife "and half-a dozen children may be a pleasant sight in an "English parsonage, but it is a standing absurdity in a Heathen "Mission-Home."

I myself spent ten years entirely alone, or with one or two celibate companions, in the midst of the people, over whose secular interests I had to watch. I remember, how greatly the work was advanced by entire freedom from family and social duties and cares, how subjects of doubt could be discussed earnestly and thoroughly, how before dawn I was in the saddle surrounded by Natives, who came to accompany me, how my heart went out to them, because they were the sole objects of my interest; if such were the case in community-life or solitary life, while employed on earthly business, how much more, when the heart is given to spiritual business by spiritually-minded men!

It remains now for all Missionary-Societies to refuse absolutely to permit the marriage of Missionaries before they have served ten years, or at least attained the age of 33. . . . A man is much more likely to make a good choice of a helpmeet, when he knows the work, which he requires help in, than if *in statu pupillari* at the Missionary-College he asks the little girl, whom he has met in the Sunday-school, or the young person in the shop adjoining that of his father, to go with him. In the first decade of Missionary-life sisters and brothers are more useful than husbands and wives. . . . If men are really called to God's special service in foreign parts, they must just make a sacrifice of their lives and comforts. A conscript soldier has to put off his marriage until his term of service is over. It is idle to talk of sacrifice, when a Missionary marries at the expense of a Missionary-Society ten years earlier than his brother in some trade or profession at home can afford to do. Even down to the day I write this, College students do not hesitate to engage themselves. In fact many of the Clergy, and some clerical members of the Committee, lay themselves out to secure Missionaries as husbands to their daughters, as there is a certain provision for the widows and children: I could name one Member of the Committee, who has three or four Missionary-sons-in-law. There is another aspect of the case: it pays.

Here is the latest effusion of the managers of the Missionary-Matrimonial-Office: Many years must pass before U-Ganda settles down to quietness: the British Government refuses to occupy the country: only a Protectorate is talked about, and no British troops: it is 800 miles from the sea, under the Equator, and yet here is the call to brave women to throw away their lives uselessly: "And not Clergymen only, nor men only. It
" is Bishop Tucker's distinct opinion, that, assuming that the
" country will now be reasonably safe, we must no longer delay
" to send up Christian women. There are, he believes, and we
" believe, strong and vigorous women, who need not wait for
" the future railway, but could take the journey now. But they
" must not be young wives. In the present circumstances of
" Africa, women must be ready, as *so many men have been ready*,
" to go with the distinct and solemn purpose of remaining
" single for a few years for the Lord's sake. The time is not
" distant, when the *beauty of English family life* may be exhibited
" in U-Ganda; but the time is not yet, and meanwhile we look
" for a bright example of self-sacrifice and absolute separateness
" to the Kingdom of Heaven to be manifested by the represen-
" tatives, both men and women, of our Protestant Church of
" England."

9. Arrogant to the Natives.

There is no reason, to suppose, that Paul and his companions lorded it over the Heathen; quite the contrary. The humble Evangelists of the time of Augustine, and Columba, and Boniface, did not do so. The Nestorians, and Moravians, did not do so. Why should the Anglo-Saxon Missionaries of this Century assert such an intolerable superiority over those, whom they go to convert? The holiest Missionary is the humblest: he works through others, not thinking of self, his own station in his native country, his acquired knowledge, his natural ability, his station in his Church, but of the Lord's work. He cries: "Let the work be done, even if I am driven out, effaced, overlooked, despised."

That pride of race, which prompts a white man to regard coloured people as inferior to himself, is strongly ingrained in most men's minds, and must be wholly eradicated by the Grace of God, before he will ever win the hearts and souls of the Heathen. Nothing is more depressing in the Reports of Missionary-Societies than this feature. Every Missionary would be better for a copy of Thomas à Kempis' "Imitation of Christ," as his constant companion. And let the Home-Committee avoid being puffed up, as if it had done something wonderful, as if its counsels had secured the measure of success, which had come to them from the Lord only. Above all, let care be taken never to talk of a man as a Hero, when living, or a Saint, when dead: he did his best: others will do the same: his place will soon be filled up: the ranks of the Lord's Army are always full.

Hear the advice of a dead Missionary, a faithful servant of God, from whose life I extract it:

1. Of all qualifications for Mission-work, Charity is most excellent.
2. Of all Methods, the only safe and sure one is to purge the heart of Vain-glory, Worldliness, and Selfishness.
3. Of all plans to insure success, the most certain is Christ's own; and becoming a corn of wheat falling into the ground, and dying.

The last is in the hands of God, but as to the first two, I can only add, Oh! that ye were wise, that ye understood this?

Hear Dr. Ellinwood, "Oriental Religion and Christianity," 1892: "The adaptation of preachers to hearers in non-Christian " lands is a task, that may well make us thankful for every help. " The Missionary is far too apt to come from the West with " exalted notions of his own superiority, and with a feeling of " condescending pity for men, who have pondered the deep " things of the Universe far more than he has. The weakness " of Christian Churches is in the temptation to arrogance, and " an abuse of superior power, and an overbearing spirit."

The European Missionary should from the beginning work with the steady policy of effacing himself, at as early a date as possible, and placing the Native Ministry in power. All buildings should be erected with that view; the European should act the part of a temporary visitor, with no intention of staying, or being a burden to his flock, or his Church at Home. He must not keep his flock in helpless pupilage, and treat them as mere children. They are wiser than him in many things. At any rate they represent the public feeling of their own people. They must be reminded from the first, that they are responsible. It may be a trial to an orderly mind to see work less well done according to red-tape, or rubrics; yet one, who loves the object, will look over the defects of the work in the present generation, in the anticipation of perfection in the next. Remember that the Syrian Church in India, the Koptic in Egypt, the Armenian, Syrian, Nestorian, and Greek in West Asia, have managed on a purely native basis to outlive oppression, and ignorance.

Mr. George Curzon, in the *National Review*, 1893, remarks, that: "Without hostility to the Missionaries it is impossible to " ignore the fact, that English Missions are a source of political " unrest, and frequently of international trouble, subversive of " the National institutions of the country in which they reside,

" because, while inculcating the Christian virtue of self-respect,
" they destroy the respect for others, which is the foundation of
" Civil-Society." I may add, that, if this shaking of dead bones arose from the stirring power of the Holy Spirit, I should rejoice, but the Missionary is accompanied by a vaunting assertion of the irresistible power of the different European Nations, whose object is commercial, or political: there can be no blessing on the work of Missionaries, while it is mixed up with Treaties, Annexations, slaying of poor Natives in Africa, Liquor-Traffic, etc. M. Michie, in his late work, "Missionaries in China," expresses sentiments not wholly to be despised: he divides the Missionaries into two categories;
" (1) men of large views, discrimination, and tolerance;
" (2) a jumble of half-witted enthusiasts, whose arrogance
" towards native officials, and intolerance towards everything
" outside their narrow horizon, may have been, and may be in
" future time, the cause of trouble: they claim tolerance for
" themselves, but deny it to the morals, customs, and religious
" views, of the inhabitants of this great Kingdom; they are
" quite confident, that they are themselves always right, and,
" what is so often remarked by others of Missionaries, they
" take credit for a perfect familiarity with the purposes of the
" Almighty; their incapacity to understand the people, and
" their arrogant bearing, is too often the direct cause of the ill-
" feeling they excite in China with sad deplorable results."
If Mahometan, or Mormon, Missionaries were to behave in the same manner in London, speak lightly of the name of our Lord, and offend the religious prejudices of a people, who at least profess Christianity, they would have but a short shrieve in spite of our constitutional tolerance.

In the Indian Manual already quoted I find the following:
" A loving manner has influence on the people of India. Vulgar
" Europeans often treat the Natives, men of high rank and
" noble demeanour, as if they were dust under their shoes:
" the same disposition is sometimes manifested by those, from
" whom better things might be expected. The Hindu should
" not be treated with contempt: the Hindu mind differs from
" ours, but will be despised only by the ignorant man."

And there is an arrogant way of presenting the Gospel of Christ. I quote from the *Calcutta Review*, January 1876: "Dr.
" Wilson of Bombay writes: 'God is Father of all mankind, and
" no God gives opposite laws for the government of his children:
" there can be but one Religion, as there is but one Sun: the
" Hindu Religion is to those, who embrace it, the road to Death
" and everlasting destruction: this may seem hard, but it is the
" Doctrine of all Reformed Churches.' This mode of repre-
" senting Christianity may be taken as a type of what was

" common, and thus represents the popular notion, which
" Hindus have of Christianity, viz., that the vast majority of
" mankind is condemned to absolute destruction by one, who is
" their Father: they never had the remotest opportunity of
" being Christians, and yet they are condemned. It is not
" acceptable to the Hindu to accept a Faith, which condemns
" all past generations to a destruction, which they could not
" avoid. They would rather, that the Churches' Faith be false,
" than that the common Father would act so partially."

Dr. Duff, in his work on Indian Missions, writes: " The truth
" of Christianity has been over and over again demonstrated
" to the entire satisfaction of thousands and tens of thousands,
" of the most rationable and enlightened men that ever lived,
" and must be admitted as true. Every other Religious System
" is erroneous, dishonourable to God, and destructive to the
" happiness of man. It is denied, that any National right exists
" to parents to teach and perpetuate a system of falsehood and
" delusion, so loathsome and deadly as Hinduism.

" The first word, with which the Missionaries used to
" commence was Damnation: their Gods were false; their
" rites were odious. These were the opening messages of the
" Gospel, which the Missionaries used to proclaim in the life-
" time of many still alive.

" No one but a very arrogant, narrow-minded, intolerant, man
" can look a Hindu honestly in the face, and say, that their fore-
" fathers, left in ignorance by the Providence of God, are
" hopelessly condemned by a loving Father."

I myself, fifty years ago, heard an American Presbyterian Missionary in an Indian Bazaar tell his audience, that their god was Cow-dung; he meant it as an insult; as a fact they saw no offence in it, as the Cow, and all connected with it, are sacred to them.

When the young Missionary arrogantly thinks, that he must be in the right (as we humbly hope that he is), and that the poor Heathen are wilfully deaf to his call, let him reflect, that the existence of so many Jews in our midst proves, that the Christian doctrines are not self-convincing, and try to find a solution, why He, who willeth all mankind to be saved, has allowed 18 Centuries to elapse without giving many of them a chance. The arrogant denial of all good in the poor Heathen, the one-sidedness of the Reports, which they send home, the tirades against Native Customs, the jeers against their religious rites, the want of pity to the poor lost sheep, show the existence in the Missionary of the same " unredeemed man," who Centuries earlier would have developed into a Persecutor. The Conversion of Europe reads as a frightful nightmare compared with the quiet, gentle, peaceful, loving conversion of the people of

Oceania, who are said to have no word for "sword" in their language.

Fifty years ago I knew an American Presbyterian Missionary in the Panjáb; he lived a long life there. I saw him a few years ago in London; he has died since. He and his colleague, Forman, were among the meekest of men. I described the latter in a Poem in 1861 as "meek as Moses and eloquent as Paul"; here is the character, written by me long ago, of old John Newton:
" For twenty years I was an official, in relation with him, and
" never heard a complaint from his lips; but I marked well
" his consistent Christian walk: there are many others of his
" stamp, and I wish that all were like them; but a great deal
" depends upon the character of the Missionary, the local
" authority, and the general population. There must be light
" and shade in the life of Missions, as in the life of man, but a
" spirit of conciliation, a practical illustration of the principles,
" that are preached, a determination not to depart from the
" Law of Love, and Discipline of Patience, except under extreme
" necessity, will work its way at last. If it does not, let us
" remember that, in all cases, it will be better to abandon the
" Mission, at least for a time, rather than to alienate the hearts
" of non-Christians, make Christianity odious in their eyes, and
" the Missionaries a disgrace to the country, which sends them
" out." As a contrast I give a quotation: I scarcely like to state from what Report, as the remark is so odious.

" Our very first preaching was opposed, a Brahmin 'with a wicked-looking face' being in the front." Have Missionaries or Christians never ugly faces, and is the face the index of the soul? Let us consider the bust of Socrates, and the outward forms of many of our most advanced Christians, and contrast with the above the fond foolish gush of the following: "In spite
" of the persecutions of all kinds, which converted Chinese
" women have to bear, their happiness is so manifest in their
" faces, that you can pick out a Christian, when you meet her in
" the street, by her bright expression."

Hear Seton Churchill's stirring words: "It was the late
" Archbishop Magee who once, in an able sermon, preached at
" the request of the Church-Missionary-Society, pointed out the
" injury, that was done to the cause of Christ by Christian
" workers *doing Christian work in an un-Christlike manner;* and
" it was the late Lord Lawrence, when Viceroy of India, who,
" after the Indian Mutiny, being asked by the officials at home
" if Missionary-work had, in his opinion, done anything to bring
" on that catastrophe, replied to the effect that, when Christ's
" work was done in a Christ-like way it could never be pro-
" ductive of anything but good. But what a suggestion is
" conveyed to us in the remarks of these two great men on the

" way, in which we workers do this work! How often, alas!
" we have to confess with shame and sorrow, that in our work
" there has been too little of the Spirit of Christ, and too much
" of the spirit of self, because we have failed to realize the
" importance of maintaining a high standard of spiritual life,
" while putting forth our hands to His work!"

In India the officials all support the Missionary in essentials, and leave him uncontrolled, and as a rule, neither English, nor American, nor German, nor French, nor Spanish, nor Dane, nor Norwegian, give the least trouble. In China it is reported, that the secular laity will have nothing to do with the Missionary. In the *New Review* I read how deep the hatred of the Chinese is to the foreigner, and that Missionary-operations are the foundation of the bad feeling: the Chinese regard their interference as impertinent, and only to be tolerated, as long as they are themselves powerless to prevent it, since they are overbearing and meddlesome: how could a proud Nation of so many Millions tolerate it? a little Nation like England with its thirty Millions would not tolerate Chinamen acting thus in our country: that is the real point at issue.

10. Deficient in Sympathy and Love and Feelings of Justice to the Natives.

In 1880 I presented to each student of the Church-Missionary-Society-College copies of the Report of the International Missionary-Congress, with the following Inscription, which explains my meaning in this Section:

On the occasion of his entering upon his Christian warfare,
May God's Holy Spirit guide him!

(1) To feel a warm sympathy in the preaching of the Gospel throughout the World, not only in his own particular Field.
(2) To recognise, that the path of the Missionary is one of failures, and chastenings, of self-abnegation, and humility, sanctified with humble prayer and renewed efforts, based upon experience as well as Faith.
(3) To know, that the great agent for Conversion of souls is Love; that the Missionary must have the tender pity, as of a father, for the Heathen sitting for so many generations in darkness; an inexhaustible patience for their waywardness and backslidings, and a sympathizing indulgence for their ancient customs, however foolish in his eyes.

I have observed in many instances the entire absence of this feeling. A Missionary should try to win his way to the hearts of the people, and should under no circumstances invoke the Arm of the Flesh for the protection of property, or accept compensation for property lost. He will find it more profitable in the long run to exhibit the patience, and charity, and unselfishness, which will disarm his antagonists. If his life be endangered, he must save it by timely flight; if imprisoned, there can be no doubt that collective intercession will be made for him in such a manner, as to secure his liberation; if he fall, " he falls a blessed Martyr." Such deaths are great victories: they convince the doubting; they stimulate the faint-hearted; they astonish the worldling. Peradventure for a good man some would even dare to die, but Christ died for sinners, and Christians are ready to die for Christ. How our hearts beat high to think, that we have known, and loved, and conversed with, and had letters from, men, destined by God's Grace to die for Him; he does no more than numerous examples have gloriously sanctioned, than the Gospel predicts, and than hundreds of his countrymen have been willing to do in every part of the World, even when the prize to be gained was but an earthly one. Persecutions were not unknown in the early days of Christianity, and yet it triumphed in the end. It is idle to expect the Crown without the Cross. There are many sufferings still unsuffered, many Crosses not yet taken up, many Crowns still to be won.

I quote again from the " Missionary Manual ":

" The Missionary should have Love, the Love of compassion,
" for the people; the Love of Jesus, who wept over Jerusalem;
" the Love of Paul, who could wish himself accursed for
" Christ, and for his brethren. Credit should be given to the
" people for their good qualities, and the Missionary, remember-
" ing his own sins against Light and Love, should make allow-
" ance for those, who from their birth have been exposed to
" so much evil influence."

I am sorry, that a Missionary should use such words as those now quoted: he had no experience, and did great mischief during his short life:

" If we have formed our estimate of the African from the
" descriptions sometimes heard at Missionary-Meetings, we
" shall be inclined to take the other extreme, and maintain, as
" Missionaries may sometimes be heard doing, that the native
" is a better man on the whole than the white man. In so
" doing we put our Mission on a wrong footing, for our hearers
" know very well, that the immense majority of natives, with
" whom they come in contact, are untruthful to a degree,
" grasping, and immoral, and often cruel and ungrateful as
" well; and any expressions of sympathy with the native, which

" we may base on contrary suppositions, only confirm their view,
" that we do not know what we are about."

How much wiser is the following extract!

" The variety of temper, temperament, thought, sentiment,
" among the races of mankind, is far greater than is usually
" supposed; and, in addition to these distinctions, the moral
" and social state of almost all non-Christian races is very low,
" their distrust excessive, and their methods of observation and
" judgment very different from our own. Of all this young
" Missionaries are usually profoundly ignorant, and therefore
" enter on the important and difficult task of converting those,
" whom they do not understand, to whom they are prejudicial
" and contemptuous, and whom they do not know how to
" approach in a suitable manner. Preparation in these direc-
" tions may save a young Missionary from grave mistakes,
" perhaps from a bearing, which is most injurious."

Even the use of such words as "devil-Priests" shows a want of human kindness: the Missionaries in China do not like being called "foreign devils." Certain Religious Conceptions are defined as "Animistic," the worship of "Spirits." Socrates used to say that he had a "$\delta\alpha\ell\mu\omega\nu$"; he would be a poor translator, who wrote, that Socrates had a "Devil."

Hear what Professor Wilson of Bombay says: "The best
" Missionary is he, who knows the people best. The more a
" knowledge of Hinduism and Hindu literature is possessed
" by any teacher, the more patiently and uninterruptedly will he
" be listened to, and the more forcibly will he be able *by contrast*
" *and concession* to set forth the authority and excellence of
" Christianity."

Hear Bishop Hodges of Travancór: "Paul's Method of
" dealing with the keen-witted philosophers of Athens may well
" be a model for the modern Missionary in dealing with the
" higher Castes of Hindus. He carried out the principle, which
" prudence suggested, of becoming an Athenian to Athenians.
" And, if we would win the Brahmins we must in like measure
" become Brahmins. We cannot hope to win men from any
" error unless we sympathize with them, and we cannot do this,
" unless we understand their modes of thought, and the principles
" by which they are guided. To do this requires patience and
" study; and these are hard to acquire, but no Missionary
" worthy of his name would shrink from the effort."

I was sorry to hear the following words from a Missionary on his return from the Field. There is nothing false in it, as I know well the place and people described; but there is an entire absence of sympathy with, or knowledge of, the Religious element. No immorality is suggested: the worshippers in the town clearly had a ritual, and observed it; the villagers had no worship,

and are called "atheists." Perhaps a few words interchanged would have indicated, that they had a Religious Conception also. Imagine a clever Japanese making a similar account of the religious practices of the better classes in London: "He
" described some aspects of the Hindu Religion, as practised at
" Delhi. With regard to worship, the most important point is
" that of bathing in a sacred river. This takes place every
" morning. Only the more religious people go every day.
" Sunday is the favourite day. The bathing is without solemnity,
" and the bathers are engaged in ordinary conversation. Some
" turn to the sun, and pour water towards the sun from their
" hands. There is no common or united worship; large num-
" bers of people are coming, as others are going. The religious
" on returning to the shore ask a Brahmin to put marks on
" their foreheads, and then go home, some of them visiting a
" temple on the way, and offering a few flowers and some water.
" There are no temples worthy of the name. Shrines are now
" only built by the mercantile classes. They allow room for
" about four worshippers and the image. They are for the
" worship of Siva, and are entirely phallic. In the villages the
" people are practically atheist, and scarcely ever enter a temple.

" He described the Superstitions added to their Religion, the
" shrines for the small-pox-goddess and other divinities, and
" shrines used on certain days of the week, and the religious
" books. He said that they were ignorant of their own books,
" and that it would be hard to find five men who knew anything
" of the Veda."

I quote the words of a wise Missionary in China: "With the
" scholarly class it is only necessary, that the Missionary know
" something of the Confucian books. Quoting from Confucius,
" or his disciples, he is at once in favour, and at once he is in
" the midst of religious and moral topics, capable of indefinite
" expansion. It is a mistake to think, that the Confucianists in
" China are the most difficult to engage in religious conversa-
" tion, though they may be most difficult of Conversion to Christ.
" But with God all things are possible. Coming to the more
" simple classes, we find, that their thoughts are ever recurring
" to religious matters, and only need the direction of the true
" Christian guide. There is inquiry in China, as is plainly seen
" by the vast number of secret sects and religious tracts and
" books. Each Missionary only needs to study the art of per-
" suasion, and so fit the truths he teaches to the people who
" hear. The ways are different, as individuality is different;
" but if the teacher be apt to teach, the truth will soon take
" effect."

And I quote a pleasant narrative of a sympathetic Medical-Missionary: " Oftentimes these are very pleasant gatherings.

"The patients appreciate them as a break in the monotony of
"their day; while the period of quiet and enforced rest gives
"them opportunity for thinking about the truths, which they
"hear. But above all, the great advantage of Medical-Mission-
"work is, that it presents such obvious facilities for showing, that
"the Christian Religion is not a mere collection of dogmas,
"that it is no barren philosophy, but a vital principle permeating
"the lives of believers. The patients can test our teaching by
"our lives. A wound carefully dressed, an extra visit, patience
"under the provocation of disobedience or ingratitude, justice
"in the control of a large establishment, the maintenance of
"cleanliness, and all that goes to make up discipline, the oppor-
"tunities for demonstrating the difference between honest work
"and eye-service, these things are more valuable than many a
"sermon. And when combined with teaching and preaching,
"they indicate, that philanthropy is not distinct from Christi-
"anity, but included in it. And thus patients are brought into
"contact with more than one side of our Religion."

If the Christian Church is to become permanent in China, it must be solidly based on National self-respect, affected no doubt by National weaknesses: Confucius will ever remain a power: such men are not produced every Century. The Literati, and Gentry, whom the Missionary is always girding at, represent the Clergy and Landowners of Great Britain, not faultless, but still respectable and exceedingly conservative. The objection to Fung Chui, or Luck, is not fictitious, and as regards houses and lands such sentiments, however ridiculous they may seem to a European or American stranger, indicate the feelings of a great Nation, which cannot be despised, and will probably survive a change of creed.

Missionaries accompany the pilgrims on their pilgrimage to the Ganges, and take the opportunity of speaking to large audiences. It can be understood how favourable such occasions are. In the Province of Canada I find the following circumstances described. There is no fear of the Missionary being degraded by such actions.

"In May the Indians all left to celebrate their annual sun-
"dance, about eight miles from the Mission. This year we
"followed them up, and pitched our Mission-tent in the midst
"of the encampment. We held school every day for the
"children, with an average attendance of eighty scholars.
"When school-hours were over, the Indians came to smoke, and
"talk, and many were the opportunities of speaking about Jesus.
"When the actual ceremony of torturing the body was about
"to come on, I spent much time in talking to the chiefs and
"head men, showing them, that such worship was contrary to the
"command of God, and that no blessing could be expected

" from it. Two men were painted, and prepared with incan-
" tations and prayers for the ordeal. The ropes were suspended
" from the top of the medicine-pole, and the medicine-man was
" about to make the incision in the breasts of the young men
" through which to place the bone skewer to which the ropes
" were to be attached. Even then we were able to prevent the
" ordeal, with the aid of the Indian Agent, by prevailing upon
" the chiefs to abandon it. To God be all the praise! For
" the first time in the Blackfoot-camp no torturing took place
" at the sun-dance. May it never again ! "

Hear what General Booth, of the Salvation-Army, says : I do not often agree with him, but I do so here.

" *The Mission of the Future, while retaining all that is essential*
" *to Godliness, will strive to adapt itself to the peculiar habits, con-*
" *ditions, and circumstances, of the different races which it seeks to*
" *conquer for Christ.*

" Strange that this common-sense Method should ever have
" been neglected, or need defending. No wonder there have
" been such miserable, and mortifying, and soul-ruining failures,
" seeing that it has been so openly and boastfully set at naught.
" This is a principle, that is acted upon every hour of our
" existence, in almost every transaction of every-day life. We
" continually become all things to all men, yielding to the
" eccentricities, ignorance, and infirmities, of those about us, in
" order to prevent any unnecessary hurtfulness to their feelings,
" or to accomplish something that we may consider of im-
" portance. This principle will be carried out in the Mission
" of the future. We shall learn to stoop in non-essential
" matters, in order to conquer in the greater things that concern
" and lead to Salvation.

" You go to lead and guide your less-favoured brethren to
" the Christ, who bought them with His Blood. Then go as a
" brother, and do not go at all unless you do. I say to my
" Officer, who is going to Holland, ' Can you be a Dutchman ?'
" to the man who is going to Zululand, ' Can you be a Zulu ?'
" to the one going to India, 'Can you be an Indian ? If you
" cannot, you must not go at all.' This principle has only to
" be acted out to prove an enormous success. The Missionary-
" Societies have only to go forward, and, with the opposite,
" setting it at naught, as in the past, in order to perpetuate the
" wretched failures, over which so many thoughtful and sensible
" Christians are mourning to-day."

A Missionary, who had been seven years among the races of the Kongo, remarked to me, that he had never met a Savage : they were capable of appreciating the exercise of the great cardinal virtues, and of being influenced by the sincere, unselfish, pure, strong, and yet gentle character, of their white teacher. It is shocking to hear and read of the tone of the Missionaries as regards their native brethren in some Missions in Africa: some of them seem to loathe and hate the Natives; and yet the Son of God did not disdain to take upon him the form of a bond-servant or slave, δοῦλος, for the purpose of saving mankind: how then can the Missionary disdain to speak, feel, and live, as the people of the country, to whom he is sent, if by so doing he can save them? Take the extreme case of the distance between the European and the Negro: how little, how absolutely nothing, it appears, when contrasted with the distance betwixt our Lord, and His Disciples! Love can never be generated, if such intimacy be not formed, if there is evidenced by the Missionary the most unjustifiable Pride, and Caste, and Contempt. Even in secular matters the value of a Public Officer amidst a subject People is estimated by the degree, to which he is loved and respected by them, and that Love and Respect is only purchased by Intimacy and Sympathy.

Mr. Spurgeon, in his last speech in Exeter Hall, in 1888, remarked on the gentleness of Christ: "Henceforth I call you not servants, but I have called you friends." "These things I have said unto you, that ye should not be offended." How different is the bearing of the European, and American, Missionary to the ancient, civilized, and peaceable, people of India and China, with their ancient literature, and traditions, and lineage! Does he call them "friends," or is he careful, that " they be not offended"?

I say with deliberation my own convictions, that Christian things should be done in a Christian manner, that there should be more sympathy in thought, word, and deed, expressed, if not felt: as it is now in the Reports, which I read, there is scarcely a breath of sympathy for the provoking non-Christian, who refuses to hear, or be convinced after hearing; there is not a grain of pity for the poor dark-skinned convert, or Mission-Agent, or Native Pastor, who after Centuries of Heathendom and Mahometanism, and one generation of a very weak Christianity, does not at once "per saltum" pass up to the level of middle-class Evangelicalism, does not keep clear of habits and weaknesses of his Heathen ancestors, which cling to his flesh: those, who judged the erring Negro Christians on the Niger, forget to be thankful for the long Centuries, and the numerous generations, through which England has passed, ere it reached the small modicum, the low-level, of Christianity, to which some small portion of its population has attained, while a majority are as much Heathens in their Religious Conceptions, and as free from moral restrictions, as our forefathers were, when they were but little advanced beyond the level of the Civilization of the Negro.

How striking are the incidental touches of the Gospel. No doubt the Jews were, in the time of our Lord, a puffed-up, egotistic people, better in their own opinion than all the Gentile world: the Jews are so still, and the Hindu, and so are many Englishmen. But the Master, notwithstanding His Divinity, allowed Himself to be influenced by the human weakness of Compassion (σπλαχνίζομαι) (to have the bowels yearning), and in one case it is specially recorded, that He, "looking upon a young man, loved him" (ἠγάπησεν), and He loved him, although He well knew, that the World had too strong a hold on him to allow him to give up all and follow Jesus: is not this an example for a Missionary?

There exists in the soul of the meanest, and most degraded, and most stupid, of the human race, a Divine Spark, the direct gift of the Creator, which spiritual intercourse with the Personal and Risen Christ can fan into a flame of goodness. No man is hopelessly bad: he has within him the seeds of goodness, if only the waters of life, conveyed by a loving and sympathetic hand, and the sudden illumination of his environment, brought about by the words of his Master, and the prayers of a true Servant of God, permit it to germinate, and bring forth fruit one-hundredfold. He may be ugly in features, filthy in his dress, rude and coarse in his utterances, still there is in him a possibility of Salvation, which discriminates him from the intelligent and beautiful animals, which gather around him, and who live only to perish. There is a sweet reasonableness in the recorded words of Christ, a sweetness and a light, which no thoughtful man, if he can be brought to think, can resist. Still there is one thing higher than the *written* Word, which retains the flavour of ancient days, of forgotten surroundings, narrow views, and physical ignorance: that thing is the living, eternal, all-powerful, Word of God in the heart of each one of us, ever fresh and ever new, adapted to the environment of every Century and every Country, every degree of Knowledge, or non-Knowledge, every round of the ladder of Social Culture, or non-Culture. Christ lives for ever, and is renewed in the same, yet seemingly different, outward form, and conception, by the Chinese, the Indian, the Negro, the Redskin, the Kanaka: it is not the perquisite, and monopoly, of the good Christian of the English middle-classes to know Christ as He is, and as He deigns to reveal Himself to the poor, benighted, intellects of Man in his deepest degradation.

11. Disloyal to Home-Committee.

Still more reprehensible is the conduct of those Missionaries, who are misguided enough to rebel against those, who sent them out, and to turn the resources, which were entrusted to them, against the Home-Committee. Cases have lately occurred, of a character, which a Merchant, a public Official, or a secular servant, could never have done, and which nevertheless a Christian ordained Missionary justifies himself in doing. If his views upon some theological point undergo a change, his duty is clear, to resign his connection with the Society, with whose principles he is no longer in accord. Instead of that, I have known cases, where the Missionary threw off his allegiance, claimed the souls of the Converts as his own private property, and, in defiance of all honour, all Christian duty, attempted to found a rival Mission, and carry on a work in antagonism to the Home-Committee, which selected him, equipped him, supported him, and to whom he promised obedience. In the case of a tribe of considerable numbers, and a low state of culture, bloodshed might be the consequence. These are no imaginary or trifling cases. They have occurred in Asia and America.

In return for the care taken of him, the Missionary should render obedience, not the slavish obedience of the Jesuit Priest, but the ready, and self-forgetting, submission of the Christian Soldier. In Secular Matters, when an order is received by a subordinate officer, he can temperately remonstrate, but, if the order be confirmed, he shall render instant and complete obedience. What a contrast is found in the conduct of some self-willed, and egotistic, individuals, who forget the cause of their work in Self, who forget to practise the precepts of the Gospel, which they preach!

Over every Mission some kind of Head-Pastor is absolutely necessary: the time has passed for placing the old and tried Agent on the same level with the inexperienced youth; the gifted man, and the man of power, on the same level with the ordinary hewer of wood. All experience shows, that in each Mission there must be some kind of Organization, some defined plan of operations, a certain grouping in centres, and detachment at outposts, a certain combination of different qualifications, a certain diversity of ministrations, and, unless there be a ruling spirit, and a governing wheel, the end must be, and in reality is, loss of power, or confusion. The leader need not necessarily be the oldest, but the ablest, one who has had the peculiar Grace of Rule conferred upon him. We find it in things secular, and we know, that it has not been wanting in things religious.

12. DEFYING LAWS AND CUSTOMS OF A COUNTRY.

It would seem incredible, that Missionaries should be charged with the heinous crime of promoting wars among Native Tribes, but I adduce the following resolution of the Aborigines-Society

as proof: "This Society, while rejoicing in the early termi-
"nation of the Zulu War, and expressing an earnest hope, that
"Cetewayo may yet be dealt with in a just and magnanimous
"spirit, desires to call the serious attention of the Missionary-
"Societies to the support, which many of their representatives
"in S. Africa have given to this wicked and unnecessary war,
"apparently under the impression, that the cause of Missions
"will be promoted by the invasion and conquest of the Zulu
"territory. This Society believes, that no idea could be more
"immoral in itself, or more calculated to prove fatal to Mis-
"sionary-enterprise in S. Africa; and it therefore considers, that
"the time has come, when it is imperative, that the Missionary-
"Societies should impress upon their Agents the duty of giving
"no countenance to a course of action so opposed to the
"principles, upon which those Societies are based, as well as
"to the traditional practice of English Missionaries, who have
"laboured among uncivilized races."

The French Protestant Missionaries openly admit, that they encouraged the Ba-Suto in S. Africa to fight against the British. It would seem, as if the Missionary-Societies on Lake Nyassa regarded with complacency the idea of a British invasion of that Region, which would necessarily be accompanied by slaughter of the people, whom they wish to convert. The Missionary should set the example of a steady and willing obedience to the law of the land: he assumes an awful and dangerous responsibility, when he encourages people, over whom he has influence, to resist the powers that be, forgetting the advice of Paul to the Romans, who dwelt under the rule of the Emperor Nero.

In U-Ganda the Missionaries went further, joined in the expulsion of the Ruler, and profited materially from the success of the alien invasion. Posterity will have to form a judgment upon this unique incident. I am thankful, that the Missionaries took no part in the Ma-Tabélé Scandal of 1893.

The Missionary should not meddle in the Politics of the Country, in which he is located; he seldom is able to appreciate the value of the forces, which are in antagonism. His kingdom is not of this world. It is monstrous, when a Missionary usurps the power of a Magistrate, or a Chief, and tries offenders, and sentences them to corporal punishment, or even Death. Within the last ten years this has happened in Africa. In a Patriarchal way he may act as Umpire to remove difficulties, or prevent bloodshed; in case of moral offences among his converts he may enforce Church-penalties, but he should carefully abstain from personal violence, and personal restraint. It may be a question, whether he is justified in using lethal weapons, or firearms, in resisting an invading band: the terrible necessity may sometimes be forced upon him to do so in defence of life and female honour, but I know of no case, where matters have come to this pass in modern times. As to the spoiling of goods by the tyranny of Officials, or petty Chiefs, or the inroads of freebooters, he must take it joyfully. As to avenging the death of a fellow-labourer or follower, he must not think of it. In many parts of Asia and Africa he carries his life in his hands, and if he is not content to do so, he had better leave the Field and go home: he clearly is not the man for such a Mission.

A Mission-Station should not be allowed to be a city of refuge to runaway slaves; it is dangerous, and is wrong. Paul did not do so. Until the Civil Power abolishes the status of Slavery, the Church can only look on in sorrow. I give instances of the inconveniences: "Reported that a catechist had lately been in " trouble through assisting a man, who had escaped from a " creditor. The man was recaptured, and told the authorities " what had been done to help him, so the catechist was fined " £3 2s. 6d., which he hoped would be repaid to him by the " Committee. The Local Committee felt unable to do this, " but the various Members subscribed £2 5s., and decided to " ask friends for the balance. A catechist was charged with " helping two slaves of an influential chief to escape, and he " demanded restitution. The matter at one time looked serious, " but appears now to be settled. Such cases show the continued " need of caution."

And again: "I asked Bishop Patteson of Melanesia to " consider, what was the sight to a Christian man, of slaves " driven off with a yoke on their necks, and whether it did not " justify armed interposition. He replied, upholding the " principle, that the shepherd is shepherd of the cruel and " erring, as well as of the oppressed, and ought not to interfere."

I found in Morocco, that an Agent for the Conversion of the Jews chose to interfere as regards the sale of slaves, forbidding husband and wife to be sold separately: this, no doubt, was a right suggestion; but what business had he to make it? It might have cost him his life, and placed the Diplomatic Representative of his Country in great difficulties. He received a caution from his Committee at my suggestion to keep to his own work.

As the Organs of the Church of Rome have openly announced the policy of arming African converts, to resist their lawful Sovereigns, and everybody else, whom they choose to oppose, it is as well to state, that such a line of conduct is totally opposed to the principles, upon which Protestant Missions are conducted, and must end in grievous trouble, and contrary to the New Testament.

Then, again, the Missionary must not set himself up as a Reformer, or a Patriot, or a friend of oppressed people against their lawful Rulers. Temperate remonstrance can do much, and his very presence is a safeguard to the people; but, if a Missionary so conducts himself in the territory of an independent Chief, how can we wonder, that the Chief forbids his entry into his kingdom, or ejects him beyond his frontier?

Then again, as regards the Criminal Law and the Police, the Missionaries are not the Judges, whether the local Governor be just or unjust, and it is a monstrous abuse of the hospitality of a friendly State for a resident alien to give shelter to a man, for whose arrest a warrant had been issued, to conceal him in the Mission-premises, and smuggle him out of the Jurisdiction. Yet such a case is reported with complacency by a Missionary, who thinks that he has done a praiseworthy act. In British India any Missionary, who acted thus, would have found himself next day in prison without benefit of clergy.

While on the one hand Missionaries should not refuse to give presents in lieu of transit-duty, and reasonable taxation to the Sovereign, or Chief of the Country, they should resist all exactions, and rather leave the country, if the demands are unreasonable: they should have about them as little property as possible, so as not to excite cupidity: under no possible circumstances should a Missionary make presents of lethal weapons of any kind, ammunition, or intoxicating liquors or drugs: he should not have such things with him to give. It is scarcely credible, but it is recorded as a fact, that Missionaries have presented firearms to Natives. They should be prohibited from doing so, either in their private capacity, or as Agents of the Society.

The Missionary should try to make the Native Chiefs exercise a rightful authority, and only give them advice. Traders charge the Missionary with usurpation of power, and meddling with politics, and trade; those complain most, who want to take advantage of Native ignorance. On the other hand, the Missionary should steadily refuse to constitute himself a Chieftain, or arrogate power and authority.

A judicious Missionary remarked to a visitor, that he placed great importance on working in such a way, as not to embarrass the Government. The wife of a rich Landowner desired to be baptized contrary to the wishes of her family. She entreated the Missionary to help her to escape from her husband's house, that she might join them. She was told, that the Christian Religion forbade him to countenance such acts: she must remain at home, and strive by gentleness and persuasion to lead her husband to sanction her desire: under any circumstances she must wait patiently.

In 1852 an emeute took place in the great city of Banáras on a local matter: I was one of the Magistrates, and accompanied a Regiment to enforce obedience, and compel the tradesmen to open their shops, and we succeeded without bloodshed.

Unknown to us a party of young Missionaries made a sudden attack during the advance of the Soldiers on the private house of a Brahmin, captured the wife of a convert, who had been withheld from him, and made her drink a cup of tea, and thus break her Caste, and live with her husband. This was a grave offence, as it might have led to bloodshed; at any rate it was a gross outrage on a private family of high Caste, and contrary to the Law of British India: no complaint was made by the outraged family, and the matter dropt: the poor child-wife died in a few months, and the convert, now a distinguished Native Missionary, has never married again. It was a lamentable mistake, and shows what a Missionary should not do: if he had been shot down or stabbed, what a loud outcry at the want of toleration would have been made!

Mr. Ashe, late a Missionary of the Church-Missionary-Society at U-Ganda, a man of good ability and experience, justifies a breach of the Peace by himself: he acted thus in the German Sphere in E. Africa: "The first matter referred to a most
" regrettable incident, which occurred during a visit undertaken
" to an Urima Chief, when I found myself compelled, by cir-
" cumstances of extraordinary difficulty and danger, to resort to
" a course of action, which at first sight might appear unjustifi-
" able, since it included the removal of a stone, which kept the
" gate of the village closed, and which had temporarily been
" placed there, and so entering the village; and which, unhappily,
" culminated in the firing of several shots, and the burning of
" three native houses; but which I shall show was a course of
" action, that the circumstances fully justified.

" There are a good many cases which have occurred in the
" annals of our own ·Church-Missionary-Society's Equatorial
" African Mission, where Missionaries, of the highest principle,
" and of undoubted Christian character, have been compelled
" under sudden and trying emergencies to resort to acts of
" violence.

" I give a little analysis of these cases, which deal with ten
" Missionaries.

" Two Missionaries threaten recalcitrant natives with revolvers.

" Four Missionaries fire on natives, wounding three.

" Four Missionaries fire on, and kill, at least twenty-one
" natives.

" In two cases three Missionaries were killed.

" In two cases, involving four Missionaries, the matter was
" referred to the civil Authorities, and in both the Missionaries
" were held to have acted with justification, while in four cases
" no further notice was taken of the matter, as far as I am aware.

" I have here only referred to cases, of which I know the
" full particulars, and have purposely omitted four other cases,

"where violence was used, in one instance with fatal results, "since I do not know the full particulars."

It is notorious, that a Presbyterian Missionary at Blantyre tried and condemned a man, and took away his life. All this shows the extreme necessity of a Missionary keeping to his own peaceful duties: if the hands of Great Britain were shortened by a long European war, the fate of many British Missionaries is sad to contemplate: they would be attacked and massacred: it is not wise to found a Mission on Musquets and Maxim-guns. A Medical-Missionary in the independent kingdom of Kashmir in North India, ruled over by a Native Sovereign, whose Father and Grandfather were my personal friends for many years, enjoyed all the hospitality, which the King could give; but he chose to get up stories of the most dreadful character, that the King had drowned many of his subjects in the lake, and published this in the local papers of North India. It is no wonder, that the King, and the British Officers, were much annoyed: such statements should have been sent confidentially to the Political Officer attached to the King's Court.

Another Missionary, to the surprise of all who knew him, took a violent part on the side of the Natives of Bengál against the European Indigo-planters: possibly his statements were accurate, but it did not lie in his mouth to make them, or to head an agrarian revolt. It ended in his being sent to Prison on a matter, which arose out of this departure of his from the proper conduct of a Preacher of the Gospel to the Heathen.

I read in the Historical Sketches of Natal and Zululand of the Society for the Propagation of the Gospel, in 1891, the following: "The hostility to Missions evinced by Cetewayo, "the Zulu-king, on the ground that he lost his subjects, led "the Bishop and clergy to consider the proposal, that they "should address themselves on the subject of Christian Missions "in the first instance to the tribal chieftains themselves, in the "hope of impressing them favourably towards Christianity, and "so of convincing them, that their people would remain firm "in their allegiance. It was felt that the partial change of "allegiance, which came to be regarded as one of the duties "of a convert, had undoubtedly hindered the spread of the "Gospel in Africa, by raising against it the entire influence "of the chiefs, whose despotism was thus menaced." Such a policy might lead to dangers of another kind, so common in the early ages of Christianity: as a fact, Conversion makes no change in allegiance.

13. Tilting against Legal Native Customs.

In the life of Mr. Venn, the secretary to the Church-Missionary-Society, given in the Organ of that Society, it is mentioned, that a feature in his character was the resolute manner, in which he ever kept clear of all extraneous questions, which were not clearly involved in the duties of the Committee: the sensational enthusiast, now called Faddist, could not convert the great Secretary to his views: according to him the Committee had one sole object to pursue, to convert the World to Christ: peculiar crazes, and collateral evils, should be ventilated elsewhere. At Jaggahnáth, the great Temple of the Vishnuites, at the time of the festival, all distinctions of Caste for the time cease. So in Salisbury Square, in the presence of the great work all idiosyncrasies, and fads, ought to disappear. I have known a downright teetotaler drink claret at the Church-Missionary-Society-luncheon with the air of a man sacrificing his prejudices out of consideration for his weaker brethren: if there be one interest, which more than any other supplies grist to the Church-Missionary-Society-Mill, it is that of the Brewer. It is, therefore, a strange feature, that of late years the *Intelligencer* of the Church-Missionary-Society has become the handmaid of the Anti-Opium-Society, and an Annual Report never appears without an attack upon the Government of India. Such attacks are, of course, like the wagging of a dog's tail, or the mop of Mrs. Partington, and very unfair on the Anglo-Indian Members of the Committee, who cannot see any cause for the interference of the Church-Missionary-Society. A Bishop was asked to take part in the Crusade : his reply was, "make the people of India " and China Christians, and they will cease to eat, or smoke, " opium, and perhaps keep clear of Tobacco and Whiskey, to " which the English introduce them."

And with regard to India, why do Missionaries run a tilt, and a very hopeless tilt indeed, against that universal custom in India, known as Caste ? It exists all over the world, in Great Britain, and in North America. The Missionary himself would shudder at the idea of his daughter marrying the Native Pastor, or of his being compelled with his wife and family to eat his meals with the men of less clean habits in the Native village : he would say, with justice, that his origin, his habits, his culture, are different: but the population of India is made up of an infinite number of races, and tribes, which never have fused together, and they shun intermarriage, and commensality. Let everything else, which is called Caste, be swept away : one Caste does not ordinarily pretend, that it is better than another, but different, and, the lower the Caste is, the more particular are the Caste-rules. The Civil Government in its Schools, its Railroads, its

Ferries, its Courts of Justice, refuses to recognise Caste: let the Missionary draw the same line, and insist, that in the School, and Chapel, and at the Lord's Table, there is no Caste, and not attempt Love-feasts, and Social-gatherings, and forcibly unite in marriages converts of different Castes. We should not tolerate such action by a Minister in any British or American Church. Each class of the Community lives its social life apart. The Missionary by the necessity of the Vernacular is tied for the whole of his life to one narrow Field: he picks out what he considers to be the great obstacle to his progress, and denounces it, without considering, that the progress of Missions in other Regions, where that particular obstacle does not exist, is not more encouraging.

Another Crusade has been made by the Missionary against the custom of Infant-Marriage, and somehow or other he desires to enforce the re-marriage of Hindu widows: he does not tell us how. We must recollect that the Family-Customs of Natives differ in different countries: how wide the difference betwixt the Customs of the Jews at the time of our Lord, and the Customs of Great Britain!

Another fad of the Missionary in China is the Crusade against Ancestral Worship: I subjoin an extract from the *Chinese Times*:
" In their attempt to introduce Christianity into China the
" Missionaries proceed by Methods, which would be condemned
" in any other kind of enterprise, moral, or material. Instead
" of looking for local allies, for existing foundations, on which
" to build, and trusting to the divine alchemy of their Religion
" to gradually transmute whatever is base into pure gold, they
" proceed on the more radical principle of destroying, in order
" that they may build anew. Scarcely have they gained a foot-
" ing in the country, than they declare war to the knife against
" its most cherished institutions, converting the moral forces of
" the nation into bitter enemies. Aiming at nothing less than
" setting up a spiritual kingdom in the hearts of the Chinese
" people, the Missionaries begin by shocking such feeling of
" propriety, as they already possess. That delicate piece of
" mechanism, the conscience, though susceptible of education
" in judicious hands possessing a nice touch, is nevertheless
" strong to resist outrage. The conscience even of the Heathen
" was acknowledged by the early Christians to have been suffi-
" ciently well adjusted to be a law to them, whereby they were
" acquitted or condemned. The plan has never succeeded of
" telling a non-Christian, that the parents, whom he revered,
" were burning for their wickedness. He will go and burn with
" them, if he have the spirit of a man, rather than follow one,
" who so outrages his feelings. So, to come to the Chinaman,
" who inherits from a hundred generations of ancestors such a

" love of them, as to be to him the warp and woof of his character,
" and bluntly tell him, that the reverence, which he shows to his
" deceased parents is a gross offence, which he must abjure, if
" he would escape the curse of God, seems the most unlikely
" way to gain him over. 'What is to be expected of that
" Heathen but amazement at the impudence of the intruder, and,
" if he stops short of reviling the Deity so presented to him, it
" only shows, that the Heathen has the virtue of forbearance,
" which is lacking to the Evangelist. Humanly speaking,
" China can never be converted to Christianity, while violence
" is done to the best feelings of the Nation; and, as ancestral
" worship is a Religion, which sits deep in their heart of hearts,
" some means of accommodation will have to be discovered
" before Christians can make any impression worth mentioning
" on this people. Hence the present attitude of the body of
" Missionaries, with a few notable exceptions, will in all proba-
" bility retard the progress of Christianity for at least a genera-
" tion. There is, however, a worse evil than even loss of time,
" for the revulsion, engendered in the minds of the Chinese by
" unprovoked assaults on the objects of their affections, is likely
" enough to keep alive, and probably deepen, their prejudice
" against the foreign Religion. If the barrier, while slowly
" wearing away physically and geographically, should be at the
" same time increasing morally, and the problem of regenerating
" China thereby becoming progressively harder, the present
" generation of Missionaries may be not only spending their
" own lives and labour fruitlessly, but actually creating obstacles
" for those, who may come after them.'"

14. THROWING UP HIS VOCATION FOR HIS OWN PRIVATE CONVENIENCE.

The Missionary in these days should ponder well over the last verse of the ninth chapter of St. Luke's Gospel. Here again the Missionary of the Church of Rome presents a bright example, and magnificent examples are supplied in the annals of every Protestant Mission. It is a life-work, which the Missionary undertakes, and he should not be always running home as a "returned empty." The contrast of those brave men, who hold on beyond their strength, comes out more strongly, when the faces of others are seen so often in England. It was not so formerly, but with the facility of communication has come a laxity of control, and an infirmity of will. Of course a medical certificate has to be complied with, as lives must not be sacrificed; but I allude to other cases.

It has been well said, that a modern Missionary's career is too often treated as a mere Profession, like that of a Soldier or a

Lawyer, whereas it should be regarded as a Vocation. This is the very root of the whole matter. How shall a man preach, unless he be sent? on the other hand, if he be sent, called of God, how can he refuse to go? In considering, then, the qualifications of a Missionary, we must ever bear this in mind, that there are diversities of gifts, but the same Spirit; and that the one sole, supreme, and absolute qualification for a Missionary is Vocation; without which, talents, zeal, nay, even personal saintliness, are of no avail.

What shall be said of the following notice? "Mr. A. A. J. " Swann, F.R.G.S., who has spent many years in Nyasaland, " in the service of the London-Missionary-Society, has resigned " his connection with that body, having accepted a post in the " British Administration of Nyasaland, under Mr. H. H. John- " ston, C.B., her Majesty's Commissioner in that region. Mr. " Swann, from his long and friendly intercourse with both chiefs " and natives in Nyasaland, has gained a wide experience in " native affairs. He leaves for his new post on board the " Union Company's steamer 'Mexican,' which sails on March " 31st. It was Mr. Swann, who brought to England the first " definite news of the murder and decapitation of Emin Pasha " by the Arabs."

I quote the following from a well-known writer: " But such " failures are not confined to foreign work: we know of them, " alas! too frequently at home. Nor are they confined abroad " to men from our Missionary-Colleges. And it is time, that it " should be said plainly, that they are not even confined to the " lower orders of the ministry: one of the chief difficulties at " present is, that so many Bishops, having put their hand to the " plough, speedily turn back. As to the right and wrong of this, " God alone can be the judge; but most certainly it forms a " very serious difficulty for us, when trying to urge upon our " men the need of an entire life-surrender to the work. If the " officers turn back from the breach, who shall venture to be " hard upon the rank-and-file?"

Hear the announcement of a Colonial Bishop in a most healthy climate: "The Doctors assure me, that my dear wife " cannot return to my Diocese without endangering her life. I " could not deem it my duty to accept a complete separation in " the evening of our lives after thirty-seven years of union. I " have no alternative but to relinquish my work here."

Tertullian would have said, that no married man should enter the ministry.

Bishop Steere, who after a long separation from his wife died at his post, remarks: " It is a very nice question of conscience, " how far a man, who leaves his post, because his wife is ill, can " suppose himself one of those, who are expected to leave

" everything for Christ. I should be ashamed to read our
" Lord's words about forsaking home and so forth, if I had
" refused, when I had a clear opportunity to do the thing,
" which He recommended."

I am obliged to lay stress upon such cases, because the younger clergy follow the example, throw up their Vocation; in some cases of University-men, or independent men, they were *legally* entitled to do so. But think of the young man, picked up from the shop, or place of business, instructed at the expense of the Society, and a very considerable expense, throwing up the service of the Lord in the Mission-Field after a few years' service, as an apprentice, rather than an efficient Missionary, because his wife is sick: his wife, whom he wilfully, and against all consideration of expediency, married at the time, that he was ordained. What blessing can accompany in their retreat such deserters from the great Army of the Lord? The Lord followed Jonah in his attempt to flee to Tarshish.

For years I have drawn attention to this subject in Committee, but it is all in vain. The head of a Missionary-College writes as follows : " On the whole, we may fairly claim, that our Missionary-
" Colleges, though by no means perfect, are doing a solid and
" useful work, if humbly, yet not ignobly. There is much still
" to be desired, both at home and abroad, in the way of self-
" sacrifice, and self-effacement. Men are apt to be drawn away
" by the all-pervading desire for ease and self-indulgence ; there
" are too many complaints, that they do not care to do menial
" offices, or to take off their coat and work, where need requires.
" We want more Hero-Missionaries of the type of Boniface,
" and Columbanus. And we need more leaders, of experience
" and education and spiritual power, under whose guiding care
" our young Missionaries might be placed on going abroad."

Look at the other side of the picture, and be thankful, that there is another even in Protestant Missions, and this is the only possible side in the Romish Missions. Rejoice that Bishops Caldwell and Sargent in S. India, John Newton in N. India, and many others at all periods have lived, and died in old age, amidst their flocks, and that many old men, like Robert Clarke, are still at work. Read the account, which I subjoin, of the funeral of a Missionary-Bishop in the Province of Canada only last year: "Saturday, January 21st, we had the funeral. The
" coffin was closed in the presence of four clergy. It was a
" lovely afternoon, almost spring-like, when the beautiful Burial-
" Service was read, and the first Bishop of Moosonee's body
" was committed to the grave before his bereaved people. The
" whole adult population went to the Church, and to the grave.
" There he was laid amongst his flock, as he had said he wished
" to be. While still lying in the Church young and old came to

"take the last farewell of the face, which they loved so well, and
"who went in and out of their homes, over forty years, as a
"Missionary, Pastor, Friend, and Bishop." Every Missionary should wish, and be determined as far as in him lies, that his last end should be like this.

When better than pearls, or shekels of fine gold, the believing man, or woman, lays himself, or herself, on the altar of Missions, forgetting Father, Mother, Husband, Wife, or children (our Lord Himself answered the question, 'who is my Mother?'), God's own fire comes down on that altar, not to consume, and destroy, but to consecrate: he or she are accepted in the Beloved; but they must not turn away from their choice a few years afterwards to suit their worldly notions: they have sold themselves, body, soul, and spirit, to their Lord, who bought them: after all in the scale of human gifts, and divine possibilities, they had little enough to offer, but the lives and service of two commonplace individuals of the middle-classes of England, totally unknown, and unvalued, in their own country: but it was their all, and God valued it, and accepted it: is it not trifling with the Giver of all good things, to say, "my wife is not strong enough for the climate, so I, the Lord's chosen, consecrated, servant, must pack up my trunk, and go back to my place," as if he had never bound himself to the Lord.

When the Crimean War broke out, a young officer sent in his papers to retire from the Regiment, which he had dishonoured by his presence: he had no stomach for the fight. He received during the next week many envelopes containing nothing but a white feather, the meaning of which was quite intelligible: his reputation as a Soldier, a Briton, and a man, was tarnished, and he had for the rest of his days to carry a white feather on his shield. In what respect does the Missionary-deserter differ from this craven, except that he has deserted a higher post, failed in a nobler duty, and thrown up a nobler service? I knew a case of a Missionary, who brought a sick wife home, and resigned. She died. He returned to his duty, and is doing excellent service, and may do so for many years more. Is it necessary, that the poor woman should die, in order to save the reputation of her husband? Should she not humbly, and yet nobly, bow to the Lord's will, and exclaim: "I had hoped to
"have served the Lord with you in *our* chosen Vocation: He
"has willed it otherwise: return to your holy life-chosen work
"without me, and be sustained by my unceasing prayer for your
"welfare." This is the age of Special Services: there should be a special service to receive such a recreant in the Committee-room: a white feather should be solemnly handed to him by such men, as Bishop French, and Bishop Stuart, who even in their old age cannot be kept back from the Holy War; and some

Missionary, who in the prime of his life, and fulness of his powers, has been forced home by the imperative order of his Doctor, because a hopeless malady has totally disqualified him for work, should describe to the deserter the sorrow, which he felt, at being torn away from his duty, his flock, and his earliest and latest love, the Saving of Souls.

I am not alone in these sentiments. Hear what the Archdeacon of London said in May, 1894: " Brothers and sisters in " Christ Jesus! There is another point, in which the Church- " Missionary-Society is of deep spiritual importance to our own " souls. It brings home to our hearts individually the lesson " of Personal Consecration. There is a tendency amongst us " Christians at home to lead easy, comfortable lives, to devote " no very great share of our thoughts, interests, or resources " to the things of God, to think a good deal of quiet reasonable " enjoyment, and with the exception of being regular and con- " sistent in our religious duties, to seem not very different from " the people of the world. As long as we exercise ourselves " to have a conscience void of offence toward God, and towards " men, it appears on a merely superficial view, that of us no " very great effort is required. With that superficial view too " many Christians are content. And then there comes to us, " like a lightning flash, the example of a Bishop Hannington, a " Bishop Parker, a Bishop Horden, a Bishop Hill. Yes! Here " he stood only last year, full of earnest hope and energy, ready " to spend his life, be it long or short, amongst heathen savages " in the service of that Lord, in whom he so utterly and entirely " believed. He might have remained at home in some pleasant " English country-rectory, and had a very useful career, and " filled his Church with devout worshippers, and visited his " schools, and tended his sick, and died in a good old age " amidst the genuine tears and affectionate regret of his people. " He chose to face death and danger in his loving sympathy " for the thousand Millions of the earth's inhabitants, who do " not yet know the way of peace ; and the death, of which he " had counted the risk, came to him with unexpected rapidity. " And other bright young lives, full of promise, were taken with " him by the same inexorable law of nature, that fever is the " Nemesis of an undrained tropical country. The examples, of " which we speak, are noble, saintly, illustrious, and worthy of " the best days of the Church. But there was no different " command laid upon them from that, which is laid upon you " and me! To you and me there is the same merciful law, ' If " any man will come after Me, let him deny himself, and take " up his cross daily, and follow Me ' ; ' He that loveth father or " mother more than Me is not worthy of Me ;' ' Ye are not your " own, ye are bought with a price.' There is no command to

"self-devotion and self-sacrifice, which applies to them, which
"does not apply to us also. We at home must be as complete,
"and heroic, in our relinquishment of our own desires, ideas,
"and wishes as they. Each of the ninety-three men, who in
"the past twelve months have been accepted by the Society, is a
"direct warning to ourselves. They are leaving father and
"mother, and brothers and sisters, and kindred and lands, ties
"as dear to them as to us, for Christ's sake and the Gospel's.
"We have chosen to stay, and fulfil our duties at home. What
"are we doing to compare with their resolve and unselfishness?
"Are we devoting the whole of our time, and energies, and re-
"sources, to the spread of the Kingdom of Christ at home and
"abroad?"

No one is more antagonistic to the doctrines and practice of the Church of Rome than I am, as is evidenced by my writings: still "Fas est et ab hoste doceri." I quote from the *Times*: "A
"venerable ecclesiastical figure in India has lately passed away.
"During 50 years Bishop Bigandet has been the Christian philo-
"sopher of Burma, and the most continuous spiritual influence,
"which the West has brought to bear upon the Burmese races.
"It is no disparagement to Judson to say, and, indeed, that
"noble-hearted American would have cordially acknowledged,
"that Bigandet had an access to the inner thoughts of the
"people, which a Protestant Missionary can scarcely hope to
"win. As a Romish priest and celibate, the Monsignor held
"the key to the institutions of a country, whose educational
"system and whole religious life are based upon monastic and
"celibate orders. The initial antagonism, which a married
"Missionary feels to such a system, and the tendency to con-
"demn it on insufficient knowledge, were to him unknown. He
"started at the point, to which many of our Protestant Mis-
"sionaries ultimately attain. While never underrating the
"differences between the native faiths and Christian Verity, he
"recognised the controlling influence, which those faiths exert
"upon the conduct of life, and his attitude was one of careful,
"but sympathetic, study of the Religions, by which that control
"is enforced."

15. HOLDING SECULAR OFFICES OR HONOURS.

Missionaries should decline to undertake any duty, that is not included in the words "carrying the Gospel to the non-Christian world": the office of Magistrate, Vice-Consul, Member of Local Board, or anything connected with the Civil or Criminal administration of the State, should be refused, if offered. It is a snare. A Missionary writes in an Annual Report as follows, from a great City in Upper India: "I am terribly deep in Municipal Com-

" mittee-matters. I am going in especially for the Conservancy
" of the City, and the Water-supply." Imagine Paul looking
after the drains of Corinth, or the water-supply of Ephesus!
These kinds of employment must destroy Spirituality, if it ever
existed. So also a Missionary should decline to take permanent
clerical duty among Europeans, which interferes with his proper
work. This will not exclude occasional services in the Church,
and visits to the sick, when called upon; but under no circumstances should he take any emolument. He should never act as
Chaplain of a Civil and Military Station, or the Medical Officer
of a Secular Hospital.

I quote from a Lagos Newspaper, 1894: it is not pleasant
Missionary-reading: "There were those, who advised that, in-
" asmuch, as Mr. Boston was unwilling to leave his J.P. honours,
" the Committee should have removed him to such quarters in
" their Mission-Field, where his Government-Commission would
" have been inoperative. Unfortunately, however, the whole of
" the Missions-Stations within the jurisdiction of the Committee
" were included within the sphere of British influence, as upheld
" by the Local Government. Besides, it is a question, whether
" the mere fact of a transfer would have rendered the Commis-
" sion a nullity, when there was nothing to prevent the Revd.
" gentleman from seeking means, whereby effect could have
" been given in the locality, whereunto he would have been
" transferred, to the Commission in question. Apart from this,
" there was the question of inexpediency. For, experience has
" taught the Church-Authorities here, if not elsewhere on the
" coast, the undesirableness of carrying on Missionary-opera-
" tions amongst the Heathens through the efforts of Agents,
" vested with the authority of a Civil Government. In such a
" case, it will be readily admitted, the Missionary-character of
" the work would be considerably impaired, as the Missionary
" would be very often tempted to overcome the difficulties in his
" way by the assistance of the power, which his other position
" gave him. It was even said, that Mr. Boston mentioned it to
" the members of the Committee, that his position as Justice of
" the Peace at Yongro would enable him the better to prosecute
" his Missionary-work more successfully in the Bullom-Shore.
" If such a suggestion were made by him, it was certainly a most
" unadvised one, and deserved to be corrected. However much
" it may be desirable to have the Heathens converted to the
" Christian Faith, any attempt to influence them beyond those,
" which we are bound to regard to be sufficiently potent, viz.,
" the preached Word, and exemplary conduct on the part of the
" Missionary, cannot be too severely deprecated. Every thinking
" mind deplores the growing Religious formality in this Colony;
" whereas in other parts of the Dark Continent, where the purely

"Missionary-Agency is employed, those, who have been plucked out of the burning have ever been known to manifest a better evidence of the Faith that is in them, than their brethren in this portion of Africa. It is an admitted fact that, though the early Missionaries in Sierra Leone were, as a whole, good and devoted servants of the Cross, yet, the effectiveness of their work in respect of Method and permanent good results, was, to a considerable extent, impaired by the Magisterial and other Civil appointments, whereby opportunities of constraining men to become Christians have been easily obtained. The re-captives were wont to relate, how some of them were in a variety of ways punished at the instance of the early Missionaries for absenting themselves from Divine Service without assigning sufficient reasons for so doing, when called upon to account. Many a time during the continuance of Divine Service, spies were sent to suspected localities, so that, as a matter of fact, many became Christians only for the purpose of preventing punishment. It is undoubtedly true, that, if the old Missionaries had confined themselves to the ordinary Methods of Christianizing the Heathen, the progress of their enterprise would have been rather tardy, while at the same time the results accrued would have been more real and lasting. It therefore behoves the successors of those Missionaries, and others responsible for the planning out of Missionary-undertakings, to take every possible precaution, in order to avoid the errors of the past."

There is not much fear of a British Missionary being troubled by British Honours, but it is interesting to read how thoroughly the French Missionary is imbued with the idea of being a Frenchman first, and a Christian afterwards, as is evidenced by the fact, that in December, 1885, M. Casális, a Missionary of the French Missions Evangeliques, in Ba-Sutoland, was decorated with the order of the Legion of Honour because : " Il a con-"tribué par ses Missions au developpement de l'influence "française dans l'Afrique Australe. Titres exceptionelles." The Periodical states, that a considerable population in the heart of a British Colony only pronounce the name of France to bless it, as it is synonymous with Goodness, Justice and Charity.

I am grieved to read in *Le Chretien Belge* of June, 1891, the following notice of a British Protestant Missionary receiving a secular order for secular services rendered to a foreign Sovereign of the Church of Rome, and receiving it personally: "A l'occasion "d'une entrevue, qu'il a eue dernièrement avec notre Roi, "M. le rev. Grenfell a été décoré chevalier de l'Ordre de "Léopold, en reconnaissance des services, qu'il a rendus au "Congo."

16. LIVING IN SOCIETY OF SECULAR WHITE MEN.

Let the Missionary shun the worldly and fashionable life of his countrymen: he will find it impossible to maintain the double position. If he cares for the Natives, as he ought to care, he must live for them, and among them. He cannot, and he ought not, to drag them up: he must condescend to men of low estate, leading a simple holy life in their midst. The residence of the Missionary, and his way of life, should be simple: his profession is a serious one, and his family should not surround themselves with the luxuries of secular life. In the Missionary-Conference at Lahore in 1862, I was amazed at the manifestation of the seeds of bitterness, already sown betwixt the Missionary and his converts, and this is one of the trials of the future. It is vain to suppose, that the man of European culture can ever be brought to the level of the Natives of Asia, Africa, or Oceania; there is the abyss of Centuries betwixt them; but the difference need not be accentuated.

I quote the remarks of a speaker of good experience: "He held, that many of the conditions of Mission-life did not support the Missionary-cause. Quite lately he had heard from a perfectly independent critic, that in his judgment many Missionaries lived in far more easy circumstances than their own families at home. Missionaries, he thought, too often yielded to their environment. Europeans visited the Missionaries, and what could be more natural, they thought, than to live as they did. But he believed that the number of men false to their Faith was infinitesimally small. He would not like to let them separate without saying, that of the noble army of Missionary-confessors there were very many who had not the simplest comforts of life, and endured many things, which the English poor were commiserated for enduring. Bishops had to mend their own stockings, paddle their own canoes, pull their own sledges across the snow, and camp out in the open air without food or fire, and yet were affectionate, and cheerful."

It is impossible for the white man from Europe and North America to attempt to live the life, wear the clothes, and eat the food of the Asiatic, African, or Oceanian. He would succumb in a few months. The modern suggestions of Brotherhoods, and Associated Evangelists, will settle that problem: It is the women, and children, and servants, and conveyances, that cost so much. During my residence in India, spreading over twenty-five years, I rejoiced in the society of Missionaries, and always sought them out. I think, that they might be more accessible to natives: perhaps in Brotherhoods this is possible. When they are in camp, nothing can be better. Here again the absence of family-ties helps them. It is really essential, that a Missionary should move about among the people. A rolling stone is said to gather no moss, but a stone, that never moves, is apt to be choked with moss. Nor on the other hand, should he itinerate too widely, but return year by year to old acquaintances. Human kindness is a key, that opens every door, however firmly it may seem to be closed against us. In the early days of a Mission, before the language is learnt, very little dependence can be placed on oral teaching, but power and influence is obtained by a consistent Christian life. Something in the manner, and voice, and general bearing, has a magic effect upon unsophisticated races, and the constant exhibition of the Christian virtues of gentleness, patience, pity, purity, can never be without its charms and its influence. We hear repeatedly of complete systems of village-itinerations and preachings, conducted by parties of male, or female, Agents separately in a patient, leisurely, and sympathetic manner. This brings the Missionary into immediate touch with the people, and has in it the elements of success, for no doubt many visitors will crowd the tent in the evening-hours, as it used to be my happy lot many years ago in my solitary tours among my people on secular duties. It is thus, and thus only, that the white man gains influence over the natives of a country in a lower stage of Civilization, who are still men with hearts to be touched, and affections gained.

17. Offending against intra-Mission Comity, Protestant, or Romish.

Gradually this principle has obtained among Protestant Missions, and it should be religiously observed. Great cities with a population of (say) ten thousand inhabitants should not belong exclusively to any one denomination, but rural districts, and market towns, should be understood to be portioned out, and intrusion should be avoided.

A well-known writer repeats the suggestion made by myself in my "Africa Rediviva," 1891 : " Speaking of the problems of " Missionary-enterprise, Mr. Buckland held, that the Comity " of Missions was one of the most important elements of the " Mission-work. He was not sure, that it would not even be worth " while to approach the Church of Rome in this matter; at any " rate, he was sure, that every effort should be made to avoid " setting opposing views of the Christian Religion before the " Heathen, for wherever a Protestant Mission succeeded, the " Romish Mission followed."

The U-Ganda Scandal has happened since, and made the problem still more acute. It is of no use for the Missionaries of either faction ignoring the facts, that hundreds and hundreds of a different phase of the Christian Faith are at work not very far off from each other. Some years back I took the trouble of going over to Tunis to see the late Cardinal Lavigerie on the subject: he entirely agreed with me, and a certain interval of distance was suggested by him between rival Mission-Stations.

I subjoin the opinion of another authority: " But, besides " this, I may venture to say, that I feel an entire sympathy with " the main principles, upon which, as I understand it, this " Society pursues its Missionary-work. Unless I entirely mis- " interpret the spirit of this Society, it desires to act on the " broadest principles of unity and concord with other Christian " Missionary-Societies in England; and it has worthily main- " tained the traditions of its founders, for we all of us know, " that the names of David Brown, of Claudius Buchanan, and " Henry Martyn, were associated in the annals of the Society " with those of Carey, Henry Marshman, and Ward. My " friends, it has often struck me, as it has, no doubt, most " seriously-minded men, who visit India, that the differences of " detail between different Societies of Christians sink into " entire insignificance when the Missionary is brought face to " face with the Hindu and Mahometan Religions. I feel " satisfied, that this principle is a sound one, and it commands " my most entire sympathy. I would venture to say one word " in favour of Romish Missions. After all, they are our fellow- " Christians. We must not forget, that some of the most " earnest and self-denying men are in their number."

Whatever the Missionaries of this generation may plan, or propose, or do, the converts of the next generation will do as seems best to themselves as regards dogma and Church-Government. The non-Christian world is large enough for all the Churches, however great may be their efforts. Educational establishments may be supported by the union of several denominations, but pure Evangelizing work must be done separately by each Church, and this leaves room for rivalry and animosity. Converts expelled from one Church might be admitted into another, and thus bad feelings would be generated. It is neither wise, nor prudent, nor Christ-like, to intrude into the Mission-Field of a Sister-Society. Seceders from one fold should not be admitted into another; Native Agents discharged should not find ready employment in another Mission. To entice an ordained Native Minister from one Church, and re-ordain him, is an outrage. A Mission-Field must be compactly occupied, one Station supporting the other with a base, either on the Sea, or on some firm and certain post: This matter should not be left to the Missionaries, but settled by the Committee, and, if they do not discharge their duty, the Board of Missions must interfere. Such things in the Church of Rome are settled by the Propaganda. A larger area should not be greedily, and selfishly, appropriated than can be actually occupied. Supervision is of the utmost importance for mutual support and friendly intercourse. Committees and Secretaries should make a closer study of Geography, Ethnology, and Language, when they determine to occupy Regions. Nothing in the history of Missions has been so foolish, and is pregnant with such danger, as the occupation of U-Ganda by the Church-Missionary-Society. No wise General would have made such a plunge: From Mombása as a basis, by gradually advancing posts, the Lake would in due time have been reached, and held in force. Every element of danger, as it is, surrounds that Mission: 1. Leaning absolutely on the Arm of the Flesh. 2. Frightful, even bloody, discord with a French Mission. 3. Entire absence of regular postal communication, or easy access.

Nothing more disfigures the Reports issued by the Societies than the attacks on the Missionaries of the Church of Rome. It is presumed, that the funds are supplied by a particular class of Protestants, who consider no Report complete without an attack on Rome, Caste, and the Opium-Trade. The solitary Missionary may pour his pique into the ears of the Secretary, but why does the Secretary publish it to the world, the non-Christian world? "How these Christians hate each other," must be the remark of the Chinese literati, and the Indian Collegian. I quote a few expressions: Church-Missionary-Society Report, 1893, p. 239:

" In a country where base, worldly Priests have long ruled, and where there is an absence of true Christian white men." The compiler of the Report forgets, that these men have given up home, family, all for their Church, while the writer of this attack is moaning over an absent wife, covering her with fulsome praise, with a kind of bathos of weak praise.

"Her influence for good seems greater than mine," which is perhaps not saying much for the degree of her influence.

I quote the words of a Ba-Suto Chief in South Africa: a Church of England Mission intruded itself without reason into a Region occupied by French Protestants. The Region is not a large one, and there are vast unoccupied Regions without a Mission, which were available.

"At the outset of the Mission a local chief, Moloppo,
" addressed curious words to the Missionary, 'I am glad to
' welcome the Church into my country. I have often heard of
" the Church of the Queen, and now I am rejoiced to find that the
" Baruti [teachers] belonging to it have come here. Hitherto
" I have only seen two kinds of Christians in the country, the
" Ma-Franze [French Protestants] and the Ma-Roma [the

"Romanists]. I have also heard of the Ma-Wesley [Wes-
"leyans], who have Stations on the borders of my country.
"But I am now glad to see the representatives of Ma-Churche
"at my house. It is good to have these four kinds of Chris-
"tians near. It is like a man having four cows; sometimes he
"can milk them all, and when some fail, he can always reckon
"on a supply of milk from the others. So Ma-Franze, and
"Ma-Wesley, and Ma-Churche, and Ma-Roma, all supply us in
"their own way with good things out of the Word of God.' It
"is to be hoped, that the Ba-Suto may not be disappointed, and
"that the spirit of Christian rivalry may not do injury. It
"scarcely seems to have been necessary for the Church of
"England to have entered, where two Protestant Missionary-
"Societies were already engaged, nor in accordance with the
"Comity of Protestant Missionary-bodies."

The Bishop of Bloemfontein urged the extension of Missions to Ma-Shonaland, but in the spirit of a Christian Statesman argued, that Ma-Tabéleland should be left to the London-Missionary-Society, who were already in evidence. I now quote with real pain, as a Member of the Church of England, the following: "Archdeacon Gaul and others are opposed to this
"abandonment of Ma-Tabéleland, and argue, that the Church
"has a Mission to countries, where other agencies are at work,
"pointing especially to the case of Be-Chuánaland, where the
"London and Wesleyan Missions have long had stations, and yet
"Mr. Bevan has gathered some 600 native Be-Chúana commu-
"nicants, and is carrying on one of the most successful Missions
"of our Church. He therefore combats the theory, that we must
"leave the people next door to us, and go after the Ma-Shona
"700 miles further on, *first*, at least, if not altogether. We
"have no right to leave to any Religious body the work we are
"commissioned to do, as *Priests and Bishops of the Catholic
"Church*." No Priest of the Church of Rome could make a more audacious non-Christian claim. Who gave the Church of England a monopoly of S. Africa?

If this be the policy in the green tree, what is it in the dry? It is very undesirable, that a Missionary Society, which collects its funds to convert the non-Christian world, should allow its Agents to waste their time in proselytizing the members of the Oriental Churches, on the ground, that their form of Christianity is dead or imperfect. It is sufficient, that members of those Churches should be permitted to attend the Schools, and Churches, of the Mission, if they are so inclined, but no effort should be made to entice them, retain them, or, with rare exceptions, to employ them. The appearance of a renegade Priest from his own Church is not calculated to advance the character of the Protestant Mission, and it is probable, that a man, who had been false to one Church, would be false to another: the eternal law, of doing unto others as you would wish men to do unto you, should govern the action of Missionaries, as well as ordinary men. Loud would be the complaints, if the Church of Rome decoyed away a promising Protestant Minister, and turned him into a Priest. Loud is the outcry, if a Romish Priest touches a Protestant lamb. Read this from the Church-Missionary-Society-Report, 1890: "Mr. " Owen received five into the Congregation, of whom four were " of the Church of Rome. The fifth was a young woman, who " was led to desire baptism through the death of her infant " child, who had been baptized, the husband being a Christian. " She said 'she wanted to go to her little baby, when she died.'"

Read the enclosed letter from a Church-Missionary-Society-Missionary in Africa: "I visit Protestants and members of " Church of Rome alike every day. The most important " Romish Chief has twice given me presents. Nineteen men " are wanted for work in the capital and in the surrounding " countries, or nine additional to those already in the Field or " expected. Besides these there should be men in reserve for " emergencies. Expenses are very small. The type of the future " Christianity of Central Africa will largely depend on the " present occupation of the country by Church-Missionary- " Societies."

The white population of the Island of Mauritius consists chiefly of members of the Church of Rome: the State contributes towards Education independent of Religion, as in British India: the contribution is adjusted to the population-returns, and yet in the Report of the Church-Missionary-Society it is stated, as a grievance, that the Church of Rome receives a greater grant than the Protestant: is it not so in Ireland also? Missionaries seem to lose all sense of common justice to those, who differ from them.

I quote again from the Church-Missionary-Society-Report with regard to British India: "The Romanists continue to give " much trouble in seeking to draw away the Christians from the " Protestant fold. One of their Priests, when expostulated with, " could only reply: 'I have to obey orders. The Bishop bids " me, and I come.' The Methods employed are thus described: " The nuns hold meetings for women, to which they refuse " entrance to Miss Parsons, or Mrs. Ghose, of the Church of " England Zenana-Missionary-Society; the class is well supplied " with light refreshments, and aid is given both in money and " clothes. Women and children are received in the Romish " Mission-village at Krishnagar, whose husbands cannot or will " not support them; girls are received in one of their two large " boarding-schools free of charge, and after a scanty education

"come out, in many cases to become the wives of our Protes-
"tants, unless we can prevent it, bigoted and ignorant; children
"are received of tender years, and put out to nurse till old enough
"to enter a school; the bishop, priests, and nuns, go to and fro
"into our Christian villages. We have sought to adopt, and
"observe (which is more difficult), more stringent rules as to
"those, who from time to time wish to return to us, *e.g.*, we
"urge the returning of part at least of the money received to
"the Italian priest; and we seek to make exclusion from the
"Church and its privileges more definite. Many have been
"enticed away. May I be forgiven if I misjudge; but I see
"everywhere a marked moral deterioration, wherever our people
"have joined the Church of Rome."

My first suggestion is, that no statements such as the above, with regard to the Missionaries of other Churches, be admitted into the Report: no possible good can come from publishing the accounts of the rents in the robe of our Saviour. My second is, that some attempt should be made to divide off Mission-Fields. In my "Africa Rediviva," 1891, I suggested it. We have the shocking fact placed beyond doubt, that a portion of our own Church of England considers, that they have a right to intrude on the Mission-Fields of English Nonconformists: one Nonconformist denomination openly says, that the "World is their Parish." This bad spirit contains the germ of Intolerance, which, if ever the heavy hand of the State were removed, would blossom into open Persecution, to the contempt and derision of the non-Christian World.

In the Dominion of Canada the Romish Missions are strong. In the Church-Missionary-Society-Report complaints are made:
"Again ascending the Saskatchewan River, Battleford is reached,
"where the Rev. R. Inkster is in charge, residing at Red
"Pheasants' Reserve. The Romish Priests have been exceed-
"ingly aggressive in this district, and have devoted their time,
"Archdeacon Mackay says, to undermining our efforts, with
"considerable success. To some of the heathen Indians the
"mutually hostile attitude of the two Missions is evidently a
"stumbling-block. They said to Mr. McDonald, 'We do not
"know what to do; the Priest tells us one thing, and you expound
"another.' Mr. McDonald says: 'By constant prayerful work,
"and the assistance of the Divine Helper, in the month of
"December I was happy to see a few more coming forward for
"baptism, while the Romanists were adding few, if any, to their
"numbers. Then began our great trouble. The Priest began
"holding nightly meetings, and giving out goods to these poor
"ignorant Indians, for the purpose of gaining their confidence,
"and undoing, if possible, the little success, that God had given
"us, till at last things looked so dark in the Reserve that I thought

"that we were going to lose all. But good sometimes comes of evil. I never lost faith in God, and by some means or other the minds of the Indians were again turned, and in January, 1890, also in February, a good many joined our Church. Yet the Priest kept giving presents to the Indians, as it were buying them over. Some of our own Indians came and asked me, why I did not do the same. I told them, that I never would pay a man to pray to his God, but, if they thought they could inherit eternal life by being paid to worship God, they had better try the Romish mode in this Reserve of gaining adherents. This had a good effect; any way, they began to think for themselves, and I may safely say, that our Indians feel, that it is for the good of their immortal souls, and not for their mortal bodies.'"

Now in the *Missions Catholiques* of Lyons, the same charge is made by the French Priests of Rome against the Protestant Ministers, and I am bound to say, that I believe neither the one nor the other.

I read again in the Church-Missionary-Society-Report, 1891-92: "To human judgment, it has appeared the leading of a forlorn hope to get Chipewyan Indians, who are under Romish power and influence, to receive or believe in the Gospel of Christ. Our Mission is not especially directed at them, but indirectly, and in the interests of the diocese and our own converts, who are constantly being attacked by Priests.

"I took advantage of every opportunity to preach Christ Crucified, and explained the Gospel-Plan of Salvation to all, who visited me. The natives have been attracted to our Mission by lantern-lectures on the life of our Lord. Upon one occasion I had about 500 natives, to whom I sang and preached, as well as I could, the old, old story, in their own tongue. Many left off going to confession, and ceased, out of deep poverty, to pay for hearing the Mass sung. Some began to show signs of doubt, and became very restless, when I dealt personally with them in the Mission-house; others went to their half-breed relations for an explanation of their fears, etc., while some became enquirers after Christ in a sincere way. At times we all felt the power of the Holy Spirit in our midst. One after another went to the French Priest with doubts and fears; some demanded letters of assurance from their Bishop as to the safety of their spiritual state. Towards spring of last year the Indians made known their intention of forsaking what appeared to them the evils of their System, among other things the confessional. This they actually did."

Hear a voice from S. Africa: Report of Free Church of Scotland, 1890: "The Trappist-invasion with its 170 monks and 120 nuns is a very serious one for all the Missions in

" Natal and the Colony at large. As yet they have not inter-
" fered with our work, but other and older Missions have not
" been equally fortunate. They work the old system of finding
" out any disaffected party, and by flattery and bribery cajoling
" such into their ranks. Of course they are the true Church ;
" there is safety alone in them ! Their wealth seems inexhaust-
" ible, and they already own an estate in Natal of 20,000 acres,
" and another in Griqualand of 50,000 acres ; and current report
" credits them with being constantly on the hunt for more.
" They are opening cheap boarding and other schools, and in
" Pretoria they collect the children to their schools morning by
" morning in carriages sent round to their homes, redelivering
" them in the afternoons." The Abbot applied to the Government of this Colony for an annual grant of £500 to the support of his educational, and industrial, schools at Marion Hill-Monastery.

The Church-Missionary-Society-Report tells us the following from Japan : " The Nagasáki Congregation, which consists of
" seventy-four baptized members and eight catechumens, was
" tried by the loss of five hopeful young men, who separated
" from it during the year. Two of them were drawn in the
" direction of Rome by the influence of a former catechist.
" This man had been received into the Romish Communion,
" but had kept the fact secret from the Rev. A. R. Fuller, who
" only learned it through a message brought to him from the
" man's death-bed by a Romish Priest. One of the two, whom
" he influenced, a schoolmaster, was baptized in the Church of
" Rome ; the other, a medical student, after studying the
" Romish system, left the Protestant Communion."

Twenty years hence the strain will be much greater : The Missionary-spirit of the Nineteenth Century has set a stream flowing, which can no longer be controlled. The Church of Rome, and Protestantism, have the Divinity of Christ, and His Atonement, in common : in the war with those, who reduce Christ to the position of Socrates or Buddha, or set him altogether on one side, it would seem to be wise on the part of those, who hold the great central Truths, to agree to a certain intra-Mission Comity, so far as to set apart Regions, as has in fact been settled in U-Ganda by the Civil Authorities.

Whether this can be secured, as a lasting arrangement, is doubtful. The arrogant ideas of the Englishman is illustrated by the annexed letter to the *Record*, 1894 : " It is impossible to
" read Captain Lugard's Book without being deeply impressed
" with the hopelessness of settled peace, and good government,
" while these men (the French Priests) are allowed the free
" hand, which they have had in the past.

" Much allowance must be made for the extreme difficulty of

"Captain Lugard's position while in U-Ganda, yet, from his own showing, it is clear, that he was completely outmanœuvred by the subtle Priests, with whom he had to deal.

"The rôle of 'Mgr.' was simple and easy, always to adopt an attitude of being wronged, and of receiving less than what was due, and to back this up with indirect menaces, the Romish native faction playing very much the part of the secret-societies in Ireland. The result was, unfortunately, attended with far too much success. It is consistent with the same policy, that the preposterous claims for compensation are now being made for losses sustained in the onslaught made on the Protestants, connived at, if not directly instigated, by the Priests themselves.

"It is earnestly to be hoped, that whoever is appointed Commissioner will at once and for ever abandon the weak and disastrous policy of perpetually trying to conciliate these men. What is needed is that firm and just government, which, it may be confidently asserted, is the invariable characteristic of a proper English Administration."

Here it is clear, that the domineering Protestant Englishman is to have his way in a British Protectorate; the Wa-Ganda are to be taught who is Master: Rome or Canterbury? London or Paris? But supposing, that the Romish Missionaries had been from Cardinal Vaughan's English Mission from Mill Hill, Hampstead, and the Protestant Missionaries had been from the Missions Evangeliques of Paris, what then? Would Cardinal Vaughan be allowed to assert, that his English Mission is the Master, and the French Protestants only there by sufferance? Does the correspondent of the *Record* write as a Protestant, hating the Church of Rome, or as an Englishman, hating the French? which thought is uppermost? Let him know, that the British Government is above all Religious partialities, and prejudices: as in British India, so in British Equatorial Africa, the Protestant, and the Pagan, the Romish Priest, and the Mahometan, are on an equality, as subjects of the Queen Empress, and must keep the Peace, or a heavy hand will fall on them without benefit of Clergy. Under this firm, strong Rule British India has become the greatest Field of Missions, that the World ever knew.

18. Ridiculing and Speaking Ill of non-Christian Religions.

Still more reprehensible is the practice of the Missionary insulting the Religious Convictions of his audience. How different was the tone adopted by Paul in his address on Mars Hill at Athens! I rejoice to say, that this error is diminishing, and in some Fields it never existed.   Hear the repentant words of an old Missionary, a true servant of God: "It was inwardly manifest to me, that " for some time past I have attacked the heathen customs, and " superstitions, of the Wa-Nika too fiercely, the sight of the " abominations moving me to indignation, and I feel now, that I " ought to preach more the love of the Redeemer for His sheep, " lost, or gone astray, or taken captive by Satan. I must show " more compassion, and my words must be more filled with " pity. It is not the gifts, nor the works, nor the words, nor " the prayers, that convert, but the Lord Jesus only."

Hear the evidence of another old Missionary in India: " I " confess, that in the beginning of my work I thought, that the " exhibition of Gospel-Truths was sufficient to make an im- " pression on the native mind, and hence, when anything like " Hindu doctrine was brought before me in conversation with " the natives, through an ill-directed zeal I was peremptory in " condemning the whole without discrimination: this was an " error: by such zeal we do, I am persuaded, more harm than " good. Asiatics will not be prepared to receive the Truth from " anyone, who haughtily and peremptorily cries down every- " thing in their books, and so long as we show, that we are " ignorant of their literature, they mistrust the correctness of " our doctrine."

Besides, in all Religions there is a substratum of Truth: why knock your head against adamantine Truth? Go back with them to the basis of their convictions, until common ground is reached. Few will deny the existence of God, the immortality of the Soul, and the future Judgment; all will admit, that Sin exists in the world: bring these truths home, and show them the better way.

The ignorant Missionary allows himself to heap unlimited abuse on the Sacred Books of other Religions, of which he knows nothing: this is injudicious: the hearers know well enough, that he is ignorant. The learned Missionary should avoid the opposite error: he should render all due praise to the noble sentiments, and conceptions, of the non-Christian Philosopher, but never for one moment concede, that he is inspired, or divine, or that his words are good for Salvation of men hereafter, though good for morals, and often elevating. None of them rise higher than Socrates. And he should be cautious in selecting passages of unequal value, and thoroughly bad in morals, from their Sacred Books: the scoffer might retort in a manner, painful to a Christian, by misquoting the Bible.

It is a low taste to exhibit the idols of the Pagan, and the statues of Buddha, to the scoffings of uneducated men, and the laughter of children: we do not so treat the remains of the beautiful ideals of Greek and Roman worship: but both the one and the other teach us, how man in his unconverted state feels after God, and of the danger of committing spiritual beliefs to material forms. When a new irruption of Goths destroys London and St. Paul's, the Reredos will be destroyed, but the Gospel-Truth will survive all earthly changes.

A Religious Paper tells us, how a returned Missionary on deputation raised a smile on the faces of some foolish persons in May, 1894. " He described what he had seen of Heathenism " at Agra and Banáras. His racy descriptions of the worship " of the household-god, when a little bell was rung to wake " him, produced some smiles, but the whole story was inex-" pressibly sad." Are bells never rang at the beginning, and during the conducting, of Divine Worship? The Household-Deity represents to the Hindu the emblem and idea of Purity and Holiness, which is found wanting in many a so-called Christian Household, unsanctified by daily Family or Private Prayer, or Reading of the Bible. In fact, in many Christian Households the very idea, as well as the worship, of God has ceased to exist. This is a thought still sadder than the story told above.

I quote from the "Missionary Manual" already alluded to: " Expose the errors of Hinduism, and Islam, certainly by a " full exposition of the truths of Christianity, rather than by a " violent Crusade on non-Christian Beliefs: who is the fanatic " then? Everything insulting should be avoided. Speak the " truth in LOVE: the surest way to bring a man to acknowledge " his errors is to give him full credit for as much as he has " discovered of the Truth. Whatever is a portion of adaman-" tine Truth in any non-Christian conception will only baffle " our efforts, if in ignorant un-Christian impatience we attempt " to sweep it away with the rubbish, which has enveloped it; if " you treat with scorn what is true in the doctrines, which you " attack, you must not complain, if your argument against what " is false in their doctrine is as highly esteemed as your scorn of " what is true. We ought gratefully to acknowledge all that " is excellent, as we welcome a spot of verdure in the Desert. " Our knowledge is not a contradiction of what is false in other " conceptions so much as a legitimate development of what is " true." God has not left Himself without a witness.

The very circumstance, that the Almighty has allowed these Systems to survive the break-up of Empires, and the lapse of so many Centuries, when with one breath of His anger He could have destroyed them, and wiped them out, is a lesson to us, that we must not in our ignorance be less merciful than God.

Hear what Dr. Benson, the Archbishop of Canterbury, said at the Society for the Propagation of the Gospel: "What I think is " absolutely necessary to further progress, and of immense im-

"portance is the forming a really clear idea of the theory of
" Missions. Missionaries themselves work isolatedly under-
" ground, often in the dark, by constant, steady, and very lonely
" work aiming at, and often in the end effecting, what seemed
" to be impossible for individuals to accomplish. But a great
" Church has to take a wide view of all Missionary-operations
" everywhere, and of the principles, on which they are con-
" ducted. It has to recognise honestly, that there have been
" mistakes in the past, and that there may be mistakes going on
" now. We ought to pass out of our mistakes, as fast as we
" can, sailing henceforth by a great Chart, which, I am afraid,
" has to a great extent to be laid down. The work of the future
" should be no more tentative or experimental, as it has been in
" the past. We have now an immense mass of facts before us,
" and like all students in science, or like politicians, we must
" study our policy, we must take a survey of the facts, and we
" must, with all the power of mind, that we can command, as
" well as with all the earnestness of spirit, clearly lay down
" what are the best lines, on which Mission-work is to be pur-
" sued. There are one or two things, which are becoming very
" plain to observers, which were by no means obvious in the
" past. It really did commend itself to many great Missionaries
" in the past, that the best Field for working in was the Field of
" the unsophisticated, the simple, and the ignorant, and no
" doubt there is beautiful work, with beautiful results, to be done
" among them; but I believe, that is not our theory now. We
" have perceived, that the reflective mind stored with knowledge
" is in the Heathen a better Field for the work of Christ than
" vacancy and ignorance. The greatest works in the past have
" been done on that principle. The Gospel itself recognises
" the fact, because it came in the Fulness of Time. It came,
" when the human intellect had attained the highest point, to
" which it has ever attained. For originality of conception, for
" keenness of investigation, the old philosophies, even if they
" have rivals in modern times, have not been surpassed."

His Grace here lays down a great Truth, which the young Missionary, or the isolated Missionary, who have not dipped into the history of the past, have not arrived at: the danger of a vacuum of the Religious Conception. Oh! that they would recollect what happened to the soul, that was swept and garnished, after the departure of the evil spirit.

" It is not so many years, that it has been borne in upon us,
" that a Religious tone of mind though heathen is a better Field
" for Christian effort than a non-Religious tone of mind. We
" are beginning to perceive, that in those regions, where our race,
" where Europeans, are destroying belief in the old Religions,
" if they have not the Religion of Christ at hand immediately to

" substitute, they are doing more harm to Religion than good.
" It is not true, that the mind from which every possible Super-
" stition has been banished, until it becomes a *tabula rasa*, is in
" a better state of receptivity for the Truths we have in hand
" than the mind, which still retains its Religious tone, even
" though it is associated with the most corrupt Religion in the
" world, even though the modes and shapes, under which it lives,
" are untruthful, and in some cases even injurious. Any Religious
" tone is the upgrowth of many generations. The Religious
" tone in any Nation has been gradually formed in it, and for
" any generation, that we may be dealing with, it is the offspring
" of the teaching of old traditions conveyed by teaching, and
" by early habits formed. I fear, that if we have one single
" generation intervening, which has no Religious habits, no
" thought beyond the grave, no tone which makes it perpetually
" look up to that which is beyond it, and above it, we shall find
" it a harder task to convert the children of that generation than
" to convert the polished Heathen, however firmly they hold to
" their old Faith. No one can go into a Mahometan place
" of worship without being struck by the evidence of sincerity,
" gravity, absorbedness, and solemnity, in the worshippers. We
" must not approach them, as if they knew that they were
" themselves deficient, and that it was only pride, and obstinacy,
" that prevented them from listening to us. We must go to
" them acknowledging, that God has brought them a long way
" on the road to Him. We must take them up where they are,
" and remember, that they do not look upon themselves as
" behind Europeans, or the English Nation. They look upon
" their Sacred Book as an advance on Christianity, and, until we
" are able to meet them on their own ground, until we have
" thoroughly mastered theirs, until we know exactly, what their
" position has been in the formation of character and thought,
" unless we recognise the deep-spring of the devotion, which
" they exhibit, unless we are prepared to find the formation of
" noble characters in their midst, we shall have no chance in
" dealing with a Religion like Mahometanism. It is a Religion,
" which requires to be thoroughly understood, and deeply
" mastered."

Hear what Bishop Bickersteith of Japan says, 1883: " The
" Mahometans denounce Christianity to their own people, who
" are ignorant: they are stigmatized as 'fanatic' and 'bigoted' by
" Christians, who call themselves large-minded, and still follow
" the mean example ": of what use is knowledge, if the weapon
used is abuse ? where are the precepts of Christ, if LOVE be laid
aside ? " The Missionary should try to appreciate the difficulties
" felt by Mahometans, and offer carefully-considered answers to
" their questions. The Gospel should be placed before the

" Mahometan in the way, in which its own Truth may best link
" themselves on to the Truths already held by the Mahometan,
" and offer the fewest difficulties to their critical and inquiring
" minds."

His colleague, Mr. Lefroy, of Dehli, in 1894, remarks, that
" Christian Missionaries must recognise the good in non-
" Christian Systems more fully than they have done: it is a
" lesson, which we must lay to heart, and this may be done
" without ignoring the errors inherent in their System. Paul
" never abused other Religions in the presence of their followers,
" but rather laid hold on all, that was in them to suggest, and
" justify, his own teaching. In the Epistle to the Romans he
" points out the corruption of the Greek and Roman Systems."

Hear what Archbishop Trench says in his Hulsean lecture,
1845: " We address ourselves in a slight and inefficient manner
" to our work, when, without discrimination, without acquaint-
" ance with those Systems, which hold souls in bondage, which
" hinder them from coming to the Light of Life, we have but one
" Method with them all, one language, in which to describe them
" all, one common charge of belonging to the devil, upon which
" to arraign them all; instead of recognising, that each province
" of the dark kingdom of Error is different from every other;
" instead of seeing that it is not a lie, which can ever make
" anything strong, that it is not certainly their lie, which has
" made them strong, and enabled them to stand their ground so
" long, and some of them, saddest of all! to win ground from
" Christendom; but the Truth, which that lie caricatures and
" perverts.

" Nor would I leave unuttered my conviction, that any other
" dealing with them than this, which, even while it wars against
" them, welcomes and honours the residue of Truth, which they
" still may retain, any ruder and less descriminating assault on
" that, which multitudes have hitherto believed, and which
" however mingled with falsehood and fraud, has been all,
" whereby they have holden on to a higher world, may, even
" when it seems most successful, be full of peril for them, whom
" thus coarsely we seek to benefit, and with unskilful hands to
" deliver. For, indeed, there is no office more delicate, no task
" needing greater wisdom, and patience, and love, than to set men
" free from their Superstitions, and yet not with this to lay waste
" the very soil, in which the Truth should strike its roots, to
" disentangle the tree from the ivy, that was strangling it, without,
" in the process and together with the strangling ivy, destroying
" also the very life of the tree itself, which we proposed to save.
" It may be, that we have not brought them even into the vesti-
" bule of the Faith, may have rather set them at a remoter
" distance from it than ever. To have taught them to pour

" contempt on all, with which hitherto they have linked feelings
" of sacredness and awe, may prove but a questionable prepara-
" tion for making them humble and reverent scholars of Christ.
" Wiser surely was Paul's Method, who ever sought a ground
" common to himself and those, whom he would persuade, though
" it were but an handbreadth, upon which to take his stand, who
" taught men to deal reverently with their past selves, and their
" past beliefs, who to the Athenians said, 'Whom therefore ye
" ignorantly worship, Him declare I unto you,' and spake of the
" Cretan poet as 'a prophet of their own'; readopting into the
" family of the Truth its lost and wandering children, however
" they might have forgotten their true descent, in whatever far
" land, and under whatever unlikely disguises, he found them."

We are dealing with a well-known subject: the Queen has fifty Millions of Mahometan subjects, hundreds of them wise, estimable, distinguished; thousands brave, clever, and industrious; all peaceful subjects; yet I quote these shameful expressions under date, December, 1892, from N. Africa: I have traversed Morocco, Algeria, Tunisia, Egypt, Syria, Transcaucasia, and know so far the Mahometans there: as to the people of India, my table-servants, my cook, my messengers, my grooms, my writers, my friends and councillors, were, to a considerable extent, Mahometans.

Their Religious Conception is called "a thraldom, fanaticism,
" arranged with wonderful Satanic skill, first to ensnare, then to
" prevent rescue: the Missionaries are described as wrestling
" against rulers of the darkness of this world, even wicked
" spirits in heavenly places. Mahometanism is a mighty System,
" invented by the Devil to counterfeit the Gospel, a masterpiece
" of Satanic ingenuity, resembling in many points other works of
" Satan, such as Romanism. Satan forged these great Systems
" of lies, and, when they get broken by the hammer of Truth,
" he will be ready to weld them together again: the love of
" *sinful ways*, and the fear of Persecution and death frightens
" converts."

Now why does the writer bring in Satan at all? Does he not see, that so gigantic and modern a System as Islam cannot have come into existence without God's knowledge and permission? Can the Ruler of the world do wrong? Do not Christians live sinful ways also? Have not all such utterances a sad lack of reality? Is it not the fool, that hath said all this in his heart?

Here what another fanatic from the Mission-Field says as regards India: "Where Mahometanism holds the people in its
" thraldom, it stands forth apparently immovable and impreg-
" nable with all the features of pride, and lust, and cruelty, which
" have ever characterized it. When in the providence of God
" its time shall come, and Islam shall bow its head beneath the

" yoke of the Cross, none can tell; that the day may be hastened
" must be our prayer, while our labours are not relaxed."

Pride! is there no wicked Pride in Christian England, and wherever the heart of man is unconverted? Lust! How about the streets of London and Paris, and the Annals of the Divorce-Court? Where Polygamy prevails among Hindus, it is nearly always the result of infant-marriages, and no lust exists there. And as regards Mahometan Polygamy, under the laws of the Koran the rights of the woman are protected: how about Christian Profligacy? Cruelty! How about Ma-Tabéleland, where poor Africans are killed for the sake of gold-dust, and to make commercial Companies pay? *Let us look at home.*

Hear what Mr. George Curzon, M.P., says as regards to China: "With rare exceptions, more liberal-minded than their
" fellows, the Missionaries adopt an attitude of implacable
" hostility to all native Religions and Ethics, ignoring alike their
" virtuous aspects and influence, the all-powerful hold, which
" they have acquired upon Chinese character, and the sanction,
" lent to them by a venerable antiquity. Particularly is this the
" case with regard to ancestral worship, with which they decline
" all parley; although a rare retort would appear to be open to
" a Chinaman in England, who accidentally found his way into
" Westminster Abbey. Such iconoclasm, in the eyes of many
" critics, could only, even if successful, lead to two results, both
" equally to be deplored: the complete disintegration of the
" Chinese social fabric, and the collapse of Chinese morality."

Hear the words of a writer in the *Quarterly Review*, 1894:
" In the present critical position of Indian thought it is of the
" utmost importance, that the Missionary should have mastered
" the Religious Systems prevalent in India, and should have
" made personal investigation into their creeds, and their
" practices, in their own homes. He should be able to under-
" stand, and sympathize with, the Oriental mind, to examine the
" Hindu Sacred Writings from their own point of view, to
" acknowledge whatever of Truth is contained in them."

At the Victoria-Institute, London, 1894, was read a paper by a late Surgeon-General in China, in the presence of a late Minister-Plenipotentiary, and now Professor of the Languages of China at Cambridge, on "Present-day Chinese Ethics, and Philosophy." The paper was replete with hints for the Missionary, and Dr. Gordon pointed out the need for care on their part to respect the feelings of a people with so ancient a Civilization. Amongst other points he showed, that the late massacres of Romish priests and nuns was caused by their own action in depriving parents of the children, whom they had undertaken to educate. The discussion on the paper was mainly occupied by Sir Thomas Wade, giving a long and careful analysis of the present position of China, and the best way, in which European Civilization may be presented to her people. In doing so, he said that some old views as regards her Customs were false; for instance, we were under a misapprehension in our idea of the Chinese Ancestral Worship; it was really confined to an annual service commemorative of the departed and their virtues, and answered to the memorial services, which have been held of late years in England, and on that occasion the Chinese graves were decked with flowers.

How is it? An imperfectly-armed gladiator, with the narrowest views of the great combat, an entire contempt for the Faith, held by Millions for Centuries, a jaunty confidence in the little knapsack of Christian Theology, and Ecclesiastical History, which he has crammed at his Seminary, and an entire ignorance of the great Truths, which underlie the intellectual and spiritual structure of man, shouts out, as the Ephesians did of old,

" Kingdom of Satan; Works of the Devil."

Damnat quod non intelligit. Instead of placing his foot on the adamantine Truth, which is the basis of all Religious Conceptions: the existence, power, wisdom, and goodness, of one only God of all the World, and the Brotherhood of Mankind, the certainty of a Day of Judgment, and the pressing need of a Saviour and a Comforter, he goes off into empty abuse, ritual observances, or denominational shibboleths.

Sometimes a preacher, who has never left England, and knows nothing of any country or race, indulges in such platitudes to Home-congregations as the following: "The World is weary
" of Natural Religion, Christianity without Christ; it is weary of
" the Religion of Humanity, for what cannot claim reverence
" cannot command conscience; it is weary of Confucianism,
" the despotism of the dead and bondage of the living; it is
" weary of Brahmanism, which is the bane of brotherhood; it
" is weary of Buddhism, morality without God; it is weary of
" Islam, God without morality."

There appears to me to be a deviation from truth in every line of the above. We could wish, that the unconverted world were weary of their ancestral forms of Belief, but not one of them would recognise their own form of worship in the above sententious apothegm, which is either unintelligible, or false.

The very use of the terms "false gods" and "false prophets" is a mistake: there cannot be a false god, for there is only one possible God in the world, and the holy word should never be used otherwise. The Jews in their early Centuries may have been "Enotheists," or "Monolatrists," admitting the existence of other divinities in other lands, though cleaving to their own.

We have passed that stage, and are Monotheists. As regards
"false prophets" it is not admitted, that Mahomet was a
prophet at all: why call him a false one, as a term of abuse?
Judging of the greatness of men by the consequences of their
having existed, it cannot be denied, that he was the greatest in
the Christian era, and that the Almighty permitted his Doctrines
to spread far beyond the limits of his wildest hopes. As regards
the Brahmanical Conception, as it was in the time of Moses,
so it is now, with two hundred Million believers; with no
desire for Propagandism, yet absorbing annual thousands, and
at all periods of its existence absolutely tolerant of other
Religious Conceptions, or of variations of its own: the Buddhist
Conception is the earliest universal Propagandist of the world,
and with the greatest number of nominal adherents. Other
Religious Conceptions are as purely National, as the Languages,
which they speak: of the population of the world a large
portion is non-Christian. Are we to believe in this Nineteenth
Century, that the Great God, who made all things, and hates
nothing that He has made, has since the days of Creation
allowed these untold Millions to pass from the Cradle to the
Grave, there to find everlasting torment, because the pious and
benevolent people of Europe and N. America never thoroughly
conceived and carried out the idea of Systematic Evangelization
until this Century? It is in vain to speculate on the plans of
the Almighty: the matter is too high for us. Can the Ruler of
the Universe do wrong? Had it been His pleasure, He could
have sent Prophets, and Evangelists, to every quarter of the great
round World, instead of restricting them to the tiny province
of Judea, with the exception of one deputation of Jonah to
Nineveh, until the Fulness of Time came.

This matter presses very much on the great civilized, educated,
people of China, Japan, and India. A Brahmin, at Banáras, is
said to have remarked: "How did it happen, that we never
"heard of this Good News until Mr. William Smith arrived at
"Banáras in 1840? We have been 2,000 years or more in the
"valley of the Ganges: why were our ancestors not informed of
"this great Truth, if it be eternal, and universal, and of such vital
"importance, as you say that it is? why did the English receive
"the Message 1,800 years earlier than we did: they were savages
"in those days, while we were then, even then, great and wise, and
"educated, composing books of Poetry and Philosophy, building
"temples, and palaces, and carving Inscriptions on the rocks,
"which remain to this day, as memorials of our greatness."
There is a great deal in this Brahmin's remark, and it is but a
poor reply to say, that all their former greatness were the artifices
of Satan, and that India is the Kingdom of the Devil.

I pass to another view of the subject: I have two Pamphlets

on my table, one published by the Society for the Propagation of the Gospel-Mission, Rewári, and the others by the Santal Mission-Press, Pokhuria. The first is entitled, "A specimen of Hinduism: How Brahma became a goose, and Vishnu a boar." The second is entitled, "Exposure of the character of the Yajúr Veda, by the Rev. T. Williams, Rewári, Panjáb."

These Pamphlets are written for circulation among the Professors of the Brahmanical Religion. I will not go into detail: their perusal would be highly offensive to a Brahmin, and might possibly lead to a breach of the peace: They are intended to expose to ridicule portions of the Sacred Books of a great Nation in their own country: can this be right? Supposing in revenge any member of the old Religious Beliefs, or of the new ones, such as Mormons, and Theosophists, were to publish in the free Press of British India a Pamphlet, describing in a scurrilous tone the life of our Lord, and the circumstances, connected with His birth, it would give pain to our weaker converts; but only imagine the results of a Pamphlet of selections from the Old Testament, such as the conduct of Lot, the conduct of Judah, and his son, passages in the life of David, and his sons, printed and placed in circulation with comical comments, such as accompany the Reverend Missionary's description, how Brahma, and Vishnu, the two members of the Sacred Triad, became a goose and a boar respectively. It appears to me quite unworthy, and may possibly lead to the interference of the Civil Government. Should we tolerate indecent attacks on the Christian and Jewish Books made by a Mahometan, or Hindu, Missionary in London? Should we not do unto others, as we should wish men to do unto us?

Professor Monier-Williams, in his paper read at the Croydon Church Congress, 1877, asks with knowledge: "Why do we meet the intolerance of the Mahometan with Christian intolerance?" He does not ask for a false tolerance, but an absence of denunciation of Mahomet, who, however fiercely intolerant of Idolaters, never uttered a word against the Lord Jesus, whose name is never pronounced unaccompanied by a blessing by any Mahometan. The Law and the Gospel are ever spoken of as the Word of God. The miraculous birth of Jesus is asserted (Sura III, 40-42). The Korán was a later revelation: here the roads part. Mahomet took his stand firmly on the ground of God's Fatherhood, and Jesus' humanity: let us start from this point, and prove the Divinity of our Saviour, the Mediation, the Atonement, the Resurrection, and Ascension. Let us reflect what example of Christian moral life Europeans set in Mahometan countries, what ideal of Christ's love Missionaries set in their indecent condemnation of Islam.

Ignorance and Superstition, the result of long Centuries of

isolation, and absence of Education, are indeed great barriers to the intelligible reception of the Gospel-Message, but they are only human barriers, and by God's Grace, working through the Love of the enlightened for their fellow-men in darkness, can be lifted up. The soul of Man opens to the teaching of his Divine Creator, as the sunflower opens to the rays of the Sun; and no cavern is so dark, no human mind so clouded, that one ray of the Divine Light cannot pierce into it, if only those, who have for generations basked in the Light, leave off idle abuse, and do their duty to their God and their Fellow-men.

19. IMMORALITY.

It goes, as it were, without saying, that the Missionary should profess, and, as far as his weak human nature permits him, act up to the very highest possible standard of Morality in everything, and to everybody. The lamentable failures of the most ordinary and vulgar laws of Morality, that have occurred lately, is appalling. In some Missions he has to live among people of a very low culture: he has to address men and women partially, if not entirely, naked, and yet they are not Savages: they have an unwritten Code of Morality, though an imperfect one.

No case of Immorality has come to my knowledge, where the Missionaries dwell in Brotherhoods, and as Associated Evangelists. No Romish Priest is ever left alone. In a jaunty way devoted, but imperfectly-informed, friends of Missions may give the lie to such allegations: I know them to be true. A certain letter, written to the Committee of the Church-Missionary-Society by good Bishop Parker, of East Equatorial Africa, and received after the news of his death had reached London, will never be forgotten by those, who read it. No allusion to such things is found in a Missionary-Report. "Bona verba quæso." If any servant of the State had robbed the Treasury, or committed a crime, it would hardly remain unnoticed in the Report forwarded by an earthly Governor. The same impartial attitude should be maintained with regard to spiritual men. No secrecy is maintained as regards the errors of Old Testament-worthies. The Bible is very outspoken. When lay and ordained Missionaries have been disconnected in considerable numbers for incontinence, the supporters of the Association should be informed: I allude to Africa.

In the accounts of the Missions in Europe in the Middle Ages I read, how the Bishop of Prague endeavoured to reform the lives of the people, who were only nominally Christian. It was uphill work. Paganism, though kept at bay, was still a living power. Such Christianity, as existed, was mixed with Pagan elements of the darkest kind. The clergy were steeped in grossest immorality; Polygamy was openly practised.

Of course it is difficult in such a Mission as that of U-Ganda to get up supplies, but anything would seem better than to employ as conveyer of supplies a Missionary discharged from the Mission for immorality, who goes backwards and forwards accompanied by his native family.

In the length and breadth of British India, during a quarter of a Century, I never heard a breath of scandal against any Missionary, Protestant, or of the Church of Rome. But in Africa my experiences are sadly different: 'Αὲι φέρει Λιβύη τι καίνον.

20. Importing Western Ideas.

Civilization is the incidental, not the primary, object of a Mission. It is wrong to expect, that Civilization should precede Evangelization; it may accompany it. Christianity can adapt itself to every phase, and epoch, of Human-Culture. Civilization may possibly choke the good seed, and retard Gospel-teaching. The Missionary should place before his eyes, as the model, which he aims at, not the British, or New England, village, with all its surroundings of European culture, but the villages of Palestine, such as they were, when our Lord passed through them. Nothing is so bad as to turn a Negro into a pseudo-Englishman. What has a particular stage of Human-Culture to do with the Everlasting Gospel?

When Paul and Peter came into contact with Greeks and Romans, the difference of their Civilization was not extreme: Paul may have been quite on the level with the very best; the other Apostles sprang from humble origin. When Columbanus, and his British colleagues, and Boniface, and his Anglo-Saxon colleagues, started on their Mission to Central Europe, there was not an excessive, if any, difference of Civilization betwixt the Missionary and his flock. If the European, or American, Missionary met the higher classes of the people of India, or China, a certain difference would be manifest, but not always in favour of the white man: but the work of the Missionary in Asia is chiefly with the lower classes, and the natives of Africa, N. America, and Oceania, are low down in the scale of Human Culture, far removed from the Culture of the white man. The Gospel is good for all, for the highly-civilized Oriental races, and the entirely uncivilized races; but it should not be accompanied by a spurious admixture of European non-essentials. The Christian Religion has its roots, and brought forth its first-fruits in Asia: the Bible is a thoroughly Oriental book: the Missionary should so far forget his country, and not drag in European, or American, notions.

There is a great danger, that our short-sighted, and imperfectly-informed, Missionaries may do a great mischief to the inferior races, with whom they come into contact, by putting into them notions of civil liberty, which has resulted to the inhabitants of the West after Centuries of struggle, but which is not a necessary ingredient of the Kingdom of God. I heard it at the time in India, that an ill-judging American Missionary put questions of this kind in his Mission-School: "What is a King?" "A bad man, who cuts off people's heads." "What is a Bishop?" "A wicked man, who bullies God's Ministers." Such are extreme, but not impossible, cases: We know, as a positive fact, that the American Mission-Schools in the Caroline Islands, in the Kingdom of Spain, had a feast in honour of the 4th of July, and the Protestant Greeks in the Constantinople-Mission were permitted to celebrate the twenty-fifth anniversary of the accession of the King of Greece. No wonder, that the Turkish Government is hostile to a hothouse of rebels: only imagine the American Mission-Schools in the Panjáb celebrating the birthday of the Emperor of Russia. All such vagaries are thoroughly wrong, and outside the circle of Missionary-duties.

Equally objectionable is the practice of urging them to change their costumes, their mode of life, and thus enclosing in an ephemeral, worldly, perishable, husk the eternal, unchangeable, spiritual, kernel of the Gospel. On the other hand, the employment of Native music, and other unobjectionable Native arts, is to be recommended.

But here again some incidents should be noticed. Fifty years ago I was the guest of Bishop Wilson, of Calcutta, at Simla: at family-prayers his Christian attendants took off their turbans, and laid them down, like large soup-plates, before them, while they kneeled bare-headed. I remonstrated at this with the good Bishop, as I remarked, that they retained their shoes on their feet: here was an entirely gratuitous departure from Oriental habit. In Public worship the same difficulties are arising: I quote from the Church-Missionary-Society-Report, 1890: "We of the Episcopal Church are thought to be un-
"bending, and desirous of planting the Church of England
"bodily in Japan. The Prayer-book, kneeling during prayer,
"and the surplice, are all looked upon as ridiculous. The
"idea is, 'let everyone do as he likes.' We are supposed to
"have a great deal of form and ceremony, and this is taken to
"be synonymous with hypocrisy. These opinions are chiefly
"rife amongst the young men, and it is they, who are noisy and
"lead others."

These objections cover a great deal of serious ground: "At
" Mandla itself the attendance at the Church-services and Bible-
" classes was 'all that one can desire' on the part of the
" Christians, while Hindu visitors, attracted by the harmonium
" and hearty singing, were often present."

In November meetings were held at Chintadrepettah and at the Mount, for lyrical preachings by a young Tinnevelly poet, the son of a Vellala convert. Mr. Satthianadhan says of one of these meetings, held at the Mount: "The hall was overcrowded, " and many were obliged to stand outside and listen through " the doors and windows. A large number of Hindu women " also were present, and listened to the music and preaching " with great interest. The meeting lasted three hours, and yet " the interest did not flag throughout. The preacher is only " twenty-five, and yet he has composed original poems on " almost every variety of Christian subjects relating to doctrine " and ethics. He also handles the violin in a masterly manner. " He thus combines in himself the rare qualifications of com- " poser, player, singer, and preacher."

In the Agenda of the Church-Missionary-Society, in March, 1894, I find a proposal to rescind a Minute regarding repairs of a pianoforte at Bombay: this really seems a waste of Committee time. In the *Missions Catholiques* I read, how a large harmonium was taken from France to Zanzibar, and then at a large expenditure carried on men's shoulders to Victoria Nyanza, shipped into a native boat, which was attacked, and sunk, by a Crocodile; and the Fathers appeal to their friends to send out another harmonium. Is not this an undue introduction of European wants among an uncivilized and very poor race? Is not the human voice better in simple congregations than harmonium, pianoforte, or violin? I have already mentioned, how a Swedish party arrived at Shanghai armed with guitars. This is only a sample of the evil, which injudicious Missionaries are working, though with the best intentions.

I subjoin some sensible remarks: "Of course that is not to " say, that all Hindu can be made good Christians; still less " that they can be brought over to the English variety of the " Faith, or the Irish, or the Scotch. Do what we will, the " Hindu will remain Hindu, and be no more English than " they will be French, Italian, or German. If we persist in the " attempt to make them Christians after the fashion of the " Book of Common Prayer and Thirty-nine Articles, of course " we shall be continually working against the grain, and attempt- " ing a work, for which neither a Divine promise, nor common- " sense, can be alleged. On the other hand, if we take the " Christian Faith, as we find it in its earliest and most authentic " form and practice, it presents no insuperable difficulty to any " Oriental intellect or sentiment. Our Faith came from the " East; and, if we are now to admit, that it cannot return to the " East, that is a confession, that we have made it a Western " thing, and overlaid it with European accretions. This is not " to be suffered for an hour. It remains now what it was "nearly nineteen hundred years ago, and there is no reason why all Asia should not become Christian."

21. UNDERTAKING WORK NOT BELONGING TO HIS DUTY.

Another caution is required. The majority of Missionaries are men of ordinary talent and acquirements, though of unblemished character, and of great self-consecration; but amidst their number in all denominations rise up from time to time men, who are giants, whose talents are of the highest calibre. These men throw a lustre in the eyes of the world over their profession, but are not necessarily better Missionaries. If their talents are linguistic, they cannot exert them too freely, or too abundantly, in the work of translations of the Scriptures, and composing of Educational and Devotional works; but, if their talents are those of the Man of Science, they should remember, that they are not sent forth at the expense of Churches, and Families, to be Geographers, or Explorers, or Botanists, or Zoologists, or Conchologists, or Geologists, or to establish Plantations, or Manufactures, or Trade, or to plant Cocoa-nut trees, or breed Ostriches, but to preach the Gospel of Christ, and they should maintain a holy restraint upon themselves, folding up their particular talents, perhaps with a sigh, in a napkin, rather than permit them to hamper the work, for which they were called and chosen. The idea of a self-supporting Mission is a dream. It distresses me to read in Stanley's "Kongo" of a Missionary, who had shot twenty-five elephants, and made great profit by the sale of the tusks. Still more distressed was I, when I came upon French Missionaries in Algeria distilling intoxicating liqueurs.

The Missionary should care for the health of himself, and his family. It has cost much to bring him to his post. Disease and death have already too many opportunities; let him not by rash exposure multiply those risks. Paul shows a tender care for the health of Timothy. Even in things secular prudence is advisable. Prudence enabled me, and many others, to pass a quarter of a Century in uninterrupted health in India, and return to our native land stronger than our contemporaries, who had never left England. The Missionary has consecrated life and faculties to his Master; let him take care of the poor, weak, earthly tabernacle, not for its own sake, for it is worthless, but as the necessary adjunct to the Spirit, which he has consecrated. The care, which the Committee takes of its Missionary, is nullified, if he himself, by false confidence or carelessness, does not take care of himself, and his wife.

I am sorry to find from the Charge of the Bishop of Mauritius, 1892, that the duties of Missionary to the Heathen, and Chaplain to the Troops and Civil Community, are combined : they seem to be entirely incompatible. In German East Equatorial Africa such duties are part of the understood business of the German Missionary.

Under the same category comes the case of a Missionary, who is sent out to convert the non-Christian world, and yet turns to proselyte members of the Greek and Romish Churches, and the smaller Asiatic and African Churches, which have survived to our time. There can be no objection to special Missionaries, properly trained and instructed, being sent to such Churches, as the Assyrian, to assist the Bishops in a friendly way in the work of instruction, but how can a Mission, sent out to convert the Mahometans at Isfahan in Persia, employ itself with propriety in attacking the Armenian Christians at Julfa ?

22. INTRODUCING NEW FADS, SUCH AS TOTAL ABSTINENCE, ETC.

Desirable as it may be to encourage total abstinence from intoxicating liqueurs (and the precepts of the Hindu and Mahometan Religions are, in such matters, on the side of the Christian Missionary), it may be doubtful, whether either Scripture, or expediency, justify an absolute prohibition. Care must be taken not to lay upon a nascent Christianity a burden, which a European, and American, Church never has accepted, and never will. Precept and example will go a long way. It may be generally stated, that the highest standard of Morality should be laid down, and practised as far as human weakness allows, but an equitable and merciful indulgence be shown to backsliders. We know who ought to cast the first stone. We read of persons denouncing Opium, and still drinking Whiskey. Mahomet forbade all forms of intoxicating drink ; the founder of the great Sikh Sect of the Hindus forbade tobacco ; the Buddhist Law forbids animal food ; the early Christian Sects forbade matrimony. All such interferences with the great law of Christian liberty are wrong, and the neo-Christian Churches will laugh at any such bondage imposed by poor weak men. We had better leave them alone.

23. INSULTING, OR MAKING USE OF, NON-CHRISTIAN PLACES OF WORSHIP.

Most dangerous in its consequences is the erection of Chapels, or Schools, in unsuitable places, close to the Temple of the Heathen, or the Mosque of the Mahometan. We boast of our tolerance in London, but would an English mob tolerate the erection of a Mosque, and the daily Calling to Prayer from a Minaret, under the shadow of Westminster Abbey? In the whole length of British India the Missionaries have been singularly discreet, and have their reward in well-earned popularity. I once had to order the demolition of a Chapel built by an ill-judging Missionary actually on the edge of a Sacred Tank, which was a grave outrage to the peaceful inhabitants of a large town. Still worse was the proceeding of a Missionary in China, who established himself upon a hill, which was held in sanctity by the people, and made a grievance, when compelled to do unto others, what he desired that men should do unto him. The Missionaries of the Church of Rome keep the French Minister at Pekin in constant hot water with the Authorities by their constant appeals to Treaty-Rights. We have heard old experienced Missionaries rejoice, that during their whole career they had never appealed to the Magistrate, or invoked the Arm of the Flesh. Missionaries must deal gently with the prejudices, which they encounter. To occupy a sacred site, and build upon it a Missionary-Residence or School, under any view of the case, is an act of extreme indiscretion, to which no lapse of years can give a sanction. To convert a Pagoda into a Christian place of worship is one of those acts, which may be resented for Centuries. We have instances of the evil consequences of such a policy written in blood in every country.

On the other hand such practices as the one described below in the Church-Missionary-Society-Report of 1893, are most objectionable: " Large audiences were addressed in Buddhist " temples, the priests making no objection, but on the contrary, " in some cases, themselves buying copies of the Gospels, and " accepting tracts."

And in the Church-Missionary-Society-Report, 1891 : " He " sought a place to exhibit his lantern-slides, and was invited " to use the devil-temple for the purpose. It was a grand time, " and the place, which had often resounded with the uncouth " shrieks and cries of devil-dancers, now rang with the sweeter " music of Christian lyrics. The occasion was rendered all the " more interesting to my mind, because the itinerating catechist, " who explained the slides, had himself at one time been a " demon-worshipper, and had even officiated as a devil-dancer. " He was now 'clothed and in his right mind,' engaged in a " holier and more heavenly service. During the exhibition a poor " woman, also a devil-dancer, pretended to have received the " 'inflatus.' She danced, and yelled, and shouted, 'They have " defiled our temple! They have defiled our temple!' But " she was speedily silenced by her Heathen-friends, who were " all eyes and ears for the story of the life of Him, who came " to destroy the works of the devil. We were thankful indeed "for this remarkable opportunity of preaching the truth from a place *where Satan's seat is*."

Christian work should be done in a Christian way, and the great principle maintained of doing unto others, what you would wish that men should do unto you. Only reverse the picture, and imagine the Cathedral of Lahór occupied by Mahometans or Hindus, and desecrated by lantern-slides of the life of Mahomet, or of Krishna, while some poor faithful Christian is the unwilling spectator of this outrage, whose sobs and cries are stopped by his renegade co-religionists, who, forgetful of the consecrated sanctity of the building, are all eyes and ears to hear the story of Krishna and the 40,000 Milkmaids. Lantern-slides are scarcely an Apostolic Method for the rousing of a sense of sin, bringing a soul to the Saviour, and sanctification by the Holy Spirit.

24. Preaching to Prisoners in Public Gaols.

As an instance of the unreasonableness of Missionaries in some cases I make the following quotation: " The Singhalese Evan-" gelistic work among prisoners has been somewhat hampered " by the enforcement of a regulation at the principal prison, " that ministers, or catechists, may only speak to prisoners, who " belong to their own denominations. This rule effectually " prevents Evangelistic efforts in behalf of the Heathen " prisoners."

Thirty years ago an attempt was made to allow Missionaries access to the inmates of the Public Gaols in the Panjáb, and I was instrumental in having the practice absolutely forbidden. That any prisoner should have reasonable access to the Ministers of his own Religion is equitable, but to allow Propagandists free entry to preach their own views to an audience compelled to listen is against all equity. Imagine the case of a Protestant inmate of a Prison in such a country as Spain, and the horror of his legal punishment being enhanced by having to listen to the solicitations of a Romish Priest. This practice is an insidious use of the Arm of the Flesh, for it is, in fact, employing the Civil Power to aid Conversions. The Christian Missionary would deem it very unjust, if one of his own converts under sentence came out of prison a Brahmoist, or a Mormonite, under influence of teaching forced upon him during his term of imprisonment.

25. Taking up New Work to the Neglect of Old.

Most open to objection is that fatal desire, that seizes some Societies, or Missionaries, to be always taking up new work, and neglecting and starving the old. In each Mission-Field there is a natural healthy internal growth, at once the evidence, and forerunner, of success, requiring annually an increase of expenditure. It is, as if the Father of a Family, instead of providing for the annually increasing legitimate wants of his own children, should waywardly adopt new children, and nourish these at the cost of starving his elder family. It sounds fair enough : some one is always found ready to pay the expenses for three or five years, but after that time the Society has to provide, or the result of the whole outlay is lost. The Scriptural advice of counting the cost before a tower is commenced, the dictates of common-sense, the example of secular administration, the warning-voice of the more prudent members of the Committee, are all set aside by the restless fervour of some enthusiasts for new work. The charge of want of Faith is cast into the teeth of those who object, forgetting that we are told to use our talents to the utmost, but not beyond our talents. The same principles, which guide the private life of individual Christian men, should guide the operations of collective Christians.

CONCLUDING REMARKS.

I have finished my task: Faithful are the words of a friend: there are not many, who could, or would, grapple with such a subject as this: Unfortunately not many Missionaries of long experience remain at their posts to the end: those who die at their posts in old age are few, for death is busy with the young and middle-aged; a percentage are disabled by failure of health: " Returned Empties," who have thrown up their vocation owing to sickness of wife, or more desirable Church-preferment at home, meet the eye at every turn: they have quite forgotten the command of the Master. The experience of the Missionary is limited Geographically: it requires prolonged, all-round, study by one entirely free from the predilections of any particular shibboleth, and who is tall enough to look over the fence, which separates Church from Church, and sees only the figure of our Lord, as He gave His parting orders on Mount Olivet.

I wish to bring home to some the state of the case, who think lightly of the blots which have been hit, by imagining a young Missionary about thirty-three years of age lying on the bed, on which he is doomed to die, and thinking sadly on the ten years of his service. He had chosen the better part, and had consecrated himself in the flower of his youth to the One Service, and yet he had married, and now was leaving wife and a large number of children, who ought never to have come into existence, to be supported by money, collected under the influence of prayer for the Conversion of the Heathen, a great deal from little children in Missionary-boxes.

Then will come back to his memory the gross abuse heaped by him upon Mahomet, and the great and wise men, Buddha, Confucius, Zoroaster, and the Hindu Sages, on the Religious Conceptions, which they had reduced to writing, and upon the poor ignorant people of Asia and Africa, who owing to the inscrutable Will of the Almighty had never had a chance of hearing of the Saviour. Had it pleased the Divine Controller of human events, the Light, which sprang up in Galilee to lighten the Gentiles, could have flashed Eastward and Southward instead of only Westward. We in the West enjoyed early blessings of Conversion, and must not blame those, who dwelt in darkness.

He will think of his meaningless attacks upon ancient Customs like Caste, Binding of Women's feet in childhood, Ancestral Worship, and the Marriage of Children in tender years; of his denunciation of the long-suffering Government of British India, of a great Agricultural Industry, and a great Commercial Traffic between two great kingdoms, and the management of the Excise of one of the greatest populations of the world, matters utterly beyond the experience of one of his antecedents, and training, in the middle-classes of Great Britain.

He could have wished, now that it was too late, that he had had his eye and thoughts fixed more exclusively on his Saviour, that his heart had been more filled with Love for, Sympathy with, Pity for, the poor, poor non-Christian.

"Faith may fail, and Hope itself remove,
"But hearts of men are won by conquering Love."

A Negro once said of William Wilberforce, the friend of the slaves, that he loved him, "because he had a black heart." The Missionary, who wishes to win non-Christian races to Christ, must show himself in that light, and many have done so.

The World is like one of those great forests described by African travellers. Ancient Religious Conceptions have grown up side by side, contending like lofty trees for superiority of elevation with each other: the birds of the air make their dwellings in the upper branches, on which the eternal Tropical Sun is shining. Down below is darkness; the inhabitants of the forest, like the believers in these Ancient Religions, move about in total spiritual darkness. Lichens and Epiphytes have covered the lower branches, and the stems of the trees. Legends and Lies have choked up whatever of Truth there once existed in these ancient Faiths. But at the roots of the tree the insect-world has long been at work, and the day will come, when the great tree will perish in one or other of two ways, by the eating away of the life, and the conduits of sap, in the trunk by its insidious enemies, or by the fire deliberately lighted by the Traveller encamped beneath, and kept alive by broken fragments of its own branches. So the Ancient Faith, the simple Primæval Conception of God's Power, and Man's Duty, is gradually eaten away by the birth of newer and more refined developments of thought, or a great iconoclast intolerant foreign Religion deliberately attacks the old effete institution, and destroys it.

Then the Great Tree, and the Great Religion, fall: no one regrets them, and a thick jungle of younger conceptions of the fertile brain of man take their place: but the end is not yet: they are only in an intermediate stage, till the time of the clearing of the soil comes, and then the living jungle of younger

Pagan Conceptions, and the dead prostrate trunk of the ancient Book-Religions, are cleared away, and an entirely new, and vivid, and more advanced, view of the relation of God to Man is introduced, and no feeling of regret, or gratitude, is felt for the dead Conception, as it had had its day.

But who is equal to the task of clearing away this *débris?* Is the average modern Missionary with his scamped Education, his narrow views, the premature burden of a sick wife and young family, and the absence of opportunity for study, or converse with men, who have made the inquiry into the variety of the modes of dealing of the Almighty with His poor creatures, equal to such a task? "damnat quod non intelligit."

A new environment is opening upon us in the twentieth Century. The heart must be softened towards our brethren, who have not had the privilege of being born Christians: the contemptuous expressions, used by the Hebrews with regard to the "Goi," or Gentiles, will not go down now: there is no advantage in quoting such expressions from the Old Testament. The people of India, and China, and Japan, are advancing in knowledge, and will not put up with insults heaped upon them: many of them read the English Periodicals, and the English will soon be obliged to read their Periodicals. The Monopoly of Benevolence, which used to be possessed by the Missionary, is being taken away, or has to be shared with Secular Institutions. The Lady-Dufferin-Fund for providing medical aid for the women of India, and to bring relief to thousands of females, and little children, who suffer needlessly, and from want of knowledge, is purely secular, and has prospered beyond what anyone would have dared to anticipate. One, therefore, of the good Methods alluded to in Part I is shared by those, who do not make use of Medical assistance, as a channel for Gospel-preaching. Education is also monopolized by the State. Preaching and Teaching in the Towns and Villages are now instruments made use of by the old Hindu, and the promoters of neo-Hinduism, by the Mahometan, the Theosophist, and the Mormonite. The Miracles recorded in the Bible can no longer be appealed to, as equally wonderful Miracles are recorded in the Sacred Books now revealed, and made accessible to the followers of each Religion by the labour of European Scholars. Martyrdom is no speciality of the follower of any particular Faith. The African Traveller, who witnesses the torture and death of the two Dervishes of the Mahdi, in the camp of Emin Pasha, comments with admiration on the fortitude evinced to the last by these Mahometan enthusiasts.

It is scarcely sufficiently appreciated, how during the last half Century there has been a mighty change in the problem. Education, and a knowledge of other countries, have taught the great Heathen Nations certain lessons : a stubborn National feeling is developing itself, the absolute necessity of the highest Morality is admitted : to those, who have studied the subject of the Religious Conceptions of Antiquity, before the great Anno Domini, and the new crop, which has since sprung up everywhere, it is clear, that we are entering into a new Epoch, that the old weapons are well-nigh useless, that the cuckoo-cry of the Missionary should be stopped. My own thoughts have been much turned to the subject, and I am engaged to read a paper at the International Oriental Congress to be held at Geneva next September on the "Old Religious Conceptions, which prevailed in Europe and Asia, and N. Africa, before the Fulness of Time came, and the great Λόγος appeared": some of these Conceptions are still living, such as the Zoroastrian, Brahmanical, Buddhist, Confucian, Taouist, Shinto, and Judaism; and some have been dead for Centuries, the Egyptian, Babylonian, Assyrian, and other Semitic Conceptions in Asia, and the Græco-Latin, and Teutonic, in Europe. In my lately-published Essay, "Clouds on the Horizon," 1891, I point out the new non-Christian Conceptions which stand betwixt the people, and the acceptance of Christianity: 1 neo-Mahometanism, 2 neo-Judaism, neo-Hinduism, neo-Zoroastrian, neo-Buddhism, neo-Confucianism, Brahmoism, Arya Samáj, Brahmo Samáj, Te Kooti, Te Whiti, Mormonism, Theosophism, in addition to the well-known European forms of Positivism, Agnosticism, Unitarianism, Theism, etc., etc.

As among professors of ancient Faiths, like those of the Hindu, Buddhist, and Confucianist, so among the Jews, God's chosen people, who have stood out against Christianity so many Centuries, a change of front is taking place : while one section of educated Jews cling to the ritual of the Pentateuch, places a value on Old-World forms, and ceremonies, and even prays, that the period may arrive, when the long-forgotten ritual of sacrifice of poor dumb animals and birds may be restored, as an atonement for sin ; another section seem to be advancing into the lines of pure Unitarianism. I quote from the *Record* a notice of one of the leaders of this section: his position is rather understated than overstated : " The name of Mr. Claude G. Montefiore, who
" edits the *Jewish Quarterly Review*, and was Hibbert-Lecturer
" in 1892, is well-known to scholars outside of the Community,
" of which he is a prominent member. His Hibbert-Lectures
" on the Religion of the Hebrews proved him to be at once a
" profound theologian, and a Jew, who approached the study of
" the Christian Religion in a singularly open-minded manner.
" A man, who can remain an active and honoured member of
" the Synagogue, while publicly expressing his belief, that the
" Judaism of the future will need to be built up on the teachings

" of Jesus contained in the Gospels, and whose dream is 'of a
" prophetic Judaism, which shall be as spiritual, as the Religion
" of Jesus, and even more universal than the Religion of Paul,' a
" teacher professing such enlightened views is a force to be
" reckoned with by Christians and Jews alike, and his utterances
" on Religious questions must always command the attention of
" serious thinkers." Old things have indeed passed away, and
all things are new.

In Exeter Hall, May 1894, Bishop Tucker expressed the feelings of many of us in the following words: " To him it was
" inconceivable, that a man should be truly religious, and yet not
" have the Missionary-spirit. When a man pleaded the necessity
" of attending to his own personal Religion, or offered the excuse,
" that there was work at home, then his personal love for Christ
" must be at a low ebb. Nor could the failure of Missions be
" urged as a reason for disregarding them. If efforts fail, did
" that make the duty less binding? Some held aloof from
" Missionary-effort, simply because they doubted of its success.
" Even if they were right in their doubts, was that any reason?
" The man of Faith would labour on in Faith and Hope. Elabo-
" rating this point he pleaded urgently with his hearers to take
" their part in the Evangelization of the World, and not to have
" to say in years to come, as he had so often heard it said,
" 'Oh, that I had my time over again! Grey hairs are upon me,
" and I cannot go now.'"

The Bishop did not add, that it is mainly owing to the unguarded utterances of Missionaries, and the peculiar character of the Publications of Societies, that the extreme unpopularity of the subject must be attributed. It is sad to think, that so many live through honoured, good, and useful lives, and yet on their deathbed they must admit, that they had never contributed a farthing, uttered a prayer, or given a thought to the extension of the Lord's Kingdom, There are whole families, and whole grades of social life, who give nothing but the miserable shilling on the occasion of a Missionary-Sermon, and yet perhaps lay down £100 for some excellent Local Charity. We cannot, with any sense of justice, call these people bad names, following the example of the Missionaries towards the non-Christian world, for the good people of the Associations, with their goody-goody treatment of the great subject, are themselves the cause of this coldness. In my daily round for the last fifteen years I have passed from the Hall of Scientific Research, or the Assembly of Local Administrators, into a Missionary-Committee-Room, and I must admit, that there is a difference, the existence of which I regret. I am myself deeply indebted to Missionary-Committee-Rooms, though perplexed by the mode, in which business is conducted. I always took a volume of Homer's "Odyssey" with me, that I might get my thoughts away from some dreary discussion on the most trivial subject, such as the marriage of a Missionary, the admission of his children into the Home, or the repairing of a Pianoforte. I write with copies of several agenda on my table.

I have said my say. This is probably my last contribution to Missionary-Literature. If I have written what is not true, put this paper behind the fire. If there be a scintilla of Truth, think over it. It cannot now be said, that we must travel onward in a mist, and that, as nobody criticized, there was no error.

I have no doubt, that my book will meet bitter criticisms: a certain famous book at the time of the Reformation, "Litteræ obscurorum virorum," was not approved by those, who wrote letters of the kind exposed to ridicule. What I should be glad to see, if I live a little longer, would be a Code of Good Methods of Evangelization, and a list of those to be avoided. I have supplied some material: let my work be the *débris* of rubbish, on which the good building will be erected. I know how hard abuses, and prejudices, die: I can almost hear the strictures, uttered in certain rooms in London, uttered by the very persons, whom I have described, though not by name, as the offenders; but it was unnecessary to mention the name, for they must feel, that to them the stricture applies. Those five Methods, Jealous retention of power by the Home-Committee, Industrial Missions, Secular high-class Education, Early Marriage of Missionaries, and the Arm of the Flesh, may in course of time be recognised, as the most powerful enemies of Evangelization.

I mentioned to a Secretary of a great Missionary-Society, that I was publishing a book, commenting severely on the Methods of Evangelization, and the conduct of Missionary-Societies: I expected to be rebuked, but I found a blessing: the reply was, "you cannot make your remarks too strong"; in fact all feel, that the present system is most unsatisfactory. Should the accuracy of my statements with regard to the Arm of the Flesh at U-Ganda be questioned, I find a singular confirmation in the account of the May Meeting of the Church-Missionary-Society, 1894. The President referred with satisfaction to the success of the efforts of the members of the Committee, and Society, in *stirring up public opinion on the U-Ganda question*; that is to say, by the instrumentality of Meetings, Sermons, Writings, the British Nation had been induced to put forth its strength, and unwisely annex a Kingdom in Central Africa, using force of arms, and slaying of men and women, in order that Christ's message of Peace might be conveyed to the Natives by two rival camps of Missionaries, each ready to destroy the other. Such a phenomenon has never been seen in Protestant Missions before.

There let it rest: liberavi animum meum. There can be no manner of doubt, that, as in Manufacture, Commerce, Navigation, and Colonization, so also in Evangelization, the Anglo-Saxon race on either side of the Atlantic is unrivalled. Prayer and Praise to the Lord of Heaven and Earth, and reading and teaching of the Word of God, are heard at every hour of the day, in all the chief languages of the world, in every part of the world accessible to the Anglo-Saxon, by every race of mankind, black, brown, yellow, red, or white, under the leadership of English-speaking Missionaries. The motive is of the best that can be found in the human breast, Love to our Fellow-creatures, Love to our God. I place them in that order intentionally: what choicest present could we make to our dearest friend? in what form could Pity for the lost and suffering more completely express itself? How small seem other acts of benevolence, or of self-sacrifice? How small seems Patriotism, when weighed in this scale?

" For we best love our God and Father, when
" We most entirely love our Fellow-men."

I lay down my pen on the eve of the great Missionary-Conference of the Church of England. At one time I was tempted to delay the publication of this volume until I had the opportunity of reading the Reports and Proceedings of this remarkable gathering. But Time is against me at the age of seventy-three, so I close my book without that advantage: if well, as I wished; if not so good, as far as I was able.

London, May 26th, 1894.

ROBERT N. CUST,

Member of Committee of Missionary-Conference of Church of England of 1894,

Lay Secretary of Board of Missions of the Province of Canterbury.

APPENDIX.

I. A Plea for the poor non-Christian World.
II. Five Signs of a True Missionary.
III. Suggestions for emendation of Missionary-Methods.

A PLEA FOR THE POOR NON-CHRISTIAN WORLD.

One word to any young man, who is starting out to be a Missionary. Of all professions his is the most noble, the most elevating, and at the same time the most difficult, and the most exposed to the risk of failure. The majority of young men are not highly educated, and have no knowledge of the world: of blameless character themselves they have not been acquainted with the blameworthy conduct of Christians exposed to temptation. They come suddenly face to face with an entirely new environment, totally different from the humdrum middle-class life, to which they have been used: all is a surprise. The man, with whom they have to deal; the language, which they have to hear and use; the Religious Conceptions, with which they have to contend, are wonderful, and undreamt of, novelties.

The native man, however humble in circumstances, and devoid of Culture, is still as much an individual as the Missionary: he has the same fundamental conception of Self, of the World, and of God: language is the vehicle of his communication with the World and his fellow-creatures: Religion is the funnel, through which his thoughts go up to God: he is perfectly innocent of having taken any part in settling the Environment, the Language, or the Religion, to which he finds himself bound from the day of his birth: it never occurs to him to change, or wish to change, either, any more than the colour of his skin, or the fashion of such garments, as he wears, if he wears any. It is of no use abusing him for being what he is: he did not make himself, or his surroundings, or his powers of utterance, or his Conception of God.

Since the commencement of the World many great, powerful, and wise, races have sprung up, blossomed, brought forth fruit in the imperishable literary and architectural Monuments, which they have left behind, and passed away without any knowledge of the true Nature of the Great God, and of His great plan of Salvation for man. Here is a great fact: they never had the chance of being Christians: we cannot believe, that they have gone to perdition. Can the Ruler of the Universe do what is not right, and not be merciful to His poor creatures? They used the talents entrusted to them, and had nothing beyond.

Since the great Anno Domini, when in the Fulness of Time came the Saviour, countless Millions have been born, lived, and died, in entire ignorance of the great Truth. Is this to be placed at their door as a fault?

Language was given to man to differentiate him from the animals, and to communicate with his fellow-creatures. Some forms of speech are mellifluous, and capable of expressing any possible idea; others fail both in euphony, and word-store: is the Missionary to abuse them, or talk lightly of them, as if they had had anything to do with selecting, or forming, their language? They used it without knowing what it was. The Missionary had nothing to do with forming his own wonderful language: it was given to him ready made.

Religion was given to man still further to differentiate him from animals, who have no future state, and to enable him to communicate with his Heavenly Father. No tribe is so debased, that it has not a sense of the Supernatural, and some Conception of a Future after Death. Their oral traditions, their practices, and their sacred books, testify to this. Through Generations and Centuries, they have adhered to their old Religious Conceptions, and still hold fast to them, as part of their very lives. Are they to be abused, because they do not at once listen to the imperfectly-stated arguments of a young Preacher from a foreign land, speaking their language imperfectly?

As time went on, their Religious Conceptions have become frightfully degraded: such is the fate of all Religions, when Ignorance accompanies it: and Priestcraft, the great curse of Mankind, comes into existence, substituting Liturgies and Ritual for Virtue, and Morality. The scathing words of Rénan in his fifth and posthumous volume of " Le Peuple d'Israel," are then, and *then only*, true:

" La Religion est une Imposture necessaire. Les plus gros
" moyens de jeter de la poudre aux yeux ne peuvent être negligés
" avec une aussi sotte race, que l'espece humaine, crée pour
" l'erreur, et qui, quand elle admet la Verité, ne l'admet jamais
" pour les bonnes raisons."

Priestcraft has degraded all the ancient Religions, and even some forms of Christianity: I have visited the Greek shrine of the Virgin at Troitska, near Moscow in Russia, the shrine of the Virgin at Loretto in Italy, and the shrine of Parbati, or Lakshmi, at Banáras in India, and I could see a resemblance in the symbols, and the worship, of all, for they all told the tale of degraded Superstition: it is the same poor grovelling human worship, whether in Europe, or in Asia, or in Africa.

But upon this in the last days of the Nineteenth Century a new complication has arisen in the birth of a brood of new Religious Conceptions, more suited to the modern human intellect; at the same time Secular Education, and Civilization, are purging the imagination of any belief in the Supernatural; the same deluge overwhelms the Veda, and the Old Testament. Nothing is believed, that cannot be proved by evidence, as in a Court of Justice.

The Missionary has to face this state of things, and he is with rare exceptions totally unfit for the combat, but he can at least abstain from saying unkind things of the poor non-Christian world, of whom he knows so little.

Let him ask himself, who is the barbarian: the imperfectly-clad African, who had never the chance of altering his lot, or the European creature, who struts down the streets of a city decorated, or clad, in the furs of a wild beast, the skin of a seal, the feathers of a bird, the manufactured fibre of a worm, or of a plant. The Art of Painting, and Sculpture, would readily prefer the nude figure of the African, or the imperfectly-clad figure of the Asiatic, to the grotesque, and ridiculous, apparel of the European. Let him ask himself, "who is the atheist and unbeliever?" the man, who never had the opportunity of knowing Christ, or the man, who, nominally a Christian, dishonours his Master by his want of Belief, or openly expresses contempt of His Precepts. A bad Christian is something infinitely worse than a bad Heathen.

The Heathen man, in spite of all his infirmities, is still formed and fashioned in the image of the Most High: and evidence, gleaned from all the races of the world, and in all times, shows, that the Heathen man feels after God, if haply he can find Him, and his heart turns to his Creator, even as the sunflower turns to the Sun, and he knows not why. In his humble way the Heathen looks forward to a Heaven adapted to his merits, or demerits, or his necessities: he has Faith sufficient to enable him to die for his Faith: he is not a Christian, because the Ruler of mankind has not ruled, that he should have a chance of being so: he is ignorant, because his environment is such, as God has ordained for him, and because his more enlightened fellow-creatures have had no thought for him, and, though they have received the parting commands of the Saviour, had not thought it worth their while to obey them. Christians are to blame, not the poor Heathen: he is an object of Pity, and Love, and Sympathy. The wonder is, that he is so good as those, who know him best, find him to be, and the reason is, that his Heavenly Father has not left Himself entirely without a witness, that His Son died for him, and all mankind, and that the Holy Spirit still hovers round, ready to take up His abode in each of God's poor children, as soon as the so-called "God's people" in Europe succeed in finding a way to their hearts by words of Human Love, and Divine Wisdom: hitherto we have failed. Much has been left undone; and much has been done badly: let us find out the more excellent way; place our hands on our mouth, and each one cry out, "Mea Culpa! Mea Culpa!"

Let all recollect, both Christian and non-Christian, or pseudo-Christian, that the knell of the Book-Religions, and the Nature-Worships, which preceded them, has rung: whether Christianity will take their place is a graver question, which may have two, or more, answers. A platform-speaker eloquently and truly described the growth of a tree destroying an old Temple in Kashmir, which had survived the attacks of Time for Centuries. Thus is Christianity quietly and gradually undermining the vast edifice of Heathenism; in the end it will topple over, as this ancient Temple will do also. During a tour in North India nearly fifty years ago I accompanied one of the wisest, and most pious, of Governors, James Thomason, in a morning-ride. We drew rein before the ruins of a Castle, and a Temple, crowned with luxurious foliage, and sinking into nothing under the gentle hand of Natural Decay. "What a lesson," said he, "this "teaches us! Temple and Tower have gone to the ground "under the pressure of the advance of Human Culture, and "Divine Influences: how much better it is, than if the one had "been desecrated by a fanatic iconoclast, and the other had "exhibited the signs of a savage bombardment!"

I close with a quotation from "Wisdom of Solomon," cap. xi. vv. 23–26; it is the last echo of Jewish thought, accepted as "profitable for example of life" by the Christian Church, and written probably in the first decade after the death of our Lord.

"But Thou hast mercy upon all; for Thou canst do all "things, and winkest ($\pi\alpha\rho o\rho\tilde{q}s$) at the sins of men, because, (in "order that) they should amend. For thou lovest all the things, "that are, and *abhorreth nothing which Thou hast made*: for never "would Thou have made anything, if Thou had hated it. And "how could anything have endured, if it had not been Thy Will? "or been preserved, if not called by Thee? But Thou sparest "all: for they are Thine, O Lord, Thou Lover of Souls."

FIVE SIGNS OF A TRUE MISSIONARY.

Dr. George Smith, "Conversion of India," 1893, p. 172, lays down the following five signs of a true Missionary:

I. Must be conscious of a Call, no secondary motive, no unworthy aim, such as love of knowledge, desire to marry, desire to travel, a legitimate hope of position, or reputation, or of pleasantly convenient work.

II. Must covet the best gifts, qualify himself for the highest efficiency; study to the full measure of his powers, considering them a shadow, and praying, that they do not prove a temptation; if not a College-man he must be master of his particular craft.

III. Must follow the more Noble Way of Love: he must love the dark races with such a Love, as that with which Christ loved the world; he must show sympathy, patience, tenderness, heavenly wisdom; he must show good temper to his brethren, and have charity to all in all its breadth of humility, self-sacrifice, and geniality.

IV. Must learn habits of order in person, study, accounts, business, so as to economize resources, and utilize time for work, rest, recreation. Want of common-sense, as well as want of charity, is an obstruction to the Kingdom of Heaven.

V. Must give himself to Prayer, and reading of the Word, and cultivation of Personal Religion.

SUGGESTIONS FOR EMENDATION OF MISSIONARY METHODS.

PAGE

1. Have nothing to do with the Civil-Rulers of Great Britain, or the United States, or the countries, where the Missionary works: never appeal to the Arm of the Flesh, either to annex a country, as in U-Ganda, to give compensation for losses, as in China, to exert political influence, as in Turkey and Oceania: it is unworthy of a Christian Missionary. He ought to trust in the Arm of the Almighty alone. (Isaiah, xxxvi, 6.) . . . . 43 to 70

2. Reorganize the Home-Committees of Administration: reduce the paid Secretaries to their proper position, *as ministers*, and limit the term of their Office to ten years: have only two grades, (1) General Committee, (2) Geographical sub-Committee: let the decision of the latter be final, unless challenged in the General: weigh votes, do not count them: let the power of the General Committee not be to overrule, but to send back to the Geographical sub-Committee for reconsideration for reasons given: admit Women as members of Committee, and sub-Committee . 125

3. Decentralize: give enlarged constitutional powers to the Local Committee in the Field, subject to report and control: this will reduce the work, and expense, of the Home-Office, and get rid of some Secretaries, and Clerks 135

4. Reorganize the Deputation-System: old men are of no use on the staff: the post should only be held for ten years, and then vacated: let more members of the Committee take a share of Deputation-work *at their own charges*. Stir up the Local Clergy, and Laymen, to help 141

		PAGE

5. Get rid of the Children's Home: where Missionaries require assistance, let an allowance be made to them, but not to those, whose friends are quite able to support their young relations. (I Timothy, v, 8, 16.) 147

6. Appoint two Members of the Association to exercise power analogous to that of the Auditors of the Local Government Board, to disallow all improper expenditure *not within the scope of the objects of the Association*, and make the Members of the Committee, who voted, pay up that amount: it will serve them right . . 157

7. Alter the style, and even the dialect, of the Reports, and Publications: omit all sermons, and lists of contributions: the account to be given is of the noblest Warfare, and most important enterprise, that the world ever saw: why tell the story in a goody-goody, Pharisaical, non-natural, sensational, style? why quote Scripture, and use common-form cant terms? why use the Divine Name two or three times in each page? to say the least it is bad literary style: no good writer of a leading Article, or a Magazine-Article, or a serious Book, would be tolerated, if he stated facts in this fashion. How comes it, that there are no failures of character, or policy? Are these Reports, and Tracts, written to deceive an emotional public? Let the Report be short: it will cost less, and be read more 159

8. Spend more money on the Training of Men, and Women, for the Work: let the Vocation be deemed a life-call, not a pastime: let the names of those, who abandon their Vocation to suit their own whims, be marked with opprobium. Nothing but a Medical certificate of absolute unfitness absolves a Missionary from the obligation, which he has voluntarily taken on himself. Consider the contrast, evidenced by the conduct of the Missionaries of the Church of Rome: there is no sneaking home in their case 195

9. Do not allow the Missionary to become a busybody, meddling with other people's affairs: let him keep to his own holy duties, and have no thought, but for Christ, and the lost sheep. (I Peter, iv, 15.) . 208

		PAGE
10.	Let no male-Missionary marry till he has had ten years' service in the Field. Encourage Brotherhoods and Sisterhoods, as a matter of administrative convenience and economy	210
11.	Let young Missionaries be taught to refrain from abusing the Natives, and their Religions; if they write home in such style, let them be reproved: at any rate let not their foolish letters be published: old Missionaries rarely do so: it is very discreditable to the good sense and Christian character of the writers, and the compiler of the Reports . . .	260

ALPHABETICAL INDEX OF PARTS, CHAPTERS, SECTIONS.

A

	PAGE
Arm of the Flesh	43
Arrogant to Natives	222
Association or Society	125

B

Bad Methods	42
Baptism of Slaves purchased	73
Baptism: new conditions	80
Barracks for Converts	99
Bible-teaching omitted	74
Board of Missions	124

C

Civil, Military, or Diplomatic Interference	43
Conversion, modes of	72
Credulousness of any new story	92
Customs: tilting against legal native	241

D

Defying laws of country	235
Degradation of Gospel-teaching	76
Deputations	141
Destruction of places of worship	68
Difficulties of Conversion	76
Disloyal to Home-Committee	234
Duty, work other than	275

E

Education, injurious Western	93
Endowments	60

F

	PAGE
Fads	276
Field, Missions in	170
Financial Department	147

G

Good Methods	10

I

Ideas, imposing Western	272
Immorality	271
Intolerance	62

L

Low Culture, and Denseness, of Converts	87

M

Marrying early, Missionaries	210
Material advantages offered	74
Material help from God	105
Material status of Converts	96
Matrimony of Converts	89
Methods not recommended	15
Missions very small	171

N

Native Agents	181
Native Church	186
New work taken up in neglect of old	278
Non-Christian places of worship	276

O

	PAGE
Opposition	117

P

Pagan notions of Converts ..	79
Parental rights of non-Christians	109
Political schemes	70
Prisoners in Public Gaols	278
Publications..	159

R

Relapse of Converts	84
Ridiculing non-Christian Religions..	260

S

Secular Methods..	16

	PAGE
Secular offices and honours ..	248
Self-supporting Missions	174
Sins of non-Christian World ..	100
Society of Secular white men ..	251
Solitary Mission-Stations	172
Spiritual Methods	27
Sympathy, absence of..	227

T

Tribal Conversion	72

U

Union of Denominations	111
Unpaid Agents	191

V

Vocation, throwing up	243

MISSIONARY WARNINGS

FOR THE
TWENTIETH CENTURY.

No. 2.

The Civil Disabilities of Christian Converts in British India.

BY

ROBERT NEEDHAM CUST, LL.D.

SERVUS SERVORUM.

ARCIS DIVINÆ SUPER MUROS HUMILIS SPECULATOR CŒLI PRÆSAGIA
PROSPICIT, ET FIDELITER DENUNTIAT.

FOR PRIVATE CIRCULATION.

1894.

MISSIONARY WARNINGS.

No. 1. *THE ADOLESCENCE OF A NATIVE CHURCH IN NON-CHRISTIAN LANDS.*

1892.

THE CIVIL DISABILITIES OF CHRISTIAN CONVERTS IN BRITISH INDIA.

There is no doubt, that, as long as the world lasts, a change made in the ancestral Religion will be prejudicial to the social status, the means of livelihood, and the domestic relations, of the person, whom his new friends hail, as a Convert, and his old associates curse, and excommunicate, as a Pervert. An American Bishop told us in one of the Sectional Meetings of the Missionary-Conference, that the Mormonite Polygamists of Utah get their extra wives in great number from Christian England, and Wales. No doubt the daughter of an English Clergyman, or a pious Layman, who was talked over to join the Mormonite Sect, would leave her home, and neighbourhood, as an object of scorn, hate, and deprivation of her share of the parental inheritance. The same would be the fate of an English youth, who became a Mahometan. We can only realize the exact merits of a case by bringing home analogous circumstances to our mind. The Christian Religion in England is comparatively modern, compared with the antiquity of the Zoroastrian, Brahminical, Buddhist, and Confucianist, Religious Beliefs in different parts of Asia.

Let us enquire what the Master says:

"In the world ye shall have tribulation," etc.—John xvi. 33.

"He that loveth Father and Mother more than me," etc.—Matthew x. 37.

"Everyone that has forsaken houses, or brethren, or children, "or lands, for My Name's sake, shall receive an hundred-fold, "and inherit everlasting life."—Matthew xix. 29.

The same sentiment appears throughout the Gospels, and the Epistles.

The professors of the Ancient National quietist Religions, and also the great worldwide Propagandist Doctrine of Buddha, were ever tolerant: if left alone, they would leave others alone. A renegade Jew would have received no quarter, no pity, no inheritance, from his own relations and countrymen: the Stoning of Stephen in the Christian era evidences this. The Greek, and Roman, were ever tolerant. Christianity began the practice in Europe of Intolerance, Confiscation, and Disabilities. Islam followed her example in Asia and Africa. Our position is singular in claiming for Converts to our own Religion immunities, which until a very late period the Church of England never allowed to the Jew, the Nonconformist, the Romanist, or the Convert from Christianity to Mahometanism.

In Turkey, or Persia, or any independent Mahometan country, Death, and Confiscation of goods, have always been the recognised consequence of change of Faith. This severity is gradually passing away, as far as the Executive Government, and the Courts of Law, are concerned, but, as outbreaks of popular fury and an enraged Priesthood have to be reckoned with, successors of Stephen are still stoned, and successors of James are still killed by the sword.

In British India, on the occupation of the different Provinces, not only absolute toleration of all forms of Religious Conceptions was guaranteed, but the Hindu and Mahometan Law, and Customs having the force of Law, as regards Matrimony, and Inheritance, were declared to be the personal Law of every inhabitant of the country, so long as the paramount Laws of the Human Race were not violated: that is to say the burning of widows, and slaying of daughters, both of which Customs were part of the Law relating to Matrimony. were forbidden, as being Murder. It has taken half a Century to tread down these Customs.

Just before the Mutinies of 1857 a Law was passed, declaring, that the succession to ancestral property was not forfeited by change of Religion: this was a very strong departure from the original guarantees: it is notorious, that in past Centuries the Hindus, who became Mahometans, did not forfeit their estates: it so happens, that Christian converts generally belong to the poorest classes, and claims to landed property, or valuable chattels, are rare.

About the same time a Law was passed, declaring the issue of a Hindu widow, who remarried, to be legitimate: the Law has been practically inoperative: I never heard of a case.

These Laws affected property and status, but the real trouble of a Convert in the Nineteenth Century is to retain possession of his wife and children, and this trouble existed in the time of our Lord, as evidenced by His Words quoted above. Can modern Christian Legislation remove the difficulty? is it wise to do so? will *true* Christianity gain by it?

The state of British India is at the present moment not satisfactory. The air is full of rumours: a period of unrest, if not of open disturbance, seems to be near at hand. The Population of the country during the half Century of Pax Britannica has increased at the rate of three Millions annually, and the general poverty has increased also: War has ceased: Pestilence and Famine are kept under control. Twenty-two Millions of Widows are the result of the Law abolishing Widow-burning: a large number of unmarried females is the result of forbidding the practice of killing daughters in high-caste families: the land is overrun with lepers, as the result of forbidding the burying-alive of lepers; and lepers have families of young children: there can be no doubt, that we were right in doing what we did, but we have to cope with the consequences. Well-intentioned, benevolent people in England have commenced a system of worrying the people of India about their Marriage-Customs, their use of stimulants, and sedatives, and now a palpable injustice has been inflicted on a great Country with a population of 275 Millions for the benefit of the Manufacturing interests of the small population of England by forbidding British India to tax imports from Lancashire. The Native Press is active, unbridled, and outspoken. Up to this time there has been no breach of the absolute enforcement of Religious Toleration, and of the respect to the Customs having the force of Law.

Now it is clear, that nothing but Legislation can remove the disabilities, or such portion of them, as come within the scope of Legislation. This implies, that a pressure is desired to be brought upon the India Office, and the Viceroy, to move them to "do something": what? To get up an association, analogous to the Anti-Opium-Society, would be the worst possible policy: it would exasperate both the Government, and the People Governed: who should bring the Pressure to bear? The Missionaries of the Church of England are inconsiderable, when brought into comparison with those of the Church of Rome, the Nonconformist Churches of India, the Churches of Continental Europe, Scotland, and America; and it would be impossible to act in concert with the Church of Rome, and very difficult to act in unison with the other Protestant Churches, who might suggest methods and remedies, which the Church of England could not approve of. To my knowledge one Nonconformist Church insists upon Converts breaking all previous Marriage-Contracts, and starting fresh in life with a new Christian wife. Such was in fact the practice of Jewish Converts in London, when admitted into the Church of England, until only a few years ago, when I helped to stop the practice.

Nor would the difficulty end here: We base our claim to Justice on the highest grounds, that a man or woman should not be deprived of their consorts and children on account of a change of their Religious Conceptions: this would apply equally to the Hindu, who became a Mahometan, or a Brahmo-Somájist, or an Arya-Somájist, or a Theosophist, or a Mormon, or a Unitarian, or any new form of Faith. The Mahometans settle the matter absolutely by declaring the Marriage-Contract made between Mahometans void, if one or other of the contracting parties cease to be Mahometan, and that condition is a matter of general notoriety. The Contract of Marriages between Hindus is indissoluble, but the Christian Convert is deprived of the society of his wife, and care of his children: this circumstance is also a matter of general notoriety. There is no legal process available for restitution of Conjugal Rights, nor would the Government dare to order the Police to seek for the wife, as for an offender, and make her over to her husband: such a course would be illegal now, and such Legislation is impossible. I put the question to the Laity and Clergy of England: if any of you had a daughter married to a man, who suddenly became a Mormonite, or a Mahometan, or joined one of the Sects, which deny the Divinity and Atonement of Christ, would not the Parents and Relatives of the wife do their best fairly, or foully, to save the wife and the little children from what appeared to them a frightful contamination? Now to my certain knowledge such is the feeling of the Hindu, and Mahometan, Parents and Relatives, when the man, to whom one of their family is married, becomes a Christian.

The alternative is to set the man free from the Marriage-Contract, and enable him to marry somebody else. As regards the Conversion to Christianity of a Hindu this has been done. In 1864-65 a Law to this effect was passed, while I was a Member of the Legislative Council of the Viceroy, and in spite of my strenuous opposition. The Hindu Convert to Christianity can cite his wife to appear before the Magistrate in camera, and to express her individual feelings on the subject, and to listen to the conciliatory advice of the Magistrate: if she does not return to her husband within a year, he is at liberty to re-marry. This presupposes, that the Magistrate is a Christian: this was the case in 1864-65: it is not likely, that a Hindu, or Mahometan, Magistrate would give advice in the sense desired by the Christian Convert.

As regards Converts to Christianity from Mahometanism no analogous law has been passed: I have consulted my friend Sir William Muir, who is an authority on such matters, and he agrees with me, that the Converts from Mahometanism should have the same privileges as the Converts from Hinduism.

So much for the Marriage-Contract: if the wife herself elects, or is compelled by her Relatives, to abandon the society of her husband, the Marriage-Contract must be declared cancelled. Personally I am, and was always, opposed to this Law: in the Missionary-Conference at Lahore in 1861 I opposed any interference; in the Legislative Council of the Viceroy in 1864 I opposed the Law, but it has been thirty years in force for the Hindu, and ought to be extended to the Mahometan.

As regards the custody of the Children of tender years, we may safely leave that question to the Courts of Law: the principles of *Jus paternum* are thoroughly understood. Protestant Missionaries should not condescend to enter into Lawsuits with non-Christians only for the sake of getting an influence over young children, and making them Christians. This is the well-known policy of the Church of Rome, which will spend hundreds of Pounds to get a child out of the clutches of Dr. Barnardo : if a man wants the custody of his children, let him sue for it ; the question of their Religion will depend on themselves.

An independent grievance is, that the Christian Convert, having become an outcast, is deprived of the use of the wells of the village. It must be recollected, that the water is drawn out of the well by letting down a brass vessel with a rope into the well, and this is a difficulty, for obviously the vessel of an outcast defiles the water from the point of view of ceremonial purity. But in most villages there are members of the sweeper, and other helot, classes, who are outcasts, and they must have some means of getting their water, which the neo-Christian should not be too proud to share. At any rate no Legislation in this question is possible. The wells were made by Hindus, or Mahometans, and are kept in repair by them, and the lawful Custom of the majority of the inhabitants must be respected. The Christian Converts must seek another dwelling-place. The Master has spoken on this subject also.

In Southern India tyrannical rules are put forward, compelling so-called outcasts to wear such-and-such a kind of dress, or abstain from wearing it ; to give way to a caste-man in the Public Road : such Customs must die out : the Christian Convert is quite able to vindicate his rights on such matters in the Courts of Justice.

A great lesson is being taught to the whole population by the entire absence of any distinction of individuals, one from another, in the State-Railways, Ferries, Schools, Hospitals, and Courts of Justice.

The conclusion, that I have arrived at, after careful reflection, is, that it is not expedient for the Board of Missions to move in this matter. The Native Churches in India are quite strong enough, if they have a grievance, to state it by Petition to the Governors of their Province, or to the Legislative Council, and to ventilate the matter in their own Public Press, or in Public Meetings called for the purpose. It it utterly impossible to concede anything to a Christian Convert, which is not conceded to any other Native of India, who changes his Religious Belief. Such a policy would be unworthy of the character of the Government, and the settled convictions of the Nineteenth Century. As stated above, large tribes of Hindus during the Mahometan Empire accepted Mahometanism, and are still in possession of their ancestral lands. Large numbers of Hindus have in times past seceded from their Ancestral Religion, and Practices, and have become Sectarians, such as the Sikhs of the Panjáb, and many others less well-known : they have kept their ancestral lands. There is now a new crop of Religious Beliefs, entirely non-Christian, such as the Brahmo-Somáj, Arya-Somáj, neo-Buddhist, Theosophist, Mormonite, Unitarian: they have all a right to the same civil privileges: before long, or even while I write, we shall have Christian Converts, of whom the Missionaries have made much account, passing into one of the new-fangled Beliefs: if the English Christian Official either by legislative authority, or executive power, tears away the children of Christian Converts from the homes of their non-Christian Relatives, what will the feelings of the Christian Church be, when the families of Christian Converts are torn away from the Christian village, and handed over to Mormonites, and Theosophists? In the proclamation of the Queen, 1858, when taking over India from the East India Company, it is distinctly stated, that we must do unto others, as we should wish men to do unto us. We are in an epoch of Intellectual, and Religious, change: when a Native Christian wishes to marry the sister of his deceased wife, and his own Pastor will not marry them, he merely joins another flock of neo-Christians, where this license is allowed, and gets married. It appears to me quite impossible for the Board of Missions of but a fragment of the great Missionary-Army to take any steps in the matter.

It does not follow, that the power of Christian Europe will continue very much longer in India. It would be a fatal error to leave Christianity in a "White Man" guise. Of all Religions in the World Christianity is allowed by those, who study Religion scientifically, to be the one, which has the greatest power of adapting itself to the religious wants of individuals, nations, and successive generations of mankind, or in other words to be the most "elastic and comprehensive": it has no "Kaaba-stone," like Mahometanism, to tie it to Arabia; no Pagan illusions, which it cannot get rid of, like Buddhism. The Government of India has always acted as the benevolent, and impartial, Ruler of its subjects, and it may be depended upon, as willing to give relief to all those, who can themselves show cause. Nothing could be so fatal to the permanence of Christianity amidst the Millions of non-Christians, as the idea, that Christianity had powerful friends, and advocates, in Europe, that it was the "White Man's" Religion: if that idea gained ground, it would fade away with the decay of European Secular Power, instead of flourishing for ever with indigenous vitality, as the Church of Christ.

ROBERT N. CUST,

Honorary Lay Secretary of Board of Missions of Province of Canterbury.

June 12th, 1894.

THE MATABÉLE-SCANDAL

AND ITS CONSEQUENCES:

BY ONE WHO

(1) REMEMBERS THE PUNISHMENT WHICH FELL UPON CAIN FOR KILLING HIS BROTHER, AND

(2) IS JEALOUS OF THE HONOUR OF GREAT BRITAIN.

"*Hast thou killed, and also taken possession?*"—1 *Kings*, xxi. 19.
What was the fate of Ahab?

Cave Cæsar, ne damnum accipias!
What was the fate of the Roman Empire?

CAMBRIDGE, FEBRUARY, 1894.

CONTENTS.

CHAP.		PAGE
I.	THE MISERABLE STORY	5
II.	DANGER TO THE EMPIRE OF GREAT BRITAIN	19
III.	INJURY TO THE MORAL CHARACTER OF THE BRITISH NATION	23
IV.	SURVEY OF AFRICA	29
V.	MEETINGS IN LONDON AND AT CAPE TOWN: INTERESTS OF THE BRITISH TAXPAYER	35
VI.	CONCLUSIONS	40

CHAPTER I.

The Miserable Story.

The British Tiger has tasted blood, and returns to the banquet of blood, as usual, under the mask of the highest benevolence. Last year was distinguished by the unjustifiable conduct of the agents of the Eastern Equatorial African Company in annexing Uganda, and slaughtering the Roman Catholic converts of the French Mission in Victoria Nyanza: that matter is not settled yet, but the usual pretences of abolition of the Slave-Trade, expansion of British commerce, possible colonization of white settlers in a region under the Equator line, and Heaven help the mark! the assistance to Christian Missionaries to preach the Gospel of Peace, and Love, were not wanting. The scene has now shifted to a portion of Africa, South of the Tropic of Capricorn, and another Chartered Company is in the field, cutting down the Matabéle, a section of the great Zulu race, plundering the country, and commencing to annex it, and confiscate the land for the purpose of settling British Colonists, and protecting the poor dear injured Mashóna: we all know what will be the position of such poor weak tribes, when the British settler is in possession, and has his heel down on them. The fate of the Maori, the Australian, the Tasmanian, and the Red Indian of North America, is well known.

The British taxpayer may well cry out to Mr. Rhodes, in the words put into the mouth of Achilles by Homer:

"What cause have I to war at thy decree?
"The Matabéle never injured me."

The Matabéle may well cry out in the words of the Hebrew, who resented the interference of Moses:

"Who made you ruler and judge over us?
"Wilt thou kill me, as thou didst the Egyptian yesterday?"

Unnecessary and dangerous interference in Egypt, unjustifiable invasion of Abyssinia, thoughtless and profitless annexation of Uganda, and now cruel and unjustifiable invasion of the Matabéle: such is the British record on the East Coast of Africa: National, Religious, and Human

Freedom has retired into the deserts of the Sudán, and there defies the British lion. The disgrace of Khartúm, and Majúba Hill, still have to be wiped out in blood. The Arab and the Boer still defy the British soldier and colonist. On the West Coast of Africa there is another Chartered Company quite ready to loose the dogs of war, if occasion offers, with a chance of booty. We read pleasant little notices, how Her Majesty's Commissioner is bombarding towns on the West Coast, accompanied by the slaughter of women and children, threats to devastate the whole country, and public hanging of a Native Chief: we are on the road back to the savage modes of warfare of barbarous ages. No quarter asked or given. Væ Victis!

If any other European State ventures to annex a region in Asia, Africa, or Oceania, there is an outburst of pious indignation on the part of the British Public: to Great Britain alone is reserved the right of invasion, confiscation, and annexation. The British are righteous in all their dealings: the French, Belgian, and Russians are unprincipled land-pirates. It is not unusual for Nations, as well as individuals, to be blind to their own defects, to see the mote in their neighbour's eye, but be blind to the beam in their own. Those, who for the last twenty years, have watched the progress of events in "Africa Unveiled," have kept a record of the thousands of women, children, and men, killed by the scientific Geographical Expeditions on the war-path across Africa, by the military expeditions on the North, East, South, and West: a town destroyed here, and abandoned, a village bombarded there: a few thousands of brave, ignorant, all but naked men, mowed down with arms of precision, and Gatling guns: behind them comes the importer of alcoholic liquors, a new engine of misery to take the place of the Slave-Trade: if Saul, the soldier, has killed his thousands, David, the Gin-Distiller, has killed his tens of thousands. The object of Great Britain is, apparently, to destroy the manhood of Africa, and we have set about it in earnest: Amurath to Amurath succeeds.

The device of Chartered Companies is an ingenious one: it is to supply a kind of buffer of crime. War is not declared in the usual way, and the Company does the work as a private concern, and reports the butcher's bill, and the expenses, to its own commercial constituents. The late Lord Chief Justice Ellenborough, in his famous decision, laid down clearly what was the moral position of a Company: in a suit an unfortunate defendant urged, that the plaintiff, a great Company, had *no conscience*: "Conscience," said the learned Judge, "how can a Company have a conscience, when it has no soul to be saved, and no backside to be kicked?" This is a great truth, to which the Baganda, and the Matabéle, bear unwilling testimony.

There is a kind of grim pleasantry in the transaction: while on the East of Africa we are slaying with the sword, and on the West poisoning with the demijohn of gin, up goes from Exeter Hall a sanctimonious cry for the abolition of the Slave-Trade, and the conversion of the poor African to Christianity. Is this the way to recommend the Gospel of Peace? The Mahometan invaded Africa accompanied by the Slave-Trade, but without the alcoholic liquour, which to him was abomination. The Christian invades Africa with the liquour-cup, and Maxim-guns, and downright slaughter, and then makes a pretence of open bibles, Christian schools, and slaves set free. The British public enjoyed last month the spectacle of an Irish Bishop in Westminster Abbey encouraging the policy of slaughtering the Matabéle: it is a singular fact, that Mr. Rhodes, the great South African Napoleon, contributed largely to the Parnell-fund to set Ireland free from the British yoke, and yet is foremost in the policy of annexing new Irelands in South Africa: wiser, however, than our fathers, he kills down the indigenous races, and confiscates their land: Queen Elizabeth was foolish enough to let the Irish live, and retain their land; so centuries afterwards we rue the consequences of this merciful policy: Bishop Alexander, of Derry, takes the opposite view, and denounces the idea of freeing Ireland from the British yoke: he still clings to the Upas-Tree of Protestant Ascendancy, and yet he has the singular boldness to urge in an English pulpit a new policy of unprovoked spoliation: and why? because he has a son-in-law among the adventurers. The wife of the Bishop of the Diocese of Mashónaland writes confidingly to *The Times* to ask for subscriptions to maintain School, Chapels, and Nurses, as if the whole country had not been occupied by an invading army, as if thousands of the males had not been slaughtered, leaving widows and orphans to mourn their loss, and detest the foreign invaders, who pretend to come for their good, but more particularly for their goods and chattels. The Bishop of Derry admits that the mothers of the Matabéle are in all cases Mashóna women.

Is any word printed in the Daily Newspapers, is any thought entertained by the readers of those Newspapers, of the welfare of the people of the country, of the occupants of the soil? who made us rulers and judges of the shortcomings of the Matabéle? Are we in these last days commissioned to kill off native races as vermin? It is well to have a giant's strength, but not to use it as a giant. "Am I my brother's keeper'?" said Cain: the modern Cain goes in to be the destroyer of any portion of the human race, that stands in his way. In the history of Britain our sympathies are with the early Britains, savages though they were, in the invasion of this Island by the Saxons, the Danes, and the Normans: we feel for King Alfred in his troubles, and there is a halo round all brave patriots, who have lived and died for their native lands; and up to this time there has been a hatred for ruthless invaders whether warriors, or adventurers: but public sentiment has changed now; the British lay claim to be the chartered libertines of the uncivilized World. The Sixth, and the Eighth, commandments do not apply to Chartered Companies, or Scientific Expeditions on the War-Path. But there is a day of Judgment for all that, *for all that*: and, if the House of Commons lets these kind of transactions pass, there is still a higher tribunal, to which slaughtered and expatriated Africans may appeal: their blood will cry out.

I hear from a friendly pen what is the policy. This is the style of writing in an English periodical of a "fin du siècle" Briton, Mr. Theodore Bent.

"Nothing but making a clean sweep of the Matabéle out "of the country, and driving them across the Zambési, can "settle the matter: then, if a series of forts is constructed "to prevent their return, Mashónaland, and *Matabéle land*, "may hope for a time of peace and prosperity."

The Roman historian centuries ago describes a settlement of this kind in the stinging words:

"Solitudinem faciunt, et Pacem appellant."

This is just how the Romans treated Spain, Gaul, Britain, Helvetia, and Germany, till the day of vengeance fell on them. The addition of the words Matabéle land show that the protection of the poor dear Mashóna would be not enough: to drive the Matabéle from their own country across the Zambési would indeed be robbing Peter to pay Paul: what would the Barotsi, and Bashukulumbi, and the British Colonies on Lake Nyasa say to such a policy?

there would be continual slaughter on the Zambési, such as in far away centuries there was on the Rhine and Danube. The ingenious device of building forts for protection was adopted by our ancestors, who erected the great Roman Walls, but their object was to keep the Picts and Scots out of Britain: but the modern Briton suggests a new use for such walls: to keep the lawful owners out of their own territory, which the modern Pict and Scot have by force appropriated.

But is the game worth the candle? the same writer tells us what makes the mouth of the adventurer, the volunteer, and colonist, water. Mashónaland contains forty thousand square miles suitable to colonisation by Europeans, having an *improving* climate (whatever that may mean) and already producing all manner of vegetables, but it is not fit for horses or cattle, being infected by the tetsé fly: but it is really the gold mines, on which the future of Mashónaland depends: without gold the country may be self-supporting, but not sufficiently rich to be valuable as a SPECULATION: so after all this great scheme of benevolence, these lofty notions of protecting the poor dear Mashóna, shrinks into " Auri sacra fames " an accursed thirst of gold, which led to the destruction of the inhabitants of the West Indian Islands by the Spaniard: the Mashóna would find themselves hewers of wood and drawers of water, workers in the mines, serfs, slaves, and vermin, encumbrances of the soil, and they would not last long: another Mr. Rhodes would polish them off.

Mr. Rider Haggard, who dwells in a region of airy romances, and charming intellectual creations of his versatile genius, of which I am an unfeigned admirer, in his letter to the *Times*, is surprised, that educated men, as some of us claim to be, experienced in public affairs, and accustomed for the space of a quarter of a century to maintain a gentle, yet firm, rule of subject Millions in India, during periods of War, Mutiny and Peace, should have such weakness of moral knees, *such enlargement of the political heart* (whatever that term may mean): he fears that such critics, whom he kindly describes as " agitated " old ladies," have " lost their grip of every principle of " common sense, and law of human nature." One remarkable reason he gives for Mr. Rhodes' policy is, that it has injured the Transvaal, and that, if Mr. Rhodes had not been on the alert, the Dutch Boers and the Portuguese, would have laid their hands on these auriferous districts: he remarks, that the only claim, which the Matabéle had to their territory, was that of the "spear:" is not the British power founded on the "big ship, the rifle, and the cannon?" The sight of these brave men hurling their naked bodies upon the white soldiers' bullets, moved even Mr. Haggard to pity. The "New Sentiment," as he describes it, turns out to be a very old one, that the robbing of land is own brother to the picking of pockets, and that Murder is slaying one of God's creatures, whether done by a garotter in London Streets, or by a scratch pack of Police, Colonists, and adventurers, under the command, Heaven help the mark! of a Medical Man, who superintends the infliction of wounds, instead of the healing. Atropos for Lucina came: Vishnu the Preserver instead of Siva the Destroyer. That, which is morally wrong, can never be politically right, whether the author of that wrong is the Emperor of Russia, the President of the French Republic, or Mr. Rhodes: and it is certain, that a Nemesis will follow the commission of wrong. The late Archbishop of Armagh remarked to me in Dublin, in 1892, that we were suffering in Ireland in this century for the wrongs inflicted on the Irish race in the last and the preceding century: and the shadows of the slaughtered victims of the Chartered Companies in Victoria Nyanza, and Matabéleland, will rise up against the British Nation in the hour of her peril, and decadence, which may be nearer at hand than the thoughtless now imagine.

The Society of Friends have spoken out in their memorial to the Government: their words are worthy of record: having been oppressed themselves in past centuries they feel for those, who are oppressed at the present epoch, whatever may be the colour of their skins, or the standard of their civilization. "We have been deeply "pained by the information communicated in the public "Press of the appalling slaughter, which has taken place "in Matabéleland by the armed forces of the Chartered "Company of South Africa. We strongly feel, that such "methods of prosecuting commercial enterprise are entirely "incompatible with the Christian religion, and we regard "it as a disgrace to our nation's profession of Christianity, "that in this, as in so many preceding instances, the "settlement of our countrymen as colonists in uncivilized "lands has been accompanied by wars of extermination. "We would press upon the Government the importance "in any future arrangements of doing nothing to sanction, "or facilitate, such military interference with the rights "and liberties of native races, children with ourselves of "one common Father. In view of the responsibilities "now devolving on our Government, we trust, that its "action may be directed to insuring the treatment of the "Matabéle, not in a spirit of hostility and greed, but of "justice, humanity, and mercy. We believe, that this "policy of justice and humanity is not only right in itself, "but is absolutely essential, if Great Britain is to be able "with any effect to exercise her influence, to prevent "similar high-handed encroachment on native races by "other civilized Powers." Mr. Gladstone's reply contains the following words :—" In any case I can assure you, that "we heartily share the desire of the Society of Friends, "that the Matabéle should be treated with justice, humanity "and mercy. I remain, dear Mr. Ellis, faithfully yours, "W. E. Gladstone."

The International League of Arbitrators has also protested against these acts of Buccaneering, and appeals to the Queen to stop all further effusion of blood, the extermination of the poor Africans, and the confiscation of their lands either by the Chartered Company, or by the adventurers in its service. Sir Wilfred Lawson remarked: "We are for an honest England, just and "humane." There is much reason to fear, that many of the Members of the House of Commons have shares in the Company actual or prospective. Other countries act in a different way: the Sandwich Islands are but the point of a pin in the great Pacific, but the President of the United States remarks, that the treatment of the Government of the Queen by the American Minister was a plain violation of International Law, and he disavows it, and condemns the offending American citizens, and endeavours to restore lawful authority. Is Great Britain to sanction the enormities committed by Mr. Rhodes? The Congregational Union has also protested against the injustice done to the Matabéle, insisting, that it is the duty of Britons to set an example of Justice and Humanity in their relation with uncivilized tribes, and begging the Government to interfere and protect the rights of the Matabéle, and protect the British Nation from the shame of in any way giving way to a pack of self-seeking adventurers, who were quite indifferent to the rights of a more feeble Nation.

The Primitive Methodists have also remonstrated. The "Christian," a well known journal, remarks, "that to treat "the so-called barbarous tribes, as if there were no distinc- "tion between Good and Evil, amounts to justify all the "infamous transactions, which in past centuries have dis- "graced mankind, and swept away all traces of many "primitive races: Such a shocking policy must re-act "on the moral views of the Conqueror, and efface from "their ideas all value of Human life."

The Marquis of Ripon received at the Colonial Office a deputation from the Aborigines Protection Society with reference to affairs in Matabéleland. The deputation submitted that, "even if the British South Africa Company has been allowed in its relations with the Mashóna and other subject tribes, as well as with the Matabéle, to usurp greater power, than it was entitled to under its charter, it is competent for her Majesty's Government to limit the company's operations hereafter to equitable exercise of the functions marked out by its concessions, and to reserve or restore to the Crown direct and complete control over the general affairs of the vast district, which has now practically become a part of the British dominions. As it was probable, that the intervention of the rainy season and other causes will delay for at least a few months the settlement on a pacific basis of affairs in Matabéleland, the Government should not allow the interval to be occupied in the development of arrangements prejudicial to the interests of the natives, and it should, with the least possible delay, take upon itself the duty of actively controlling the course of events."

Lord Ripon expressed his entire sympathy with the deputation: he was opposed to the principle of Chartered Companies: the public opinion of South Africa must also be considered, though Mr. Rhodes and his Company had no Sovereign rights, and that nothing could be done as regards the settlement of the country without the sanction of Her Majesty's Government.

There is no evidence whatever, that some of the poor Africans mercilessly cut down were more than agriculturists, compelled to join in a national defence of their country and their lives. Great sympathy has been expressed for Captain Wilson and his party, who pushed on too far, were surrounded and killed: so it happened at Majúba Hill and Khartúm; sometimes in a house in London armed intruders are killed by the infuriated householder, roused to madness to protect the lives of himself and his family, and his property. Those who fell had no commission from their Sovereign to wage war according to the manner of civilized warfare: they took no prisoners: they spared no one: the tigers, who leap into a fenced enclosure to get at the cattle, are killed. No one pities the tiger: shall we pity the man-tiger?

Mr. Selous in his letter on landing in Great Britain puffs up the brave men who fell, but he forgets, that it is not the dying, *but the cause for which Death is met*, that ennobles the dead. Mr. Selous has probably not studied the legacy of Hebrew, Greek, and Roman history, and the immortal songs over those, who fell fighting against Sisera, and the Ammonites, invading the land of the Hebrews, or the Greek youths who fell at Thermopylæ to save Athens, and over the Romans who fell fighting against Hannibal. Great Imperial Nations must have Imperial instincts; the highest self-control, an entire absence of greed and lust for gold, a pity for the wounded and slain. Rhodes' emissaries had no such pity, or self-restraint. Gold, Gold, Gold: Pasture-land was their object: adventurers from the Mother Country wanted to amass fortunes. Do we feel any pity for the Italian and Sicilian bandits, who are cut down by the National troops in the act of pillage and rapine?

No sooner is the fighting over than we come into scenes worthy of the camp followers or suttlers of a great army: the soldiers would not condescend to such actions.

"The volunteers, who have served during the campaign "are already selling their rights to farms, at prices varying "from £40 to £60. A large number of wagons, loaded "with goods, are now on their way up to Matabéleland. "Horse sickness has broken out in that country."

"On the 22nd, at daybreak, a small force arrived with "a day's rations, and we ate like wolves, the whole lot at "one meal. Some of us went on patrol, and captured "600 head of cattle, and killed about a dozen Matabéle, "but were too weak to do more, physically and numerically "weak."

"Referring to the land settlement, Mr. Rhodes said, that "after the pioneers had made their choice, 3,000 morgen "would be allotted to each. The Chartered Company would "encourage settlers, but would sell no land under 3s. per "morgen."

"The pegging out of mining claims is proceeding rapidly. "Numerous old gold workings have been discovered. In a "fortnight or so I shall start *viâ* Tati, Palapye, Mafeking, "and Vryburg for the Cape, to stay there in the sun, for it "is midsummer there, for a month, and then home, sweet "home. My syndicate has got 90,000 acres of the best "grazing-land in the country. We are going to stock it at "once, and work it later on. I have got twenty miners' "claims, which a prospector here is going to peg out for me "on the main reef below Buluwáyo, as soon as possible. "My ten claims in Mashónaland will be pegged out before "Christmas, and all these things point to the fact, that the "year has not been wasted, but that I shall have to return "here, if necessary, next year, and certainly the year fol-"lowing."

A special communication to the *Cape Times* from Buluwáyo states, that since the throwing open of the country to settlers on December 15th, a good deal of land has been staked out for farms, amounting in the aggregate to 100,000 acres. Several promising gold-properties have also been " claimed."

The King's late secretary, who had been liberated on parole, has been arrested for inciting the friendly natives to waylay and murder the whites, who are prospecting near Buluwáyo.

I have been present in great battles, and celebrated campaigns, but I never heard of circumstances such as these even in an enemy's country.

It is distinctly stated by Mr. Alexander Bailey, of Johannesberg, in his letter to *The Times* of Nov. 6, 1893, that Lo-Bengúla's men were attacked and killed at Fort Victoria on July 18th, before any declaration of war, and notwithstanding this departure from all civilized precedent, Lo-Bengúla sent every white man, woman, and child safe out of his camp: he may be a barbarian, but he is not a monster. The Bishop of the Diocese, as Church Militant, joined the invading party, and in his letter to *The Times* he calls himself the Bishop both of the invaders and invaded: at any rate he seemed to sympathise with the invaders, and accepted a large grant of land confiscated from the other members of his diocese, " in partibus infidelium." He appears to be a survival of the Mediæval Bishops, who converted Europe by the help of the sword, and in the hope of grants of fat acres. I conclude that the sixth and eighth commandments are no longer read in his diocese, and the Books of Judges and Joshua are the parts of Scripture most suitable for distribution to the environment: the British and Foreign Bible Society will not publish such an edition.

In December, 1893, a Missionary entertained a Religious Committee with an account of Mashónaland, from which he was lately arrived. He stated that three (3) thousand acres of land had been granted to his Mission by the Chartered Company: when asked by one of the Committee what authority the Company had to give away land, which by ancient custom belonged to the tribe collectively, his reply was that Lo-Bengúla had made the concession in Mashónaland: in a few weeks the king, who granted this land, was turned out by the Company, and his kingdom annexed. The Missionary remarked, that the country round Fort Salisbury was very unhealthy, that everybody was down with fever, and that it was quite unfit for a European Colony, as all children died.

The words of the Bishop of Mashónaland are worthy of record, and are given in justice to himself. " Here at " Buluwáyo," the Bishop proceeds, " a trader's house has " been turned into a hospital, and two rooms are full of " Europeans only. Lobengúla, the Matabéle king, savage " as he is towards his own people and other natives, has " been most considerate in not allowing houses, belonging " to missionaries or traders, to be touched, or any European " who stayed in his country, while the fighting was going " on, to be injured. Even after Matabéle villages were " burnt by the Europeans on the line of march he made " no retaliation. He says he has given his word. I have " volunteered to go and see the King and try and arrange " something, that may bring peace to the people, and I " also wish to explain to him my neutral position. Before " he left Buluwáyo he asked where I was. He calls me " the ' Induna (captain) of the teachers.' They told him " they did not think that I was with the white men coming " into the country. He seems to have said something " expressing his satisfaction. No white man has tried to " get to see him yet. I thought that I could reach him, " but they think, that I should be killed by the regiments " round him, and so the offer that I made of going was " not encouraged. But I have left it open, as I think I " could explain sufficiently quickly even to those, who do " not know me. I do not know, that I should be of any " value to the Company by going, for I could only re- " commend Lobengúla to accept terms, that I consider as " advantageous to him as to them. I entirely and emphati-

"cally repudiate any share in the sentiment that 'the
"sword' is a necessary factor in the Christianizing of these
"savage nations, or that the only road for the preaching
"of Christianity is cleared by destroying their power; and
"I here distinctly assert, that no letter written or speech
"made urging on a war with the Matabéle has ever had
"any sympathy whatever from me. I hoped to the very
"last it would be avoided. The more rapid reception of
"Christianity may be the outcome of all this; but rapid
"reception is not always most solid. I can only trust
"that God will, in His good providence, overrule for good
"all that may be wrong." Still he does not see the gravity
of the case, for he tells us that he had Church-Parade,
and the Holy Communion afterwards. Did he recollect
the conduct of Ambrose, Bishop of Milan, who refused
entry into the Church to the Emperor Theodosius, whose
hands were dyed in blood?"

The *Cape Town Times* of October 18, 1893, gives a letter from one of the volunteers hired at Cape Town for the purpose of murder and spoliation:

"I am one of the Frontier Police: there are sixty of
"us: we are encamped four miles from Fort Victoria: we
"are to receive no pay after we have crossed the frontier,
"but to any of us, who outlive the scrimmage, will be given

"(1) Three thousand (3000) acres of pasturage land
  "in Matabéleland.
"(2) Five (5) shares in a gold mine.
"(3) A share of the plundered cattle, etc. Power of
  "sale, or hypothecation of the shares to the
  "Company, is reserved."

This implied, that the whole country was to be parcelled out among the invading army: no one cared for the Matabéle, and at the time, that this iniquitous engagement was made, war had not been declared. The terms of the engagement carry us back to the simple time of Deborah and Barak, when the mother of Sisera expected her son's army to come back "each with a Hebrew damsel "or two." Women in Matabéleland do not go for much, and can always be purchased for six head of cattle. The mothers and wives of the slaughtered Matabéle were all Mashóna women, so there must have been a plethora of widows in the market.

A correspondent of the *Gazette de Lausanne*, who has been settled several years in South Africa, and who apparently is not of the Rhodes-party, and clearly has not come in for a share of the mines, or of plundered cattle, or rich pasturage, writes that at the cost of some expenditure of men and money, the Company has become absolute proprietor of Matabéleland and Mashónaland: the Colonists will now cultivate their land without danger: the Miners will dig out their gold without hindrance: the Shareholders at home will touch large dividends: the influence of Great Britain, or possibly of the Africander Republic, will become supreme in South Africa. If to attain this object it has been necessary to confiscate the land of several thousand blacks, to cut down and massacre the native soldiery, these are mere incidents of British Christian Colonial life. There will be a cry in Exeter Hall: there will be a few Newspaper-Articles, and a few Pamphlets, and then no more will be thought of it: the wheels of the Jagarnath car of British Christian Civilization will pass over the lifeless bodies, and the incident will be forgotten. The success will be made the most of, and the means used will only be spoken of in a whisper. The black must give way to the white: the African Bantu to the European Anglo-Saxon. No one dreams of applying the maxims of the Rights of Nations to Africa: Some may think, that principles of Justice and Right should apply to all God's poor children, without reference to their colour or culture, and that a brown or black man is still made in God's image: Mr. Rhodes' friends class them among the "feræ naturæ."

The war, and the scheme of annexation, was clearly planned long before: there was no sudden conjuncture of circumstances compelling a desperate policy, as sometimes happens. Agents of the different Syndicates, jealous of each other, had come from London to accompany the forces, and lay hold of their shares of the "loot:" the war was settled upon long before any "casus belli" was formulated, before the tender hearts of the adventurers were touched by the woes of the poor Mashóna, the maternal relations of the Matabéle: all the friends of the Company were ready for the snatching. The British Nation has often—too often—extinguished the Sovereign rights of Native Potentates, *ex.g.* the Panjab, Oudh, and Burma, but the subjects of the ejected Potentates have retained their private property: nothing so mean has occurred in the annals of Great Britain as this new phase of Annexation. The Germans conquered the French Provinces of Alsace and Lorraine, but did not expropriate private owners.

In December, 1890, Mr. Maund, one of the Pioneers of South Africa, three years ago spoke in the following terms to the Chamber of Commerce of London: that in addition to the cultivated and pastoral land, the out-turn of gold would make Mashónaland one of the richest acquisitions of the British Empire, and that there would be a rush of immigrants in that direction without parallel in the History of Africa.

Mr. Colquhon's utterance is as follows: He had faith in Mashónaland and Matabéleland, and believed, that the Colony founded in 1890, with settled government replacing a cruel and despotic barbarism, was destined to be the home of hundreds of thousands of our fellow-countrymen. This was no vulgar annexation to gratify territorial greed. (Cheers.) The extension of our Empire was a national and a social necessity; and wherever, *without violating conventions or existing rights*, we could prepare the way for our kindred to live and spread under conditions, which promise prosperity, it was the most urgent of all duties to seize such opportunities as they arose. The Providence, which had guided our destiny so far, had by the mere force of circumstances rendered our Imperial duties imperious duties. For we were not as other nations are. Not only were our own islands too small for our people, but the course of our commerce and industry had been such, that we were increasingly dependent for their maintenance on a trade, against which incessant war was waged, as if we were the Ishmael of civilized nations. As we could not grow our own food, we must either send our people to distant countries in search of it, or find ever new customers for our manufactures. We, in fact, resorted to both alternatives, but were still not able to keep pace with the national growth of our people and the requirements of advancing civilization. There was no object, which a British statesman could set before himself comparable to the central necessity of providing for the development of our own race. If that were a national selfish policy, might our statesmen be saturated with such selfishness. And no nobler contribution to the ways and means of such a development had ever come across the national path than this opening up of South Africa, which was to crown a century of Imperial achievement.

CHAPTER II.

Danger to Great Britain's Empire.

There was a period in the History of the Great Roman Empire, when the wise councillors of the wise Emperor Adrian recommended, that the limits of the Empire should be fixed and surrounded by a wall of Military Posts: otherwise they saw breakers ahead, and that the great Empire "mole ruit suâ": thus the River Euphrates, the Danube, the Libyan Desert, the Atlantic, and Britain, were declared to be the boundaries. Let Great Britain pause and think. Take care, Cæsar, lest you suffer loss! Large Colonies are ready to break away: India is only held as a man holds a wolf by its two ears. It is well to have the strength of a Colossus, but not to use it like the Colossus of Rhodes: our sons may blush at the conduct of their sires at this epoch, for we have arrived at the parting of the ways. Francis I of France, after the battle of Pavia, wrote to his mother that he had "lost everything "but Honour": we are in a fair way of losing all, including Honour, as well as the sense of Christian Justice betwixt Man and Man. At the time, when the hungry classes of the British Nation are looking with eager eyes at the lands, and accumulated property of the wealthier classes, we are giving them object-lessons in murder and annexation: the appropriation of other people's property is a tendency, which is attractive, and the proletariat of the 20th Century may well point to our conduct in Africa, of the disappearance of "meum" and "tuum," and the necessity of a new distribution of material resources. What is sauce to the goose is sauce to the gander: If spoliation be legitimate in the green tree of the infantine civilization of Africa, how much more appropriate it is in the old dead tree of worn out European Society! Mr. Rhodes is an arch-socialist, and desires the happiness of the many, and I admit that there are strong arguments in his favour, if worked out in their entirety. We had better have left Africa alone, and not spent so much money in redeeming Slaves, if we intended to enter on a career of slaughter and spoliation by the aid of Chartered Companies. The last state of Africa will be worse than the first.

Already the good ship "Great Britain" is overladen, and in Asia, Africa, Oceania, and America a time of trial is at hand. When a Province is cut away from France, the population of that Province cannot be reconciled to the divorce: witness Lorraine and Alsace: when a Colony or Province is given up by Great Britain, it gladly accepts the change: witness the Ionian Islands, the United States, and the desire of Ireland to dissolve a union of six Centuries and to get away. In the case of a European war what would be our position? our interests are spread over an enormous area: our Colonies are held to the Mother-Country by a thread ready to snap: British India is on a volcano, held by a vast British Army, which owing to the climate sensibly wastes every year, and has to be supplemented by drafts of fresh soldiers. Of what profit imperially, except for the purpose of boasting, are Uganda or Matabéleland? will the inhabitants, who wear no clothes at present, consume our manufactures, if any inhabitants at all in the latter country survive the introduction of British Colonists. Up to this time liquour has not been admitted, but the Distillers are on the march, and the arrival of the first Demijohn of Gin may soon be expected. Liquour accompanies the British Colonists just as fleas accompany the dog, and the tick accompanies the sheep: they cannot exist without each other, and the natives fall ready victims to the new and seductive drink of the white man, so much stronger and more deadly than their own.

And yet we read what a young Settler writes home, that his parson calls the Company's Military enterprise an "Apostolic Mission," and that South African sentiment "is pretty well voiced by that reverend gentleman:" we in England are hardly convinced of the justice of the shameless attack on Lo-Bengúla's kraal, though justifiable on principles of African Warfare. "First come, first kill," is scarcely apostolic, or even British, in its character. It has more of the reputed character of the Zulu, or Ashanti, king. The periodical, from which we quote, writes "that "it looks very much, as if Mr. Rhodes had made up his "mind, that the Matabéle horde must be smashed, and that "since the Home Government would not let him begin the "process, unless he were first attacked, he did not need or "want to wait for more than formal provocation. Mr. "Rhodes is represented as the very embodiment of "commercial unscrupulousness, only eager to extend the "domain or bolster up the fortunes, or *avert the exposure* "of the British South African Company, and careless what "lofty purpose he simulates, or what *blood he causes to be* "*shed*: on the other side he is called the apostle of "civilization, the patron of Christian Missions, who is "engaged in executing long delayed *Justice* on a murderous "and treacherous people." Perhaps the term, Political Opportunist, will suit him: We quote the above words, but do not endorse them: we care nothing for the Company, but very much for Africa.

The Hospital Nurses at Fort Salisbury write, that Mr. Rhodes is the darling of fortune, and that blind goddess does not often select men of his stamp for the Sunday School: this opinion is a sweet admixture of Paganism and Christianity. Some call him the Colossus of Rhodes, some the modern Napoleon, or Cortes: shall we add Dick Turpin? Some propose to give him the same title, that was granted to Scipio, and call him Africanus. Mr. Selous, the well-known traveller, is credited with the gift of "never telling a lie," which is but faint praise to a man who is a gentleman, unless Truth is a rare gift in South Africa. But of the Colossus of Rhodes himself it may be well asserted, that he does bestride this narrow world, while his friends the Doctor, the Captain, and the "great slaughterer of great game in Africa" walk under his huge legs, and annex territories with a wave of the lancet larger than France and Italy united.

One thing is clear, that the power of waging war must in future be reserved absolutely and exclusively to Her Majesty's Government, or delegated Governor, such as the Viceroy of India. The character of the Empire must not be left in the hands of such men, however fit they may be to conduct the affairs of a Commercial Company, or to bleed a Patient in the Hospital.

But it may be retorted, that these new Companies of the 19th Century are but following the steps of the Great Company of the last two Centuries, which conquered British India. The circumstances were totally different: the East India Company began as a Commercial Company: when Empire was forced upon her, she ceased to be Commercial and became Imperial: there was no land-grabbing, no mining for gold, no stealing the property of the Natives: Look round India, and point out the European Colonist, who has ousted any Indian from his land, his home, and his rights. Ask whether the population has shrunk. Does not the last Census show, that it increases thirty Millions in a decade, that all the vast waste land, which we found in the plains, are now occupied by indigenous cultivators. If there were fighting, there was the fair fighting of civilized Nations: if there were Native Chiefs, they were warned to abstain from doing such things, as we the paramount power disapproved of, before they were attached: they were not driven across the boundary-Rivers, and their lands made over to Britons. Many of their Chiefs were sprung from the people quite as barbarous, quite as unscrupulous, quite as much at the mercy of their troops, as Lo-Bengúla is described as being, yet no such exterminating barbarous policy was adapted to them as is now proposed. Lo-Bengúla might have been talked over: the example of Chetewayo should have warned us: the example of Khama, once quite as great a savage as Lo-Bengúla twenty years ago, should have encouraged us: but that would not suit the Colonist: his was an earth-hunger: he wanted the land itself, and its potential vegetable and mineral resources, not the Government of the country, which satisfied the East India Company.

CHAPTER III.

INJURY TO THE CHARACTER OF THE BRITISH NATION.

CHARACTER does not go for much in these days: but still amidst all classes, as in all clubs, there is a standard, which if transgressed causes ostracism and expulsion.

We have to think of the effect of these proceedings on the population of these Islands: the Roman populace got accustomed to the sight of blood by the never ending slaughter of men and beasts in the great Flavian Amphitheatre: it gave them a taste for blood: the women did not shrink from seeing a dagger thrust through the bosom of an unsuccessful gladiator, whom they might have saved by a motion of their hand: our daily papers tell us how these volunteers slew their hundreds: Britons read in the train with a kind of wild interest, how the poor naked Africans were shot through and their bodies left to the fowls of the air: it sounds like one of Rider Haggard's novels. It is notorious, that there is no authority from the Sovereign for these misdoings: the Premier in the House of Commons tells us, that he has no certain information of what has been done. There is a kind of solemn glory, that surrounds real war, when Nation meets Nation: we feel sure, that there will be no killing in cold blood of ambassadors; no giving the *coup de grace* to poor wounded fellows on the field, for it must be noted, that the victorious army in South Africa is not encumbered with prisoners, and has no field-hospitals for the wounded: it is out on the war-path pure and simple: the Doctor packs away his lancet, and buckles on his sword and pistol: all this hardens the public mind. In the same issue of the *Times*, that records the slaughter of the Matabéle by the Company's agents, we have in another column the annual report of the commercial proceedings of the Company, and the dividend liquidated in blood. The name of Lo-Bengúla will go down to posterity in the same bracket with that of Boadicea, Caractacus, and the Athenians, and Romans, who died to protect their country from the invader. It matters not on the ground of Morality, and on the unchanging law of Right and Wrong, that Lo-Bengúla was a barbarous Chief on the lowest round of human civilization, whose father Moselitcatze had risen from the rank of a common Zulu spearsman to the position of a King: Ranjit Sing, the Lion of the Panjáb, the reputed father of Duleep Sing, did the same. It matters a great deal on the score of Morality, that this unprincipled invasion of an independent territory is made from the most sordid, and lucre-desiring, motives by the agent of a Chartered Company, assuming the authority of the Sovereign of a great, highly civilized, Christian country, which places Religion before Lust, and Justice before arbitrary Spoliation; at least it has hitherto been supposed to do so. The throne of the Queen is based on Righteousness.

Mr. Rider Haggard attacks those, who have spoken out, such as the Editor of *Truth*, as enemies, and maligners of their own country: but such is not the case. The House of Commons have not as yet accepted this policy of Murder and Rapine: the great director of the Company has not yet been made a Baronet, though he has qualified himself for the honour by providing himself with a bloody red hand independent of the Herald's office. It is very well for a Missionary of the London Missionary Society to state in the Newspapers, that the Matabéle are worthless and incorrigible. Are all worthless folk to be destroyed on that plea? Is it well to wade through slaughter to a gold mine? Was every possible expedient of conciliation exhausted? Should we apply such principles to the men on strike in the coal mines, the Anarchists, and Socialists, of this country? The poor ignorant Matabéle acted in entire ignorance of the change of environment, which had happened to them: they had unconsciously passed over a great gulf of centuries as far as regards civilization.

The *Times*, in its issue of Nov. 24, goes too far: if Lo-Bengúla was so contemptible a power, that an M.D. with his lancet was able to dispose of him, then why all this sensational writing in its own columns? It is supposed, that the Matabéle bladder has been pricked by the lancet, and that the country is now open to the gold digger: but we read, that the great Zulu race spread Northward from Zululand, and under different names, Matabéle, Angóni, Wagangwára, even up to the confines of Victoria Nyanza, carried on their depredations: that the gangs were not all pure Zulu by race, though dressed, or undressed, as Zulu, for the youths of kindred tribes, who loved plunder rather than work, became enrolled in their ranks, so that in fact, a Zulu camp was a cave of Adullam. We may hear more of them still. It would have been safer to have followed the example of wiser statesmen, and have fixed some limits to the sphere of our ubiquitous interests. In the *Times* of Nov. 23, we read how that redoubtable chieftain, Capt. Lugard in his new book recommends the annexation of Zanzibar, and the extinguishment of the Arab interests on the Continent. Treaties do not go for much with such filibusters. When Lt. Mizon, and the French Press, put forward analogous claims, affecting the sacred, inviolate, twenty years old, rights of Great Britain, and hints are made as to the rights of France to Lake Chad, how deeply indignant is the British Press, and yet, when it suits an influential personage, a monied interest, a political party, to sweep away a nation, unhappily a black-skinned nation, scarcely a single person is found to beg for a little delay, and a calm consideration of the consequences.

In future generations, when the conduct of Britons of this century, their brutal treatment of inferior races and their unbounded rapacity, so shamelessly evidenced, their earth-greed, diamond-greed, gold-greed (quôcumque modô rem) is discussed, it will seem as nothing compared with the shameless hypocrisy of the middle classes, so-called pious, and making a pretence of benevolence, preaching peace, yet practising war, and hounding on their countrymen to plunder and rapine : there will be heard one or two voices asking, can this be right ? Have Britons received a commission from their God Mammon, analogous to that, which the Hebrews received by the voice of Moses, to occupy lands belonging to others, take possession of vineyards planted by others, and slay the owners of the soil ? Is it right to teach the young men, not soldiers by profession, but merely adventurers, and hunters of wild game, to whet their spears in African blood ? And yet after all, when Rhodes has disappeared it will be manifest, that there is a God, who judges the Earth, and the British Nation, to whom so much of material power and wealth has been granted, is required to evidence a much greater amount of self-restraint, noble abstention from blood and rapine. Can we do such great wickedness and sin against God ? Some humiliation would be the just punishment of this National sin.

It is no new idea, no bran-new conception of Mr. Rhodes' fertile genius, to kill out as vermin so-called inferior races for the sake of their land and their gold. The Spaniards were before us in the career of extermination :

what is Spain now? A telegraphic line from Majúba Hill to Khartúm would merely be a connecting link of shame. The Poet Horace writes nearly two thousand years ago of the

> "juvenum recens
> "Examen, Eois timendum
> "Partibus, oceanoque rubro."

Young men commencing their career as slaughterers of game, and then rising to the glory of slaughtering naked Africans. The English Poet Byron in his "Childe Harold" seems to have foreshadowed this, and his lines are readily parodied:

> There are the Matabéle all at play,
> Butchered to make Associations pay.

If anything can be worse than killing men to make a holiday, surely it is to kill them to run up the dividends of a Commercial Company. Another English Poet, Cowper, puts into the mouth of Boadicea, the Queen of the Britons, what may apply to Great Britain now:

> "Rome shall perish: write this world
> "In the blood which she has spilt:
> "Perish, hated, and abhorred:
> "Full of vengeance, full of guilt."

A Danish lady called a few days ago, and casually remarked on the wonderful success of the Matabéle-campaign: her hostess asked, whether she, being a foreigner, and free from National Chauvanism, had ever reflected on the criminal side of the proceedings. She naively remarked, that this view of the subject had not occurred to her: all that she knew about the matter was that she had invested all her savings in the "Rudd" portion of the South African Company, and that Mr. Rudd was a delightful man.

A lady called on another day, full of grief, because the son of a neighbour had been killed in Capt. Wilson's party: she spoke of the Matabéle-king as a murderer. Had the poor Matabéle, who were killed in hundreds, no Fathers or Mothers, or wives, or little children? and yet they were mowed down by Gatling guns, because they had the misfortune to tend their herds in a country with auriferous deposits.

The white man first approaches the African chief as a cringing mendicant, and asks humbly for leave to occupy certain portions of the tribal land. The African chief knows well enough, that he has no authority to give away an acre, yet he is tempted by pecuniary offers: he can neither read nor write: he is a helpless infant as far as legal matters: the mendicant then turns into a bully: if the Chief attempts to protect his own country, customs, and rights, he is called a barbarian: no doubt Julius Cæsar called the ancient Britons barbarians, and treated them as such. History repeats itself. Julius Cæsar was not a Christian: and the last century before Anno Domini cannot fairly be compared with the 19th century, A.D.

Then comes the difficulty of securing immunity to ambassadors: at any rate Lo-Bengúla has not failed here. He, however, sent ambassadors to the British camp: their fears were roused, and they attempted to escape: the sentries shot them down: of course it was a mistake.

Tati, Jan. 10.

"The investigation made by the court of inquiry into the circum-"stances of the shooting of Lobengula's envoys near this place has "resulted in the complete acquittal of the men concerned.

"Major Gould-Adams attributes the occurrence to the negligence "of Mr. James Dawson, who was in charge of the indunas, and his "omission to inform the officials, that Sir Henry Loch has asked "Lobengula to send envoys, and that they might, therefore, be "expected. The evidence agrees with the account given by Ingubu-"gubo, the King's brother."

If Lo-Bengúla had killed a white ambassador, *only by a mistake*, we should not have heard the end of it. A French officer appears to have been killed in another of our war-paths by a mistake on the part of the British forces: every kind of excuse is offered: if Africans are cut down by the hundred, who cares a straw? If an African chief starts on the war-path on his own account, to extend his dominion, he is called a barbarian, and an enemy of civilization: but if a British, or French, adventurer commits the same atrocity in a foreign country, specially in Africa, he is supposed to be full of benevolence, though he slay innocent thousands.

A continental Journal asks, whether there is any reason to believe that the Jacks and Toms, who have suddenly become not only rulers of Lo-Bengúla's kingdom, but owners of the soil of all his subjects, will be in any degree more just and considerate towards the ousted proprietors than the Matabéle were to the Mashóna in their day? Will they pay the men, who are forced to labour in their mines, and then are kept in confinement lest they should abscond? Do the enthusiastic adventurers of South Africa think, that the world was only made to serve their purposes, or in the Poet Wordworth's words:

"The grand old rule,
" Suffices us, the simple plan,
" That they should get, who have the power,
" And they should keep who can."

The Dukes of Abercorn and Fife are full of compliments to Mr. Rhodes for enhancing the value of the shares of their Company by working the mines so cheaply: How is it done? we dare not say. Other Colonists, having destroyed with their cannon the Matabéle Tribe, have taken possession of the boundless pasture grounds, their flocks, and metallic deposits, for the profit of the Company: Lucky shareholders! their shares are rising in value: they are laying up treasures, dabbled in blood, in this world: will it be well for them in the next? perhaps they are Sadducees and Agnostics, and have no future at all, at least for them. In a few years an important history will be written, very different from the eulogiums of Dukes, and hungry shareholders, under the title of

AURI SACRA FAMES.

No such lamentable incidents have occurred in the history of the British Nation during this century.

In the Critias of Plato (113 B.) the position of Great Britain seems to be described prophetically under the fable of Atlantis, an island outside the straits of Gibraltar of unrivalled greatness. Every product of the Earth was gathered to the harbours of this famous people, the protegees of Poseidon: their docks were of marble: their palaces and storehouses of stupendous size and beauty: their harbours were crowded with vessels from every quarter of the world, and filled day and night with the sound of the voices of merchants and the din of traffic. For a time they bore meekly the large measure of their prosperity. But at last the divine element within them was overpowered by base passions: Unjust aggrandizement, and lust of power, seemed to them the greatest of blessings, and they became blind to their own shame.

Vengeance fell upon them: convulsions of Nature took place, and the great Island beyond the pillars of Hercules sank beneath the Sea, and all were destroyed. They were unworthy of Liberty and Life, because they ceaselessly, for their own mean selfish objects, desired to destroy the Liberty and Life of others: they coveted other men's lands, goods, cattle, and gold, and lost their own, like great Tyre of old, and they disappeared hated and unlamented.

Let us take warning in time.

CHAPTER IV.

Survey of Africa.

BURKE in his denunciation of Warren Hastings, a century ago, spoke thus: "Animated with all the avarice of age, "and the impetuosity of youth, the Britons rolled into "India, one wave after the other, and there was nothing "before the eyes of the people of India but an endless, "hopeless prospect of a new flight of birds of prey with "appetites continually ravening for food, which was con- "tinually wanting: we boast now of living in an age, when "consciences are more sensitive, and in which there pre- "vails a greater regard for the rights of others than in "the past. I trust that our conduct as a people with "respect to India now may justify this boast."

What would Burke say now with regard to Africa? When Lord Aberdare quoted these words at the Royal Geographical Society in 1883, with regard to New Guinea, he, the President of the Niger Company, added "Let us "know more about these people, and not fall back on the "plea of ignorance to justify National indifference to the "violation of their rights, and the sacrifice of their lives." What does Lord Aberdare say with regard to Mr. Rhodes' proceedings?

Lord Palmerston wrote to Napoleon III. as follows: (quoted from *Fortnightly Review*, February 1887, p. 174) "How could we combine to become the unprovoked "aggressors, to imitate in Africa the partition of Poland, "the conquest of Morocco for France, of Tunis for Sardinia, "and of Egypt for England, and how could England and "France, who have guaranteed the integrity of the Turkish "Empire, turn round and wrest Egypt from the Sultan." What would Lord Palmerston say to Mr. Rhodes?

The Poet Pope, in his Epistles dating back nearly two hundred years, in describing the unhappy position of the North American Indians, then crushed out of existence by the white man, describes the hopes of those poor savages.

"Some safer world in depths of woods embraced,
"Some happier island in the watery waste,
"Where slaves once more their native land behold,
"No fiends torment, NO CHRISTIANS THIRST FOR GOLD."

What would the Poet Pope have thought of the rush of colonists to secure allotments of gold diggings, of the slaughter of the Matabéle, and the violent spoliation of a country, not by a recognized Government, but a Company of Commercial adventurers?

Years ago I visited Horace's villa near Rome, and my thoughts carried me back to one of the Poet's entertainments, when he received Mœcenas, the Orators, Poets, and Generals, of the day. News was coming in from the Danube, the Euphrates, the African Sahára, Spain, and distant Britain: it was one continuous conversation of bloodshed, inflicted by, or suffered by, the Parthians, the Teutons, the Iberians, the Gauls, and the Britons. In their idle hours the guests solaced themselves by the spectacle of Barbarians killed in the Amphitheatres. Is it not the same now with the British Nation as regards Africa? All round the Continent the poor Africans are sustaining an unequal conflict against the Colonist, the Soldier, the Geographical Explorer, or the importer of deadly liquour: killing, killing, killing, is the order of the day: in former generations the Anglo-Saxons stole a few thousand Africans from Africa: in this generation they are stealing Africa from the Africans, and killing by millions. The fight is over in Australia: there is not a native surviving in Tasmania: in Polynesia the natives are dwindling in number. In Melanesia the Kánaka are being sacrificed to Queensland.

In Africa we have read about the Matabéle: cross the Zambési, and come upon the field of the Slaughter of Lake Nyasa. It was understood, that when the boats were ready signal vengeance would be taken on Makanjira for the treachery practised upon Captain Maguire. A few weeks later news was received, that Makanjira himself had been shot by his nephew, but that a second Makanjira reigned in his stead, and that the situation was in no way altered. A strong slave-raiding power, holding positions on the south and south-eastern shores of the Lake, still defied British authority, and refused to make reparation for the massacre of Captain Maguire and his companions. The destruction of this power appears from the telegram received last month to have been accomplished. The expedition, which was commanded in person by Mr. H. H. Johnston, was composed of the Indian troops, under Major Johnson and Captain Edwards, and of the sailors of the two gunboats, under Commander Robertson and Lieutenant

Villiers, and it has been a complete success. All Makanjira's positions were captured, a number of slaves released, and a fort to be called Fort Maguire has been established on the site of Makanjira's village. The exact date of the operations is not known.

Hear the Archdeacon. "Let him be wiped out," whatever may be thought of it, is the sentiment universally expressed by the great chiefs of Yaoland. This drastic recommendation does not find favour with the Archdeacon. "It cannot be doubted, that if Makanjira's people escape "punishment, or get off with just their houses burnt down, "and a hundred or so of their people killed"—in another part of the letter it is written, "with only the loss of two "or three hundred men"—"the whole country to the east "of Lake Nyasa will be shaken in its growing belief in "British force and British resource, and will cause trouble "for many years to come. We would like to ask, if force is "only to be shown on the broad waters of the Lake and "its shores?" Doubtless, away from the protection of the gun-boats and troops on the west coast of the Lake, travellers might have to take their lives in their hands, but for all that, the utterance of the Archdeacon is to be deprecated. It is consistent neither with the work of inaugurating missions, nor with the spirit, which should preside over Christian enterprise.

More explanatory of the situation, and calmer in its terms, is the letter written by Bishop Hornby on the same day. "We certainly," says the Bishop, "seem to have "arrived at a very interesting, if not a very critical, "moment in the development of this part of Central "Africa," and, employing similar terms to those of the Archdeacon, proceeds to describe the condition of the country. "Now, for the first time, the tribes which "people the borders of the Lake seem to be awaking "suddenly to the fact that they are face to face with an "aggressive military Power, a Power that is requiring "from them a submission and obedience in forms that "are strange to them, and must for the time seem unreason- "able. The question is, Will these forces be carefully "directed? There is no reason to suppose that they will "not be. But as they are now for the first time to be put "methodically into action, backed by two gunboats now "afloat, and two hundred trained Sikh soldiers, with native "additions, we cannot help feeling anxious for the ultimate "result." . . . "So you see we have some reason for "anxiety, but not for fear." In a very guarded way the Bishop hints, that it is advisable to maintain friendly relations with the Yao tribes, who, if driven from the Lake border, will become not only slave-dealers, but, away in their mountain fastnesses, slave-raiders. No doubt the position is one of extreme difficulty, which can be surmounted only by great tact, forethought, and patience.

The Missionary here has clearly no stomach for the fight, and the remark is made, that in that quarter they have not got used to the sight of bloodshed: the Arm of the Flesh must do its work, though in doing so much may result, which the Missionary will bitterly deplore: however, the appetite comes in eating: on the Nyasa there is still a certain squeamishness: they cannot with any consistency hail the Arm of Flesh, to which they can appeal in time of danger: at Uganda the Missionary, Protestant and Romish, have got over that feeling of squeamishness, and are quite ready to fight even with each other, burn each other's stations and chapels: one Missionary actually set fire to a village, and on his return to England published a pamphlet justifying it. The so-called Arab is looked upon as a most unjustifiable intruder into Equatorial Africa, but he was there centuries before French, British, or German, and belongs to the people, being an Arabized Swahili, while the Europeans are strangers. The audacity of the Equatorial Company far exceeds that of the South African: the climate in the latter is propitious; Uganda is nearly under the Equator: it is to be hoped, that the British Government will be wise in time and clear out of it: its retention will be a lasting thorn: the death of the two Portals, deputed only to visit this Region, from climatic causes, ought to be an object-lesson to the Foreign Secretary: let us be wise in time, ere we read of more slaughter, more valuable lives lost. It sounds strange to those familiar with British India, and its fifty Million Mahometans, that it is proposed by some to exclude professors of Islam from Uganda: this is, indeed, a new departure.

In the Kongo Free State there has been fighting and slaughter, and more is expected: A remarkable expression is used in one of the notices from Brussels, complaining that one African was shot instead of receiving a "traitor's" death: it is not stated, what that form of death is, and how an African fighting for his own country can be called a traitor to a petty European Sovereign, dwelling thousands of miles away? The occupation of that Region so far away from the Sea on either the East or West Coasts, seems improbable. The usual mode of chastisement of an offender is to burn his villages, which of course entails destruction of female and infant life.

From West Africa reports tell us that 200 Sofa were killed : four days previously fifty more had been killed : there is every chance of there being further slaughter. The view taken of African life is shown in the enclosed :

> "Such are the black *reiters*, whom the English Soldiers are about to fight on the borders of Sierra Leone. They have perpetrated the same crimes on the territory of this colony as in French territory, and they are about to be unearthed by the English troops with the same energy that our Senegal troops have displayed against them. That is a piece of intelligence, which can only be received with the greatest satisfaction alike in France, in Senegal, and in the French Súdan. England will have deserved well of civilization and of humanity when, in her turn, she shall have rid the regions of the Upper Niger of this scourge, which ruins them."

Thus it is coldly determined to exterminate a race occupying their ancestral lands, and the policy is made known to the British Nation and the World : When Dr. Pasteur proposed to exterminate rabbits, a feeble protest on the part of a small Association was heard, but no one protests against this deliberatly proposed vivisection of Africans.

Lo-Bengúla fled and died : why did he not surrender ? the fate of his Ambassador, as reported to him, warned him. The French have a different record. "Pursued by "our troops, and by the population, which had rallied to "the new King, abandoned, moreover, by all the members "of the Royal Family, Behanzin, in dread of being captured, "surrendered unconditionally yesterday at Ajego, north-"west of Abomey. He is at present at Goho. He will be "despatched according to your instructions to Senegal by "the Segond. The Ministers will be sent to Gaboon." The *Debats* remarks that "Behanzin has certainly reckoned "on our generosity, and he was right. He has fought "bravely ; he has defended his kingdom with a tenacity and "courage to which we have always rendered homage. He "is now vanquished. We owe him honourable treatment. "He will find it in Senegal."

Perhaps the Germans in the Cameroons outdo the English in their mode of dealing with the poor African. I quote the Newspaper-Report. Herr Leist's report of the mutiny in the Cameroons is now published by the official colonial organ. It contains nothing further of interest than what is already known. There is no doubt, that he greatly misused his powers in causing the native women to be flogged. The *Kölnische Zeitung*, however, is in a position to state, that Herr Leist confesses in his report that he caused the wives of the native soldiers to be flogged, because they had neglected their work. Dr. Kayser's honest and straightforward reply, promising a thorough investigation and the punishment of the guilty, will doubtless temporarily allay the storm of indignation aroused by this unfortunate incident. But one may venture to doubt, whether the flogging of women in any circumstances is calculated to hasten on the reign of European civilization in Africa.

Further Expeditions and Murders are contemplated in the Nile Basin: Some enthusiasts write about the occupations of Lado at a considerable expense to the British Government: it is to be hoped, that the matter will be dropped: This is but another proof, that the lust of annexation is like the thirst of the confirmed drunkard.

"Quo plus habeas, eo plus cupias."

The strange feature is, that in all these reports, the African Patriots, who fight like Bruce and William Tell, for their hereditary land, are called "rebels," and, if they happen to kill any of their ruthless invaders, it is called "Murder," while the white man, who kills the African is called a Hero: the time will soon come for carrying away scalps. This indicates how very low have fallen in certain quarters the moral opinion with regard to taking away human life, and stealing other people's property.

CHAPTER V.

Meetings in London and Cape Town: The British Taxpayer.

The South African Commercial Companies held their periodical meetings in London: It is a strange feature to hear of slaughter and annexation, as part of the assets and profits of a Company established by Charter: yet so it is: no blame attaches to the Shareholders, but to the Directors: The Directors of some Companies err by being too *sanguine* in their operations: the Directors of these Companies err by being too *bloody*. Among other Meetings was one held of the London Chamber of Commerce, to hear a well known globe-trotter describe Zambesia, to which he had paid a short visit: he naively describes how the ball of annexation was set rolling. The opening of the Suez Canal in 1869, and the Brussels Conference of 1876, were among the principal causes, that led to the re-discovery and partition of South and Central Africa. It was only when some of the European Powers, developing colonial aspirations, began to partition Africa, that Britain took steps to secure a portion of the regions rapidly being appropriated. Germans, Boers, and Portuguese being ready to lay hands on Matabéleland, it became evident, that no time was to be lost, if Britain were to secure the Zambesi as the northern limit of her South African extension. He then referred to the treaty of amity and peace, which was concluded with Lo-Bengúla in 1888, and afterwards alluded to the growth of the British South Africa Company out of the concession then obtained by Mr. C. D. Rudd and others. It is just as if a burglar forced himself into a house, and then excused himself to the Magistrate on the plea, that if he had not committed the burglary some one else would have done it. Incidentally he tells us among other facts: (1) that Matabéleland is only the first mouthful, and must lead on to advance Northwards and the conquest of all Zambesia, (2) that Matabéleland is "a white man's country": this is not confirmed by the experience of Mr. Pelly, the Missionary quoted above. While carefully avoiding any extreme view, so far as he possibly could, he thought it his duty to state, from personal observation, that the Colonial Sentiment was one, that must be reckoned with, whether at times it were palatable in this country or not. Recent news from South Africa tended to strengthen his opinion, and it was certain, that, whatever the ultimate settlement of Matabéleland might be, the colonists on the spot would claim the management of their own affairs. He then speaks of South Africa as the "inheritance" of the British People almost in the terms used by Moses as regards the country of the Canaanites, etc., which were given to the Hebrews. This is indeed a doctrine subversive of all Rights of Nationality, or Property, all the dictates of Religion and Justice. The superabundant population of Great Britain must wade through blood to a competency: the markets of South Africa must be kept open for the manufacturers of Great Britain at the price of the slaughter of all the inhabitants: and this is the Nineteenth Century!

From Cape Town comes the report of still more interesting speeches: Why should the British Taxpayer pay in future one single farthing to support so-called British interests in South Africa, which are really only Africander interests? The speaker quoted above says so distinctly, but the Imperial Secretary of Cape Town, presumably only a British official of the Colonial office, speaks thus at the Rhodes banquet: "It has been the life's labour of our "distinguished guest to remove the bolster from between "the various States and various races of this great country, "to induce your neighbours to say 'God bless you,' and to "prove to the world, that a man may be at once a good "Imperialist, and a good Africander. All honour to him "for it, I say; all honour to him! And now that South "Africans have composed their differences, or are in a fair "way to do so, now that English and Dutch have shaken "hands and agreed to combine for the common good, "we are beginning to find our bed too narrow for us." This renders expansion, confiscation, slaughter, necessary. Great Britain is to be used as a cat's paw to pick the chesnuts out of the fire, in order that the Africander may enjoy their eating. It appears that £100,000 per annum are paid by the British taxpayer for expansion in Bechuana. Railways are subsidized, other expenditure is incurred, and all this is done, not for the benefit of Great Britain, but to improve the resources of the Africander Republic. Surely the time is come to button up our pockets, and send no more money to Africa, than we do the United States.

Mr. Rhodes in his speeches is very bold: With one

foot in Fort Salisbury, and the other on Table Mount, he claims to be a kind of duality: "L'état c'est moi." In Matabéleland he is a blood-stained conquerer: at the banquet at Cape Town he is the Prime Minister of a Colony with a Parliamentary Legislature. In his " Facing-"both-ways" attitude he is an Imperialist from one point of view, and an Africander from another. Such kind of politicians generally come to an untimely end: many such a bloated self-seeking figure has disappeared suddenly, both in ancient and modern times, and share the fate of those, who seek their own interests. He contemplates visiting England in the spring, and it is important to watch carefully the utterings and doings of this Political Proteus, who is acting the part of being two gentlemen at once. The Mayor of Cape Town, in proposing his health, likened him to the Three Calendars, passing as a good Briton, a good Colonist, and a good South African at the same time. Mr. Rhodes' first remark was startling. He had for twelve years held, that the *Hinterland* was a reversion to the Cape. Be it so, but Reversion is not Possession. France has the Reversion of the Kongo Free State, if Belgium gives it up. Mr. Rhodes is living upon *post obits*. The Chartered Company holds under a charter granted by the Queen of Great Britain. He darkly remarks—" The British Government possessed but a small " majority in the House of Commons, and it had an ex-" tremely irate section of its forces arrayed against it on " this matter. It might be, that this would result in the " dictation of a settlement, and that such terms would be " demanded from those, who had shed their blood in the " conquest of the country, as would be unfair to them and " contrary to the South African ideal. Should such an " event occur, he knew his duty as first Minister of the " Crown elected of the people. If, unfortunately, he had " to fight such a cause, he would earnestly and resolutely " fight it on constitutional lines on behalf of the people of " this country, who were the children of English people, " and in that cause he would appeal for support to the " people of South Africa." His speech contains some other noteworthy expressions: he had contemplated the annexation of the whole country up to the Zambesi, and beyond, even to Lake Tanganyika, and had discussed the matter with the late Governor, Sir Hercules Robinson: it was his " Hinterland," that word, which has caused so much bloodshed all over Africa: he talked of the destruction of "the last ruthless power in South Africa," forgetting that his own power was as ruthless, and his methods were as barbarous, as were those of the Zulu: what can be more ruthless than stealing another man's land? what more barbarous than massacring the inhabitants?

He boasts, that he went into Matabéleland with the support of every religious denomination in Mashónaland: so much the worse for the religion of those denominations: they were wolves in sheep's clothing: he had squared the English Episcopal Church by a grant of three thousand acres of land, as was stated by a Missionary in his Committee room. He laughs at the Aborigines Protection Society, and naturally so, for he is the President of the Aborigines Destruction Society: he then attacks Mr. Labouchere, but that gentleman is quite able to defend himself, especially when he has so good a cause: he calls Mr. Labouchere a cynical Sybarite: he might as well have called him a Crocodile; at any rate he is not what Mr. Rhodes certainly is, an unscrupulous annexer. He concludes his speech by drawing a vivid picture of the future United South Africa, or Africander, Republic, as hostile as possible to Great Britain, a great slaughterer of the indigenous population, and a compound of Anglo-Dutch adventurers, with a mixture of Griqua and other half castes, men with Hottentot mothers. It would be better far for Great Britain to let the Colony depart, and do her own dirty work of Slaughter and Plunder. .As it is, Great Britain, in the eyes of the civilized world, covers herself with shame with no intention on her part, and no possible advantage, in order that a sucking Republic may extend its boundaries.

Mr. Rhodes speaks contemptuously of "little England": like a bad bird he fouls his own nest, if he be indeed of English blood: his tastes savour more of the Zulu and the Hottentot, with a streak of Ashanti: he poses not only as a Colonist, but a Prophet, and predicts great things for the marvellous country of the Matabéle. No doubt the prophets in attendance on Sennacherib and Nebuchadnezzar made similar utterances in the ears of their monarch. Mr. Rhodes baited his trap for his friends at Cape Town by promising the sole trade of Matabéleland to the Dutch at the Cape, forgetting the lateral railways to the Eastern Coast, and possible access to the Zambesi. We hear nothing in his speech of the poor dear Mashóna, for whose sake the war was ostensibly undertaken: they will soon be working in the Africander gold mines, and going the way of the poor wretched indigenous inhabitants in the Spanish Colonies in South America. He then, in his Colossal style of eloquence, talks of being at Blantyre on the River Shiré in six months, and before we know where we are, at Uganda on the Equator; and if he be unable on this occasion to exterminate the Mahdi and his Dervishes of the Súdan, and then open the Basin of the Nile, he will turn off to Mombása: the advantage of telegraphic communication over land is not obvious, when there are sea-cables available. At any rate he will cease to be South African, and be entitled to the full title of Africanus.

He then enters on the subject of managing natives: he (Rhodes) is the native Minister, and has under his control 1,200,000 souls: he points out how the destruction of Lo-Bengúla will enable him to deal "thoroughly" with the Pondo, and other tribes, as Strafford dealt with the Irish. One Act of Murder and Plunder will follow another, till the white man reigns alone: it does not enter into his calculation, whether God will permit the extermination of all his poor black children. He calls himself unselfish, but the pronoun "Ego" governs all the words in his sentences: he is the man, who is to leap over many fences: he is the man who is to add to his present titles of "Colossus," and "Bloody Red Hand," the title of First President of the South Africander Republic. Do such men live to work out such dreams? Washington was a man of a totally different type: he never slaughtered Red Indians, or confiscated their lands. This "petit Napoleon" has more of the spirit of the Attila and Genghis Khan, who piled up pyramids of skulls outside City walls. There is an island on the other side of the Atlantic, of which Toussaint L'Ouverture, a negro slave, got possession, and allowed no whites in the Island; but it did not answer; nor will Mr. Rhodes' policy of having no blacks in South Africa be carried out. The Negro Races of Central Africa are increasing in number, and the law of territorial expansion will apply to them as well as to the white Colonists. Already the Native labour-question is coming to the front: it is admitted that native labour in South Africa is the dearest in the world. The slave can be made to work: the free African is described by a Bishop as wishing to live like an idle gentleman.

CHAPTER VI.

Conclusions.

THE writer of these lines possesses a general knowledge of the whole of Africa, the result of a quarter of a century's close observation, perhaps unsurpassed by many : others may know a corner of the great patchwork better, but nothing of other portions. It is some slight qualification to have watched for many years the proceedings, as regards Africa, of French, Spaniards, Portuguese, Germans, Italians, and English, as narrated in their own language by their own people : each nationality is most satisfied with the conduct of its own countrymen, and highly critical—often bitterly—of the proceedings of other Nationalities. In considering the interests and sufferings of this God-forgotten Continent, the writer has no prejudices, or partialities, of Nation, Language, Religion, Civilisation, Politics, or Commerce in his opinion : what is morally right, is right : what is morally wrong, is wrong, whether the actors of the particular drama be French or English, Negro or Bantu, Mahometan or Roman Catholic. All his special knowledge of these unhappy transactions is derived from the Blue Book of November, 1893, the Debates in Parliament, and the Pages of the *Times*. He has heard, that a Daily and Weekly Paper have violently attacked the Company on the financial as well as political side, but he has not seen them, or cared to do so. They may have possibly been dictated by commercial rivalry, pique, or personal rancour. He has never seen any one of the actors in this lamentable drama ; he has no shares or interests ; or knowledge, of any African Company, and no relation or friend who has shares or interests. He is not blaming those, who have interests ; he is not aspersing the characters of the Companies, of which he does not even know the names. In the words of Horace—

"Sunt qui non habeant : est qui non quærit habere."

He is entirely free from prejudice or partiality, but he stands up for the Native Races against Governments, against the white man, against Missionaries, and indignantly rejects the idea, that any white man has a right to lord it over the black man, whether he comes as a Traveller, a Merchant, an Emigrant, or a Missionary. He is obliged to speak plainly upon this subject. The Albocracy of the age is terribly heartless. The utterances of Lord Ripon and Sir H. Loch are worthy of all praise. Not much confidence can be placed in the reports of the agents of the Company. They were neither Soldiers, nor Political agents, nor experienced administrators of Civil affairs: their existence depended on their commercial success. The officials in British India, when placed in difficulties, have no fear of an adverse vote of an Annual Meeting of a Commercial Company, enraged by having no dividend, and exasperated by a call for further payments. The Indian official does not much care also for a debate in the House of Commons: he acts from Imperial motives, according to his orders, and for the good—as far as he can see—the *real good*, of the great Native population, whose interests are in his hands: *he detests slaughter*: he has no slaughterers of mankind under his own orders; he invites no shooters of big game to help him: and he has to answer to the Government, if he call out the Military forces without due cause, and to God, if he misuse his power: he has a permanent interest in the welfare of his people. Had these adventurers any interest?

What became of the Colonial power of Spain after the atrocities of Cortes and Pizarro, after the wholesale extinction of Native Races, the plunder of National wealth, whether in precious metal or in cattle? In the *Times* of November 24th it is recorded that the Company captured 1000 head of cattle.

Is the present political position of South America encouraging? The iniquity of the Spaniards reacted on themselves and what is Spain now? It was not the fault of Lo-Bengúla that he was naked and barbarous: so was Khama in his youth, and so was Khama's father in his old age: had Lo-Bengúla been approached by conciliating Britons, and treated as Khama was, he would have become what Khama is: it would take time, longer than the Company could spare! the process would not give a good, or an immediate, dividend! Khama must now shake in his shoes: a new administrator may come, a new turn of the wheel, and he and his children will be "eaten up" by a new Director of the Company. There was no inequality of force in the contest, no display of gallantry of a few against many. The High Commissioner remarked before any attack was made, that mounted men and machine guns, if properly handled, would be in an open fight equal to many thousand Matabéle: and so it proved. When the King was offered the instalment of his pension of £1200, he promptly refused it, saying "that he would "receive no more blood money, as it was the price of his "blood": so it was: the rope was being twisted round his neck: he found out too late that to let in one European is like the letting in of a stream of water, or rather of blood: it was obvious, that the difficulty of asylum to refugees would arise. No Englishman would willingly surrender women and children to certain torture and death, and to refuse this, is to a barbarian Chief an intolerable wrong. The mistake was to allow such a state of affairs to come into existence. It could never have happened in British India, or even Burma.

The High Commissioner deplored the sensational Press telegram sent by the Company's officers to Cape Town. Mr. Rhodes, the Prime Minister of the Colony, declined to interfere: in fact the Company was blowing up the fire in the furnace. The High Commissioner throughout sincerely desired peace; "the sentence of Moloch was for open war." The High Commissioner evidences throughout the feelings of a responsible Statesman, ready to strike at the last, if he were compelled; but the scratch-pack of Doctors, gold diggers, hunters of great game, were desirous to "get up "a row," as it is described in the Blue Book, and they strove to form a public sentiment in their favour, and have succeeded.

Sir Hercules Robinson, an ex-High Commissioner, with perfect knowledge of the circumstances, expresses his confidence, that the Company would never seek the extermination of the Matabéle, or their expulsion from their own native country: but Mr. Theodore Bent, whose only connection with the Region was that of an archæological explorer, in the words quoted a few pages back, recommends their extermination: and in fact they have been slaughtered by thousands, and Mr. Bent only expresses the feelings of his friends at Victoria.

In one of the telegrams of the Blue Book we read the cry of Lo-Bengúla: "What great wrong have I done"? The unlettered barbarian, with a range of ideas limited to South Africa, did not know that in the eyes of the white man on the war-path the possession of land and mines, even by an angel, would mean, that the owner of such wealth was doing wrong by daring to exist! Fortunes have to be made by daring adventurers, the younger sons of needy families of the middle classes:

"Si possis rectè: Si non, quocumque modô Rem."
This is the motto in all climes, and ages, of the Adventurer and Colonist.

As late as August 17th, 1893, Lo-Bengúla is described by the High Commissioner, as apparently anxious for peace, and doing his best to restrain his people, and protect the lives of Europeans at Buluwáyo. On August 16th, Dr. Jamieson telegraphs, that there is further evidence of the King's "lying and duplicity." Clearly there were two distinct categories of public officers: the High Commissioner desired Justice; the Company's administrators desired Annexation and Plunder. Lo-Bengúla sent ambassadors more than once to the High Commissioner: two were killed on their journey by British armed men; one fell seriously ill, and the delay was to be regretted; but no white man, such as Mr. Moffat, of a conciliatory disposition, and with a knowledge of African languages, was sent actually to the King, just as Sir Mortimer Durand has been sent this year to the Amir of Afghanistan. No white man, though there were several in his power, was killed by Lo-Bengúla: the agents of the Company have killed thousands of black men Lo-Bengúla never interfered with the affairs of Be-Chuanaland, Transvaal, or the Portuguese Colony: the English forced themselves into his recognised dominions, coming first to ask for concessions and treaties, and having secured a footing killing his subjects with all the air of men fighting for their own hereditary possessions. Imagine the English concessionists of the Rio Tinto mines near Seville in Spain turning round on the Spanish authorities, and driving out the King of Spain.

If on one side Lo-Bengúla was unable to control his young bloods under the extreme provocation, to which they were exposed, it appears from a memorial quoted in the Blue Book that the inhabitants of this ridiculously mushroom and tiny town Victoria placed similar pressure upon the redoubtable Mr. Rhodes: he was told by them pretty clearly in July, 1893, that he must take the favourable opportunity once for all of settling the Matabéle question, *i.e.* "killing them," and, if he did not take the initiative, a very large proportion of the inhabitants of this goodly city, which had dropped down a few years back in a foreign and independent State, were determined to take the matter into their own hands, and arrange for compensation for their losses. The agricultural losses amounted to fifty oxen, two hundred and eighty sheep or goats, ten asses, and fifteen pigs, and for losses such as these the slaughter of thousands of free independent Africans was determined upon, the prime mover of the transaction being a son of Œsculapius, the great healer.

No more iniquitous arrangement was ever made than the Partition of Africa. The different gangs of land-grabbers, hailing from Paris, London, Berlin, or Brussels, are on the jealous watch of each other. Men are cut down, in order that dividends may rise. The Twentieth Century will sit in judgment upon us, as we judge the Spaniards of the Sixteenth Century. The Roman mob in the time of their decadence shouted for "Panem et "Circenses:" the cry of the British Speculator is, "African "Skulls and Gold Dust." This is the outcome of the Christian benevolence of the age. The British Matron, reading her paper at the breakfast table, remarks that two thousand more Savages have been killed. "A rise "of ten per cent. in Mine Shares," is the rejoinder of Pater Familias. Geography will be taught to the rising generation in lessons of blood. Uganda, says the teacher, is the place, where the Protestant British Mission slaughtered the French Roman Catholic Mission, and burnt their chapels. Matabéleland, says the teacher, is the country, which Mr. Rhodes conquered, and divided among his gold-digger friends, driving the king away, killing his ambassadors, slaughtering his subjects, and confiscating his land: the teacher would then delineate the geographical features of the country in blood instead of chalk.

Mr. Labouchere in one of his speeches described it as a battue rather than a battle, which will suit the taste of the authors of "Great Game in East Africa," who arrived opportunely, as well as Mr. Selous, the great hunter. Black game of the ethnological Bantu race takes the place of Lions or Bears: and poor ignorant Peasants supply the place of Pheasants.

There has been one great omission up to this date: there has been no massacre on Lake Chad: this really is a *casus omissus*. The Roman said proudly, that there was no shore untinged by Roman blood: the Briton may say, that there is no Region, or Lake, or River, in Africa, in which he has not shed the blood of the unfortunate Native Races. Something ought to be done for the honour of Lake Chad! Captain Lugard from the Lake Nyasa and Victoria Nyanza has more experience of lacrustine slaughter. Dr. Jamieson's lancet is better able to draw blood in the High Veldt.

I never saw Mr. Labouchere, but I welcome any friend of Justice and Mercy, and quote his words. Mr. Labouchere addressed his constituents at Northampton Town Hall lately. Referring to Matabéleland, Mr. Labouchere said that "he had never seen why English people should "treat Africans as though they were not human beings. "It was said that 3,000 of the natives had been killed and "wounded, and he had asked where were the 2,000 wounded? "An African chief called Khama, who was a Wesleyan, "withdrew his troops from assisting the English, because he "disapproved of the way the English were carrying on the "war. Was it not a preposterous thing, that the English "flag should be disgraced in that manner, that these mere "stock-jobbing, money-mongering people should drag our "flag in the mire in Africa, and that they should kill and "murder in order to send up their miserable shares on the "Stock Exchange? For his part he meant to stick to this "question. There was too much in the House of Commons "of turning the blind eye to what was going on in those "distant parts."

In this unhappy Matabéle Scandal all traditional feelings, customs, and moralities are reversed. In British India the Medical Officers, though brave men, are called non-combatants: in Africa they appear to take the command of Military expeditions: the combination of syllables, which make up the name of this particular militant-medico recalls that of one, who if the charge against him be true, is the greatest criminal of the Century, as an eye-witness, whose evidence is reported by the greatest of African Explorers, states that he bought a little negro girl, and had her cut up and eaten in his presence in order that he might make a picture of the incident, a sensational sketch for an evening paper. The conscience of British Christianity refuses to give credence to this story, but

" pudet hæc opprobia nobis
" Aut dici potuisse, aut non potuisse repelli."

The old Greek writers tell us, that Africa had always something new to communicate to the world, and so it is to this day. The Matabéle Scandal has a quaint novelty about it, because there was a pretence of benevolence in protecting the poor dear Mashóna, the maternal relatives of these very wicked Matabéle, who owned a territory with auriferous deposits, which were coveted by the Anglo-Saxon. The atmosphere of Africa is impregnated with crime. King Mtesa, and Mwanga, of Uganda could not have existed in Asia. It was the same climatic influences, which made them so cruel, and has the effect of making young men of Great Britain sweep away the restraints of the sixth and eighth Commandments, and go in for Killing and Loot.

Let Great Britain pause in this career of cruelty and crime; let the Africander Republic rather look to the history of the United States of North America, than to the examples of the Republic of Mexico, Peru, and the Argentine: it is as well to be honest and merciful.

My pamphlet will perish, as it deserves. One or two copies may survive on the shelves of the Library of the British Museum, and the two great Universities, to record the fact that there were a few voices in 1894 crying in the wilderness to denounce crime, even when committed by their own countrymen.

February 1st, 1894.

www.ingramcontent.com/pod-product-compliance
Lightning Source LLC
Chambersburg PA
CBHW020227240426
43672CB00006B/443